THE BLUE GUIDES

Albania
Austria
Belgium and Luxembourg
China
Cyprus
Czechoslovakia
Denmark
Egypt

FRANCE
France
Paris and Versailles
Burgundy
Loire Valley
Midi-Pyrénées
Normandy
South West France
Corsica

GERMANY
Berlin and Eastern Germany
Western Germany

GREECE
Greece
Athens and environs
Crete

HOLLAND
Holland
Amsterdam

Hungary
Ireland

ITALY
Northern Italy
Southern Italy
Florence
Rome and environs
Venice
Tuscany
Umbria
Sicily

Jerusalem
Malta and Gozo
Mexico
Morocco
Moscow and Leningrad
Portugal

SPAIN
Spain
Barcelona
Madrid

Sweden
Switzerland

TURKEY
Turkey
Istanbul

UK
England
Scotland
Wales
London
Museums and Galleries
  of London
Oxford and Cambridge
Country Houses of England
Gardens of England
Literary Britain and Ireland
Victorian Architecture in
  Britain
Churches and Chapels
  of Northern England
Churches and Chapels
  of Southern England
Channel Islands

USA
New York
Boston and Cambridge

Vendôme: detail of the west front of La Trinité

The publishers and the author welcome comments, suggestions and corrections for the next edition of this Blue Guide. Writers of the most informative letters will be awarded a free Blue Guide of their choice.

BLUE GUIDE

The Loire Valley

John McNeill

A&C Black
London

WW Norton
New York

1st edition 1995

Published by A & C Black (Publishers) Limited
35 Bedford Row, London WC1R 4JH

A CIP catalogue record of this book is available from the British Library.

ISBN 0–7136–3872–9

Published in the United States of America by
WW Norton and Company, Inc
500 Fifth Avenue, New York, NY 10110

Published simultaneously in Canada by
Penguin Books Canada Limited
10 Alcorn Avenue, Toronto, Ontario M4V 3BE

ISBN 0–393–31268–2   USA

Maps and plans drawn by Robert Smith

Photographs by John McNeill

The author and the publishers have done their best to ensure the accuracy of all the
information in Blue Guide The Loire Valley; however, they can accept no responsibility
for any loss, injury or inconvenience sustained by any traveller as a result of information
or advice contained in the guide.

John McNeill was educated at the University of East Anglia and the Courtauld
Institute of Art. He now teaches at London University's Centre for Extra-Mural Studies,
and has extensive experience of devising and leading art and architectural tours to
France, Italy and Spain. Among his previous publications is Blue Guide Normandy.

Printed and bound in Great Britain by
Butler & Tanner Ltd, Frome and London

CONTENTS

Maps and Plans

ACKNOWLEDGEMENTS

Without the friendly interest and goodwill of all I met in the Loire Valley this volume would have been impossible. I should particularly like to thank Paul Ligtenberg of the Western Loire Tourist Board, Elisabeth Lorans, who introduced me to the mysteries of Touraine archaeology, and Annick Chupin, for putting me right on Cormery and much else besides. Antoine Ruais was magnificent, and the generosity with which he shared his insights into medieval Angers will not be forgotten. Valérie Coiffard was equally supportive in Vendôme, and among a formidable cast to the south, Daniel Pringent, Soeur Chantal and Susanna McGrath must be singled out.

In April, 1994 I also took a group of extra-mural students to the region, whose conviviality, alertness and pertinence kept me honest. I thank them wholeheartedly. Others, whose advice or encouragement was a source of strength, include Lesley Scouller, Martin Randall, Nigel Clubb, Brian O'Callaghan, and Pamela Ward. Michael Brown cast a professional eye over my initial findings, and his resourceful and level-headed suggestions filled me with admiration. To him I owe a great debt. The most historic debt is owed to my parents, who first introduced me to France. My father accompanied me as 'clerk of works' on my final visit to the region, never worrying at my haphazard timings, sociable, engaging, and a marvellous companion. It is a memory I cherish.

INTRODUCTION

To a 19C English traveller the Loire valley offered a vision of French art and culture that was not only exemplary, but unrivalled outside Paris. This notion of the Loire as a paradigm of north-western European culture—as central to the identity of France as is Tuscany to Italy—came under attack during the 1950s and 60s, as the rhetoric of Modernism was unleashed on any historical or cultural model that failed to conform to centralising, and predominantly urban, strictures. Inevitably, the pendulum is once more swinging towards the view that the Loire was more than a mere playground for a displaced French monarchy, a rural backyard, and many scholars of the Middle Ages and Renaissance are now turning their attention to the area. Any region which witnessed the birth of feudalism, played host to the most extravagant Renaissance court in northern Europe, suffered the Vendéen war and was responsible for introducing architectural forms as influential as the castle and the apartment block, is bound to sustain monuments of interest to the specialist. Whether it will entertain the general traveller with an eye to a holiday is a more open question. If you have a liking for river valleys, for *la France profonde*, you have an answer, for the area is distinguished by one of the great river systems of western Europe and enlivened by some of its finest market towns, sociable, pastoral, beautiful.

The initial problem faced by any guide to the Loire valley is not one of cultural significance, but one of geographical definition. The Loire rises on the slopes of Mont Gerbier de Jonc, in the southern Massif Central, and flows through the Auvergne, Lyonnais, Burgundy, Orléanais, Blésois, Touraine, and Anjou, before emptying into the Atlantic to the west of Nantes, in Brittany. Although the river may be said physically to link towns such as Roanne and Nevers with Blois and Saumur, its length (1020km) and the difficulty of navigation above La Charité-sur-Loire, mean that the historical and geographical realities which shaped the upper and middle Loire were very different from those experienced in the downstream reaches. Furthermore, the culture of the major tributary valleys of the western Loire—the rivers Sarthe, Loir, Vienne, Indre and Cher—cannot be disentangled from that of the principal watercourse. They were subject to similar political and economic pressures, and have come to share a common outlook. The guide confines itself to this western stretch of the Loire, covering the whole of the Blésois, Touraine and Anjou (what are now the modern *départements* of Loir-et-Cher, Indre-et-Loire and Maine-et-Loire, with their *préfectures* at Blois, Tours and Angers respectively) and touching on those sections of the rivers Sarthe and Loir which flow through south-eastern Maine (now the *département* of Sarthe). Nantes and the mouth of the Loire are dealt with in the forthcoming Blue Guide *Brittany*.

The volume adheres to the usual Blue Guide method of dividing the area into a series of routes, the majority of which either follow river valleys, or explore smaller regions unified by reason of topography or historical circumstance. They are arranged as a series of interlocking circuits or journeys, and are intended to be suggestive of the main points of cultural interest, though none is constructed so as to indicate a vital and orderly progression. It is unlikely that their elaborate detours would be useful to anyone who is not spending several days in a particular *pays*, or who does not have a specific goal in mind. If you want to follow your own plan there is a detailed index to enable you to use the guide in its proper role, as a secondary resource.

Driving is essential if you wish to tour a sizeable area conveniently or in any detail. The headnote to each route gives a summary of road directions, with distances between the main towns. Detailed road directions are confined to the text itself. The larger towns are described in some detail and the text is organised with the pedestrian in mind, with the major streets and monuments indicated on the town plans. The accounts of places concentrate on their art, architecture and history, though without assuming that these belong in some special category apart from contemporary life. Equally, as the current identity and shape of the region owes most to its landscape and history, the discussion of this is integrated into the main body of the text. For quick reference, however, there is a brief chronology of regional history on page 25.

Although the Loire valley did not suffer the intensity of Second World War aerial and artillery bombardment that so devastated Normandy and northern Maine, the damage was real enough, and the great late medieval river fronts of Tours, Saumur and Angers have been lost. Despite this—and the huge 20C housing estates and industrial centres which now ring Blois, Tours and Angers—the urban fabric of most Loire valley towns and villages was laid down between the 11C and the 16C. It is even the case that the *Bocage* farmers of the Mauges rely on a landscape whose field systems, and balance of woodland and pasture, were largely developed during the late Middle Ages. This abounding late medieval prosperity is perhaps the most striking aspect of the Loire, the fundament from which the grander royal châteaux of the 15C and 16C grew, the backdrop to the new town schemes of the 17C and 18C. The landscape of Touraine and the Blésois has changed, it is true, as large-scale monoculture becomes the norm, but most towns still bear the marks of their late medieval walls, and most châteaux offer clues to their medieval identity.

This latter point often comes as a surprise, as does the discovery that great Baroque or neo-classical houses, such as Brissac-Quincé, Cheverny or Montgeoffroy, are rare, and, as most visitors are likely to encounter a number of châteaux, it is as well to nail a few possible misapprehensions. First, there are two main lines of development, and the major 'châteaux of the Loire' are not the French equivalent of the English stately home. Those châteaux that actually stand on the Loire, or in its immediate vicinity—Blois, Amboise, Langeais, Chinon, Saumur, Angers—are in towns and are easily defended. All rise above natural outcrops, overlook a river, and either incorporate or stand on earlier fortifications. Even Chaumont and Azay-le-Rideau conform to four out of five of these characteristics. There is, however, a second category of châteaux whose origins lie not in 11C and 12C medieval castles, but in rural manor houses. These are not as well-known—they include houses such as Fougères-sur-Bièvre, Le Moulin and Plessis-Bourré—and, though they borrow motifs from the great urban residences, their underlying structure—moats, gardens, comfortable accommodation—is wholly different. Inflated to colossal size, they are the source of the mighty pleasure palaces of the 16C, of Chambord and Chenonceau.

A more detailed description of the vast majority of those châteaux open to the public can be found in the main body of the guide. The rest of this section deals with practical matters: ways of getting to the Loire and travelling around it; maps; accommodation; restaurants, food and wine; and details of access to châteaux, churches and museums. Addresses and phone numbers of the main tourist offices, and of local *Syndicats d'Initiative* and *Maisons du Tourisme*, are listed on pages 21–24.

Highlights of the Region

Landscape
Outstanding: Valleys of the Sarthe and Loir, Saumurois
Very Good: Lower valleys of the Indre and Vienne, Sologne, Vendômois

Cities and Larger Towns
Outstanding: Angers, Chinon, Tours, Vendôme
Very Good: Blois, La Flèche, Romorantin-Lanthenay, Saumur

Smaller Towns and Villages
Outstanding: Asnières-sur-Vègre, Crissay-sur-Manse, Loches, Le Lude, Parcé-sur-Sarthe, Richelieu, Le Thoureil
Very Good: Baugé, Beaufort-en-Vallée, Blaison, Cormery, Le Grand-Pressigny, Lavardin, Le Louroux, Mennetou-sur-Cher, Montrésor, Montreuil-Bellay, St-Aubin-de-Luigné, Vaas

Museums and Art Galleries
Outstanding: Angers (Musée David-d'Angers)
Very Good: Angers (Musée des Beaux-Arts), Chinon (Musée du Vieux-Chinon), Cholet (Musée d'Art et Histoire), Tours (Musées Archéologique and des Beaux-Arts)

Roman Sites
Very Good: Cherré, Gennes (amphitheatre), Luynes (aqueduct), Thesée-la-Romaine

Major Châteaux
Outstanding: Angers, Azay-le-Rideau, Blois, Brissac-Quincé, Chambord, Chenonceau, Chinon, Langeais, Montgeoffroy
Very Good: Amboise, Champigny-sur-Veude (chapel glass), Chaumont, Cheverny, Loches (Donjon and Logis Royal), Montreuil-Bellay, Plessis-Macé, Ussé

Smaller Châteaux and Town Houses

Outstanding: Angers (Hôtel Pincé), Beauregard, Blois (Hôtel Sardini), Fougères-sur-Bièvre, Château du Moulin, Plessis-Bourré, Talcy, Tours (Hôtels Beaune-Semblançay and Goüin), Villesavin

Very Good: Manoir de Bonaventure, Coudray-Montbault, Gué-Péan, Manoir de la Possonière, Château des Réaux, Saché

Gardens

Outstanding: Maulévrier, Villandry

Major Churches

Outstanding: Angers (Cathedral and St-Serge), Cunault, Fontevraud, Tours (cathedral and remnants of St-Martin), Vendôme (La Trinité)

Very Good: Angers (Ronceray), Blois (St-Nicolas), Bois-Aubry, Candes-St-Martin, Chinon (St-Mexme), La Flèche (college chapel), Loches (St-Ours), Le Puy-Notre-Dame, Roches-Tranchelion, Saumur (Nantilly and Notre-Dame-des-Ardilliers), St-Florent-le-Vieil, Selles-sur-Cher, Tours (St-Côme)

Lesser Churches

Outstanding: Luché-Pringé, Montrésor, Nouans-les-Fontaines (Fouquet panel painting), Pirmil, Sablé-sur-Sarthe (glass)

Very Good: Azay-le-Rideau, La Bruère-sur-Loir (glass), Cravant-les-Côteaux, Genneteil, Meusnes, Mulsans, Pontigné, Pringé, Restigné, Saché, St-Denis-d'Anjou, St-Loup

Wall Paintings

Outstanding: Angers (Préfecture), Montoire, Tavant, Trôo (St-Jacques-des-Guérets), Vendôme (Chapter house, La Trinité)

Very Good: Lavardin, Le Liget, Le Lude (Château), Pontigné, St-Aignan-sur-Cher, St-Denis-d'Anjou, Selles-St-Denis

Getting There

By car and ferry. The most direct ferry routes are those which run between the south coast ports and either Normandy or St-Malo. **Stena Sealink Line** operate ferries from Newhaven to Dieppe (4 hour crossing time), and Southampton to Cherbourg (5 hours). Their UK address is Charter House, Park Street, Ashford TN24 8EX, Kent. For reservations phone 01233 647047. **P&O European Ferries** sail from Portsmouth to Le Havre (approximate crossing times: 6 hours during the day, 7 hours at night) and Portsmouth to Cherbourg (5 hours during the day, 7 hours at night). For further information contact P&O European Ferries, Continental Ferry Port, Mile End, Portsmouth PO2 8QW. For reservations phone 01705 827677. **Brittany Ferries** operate from Portsmouth to Caen (average crossing time 6 hours), Poole to Cherbourg (4½ hours) and both Portsmouth and Poole to St-Malo (8–9 hours). For further information contact Brittany Ferries, The Brittany Centre, Wharf Road, Portsmouth PO2 8RU. For reservations phone 01705 827701. The short sea routes to Calais and Boulogne may also be useful. For information on these, the above telephone numbers should be supplemented with: **Hoverspeed**, reservations on 01304 240241. For P&O services from Dover phone 01304 203388. The final contender for your custom is **Eurotunnel**, whose car and passenger service, Le Shuttle, runs between Folkestone and Sangatte (Calais) 24 hours a day. The crossing time between platforms is approximately 35 minutes. General enquiries are fielded on 01303 271100. Tickets can be purchased in advance but the service is designed so that you can 'turn up and go'.

By train. The Eurostar service from London (Waterloo) to Paris (Gare du Nord) via the Channel Tunnel takes about 3 hours. You will need to cross Paris in order to pick up the TGV-Atlantique from the Gare de Montparnasse, with a good choice of fast trains to Vendôme (in just under one hour), Tours (in just over one hour, though services to St-Pierre-des-Corps, some 4km west of the city centre, are more frequent, with connecting services to Tours), and Angers-St-Laud (in approximately 1½ hours). Slower services to Blois, Tours, Saumur and Angers leave from Paris-Austerlitz. Further information can be obtained from Eurostar Bookings and Reservations (phone 01233 617575) and the UK office of SNCF (French Railways) at 179 Piccadilly, London W1V 0BA (timetable enquiries answered on 0891 515477).

By air. As Air-Inter no longer fly from Paris to Tours, the only convenient route is to fly from London Gatwick to Nantes, and either hire a car or take the train from there. Air-France operates the service in conjunction with Brit Air, and handles all reservations and enquiries (Colet Court, 100 Hammersmith Road, London W6 7JP; phone 0181 742 6600). There are three flights daily in summer and two in winter.

Touring the Region

Driving is essential if you aim to exlore the region in any detail. If you are arriving by train, Blois, Tours and Angers offer a number of car-hire firms, including Avis, Europcar and Hertz, while the same is true of Nantes for those arriving by air. In budgeting for driving expenses remember that petrol prices are higher in France than in the UK. The petrol stations attached to supermarkets usually offer the keenest prices. Unleaded petrol (*sans plomb* or, colloquially, *le vert*) is a bit less expensive than *essence*, but can still be hard to find away from the larger towns and autoroutes. The road network is extremely well maintained, with the larger departmental roads (given the prefix D to distinguish them from the national system, which carry N numbers) offering fast and uncongested journeys.

The rail network is patchy away from the relevant sections of the new TGV-Atlantique line (Paris–Vendôme–Tours, and Paris–Le Mans–Angers), and the old Loire Valley main line (Paris–Orléans–Blois–Tours–Saumur–Angers). A reasonably fast service runs along the Sarthe valley, from Le Mans to Angers via La Suze and Sablé, and connects with trains to Cholet, but, as with most rural lines, trains are infrequent. Rail services also connect Tours with Montrichard and St-Aignan, Tours with Loches via the Indre valley, Tours with Chinon, and Château-du-Loir with Saumur. In summer it is also possible to travel between Richelieu and Chinon by steam train, courtesy of the local preservation society *Trains à vapeur de Touraine* (enquiries about services are handled at the Gare de Richelieu, 37120 Richelieu; phone 47.58.12.97). Timetable information can be obtained from any SNCF station, or from the UK office of SNCF at 179 Piccadilly, London W1V 0BA (0891 515477).

Cycling is also a popular way of exploring a varied region, especially in a country where the bike is close to the national soul. Bicycles can be hired by the day or week from some *Syndicats d'Initiative* and most railway stations. Cycling holidays, known as *Vélo Bleu Vélo Vert*, are also available in the west of the region under the auspices of the Comité Régional de Tourisme, Place du Commerce, 44000, Nantes. Tel: 40.48.24.20. Further information and advice about routes can be obtained from the Fédération Française de Cyclotourisme, 8 Rue Jean-Marie-Jego, 75013 Paris. Tel: (1) 45.80.30.21.

Walking has received a considerable boost from the development of a series of long-distance footpaths, known as *Sentiers de Grande Randonée* and given route numbers commencing with a GR. The finest is the GR3, which follows the Loire from its source to the sea, the section from Blois to St-Florent-le-Vieil being particularly beautiful. All long-distance paths are described in a series of 'Topoguides' published by the Fédération Française de Randonée Pédestre, 8 Avenue Marceau, 75008 Paris. Robertson-McCarta have translated into English a selection of Topoguides to the region under the title *Walks in the Loire Valley: Paris to Saumur.*

Maps

Michelin and the *Institut Géographique National* (IGN) both produce a good set of maps. The minimum useful scale is 1:250,000 (1cm to 2.5km) if you are to find all villages and most hamlets marked. Michelin's yellow regional maps are excellent at 1:200,000, though number 232 (Pays de Loire) only runs as far east as Tours and needs supplementing with number 238 (Centre) if you intend visiting the Blésois and southern Touraine. The IGN Série Rouge number 106 (Val de Loire) covers the area well, though is notoriously generous in its definition of significant ruins and monuments. If you are walking or cycling you will need one or more of the following series of IGN maps: the Série Verte at 1:100,000 (1cm to 1km), numbers 24, 25, 26, 27, 33, 34; the Série Orange at 1:50,000 (1cm to 0.5km); or the Série Bleue at 1:25,000 (1cm to 250m). See also the remarks about the Topoguides above.

Accommodation

Hotels in France are officially classified by a system of stars, running from one to four, indicating the range of amenities offered. There are also many unstarred hotels, particularly away from the larger towns, which provide comfortable and clean accommodation. The star system is only a rough guide to prices, which vary considerably in each category, but as a general rule you would rarely pay more than FF400 for a twin room in a two-star hotel (1995 prices). Prices are usually quoted per room and not per person. Hotels often list their tariffs in the reception area, and are required by law to post the price of each room within the room itself. The figure rarely includes breakfast, and in the larger towns hotels might levy a charge for off-street parking. Guests at smaller hotels would be expected to dine, so if you are watching your budget ask what the half-board rate is before committing yourself. Most such hotels will produce excellent food at reasonable prices, but it is not unknown for modest hotels with good restaurants to charge a lot more for food than for accommodation.

The *Comités Régionaux du Tourisme* publish brochures listing all hotels in the region. This is particularly useful if you are travelling in July or August, when it may be worth booking hotels in advance. At any other time of year you are unlikely to encounter any difficulties in finding accommodation, though it is advisable to start looking by 6.00pm. The big hotel chains tend to be represented only in the larger cities, such as Tours and Angers. Prices here, and in popular tourist destinations such as Amboise, Chinon, and Saumur, are higher than in less publicised areas such as the valley of the Sarthe and eastern Anjou. Hotels of any sort are also thinner on the ground away from the main river valleys, and particularly in the Mauges.

The most reliable group of hotels are those affiliated to *Logis de France*, an umbrella network of small, independent establishments rating between one and three stars. The region boasts almost 200 of them, and their distinctive emblem of a yellow fireplace on a green crest makes them easy to spot. Prices vary widely, but most rooms cost between FF150 and FF400 (1995 prices). Full details are given in the annual *Guide des hôtels-restaurants Logis de France* available from the French Government Tourist office in London for £8.50, or on sale in most French bookshops. Other useful sources of information are the annual *Michelin Red Guide* and the *Routiers Guide to France* (available by post from Routiers, 25 Vanston Place, London SW16 1AZ). Personal callers at the French Government Tourist Office can consult its computerised register of hotels.

Gîtes, or self-catering accommodation, provide a convenient base in rural areas. They are particularly useful for families or groups of more than two people. Typical weekly prices for a gîte capable of housing four people are FF1500–3000 in season and FF1000–2000 out of season (1995 rates). You can join the official booking service, *Gîtes de France*, for a small annual fee and receive its handbook of listings by contacting the French Government Tourist Office in London. The various *départements* also have a branch of *Gîtes de France* which will issue listings and handle bookings. The relevant addresses are: **Indre-et-Loire**:

Chambre d'Agriculture, BP130, 38 Rue Augustin Fresnel, 37170 Chamray-lès-Tours (phone 47.48.37.12); **Loir-et-Cher**: 11 Place du Château, 41000 Blois (phone 54.78.55.50); **Maine-et-Loire**: BP2148, 49021 Angers (phone 41.20.09.99); **Sarthe**: Préfecture de la Sarthe, BP21X, 72040 Le Mans (phone 43.76.05.06). These services also cover *chambres d'hôtes* (bed and breakfast), *fermes auberges* (farmhouse inns), *camping à la ferme* (farmhouse camping), and *gîtes d'étapes*. The Comités Régionaux de Tourisme publish lists of all camping and caravan sites.

Restaurants and Food

The cuisine of the Loire valley was described by Curnonsky, the great early 20C writer on French food, as 'clear, logical and straightforward', for which reason it is less well known than the cuisine of, say, Burgundy or Provence. Sauces are rare, ingredients fresh, and Curnonsky's precept—'in cookery, things should taste of what they are'—immeasurably enhanced by the availability of exquisite local fruit and vegetables. In short, there is ample opportunity for eating well at reasonable prices. The whole region is well-endowed with rural auberges, and most larger villages boast at least one restaurant in addition to those cafés which provide snacks throughout the day and a *plat du jour* at lunchtime. Any town worth the name will offer a choice of restaurants and will have so organised the *jours de fermeture* (all restaurants must by law close on one day per week, traditionally a Monday) that on any given day two out of three will be open. The fixed price menus are nearly always a better bet than eating *à la carte*. All restaurants offer them and most offer three or four, ranging from perhaps FF85–200 in the majority of establishments, though it is possible to spend FF500 on a seven course spectacular at one of the grand *restaurants gastronomiques*. The choice is greater with the more expensive menus, which will generally include both cheese *and* dessert, rather than cheese *or* dessert. The set price menus are prominently displayed in the windows of most restaurants and, unless otherwise specified, exclude drinks. The service charge is included in the price but it remains the habit, if pleased, to leave a modest tip.

The most complete restaurant guides are the *Michelin Red Guide* and the *Routiers Guide to France*, the latter offering a more comprehensive picture of the cheaper establishments. It is also worth consulting the locals, who are invariably discerning and well-practised judges. Finally, the old axiom that busy restaurants are good restaurants remains truer in France than anywhere.

The Loire is justly famous for its pâtés, fish, fruit and vegetables, traditionally taken with a bottle of light, fresh wine and rounded off with a glass of fiery Marc. The underlying limestone and silty soils encourage orchards and market gardens, leading François Rabelais to describe the area as the '*jardin de France*'. Artichokes, asparagus, fennel, peas, chervil, lettuce, black-skinned potatoes, strawberries, plums and pears are widely cultivated, and in addition to being used in salads and desserts are often found as accompaniments to the staple fish, game and pork. The basic culinary principle is that ingredients should be combined in such a way as to show off their particular flavours, a conviction which accounts for there being only one indigenous sauce, *Buerre Blanc*, made from butter and a reduction of vinegar and shallots, which has been widely adopted outside the region. The following list identifies some of the local dishes you are most likely to encounter.

Pâté. *Rillons*—pieces of pork breast stewed in lard, Tours and Saumur having the reputation for producing the best. *Rillettes*—Rillons shredded into a paste. *Pâté de Lièvre* (hare), *Pâté de Sarcelles* (teal).

Fish. *L'alose de Loire au buerre blanc*—Shad served in a butter and vinegar sauce. *Matelot d'anguille*—eel stewed in red wine, in medieval and Renaissance times accompanied by prunes, a combination now rare. *Brème farcie*—stuffed bream.

Meat. *Noisettes de porc aux pruneaux de Tours*—morsels of pork and prunes in cream and white wine. *Charbonée*—pork offal stewed with onions and spices in red wine and blood. *Cul de veau*—rump of veal, very much a speciality of Montsoreau. *Fricassée de géline*—a géline is a small breed of chicken, otherwise cut into pieces and cooked with onions and white wine.

Game. *Lièvre de Sologne*—Hare from the Sologne, usually pot roasted. *Sanglier*—wild boar.

Mushrooms. The Saumurois is responsible for producing 75 per cent of the cultivated fungi eaten in France, so button and gill mushrooms abound, but there is no shortage of delicate wild mushrooms, which are often used to accompany game. *Coulemelles* (parasol mushrooms), *Girolles* (a type of chanterelle), *Cèpes*, and *Trompettes de la mort* (horns of plenty) are in plentiful supply.

Cheeses. The Loire is best known for its goat cheeses, though those produced by the larger cheesemakers can be disappointing, and heavily oversalted. Farmhouse cheeses usually carry the word *fermier* on the label, and are almost always the more satisfying. The most frequently encountered goat cheeses are *Ste-Maure*, which comes as a cylinder with a piece of straw running through the centre, and *Valençay*, shaped as a pyramid and sprinkled with powdered charcoal.

Pastries and Sweets. Given its extensive orchards the Loire has developed a number of recipes using apples or pears. The most ubiquitous is *Tarte Tatin*, an upside-down caramelised apple pie now found throughout France, but originating in the Loire. *Gourmandise Domfrontaise*, a delicious confection of fresh pears baked with pear brandy and cream, is by origin a south-western Norman dish, but sometimes finds its way onto late summer menus in Anjou, and is well worth seeking out. The better known pastries are *Fouace*, a bun mid-way between a brioche and a sponge, and the celebrated *Macarons de Cormery*.

Wine

The Loire valley is among the most northerly regions of Europe to produce wine on any scale. In absolute terms Champagne and Alsace are further north, but the Loire is susceptible to cool, wet Atlantic winds, dragging the summer temperatures lower and rarely allowing the grapes to ripen fully until dangerously late in October. One result is that most Loire wines have a sharpness and intensity of fruit that is unrivalled elsewhere in Europe, and an immediacy of flavour which is quite unmistakable. The wines produced upstream of Orléans, notably Pouilly Fumé and Reuilly, can develop a certain complexity, but, with the exception of a very few sweet whites, the appeal of most Loire wines is their straightforwardness. The locals describe them as *gouleyant*, meaning they slip down easily, and there are few better areas in which to succumb to the charms of good quaffing wines than the Loire valley.

The major grape varieties are *Chenin Blanc* (also known as *Pineau de la Loire*), *Sauvignon* and *Muscadet* for white wines, *Pinot Noir* and *Cabernet Franc* for rosés, and *Pinot Noir, Cabernet Franc, Gamay* and *Cot* for reds. The whites are best known abroad, particularly those produced just to the west of Tours, at Vouvray and Montlouis. Both are made from the *Chenin Blanc* grape, and, at their best, bring out the celebrated 'honeyed' quality associated with this grape, the wines of Montlouis tending to be softer and sweeter, though both *appellations* range from bone dry to medium-sweet. Further north, in the valley of le Loir, the *Chenin Blanc* is also used to produce Jasnières, described by one vigneron as 'all fruit on the palette and flint on the nose', and the increasingly popular Côteaux-du-Vendômois and Côteaux-du-Loir, the latter being the more interesting of the two. Sparkling wines made from the *Chenin Blanc* have become something of a speciality of Saumur, marketed under both the *Saumur Mousseux* and *Crémant de Loire* labels, and are quite capable of vying with non-vintage champagnes. The major white wine producers in Anjou lie to the south-west of Angers, and all, again, make use of the *Chenin Blanc* grape. There is a cluster of small *appellations* in this corner, Côteaux-du-Layon, Quarts-de-Chaume and Bonnezeaux in the Layon valley, Savennières on the north bank of the Loire, all exploiting the frequent morning mists to encourage the formation of 'noble rot' at harvest, and so give the wine an unaccustomed sweetness and depth. The Layon valley wines are exclusively sweet, but those from Savennières combine a honeyed bouquet with a dryness and bite on the palate, qualities which have made the single vineyard *appellations*, such as Coulée-de-Serrant and La Roche-aux-Moines, much sought after.

Of the other two types of white wine, Sauvignon de Touraine is an umbrella term given to any wine made in Touraine from the *Sauvignon* grape. It is inexpensive, reliable, and perfectly suited to drinking by the glass on a café terrace. Muscadet probably requires little introduction, as it has become the most popular French white wine in the UK, though there are a few ground rules it may be worth observing. All Muscadet comes from the mouth of the Loire, the *pays Nantaise*, in Brittany, and at its heart lies an area known as *Sèvre-et-Maine*. It is here that the best Muscadet is made, and here that the method of leaving the wine to mature on its lees until such time as it is bottled was first adopted. This style of wine, known as *sur lie*, improves the depth and quality of an otherwise extremely acidic drink, made from a grape variety which was first imported from Burgundy in order to produce a base wine to distil into Dutch brandy. *Muscadet AC*, the common or garden stuff, still tastes like a base wine, but this does not mean all *Muscadet-sur-Lie* is worth a few extra francs a bottle. In order to get the best out of the lees method, the wine should be bottled direct from the cask in the grower's cellar. If it is moved for bottling by a *négociant*, the lees will be disturbed and the flavour spoiled. As such it is always worth looking for the term *mise en bouteille au domaine* on the label.

The vast majority of rosé wines are made in Anjou, whose sweet, pink café wine, *rouget*, became a national hit after the Second World War. Tastes have since changed, and the rosés you now encounter are less cloyingly sweet than they used to be. Even so, production is on a downward trend, and a number of the bigger growers have now entirely switched to producing red wines.

The Loire's red wines are nothing like as well known outside the region as its whites, and, while none aspire, to any great depth of flavours they can be extremely pleasant, at their best a good match for the better known light red wines of Beaujolais and the Rhône valley. The finest are made from the *Cabernet Franc* grape (cut with a little *Cabernet Sauvignon*) in Chinon and Bourgeuil, with the *appellation* St-Nicolas-de-Bourgeuil being a lighter version of Bourgeuil. Chinon produces the fresher of the two main *appellations*, with a wonderfully soft bouquet, and what is usually described as a hint of violets on the palate. Bourgeuil is more austere, and ages better; it is worth leaving for a good three or four years before drinking. Saumur-Champigny also makes use of the *Cabernet Franc*, and, like Sancerre, became briefly fashionable in French restaurants during the 1980s. Prices are now back to where one suspects they should be, roughly comparable to Chinon, and, if you like open, fruity reds, it is an enjoyable wine. The one other red you are likely to encounter is Gamay de Touraine, production of which, despite the generic title, is concentrated around Amboise and Mesland. Like Beaujolais it is made from the *Gamay* grape, producing a wine every bit as reminiscent of strawberries, but, lacking the sun of southern Burgundy, tending to be thinner.

Visiting Châteaux, Museums and Churches

Opening times are only quoted in this guide where they are exceptionally restrictive, and even here it may be worth checking before going out of your way. Up-to-date information can easily be obtained from local *Syndicats d'Initiative*, and from the annual broadsheets issued by each of the four *Comités Départmentaux de Tourisme*. Their addresses and phone numbers are listed on page 21.

A few general rules should be remembered. Many châteaux and most smaller museums are closed outside the tourist season, which stretches from Easter to October and reaches its peak in July and August. Tuesday is the closing day for municipal museums and any properties staffed by public employees, as well as for an increasing number of privately owned properties. Smaller places may only open in the afternoon or at weekends, and virtually all châteaux, museums and churches close for lunch, usually from 12.00 to 14.00. Village churches are often kept locked and will post a notice indicating where the key might be obtained (instructions are supplied for places mentioned in the text where this is not obvious). If not, then an enquiry at the nearest house or café will usually elicit the address of the custodian, but one should observe the proprieties, and the key-holder will not appreciate being interrupted during lunch.

The annual *Portes Ouvertes* day, usually a Sunday in September, gives the public access to *Monuments Historiques* (listed buildings and sites) not otherwise open, and organises special events at those which can usually be visited. Details are available from the *Comités Départmentaux de Tourisme*.

Access to churches and châteaux does vary enormously. The *Monument Historique* signs which point the way to notable monuments from major roads indicate nothing more than that a building is listed. They do not signify that a place is open, or even generously inclined towards the occasional visitor. Nor, in the case of small privately-owned châteaux, do advertised opening hours constitute a guarantee—business, family affairs, or disrepair can cause owners to lock up their premises and abandon visitors to a baffled stroll around the front gate. When access is obtained it is unlikely you will be given free rein to wander at will. The guided tour is still the preferred form in all but the largest châteaux. These usually last about an hour and tend towards the 'historical-anecdotal', though in summer the availability of bright, enthusiastic and well-informed students can transform a visit. The latter will often speak English, either conducting the tour bilingually or, if the demand is there, taking you round as a separate party. Out of season you will rarely encounter English-speaking guides, except at places such as Angers, Blois, Chinon and Amboise.

Access to churches is more straightforward, the major complication being caused by restoration projects. Guided tours are available to Tours and Angers cathedrals, La Trinité, Vendôme and Fontevraud. Details are usually posted at the west end of the nave. To visit the abbeys of Cormery and Asnières, and the cloister at Tours cathedral, a guided tour is obligatory. Otherwise one is free to roam, or combine a guided tour with a more leisurely exploration.

Weekly Markets and Calendar of Events

The list of markets and festivals below makes no pretence at covering a crowded programme fully, and notes only the largest of the local fêtes. Local tourist offices will supply details of these events, as well as the precise dates of the moveable feasts.

Markets

The following is a summary of the larger markets, most of which start before 9.00 am and are usually running down by lunchtime.

Mondays:	Baugé (afternoon), Montrichard, Sablé-sur-Sarthe, Richelieu, Tours (St-Paul)
Tuesdays:	Bourgueil, Chalonnes-sur-Loire, Marchenoir (afternoon)
Wednesdays:	Amboise (glass market), Azay-le-Rideau, La Flèche, Fontevraud, Loches, Montoire, Tours (butter market, Place des Halles; flower market, Boulevard Béranger)
Thursdays:	Bracieux, Chinon, Le Grand-Pressigny, Le Lude, Montlouis, Selles-sur-Cher, La Suze-sur-Sarthe, Tours (local specialities and artisans' work, Place de la Résistance)
Fridays:	Amboise, Chalonnes-sur-Loire, Montrichard, Ponts-de-Cé, Ste-Maure-de-Touraine, Richelieu, Tours (general market, St-Paul), Vendôme
Saturdays:	Amboise, Angers (general market, Boulevard Bessonneau; flea market, Place Imbach), Château-du-Loir, Chinon, Fontevraud, Tours (butter, fruit and vegetables, Place des Halles; cloth market, Place de la Victoire)
Sundays:	Blois, La Flèche, Joué-les-Tours, Langeais, Tours (Place Rabelais)

Events

January
Angers: Film Festival (usually mid-month)

February
Angers: Honey Fair (Boulevard Foch)
Bourgueil: Wine Festival (first Saturday in month)
Chalonnes-sur-Loire: Wine Festival (last weekend)
Saumur: Wine Festival (second weekend)

March–April
Angers: Food Fair (first Sunday in March)
Solesmes: Easter Ceremonies

May
Chambord: 'Festival de Chambord' (theatre, music and dance festival, late May–end June)
Saumur: International Horse Show (first weekend of month)
Tours: 'Florilège Vocal de Tours' (International choir festival, end of month)

June
Blois: 'Floréal Blésois' (carnival and river regatta, mid-month)
Chinon: Series of lectures by the *Entonneurs Rabelaisians* (Rabelaisian Imbibers)
Saumur: Festival of Military Music (odd-numbered years) or Flower Festival (even years)
Tours: 'Fêtes Musicales de Touraine' (International Music Festival, last two weekends in month)

July
Amboise: Summer festival of music and drama (continues into August)
Angers et al: 'Festival d'Anjou' (theatre, music, drama and dance throughout Anjou)
Doué-la-Fontaine: 'Journées de la Rose' (Rose Festival, mid-month)
Loches: 'Festival de Théâtre Musicale' (middle of month)
Le Puy-Notre-Dame: Wine and Mushroom Fair (first Saturday)
Saumur: 'Carrousel' (equestrian tattoo held each evening during the last fortnight of the month)

August
Chinon: Medieval Market (first weekend of month)
Montoire: World Folklore Festival (second week)
Rochefort-sur-Loire: Anjou Folk Festival (mid-month)
Vouvray: Wine Fair (also at Montlouis, 15th August)

September
Angers: International Folk Festival (second week)
Château-du-Loir: 'Comice Agricole' (agricultural show)
Fontevraud: 'Art et Lumière' (drama, music, dance, end of month)
Le Lude: 'Foire du Raillon' (general fair, second Thursday in month)

October
Angers: Festival of 20th Century Music
Azay-le-Rideau: Apple Fair (first or second weekend of month)
Bourgeuil: Chestnut Fair (mid-month)
Preuilly: Plum Fair (mid-month)
Romorantin-Lanthenay: 'Foire Gastronomique de Sologne' (Series of days given over to eating at the end of the month)
Tours: 'Crea-Cité' (Exhibition of Contemporary Art held in the Mairie)

December

Angers: 'Foire aux Chiens' (major dog show, second Sunday of month)

Anjou: 'Messe des Naulets' (Mass and Carol service held in a country church on Christmas Eve, the carols, in Angevin dialect, being sung in a different church each year)

Tourist Information Offices

French Government Tourist Offices abroad

UK: 178 Piccadilly, London W1V 0AL. Phone 0171 491 7622; fax 0171 493 6594

USA, New York: 610 Fifth Avenue, Suite 222, New York NY 10020. Phone 757 1125; fax 247 6468

USA, Middle West: 645 North Michigan Avenue, Chicago, Illinois 60611. Phone 337 6301; fax 337 6339

USA West Coast: 9545 Wiltshire Boulevard, Beverly Hills, California 90212. Phone 271 7838; fax 276 2835

USA South: 2305 Cedar Springs Boulevard, Dallas, Texas 75201. Phone 720 4010; fax 720 0250

Canada, Montreal: 181 Avenue McGill College, Suite 490, Montreal, Quebec H3A 2W9. Phone: 288 4264; fax 845 4868

Canada, Toronto: 30 Saint Patrick Street, Suite 700, Toronto, Ontario, M5T 3A3

Local Tourist Information Centres (Syndicats d'Initiative and Offices du Tourisme

Indre-et-Loire

Amboise 37402, Amboise Cédex. Phone 47.57.09.28, fax 47.57.14.35

Azay-le-Rideau 37190, B.P.5 Place de l'Europe, Azay-le Rideau. Phone 47.45.44.40, fax 47.45.31.46

Bléré 37150, 8 rue J.J. Rousseau. Phone 47.57.93.00, fax 47.23.57.73

Bourgeuil 37140, Les Halles, B.P. 33. Phone 47.97.91.39, fax 47.97.91.39

Château-la-Vallière 37330, Place d'Armes. Phone 47.24.14.31, fax 47.24.00.57, Mairie, phone 47.24.00.21

Chemillé-sur-Indrois 37460, Mairie. Phone 47.92.60.75, fax 47.92.64.64

Chenonceaux 37150, 13, rue du Château, B.P. 1. Phone 47.23.94.45

Chinon 37500, 12, rue Voltaire. Phone 47.93.17.85, fax 47.93.93.05

Cinq-Mars-la-Pile 37130, Mairie. Phone 47.96.43.33

Cormery 37320, 13, rue Nationale. Phone 47.43.30.84

Descartes 37160, Mairie. Phone 47.59.70.50, fax 47.59.72.20

Genillé 37460, 17, place A. Sorel. Phone 47.59.57.85, fax 47.59.59.78

Le Grand-Pressigny 37350, Rue du Collège. Phone 47.94.90.37

Joué-les-Tours 37300, 2, boulevard des Bretonnlères. Phone 47.80.05.97

Langeais 37130, B.P. 47. Phone 47.96.58.22, fax 47.96.83.41

Ligueil 37240, 49, rue A. Briand. Phone 47.92.06.88

Loches 37600, Place de la Marne. Phone 47.59.07.98, fax 47.91.61.50

Luynes 37230, Maison XVe, B.P. 1. Phone 47.55.50.31, fax 47.55.52.56

Montbazon 37250, B.P. 2, 11, avenue de le Gare. Phone 47.26.97.87,, fax 47.34.01.78

Montlouis 37270, Place de la Mairie. Phone 47.45.00.16

Montrésor 37460, Maison de Pays. Phone 47.92.71.04/47.92.60.19, fax 47.92.71.11

Richelieu 37129, 6, Grand Rue. Phone 47.58.13.62/47.58.10.13,

Rochecorbon 37210, Place du Croissant. Phone 47.52.80.22, fax 47.52.57.57

Ste-Catherine-de-Fierbois 37800, Mairie. Phone 47.65.43.46

Ste-Maure-de-Touraine 37800, Rue du Château. Phone 47.65.66.20

Savonnières 37510. Mairie. Phone 47.50.12.66

Tours 37042, 78 rue Bernard Palissy, Tours Cedex. Phone 47.70.37.37, fax 47.61.14.22

Les Vallées-de-la-Manse 37800, Maison de Pays d'Accueil, 33, Grand Rue, Saint Epain. Phone 47.65.84.653

Vouvray 37210, Mairie. Phone 47.52.68.73/47.52.70.48, fax 47.52.67.76

Loir-et-Cher

Blois 41000, Pavillon Anne de Bretagne, 3, Av. J. Laigret. Phone 54.74.06.49

Bracieux 41250, Mairie. Phone 54.46.42.37

Celle 41360, Mairie. Phone 54.23.72.09

Cellettes 41120, 2 rue de Rozelle, Mairie. Phone 54.70.30.46 (summer) 54.70.47.54 (winter)

Chaires-sur-Cher 41320, Mairie. Phone 54.98.03.24

Chaumont-sur-Loire 41150, Maison du Tourisme, rue du Maréchall Leclerc. Phone 54.20.91.73

Chemery 41700, Maine. Phone/fax 54.71.80.24

Cour-Cheverny 41700, 4 Av. de Cheverny, Cidex 403. Phone 54.79.95.63

Droué 41270, Rue de la Poste, Maine. Phone 54.80.15.04 (summer), fax 54.80.50.39

Lamotte-Beuvron 41600, Mairie. Phone 54.88.00.28

La Ferté-Imbault 41300, 26, rue Nationale, Cidex 158. Phone 54.96.26.82

Les Montils 41120, 1, route de Candé. Phone 54.44.05.07

Mareuil-sur-Cher 41110, Mairie. Phone 54.75.15.13, fax 54.32.79.51

Mennetou-sur-Cher 41320, 1, Grande Rue. Phone 51.98.12.29

Mer 41500, Mairie. Phone 54.81.02.03

Monthou-sur-Cher 41400, Mairie. Phone 54.71.43.17

Montoire-sur-le-Loir 41800, Mairie. Phone 54.85.00.29

Montrichard 41400, 1 rue du Pont. Phone 54.32.05.10 (summer)

Mur-de-Sologne 41320, Mairie. Phone 54.83.81.15

Nouan-le-Fuzelier 41600, 29, rue du Bourg Neuf. Phone 54.88.72.23

Noyers-sur-Cher 41140, Mairie. Phone 54.75.02.35

Onzain 41150, Mairie. Phone 54.20.72.59

Pontlevoy 41400, 5, place du Collège, Mairie. Phone 54.32.60.29, fax 54.32.50.43

Romorantin-Lanthenay 41200, Place de la Paix. Phone 54.76.43.89

Saint-Aignan 41110, Maison du Tourisme. Phone 54.75.22.85 (summer), 54.75.13.31 (winter)

Salbris 41300, 27, boulevard de la République. Phone 54.06.15.52

Selles-sur-Cher 41130, Mairie. Phone 54.97.40.19

Suèvres 41500, Place de la Mairie. Phone 54.07.05.27

Trôo 41800, La Croix Verte. Phone 54.72.58.74, fax 54.72.51.27

Vallée de la Cisse, 16, Av. du Mal de Lattre de Tassigny, 41190 Chambon-sur-Cisse. Phone 54.70.02.16

Vendôme 41100, Hôtel du Bellay, Le Saillant, Parc Ronsard. Phone 54.77.05.07

Maine-et-Loire

Angers Cédex 49051, Place Kennedy/BP 5157. Phone 41.23.51.11, fax 41.23.51.11

Baugé 49150, Place de l'Europe. Phone 41.89.12.12, fax 41.89.12.12

Beaufort-en-Vallée 49250, 13 rue de Général Leclerc. Phone 41.80.30.01, fax 41.57.42.30

Beaulieu-sur-Layon 49190, 3, rue St Vincent. Phone 41.78.31.30, fax 41.78.65.07

Beaupréau 49600, Mairie. Phone 41.63.00.47, fax 41.63.00.47

Blaison-Gohier 49320, L'Airault. Phone 41.57.17.57, fax 41.57.17.57

Brissac-Quincé 49320, Mairie. Phone 41.91.22.13, fax 41.91.22.13

Chalonnes-sur-Loire 49290, B.P. 81. Phone 41.78.13.22, fax 41.78.26.21

Chateauneauf-sur-Sarthe 49330, Qu. Sarthe (or Mairie). Phone 41.69.84.20, fax 41.69.82.89

Chemillé 49120, 5, rue Arzillé (or Mairie). Phone 41.30.35.17

Chênehutte-Trèves-Cunault 49350, 22, rue Beauregard. Phone 41.67.92.70

Cholet 49306, Pl. Rougé/BP 636. Phone 41.62.22.35, fax 41.62.22.35

Doué-la-Fontaine 49700, 30, pl. Champ-de-Foire. Phone 41.59.11.04, fax 41.59.20.49

Durtal 49430, Mairie. Phone/fax 41.76.30.24, 41.76.30.24

Fontevraud-L'Abbaye 49590, Avenue Rochechouard. Phone 41.51.71.21, fax 41.51.79.45

Gennes 49350, Pl. Etoile (or Mairie). Phone 41.51.81.30, fax 41.51.81.30

Maulévrier 49360, La Tuilerie. Phone 41.55.00.29, fax 41.55.09.60

Mazé Montgeoffroy 49250, Mairie. Phone 41.80.60.19, fax 41.80.60.19

La Ménitre 49250, Anc. Gare SNCF (or Mairie). Phone 41.45.63.63, fax 41.45.67.51

Montjean-sur-Loire 49570, Mairie. Phone 41.39.80.46, fax 41.39.80.46

Montreuil-Bellay 49260, Pl. Ormeaux (or Mairie). Phone 41.52.33.86, fax 41.52.32.39

Montsoreau 49730, Av. Loire (or Mairie). Phone 41.51.70.15, fax 41.51.70.22

Pouancé 49420, 2, rue Porte Angev. (or Mairie). Phone 41.92.41.08, fax 41.92.45.86

Le Puy-Notre-Dame 49260, Mairie. Phone 41.52.26.34, fax 41.52.26.34

Rochefort-sur-Loire 49190, Grand'Cour (or Mairie). Phone 41.78.70.24, fax 41.78.81.70

Les Rosiers-sur-Loire 49350, Pl. Mail (or Mairie). Phone 41.51.80.04, fax 41.51.85.59

Saumur 49400, Place de la Bilange/BP 241. Phone 41.51.03.06, fax 41.51.03.06

Seiches-sur-le-Loir 49140, 5 Square Georges Brassens. Phone 41.76.20.37, fax 41.76.20.37

St-Aubin-de-Luigné 49190, Embarcadère (or Mairie). Phone 41.78.33.28, fax 41.78.52.98

St-Florent-le-Vieil 49410, Carref. Tourist (or Mairie). Phone 41.72.50.39, fax 41.72.52.37

St-Mathurin-sur-Loire 49250, La Marsaulaie. Phone 41.57.08.18, fax 41.57.01.82

St-Rémy-la-Varenne 49250, Mairie. Phone 41.57.03.94, fax 41.57.03.94

The Sarthe

Bazouges-sur-le-Loir 72200, Mairie. Phone 43.45.20.30, fax 43.45.32.20

La Chartre-sur-le-Loir 72340, 'La Basse Pointe'. Phone 43.44.40.04, fax 43.44.40.04

Château-du-Loir 72500, Hôtel de Ville. Phone 43.44.00.38, fax 43.44.56.68

La Flèche Cédex 72205, Hôtel de Ville. Phone 43.94.02.53, fax 43.94.02.53

Le Lude 72800, Place François de Nicolay. Phone 43.94.62.20, fax 43.94.62.20

Malicorne-sur-Sarthe 72270, Rue des Sablons. Phone 43.94.80.09, fax 43.94.74.45

Sablé-sur-Sarthe 72300, Pl. Raph. Elizé. Phone 43.95.00.60, fax 43.95.00.60

Chronology of Regional History

52 BC	Julius Caesar conquers Gaul
1C AD	Caesarodunum (Tours) founded
c 275 AD	First barbarian invasions of the Loire by Franks and Suevi
304	Gatien described as bishop of Tours
372	Colony of hermits established at Marmoutier
397	St-Martin dies at Candes
470	Cathedral of Angers moved within the city walls
507	Clovis, King of the Franks, defeats Alaric II, Arian King of the Visigoths, at the battle of Vouillé
573–94	Gregory, author of the *Historia Francorum*, is bishop of Tours
732	Charles Martel defeats a Moorish army on the plain of Ste-Maure
791	Ithier founds the abbey of St-Paul de Cormery
796	Charlemagne instals Alcuin as abbot of St-Martin at Tours
853–54	Norse invasion fleet sacks Angers
898	Foulques le Roux seizes power in Anjou and takes the title 'count'
903	Martinopolis (Tours) destroyed by fire
950	Thibaud le Tricheur described as count of Tours and Blois
987–1040	Foulques Nerra as count of Anjou. Earliest castles of which fragments still survive in the region erected at Langeais, Loches and Montbazon
997	Hervé begins the new church of St-Martin at Tours
1026	Saumur falls to Foulques Nerra
1032	Abbey of La Trinité, Vendôme founded
1044	Annexation of Touraine by Geoffroy Martel, count of Anjou
1101	Robert d'Arbrissel establishes the monastery of Fontevraud
1109	Maine united with Anjou
1133	Birth of Henry II (Plantagenet)
1144	Geoffrey Plantagenet seizes Normandy
c 1148	Ulger begins rebuilding of Angers cathedral
1152	Henry Plantagenet marries Eleanor of Aquitaine
1154	Henry Plantagenet ascends the English throne as Henry II
1168	St-Ours at Loches completed
1175	Henry II founds the Hôpital St-Jean at Angers
1180	Philip Augustus ascends the French throne
1189	Henry II dies at Chinon
1199	Richard Coeur-de-Lion buried at Fontevraud
1202	Anjou falls to Philip Augustus
1205	Hubert de Burgh surrenders Touraine to the French crown
c1210	St-Serge, Angers begun

1230	Blanche of Castille begins work on the new château at Angers
1246	Charles, brother of Louis IX, created count of Anjou
1279	Choir of Tours cathedral completed
1307	Suppression of the Order of Knights Templar
1318	Choir of La Trinité, Vendôme completed
1348	Black Death
1356	English victorious at the battle of Poitiers, King Jean le Bon taken into captivity
1360	Louis, brother of Charles V, made Duke of Anjou
1371	County of Vendôme acquired by the Bourbons
1377	Louis d'Anjou commissions the Apocalypse tapestries
1392	Onset of the madness of Charles VI
1409	René d'Anjou born at Angers
1422–61	Reign of Charles VII
1427	Charles VII moves the court to Chinon. West front of Tours cathedral begun
1429	Joan of Arc relieves the siege of Orléans
1453	English expelled from France
1454	University law school at Angers expanded to admit 1000 students
1461–83	Reign of Louis XI
1465	Louis XI begins the new château at Langeais
1476	First printing press in the Loire valley established at Angers
1483–98	Reign of Charles VIII
1491	Charles VIII marries Anne of Brittany at Langeais. New building programme launched at the Château d'Amboise
1494–96	First Italian campaign
1498–1515	Reign of Louis XII
1498–1501	East wing of the château de Blois constructed
1498–1510	Château de Chaumont completed
1507	West front of La Trinité, Vendôme completed
1515	Châteaux de Chenonceau and Azay-le-Rideau begun
1515–1547	Reign of François I
1515–24	North-west wing of the château de Blois constructed
1516–1519	Leonardo da Vinci at Clos-Lucé
1519	Château de Chambord begun
1524–26	François I imprisoned at Pavia
1530	Hôtel de Pincé, Angers begun
1547–1559	Reign of Henri II
1560–1574	Reign of Charles IX
1572	St Bartholomew's Day Massacre
1574–1589	Reign of Henri III
1576	Henri, duc de Guise, founds the Catholic League
1588	Henri de Guise murdered at Blois
1589–1610	Reign of Henri IV
1589	Vendôme sacked
1598	Edict of Nantes guarantees religious toleration
1599	Philippe Duplessis-Mornay founds the Académie Protestante de Saumur

1600	Henri IV marries Marie de Medici
1604	Royal College of La Flèche founded
1606	Château de Brissac-Quincé begun
1610–1643	Reign of Louis XIII
1625	Château de Cheverny begun
1626	Gaston d'Orléans, brother of Louis XIII, granted Blois
1635–38	South-west wing of the château de Blois constructed
1643–1715	Reign of Louis XIV
1648–53	Civil War (the Fronde). Angers placed under direct royal control
1684	Revocation of the Edict of Nantes
1693	Notre-Dame-des-Ardilliers, Saumur completed
1715–1774	Reign of Louis XV
1756	College of Surgeons established at Tours
1767	Cavalry School created at Saumur
1770	Duc de Choiseul exiled to Chanteloup
1773	Château de Montgeoffroy begun
1774–92	Reign of Louis XIV
1789	Storming of the Bastille
1792	Proclamation of the Republic
1793–95	Vendéen War
1804–1815	First Empire under Napoleon Bonaparte
1807	Demolition of the medieval walls of Angers begins
1825	David-d'Angers carves the memorial to the Marquis de Bonchamps at St-Florent-le-Vieil
1845–47	Tours and Angers connected by railway
1848–70	Second Republic
1868–71	Théâtre Municipal at Angers built
1914–18	First World War
1939–45	Second World War
1952	First *son et lumière* performed at Chambord
1970	University of Tours founded
1991	TGV-Atlantique services inaugurated, connecting Tours with Paris in just over one hour

Further Reading

The following is not intended as a bibliography, but as an informal list of suggestions which concentrates as much as possible on works in English.

History. Questions of Plantagenet rule and the experience of a Valois court on the banks of the Loire have understandably attracted the most attention. Bernard Bachrach's long-awaited study *Fulk Nerra, the Neo-Roman Consul, 987–1040: A Political Biography of the Angevin Count* promises to shed light on the early feudalism of the area, as well as offering a much-needed analysis of a seminal figure. J. Gillingham's *The Angevin Empire* (London, 1984) probably underestimates the flaws in Plantagenet government but remains a useful general account, while W.L. Warren's *Henry II* (Eyre Methuen, 1973) and D.D.R. Owen's *Eleanor of Aquitaine* (Blackwell, 1993) are the best of the biographies. Anyone with an interest in primary sources should certainly consult R.W. Eyton's indispensable *Court, Household, and Itinerary of King Henry II* (Taylor & Co, 1886). K. Fowler's *The Age of Plantagenet and Valois* (London, 1967) offers a narrative treatment of the later Middle Ages, which might be supplemented by E. Perroy's *The Hundred Years War* (London, 1965), a dated but immensely readable account. More focused 15C insights can be found in M.G. Vale's biography, *Charles VII* (London, 1974), and Michael Jones' translation of the writings of Louis XI's Governor of the Château de Chinon, *Philippe de Commynes: Memoirs* (Penguin, 1972).

A plethora of books dealing with the Loire during the 16C have appeared in the last 30 years. R.J. Knecht's *French Renaissance Monarchy: Francis I and Henry II* (Longman, 1984) was conceived as a sixth form primer, and has the advantage of succinctness, but those in search of more detail would be better with Knecht's magisterial *Francis I* (Cambridge University Press, 1982). The later 16C is admirably treated in J. Héritier's *Catherine de Medici* (Allen and Unwin, 1963) and M.P. Holt's *The Duke of Anjou and the Political Struggle during the Wars of Religion* (Cambridge University Press, 1986). Finally, for a first-rate account of the French Revolution you need look no further than Simon Schama's *Citizens: A Chronicle of the French Revolution* (Penguin, 1989), while Jacques Godehot's broad and theoretical *The Counter-Revolution* (Routledge, 1972) provides a good background to the Vendéen War.

Art and Architecture. Appallingly little has been published in English, excepting articles in specialist academic journals, a situation which is unlikely to change for some time. Charles Lelong's *Touraine Romane* (Zodiaque, 1977) contains a précis in English, is handsomely illustrated, and ranks among the better in the series, though the text of Jean-Marie Berland's companion *Val de Loire Roman* (Zodiaque, 1980) may disappoint the scholarly. Marcia Kupfer's *Romanesque Wall Painting in Central France* (Yale, 1993) is exclusively concerned with painting in the diocese of Bourges but contains a useful discussion of the crypt cycle at St-Aignan. Another study which just touches on Romanesque forms in the region is *The Romanesque Frieze and Its Spectator* (edited by Deborah Kahn; Harvey Miller, 1992), with a good essay on Selles-sur-Cher. The relevant entries in Grodecki and Brissac's *Gothic Stained Glass: 1200–1300* (Thames and Hudson, 1985), Jean Bony's *French Gothic Architecture of the 12th and 13th Centuries* (University of California, 1983), and Christopher Wilson's *The Gothic Cathedral* (Thames and Hudson, 1990) are all worth consulting. The same can be said for Wim Swaan's *Art and Architecture of the Late Middle Ages* (Omega, 1982), a seriously neglected area of study when it comes to the Loire valley, indeed when it comes to northern France. Erwin Panofsky's *Early Netherlandish Painting* (Icon edition, 1971) and G. Ring's *A Century of French Painting: 1400–1500* (London, 1949) also have a lot to offer on the Angers Apocalypse Tapestries and the work of Jean Fouquet.

The Renaissance, by contrast, is well served by books in English, the main lines of research having been admirably synthesised in Anthony Blunt's *Art and Architecture in France: 1500–1700* (Penguin, 2nd edition, 1981). Blunt's bibliography on pp 447–53 is worth exploring for further suggestions, though two other works should be mentioned: Joan Evans' *Monastic Architecture in France from the Renaissance to the Revolution* (Cambridge, 1964) and Marcus Binney's *Châteaux of the Loire* (Viking, 1992), the latter serving as a useful introduction and general gazeteer.

Works in French. Here you are spoilt for choice. Jacques Mallet's *L'Art Roman de l'Ancienne Anjou* (Picard, 1984) is an excellent general survey, while André Mussat's *Le Style Gothique dans l'Ouest de France* (Paris, 1963) at least deals with a subject—Angevin Gothic Architecture—which intrigues a great number of scholars, but on which no one seems prepared to publish. Denis Jeanson's *La Maison Seigneuriale du Val de Loire* (Garnier, 1981) covers feudal architecture, while more specialised areas are well-served by the appropriate volumes of *Le Guide des Châteaux de France* (Hermé) and *L'Architecture Rurale Française: Corpus des Genres, des Types et des Variants* (Berger-Levrault). For ecclesiastical architecture the relevant volume of the *Dictionnaire des Eglises de France* is *Val de Loire, Poitou* (Paris, 1968). The *Corpus Vitrearum Medii Aevi* have also published the medieval stained glass in the region in the volume *Les Vitraux du Centre et des Pays de la Loire* (CNRS, 1981). François Eygun's *Arts des Pays de l'Ouest* (Arthaud, 1965) and François Lebrun's *Histoire des Pays de la Loire* (Paris, 1972) remain useful background surveys.

Glossary

ABACUS: flat slab seated above a capital

APSE-AMBULATORY: semicircular aisle terminating a church to the east, generally used for processional purposes

APSE-ECHELON: arrangement of apses forming an inverted V at the east end of a church

BARBICAN: defensive work attached to the outside of a town or castle, particularly applied to a double-tower erected over a bridge or gate

CHARTRAIN: derived from Chartres, and particularly from Chartres cathedral

COLOMBIER: dovecot

COMMUNS: outbuildings, usually including stables

COMPOSED WINDOW: two lancets surmounted by an oculus

CORBEL: projecting block, usually stone, supporting a beam, roof or shaft

CORPS-DE-LOGIS: the major residential block of a château, as distinct from pavilions or wings

COUR-D'HONNEUR: courtyard giving on to the 'corps-de-logis'

DONJON: fortified tower (origin of the English term 'dungeon')

EXTRADOS: outer surface of an arch

GRISAILLE: monochrome painting, the term often applied to lightly tinted stained glass

HALL CHURCH: church with a single storey elevation, i.e. where the aisles are approximately the same height as the central vessel

HÔTEL PARTICULIER: large private townhouse

INTRADOS: under surface of an arch

LOUVRE: overlapping wooden shutter designed to admit air and exclude rain

LUCARNE: any gabled opening in a roof or spire, often applied to dormer windows

MACHICOLATION: parapet projected on brackets with openings in the floor so as to allow missiles, boiling oil, etc, to be dropped on anyone unfortunate enough to be below

OPUS MIXTUM: alternate bands of stone and brick

OPUS RETICULATUM: diagonal arrangement of squared stones

PETIT APPAREIL: small pieces of stone, semi-dressed and roughly coursed

PILIER CANTONÉE: pier with four attached shafts on the cardinal faces

RETABLE: painted or carved screen standing on or beneath an altar

SOFFIT ROLL: roll moulding carried round the undersurface of an arch

SPANDREL: triangular space between the side of an arch and the adjacent horizontals and verticals

STRINGCOURSE: horizontal band dividing one register from another

TRIBUNE: spacious gallery, usually situated above the aisle of a church (often mistakenly used to describe any intermediate storey of the elevation)

TRIFORIUM: arcaded wall-passage found between the arcade and clerestory of a church elevation

TRIRADIAL: vaulting device making use of three equal ribs

TRUMEAU: post or statue supporting the centre of a lintel

TUFFEAU: a soft, calcarious limestone quarried along the banks of the rivers Loire, Loir, Indre, Cher and Vienne and widely used in building

VANITAS: moralising still-life in which objects are arranged to suggest the transience and uncertainty of life

VOLUTE: curved scroll or leaf-tip at the corner of a capital

VOUSSOIR: wedge-shaped stone around an arch

1

Blois, the Petit-Beauce and the Loire to Tours

ROAD (176km): Blois N152, 16km Mer; D15, 9km Talcy; D15/D917, 9km Marchenoir; D50, 10km Villexanton; 19km Blois; D751, 20km Chaumont; 15km Amboise; 14km Montlouis; 8km Tours; N152, 7km Vouvray; D46, 4km Vernou-sur-Brenne; D1/D58, 29km Onzain; D58/N152 16km Blois.

The above routes describe two unequal circuits, looping respectively to the north-east and south-west of Blois. The area they cover would once have been known as the Blésois, the term having been used during the Middle Ages to describe the old county of Blois, but the use is now generally restricted to the vicinity of Blois itself. In fact, both the words Blois and Blésois derive from *Bleiz*, a Celtic term for wolf, and are rooted in the vast forest which once covered the whole region. Pockets of this woodland still survive, particularly to the south and west, but both the land to the north and much of the Loire valley downstream to Tours was cleared between the 15C and 18C. There are also marked disparities between the sort of settlements which grew up along the banks of the river and those of the Petit-Beauce, a fact reflected in the very different treatments given to each below.

Blois

History. Although the date at which this stretch of the north bank of the Loire was first occupied is uncertain, it seems likely that by the 1C AD a small trading station had been constructed where the Roman road from Chartres to Bourges crossed the river. This incipient town was developed under the emperor Septimus Severus during the early 3C, acquiring baths (evidence of which has been uncovered beneath the Place Valin-de-la-Vaissière), a port, and necropolises on the high ground around the present cathedral. It was never a large Gallo-Roman town, but in 584, in the wake of the barbarian assimilation of the old Roman centres, Gregory of Tours could report that the *Biesenses* (people of Blois) entered into an alliance with the *Orléanais* against the *Dunois* to the north. And, under the Merovingian monarchy, Blois became the administrative and judicial centre of a *pagus*, answerable to the *cité* of Chartres, boasting a mint and a Benedictine abbey, Notre-Dame-de-Bourgmoyen, which was dedicated to the Virgin in 696.

Its status began to shift after the Norse raids of 854 and 857, and with the weakening of Carolingian authority the more powerful local families allied themselves initially with Louis the Pious, and eventually with the Robertian forbears of Hugh Capet. By 950 Thibaud le Tricheur described himself as count of Tours and Blois, and though this vast fiefdom was trimmed by Foulques Nerra, count of Anjou, it established Blois as one of the principal towns of the middle Loire. On inheriting

Champagne in 1019, Eudes II united Blois with his lands to the east, effectively encircling the southern half of the royal domain. And after Thibaud IV's brother Stephen assumed the English throne by virtue of his father's marriage to Adèle (the daughter of William the Conqueror), the house of Blois-Champagne boasted powerful friends indeed.

All this had an impact on the shape of Blois itself. A *castrum* was described as occupying the site of the present château as early as 903, and in 978 Thibaud le Tricheur was reported to have built a fortified tower there. A number of quarters were also developed along the axis of the road, often taking their titles from their principal churches. The *Bourgmoyen* grew along the river, to the north of the present bridge, with the *Foix* just to the west, around the old Benedictine abbey of St-Laumer. The *Haut-Quartier* took up residence on the rocky spur supporting the church of St-Solenne, with the *Bourg-St-Jean* between the castle and the priory of St-Jean, and the *Faubourg de Vienne* on the south bank of the river. Finally, in 1190, the *Bourgneuf* was constructed astride the road to Chartres.

But this must have seemed as little compared to Blois' late medieval prosperity. In 1392 Louis d'Orléans acquired the county and, on the death of Charles VIII at Amboise in 1498, his grandson, Louis, acceded to the throne as Louis XII. Louis had been born in Blois, favoured the town and established it as his winter residence, launching the first great wave of works which were to transform the château. His successor, François I, married Louis' daughter, Claude de France, and until Claude's death in 1524 Blois shared with Amboise the title of principal royal residence. The results of this royal interest are evident in the château de Blois, but the spectacle of the court in residence also brought lawyers, merchants and financiers to the town, and resulted in a rash of new and splendid townhouses. This is something of which one is less conscious today, as the result of the big mid-19C urban development programmes, and the bombardments of 1940 and 1944, has been to confine these dwellings to a few streets between the cathedral and the river. But it is as a great early 16C town that Blois is most profitably approached.

Town Tour. The best place to begin an exploration of Blois is in the **Jardins de l'Evêché**, banked against the high ground to the rear of the cathedral and at the north-east corner of the old town. From here the natural advantages of the site become apparent, as the bluff falls away south-westwards towards the river, before rising to form a secondary ridge supporting the château. The finest views are from the far end, by Anna Hyatt's 1921 equestrian statue of Joan of Arc, where you can make out the contours of the ridge as it runs west, past the garden façade of the Evêché and down towards the towers of the earlier Benedictine monastery of St-Nicolas. The views are part obscured by a magnificent ash tree, rising to shade the bishop's palace, but this eastern quarter of the town can be seen in full, gathering in height and grandeur before it falls away to meet the bridge. This, the **Pont Jacques Gabriel**, was built to replace a medieval structure swept away in the floods of 1716. When complete in 1724 it was once more the sole bridge to span the Loire between Amboise and Beaugency.

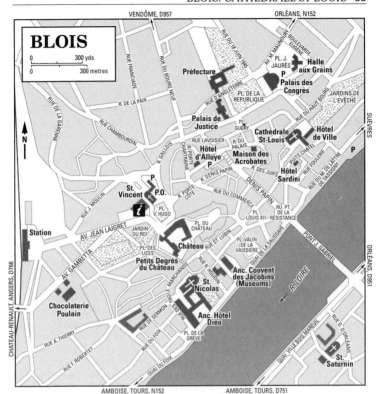

Jacques Gabriel was also responsible for the bishop's palace, **L' Ancien Evêché**, designed for Bishop de Bertier in 1698 as a rectangular block, set against the bluff to create a garden front some two storeys higher than that of the main façade. It now houses the Hôtel-de-Ville, the interiors having been refurbished in sober office fashion; but the principal façade survives as an impressively modulated design, balancing the flat treatment of the main elevation with the fuller-bodied stonework around the entrance block.

A brief stroll to the west quickly brings you along the north flank of the **Cathédrale St-Louis**, and into the Place St-Louis. Excavations have shown the Place to have been just to the east of the Gallo-Roman town, and the discovery of a cemetery here suggests the site was favoured by Blois' early Christian community. A small chapel dedicated to St Peter may have been built as early as the 6C, and certainly existed by the 10C, when contradictory accounts of miracles witnessed around the sarcophagus of St-Solenne begin to surface. The earliest account suggests that the coffin belonged to St-Solennis, a 9C Tourangeau hermit about whom little is known, but the most popular legend conflates this figure with the great early 6C bishop of Chartres, St-Solenne, who died in 507 accompanying Clovis on his campaign against Alaric the Goth. This story has it that the remains of Solenne had been discovered in the Poitou and were being transported north to be returned to the cathedral of Chartres. Having crossed the Loire at Blois, the sarcophagus was placed overnight in the chapel of St-Pierre, but in the morning—a common twist in medieval reliquary literature, this—the coffin became so heavy that no one could lift it. Honouring the saint's evident wish to remain at Blois, the widow of Count Thibaud le Tricheur built a new collegiate church on the site.

Whatever the identity of the saint, a church was undoubtedly built here in the late 10C, which was expanded after 1132, when the earlier canons were replaced by a congregation of Benedictine monks from the nowdestroyed abbey of the Bourgmoyen. The old foundation lost its independence, and from 1132 until 1697, when it was made a cathedral, its status was that of a priory, answerable to the abbot of Bourgmoyen. The downgrading does not seem to have lessened its attraction as a pilgrimage centre, nor to have dissuaded François I from reconstructing the wooden-roofed building. With the exception of the main apse piers, west front, and upper stages of the lantern tower, the whole of this early 16C church was destroyed by a hurricane in 1678. The greater part of the present structure is that undertaken between 1679 and 1702 and financed by Marie Charron, the wife of Colbert and a native of the town. Blois was finally given a bishop in 1697, and the church was rededicated to St-Louis.

The 17C church is certainly on a cathedral scale, rising without transepts, but with a full run of nave chapels which lend breadth to an already spacious design. The architectural idiom is perhaps even more selfconscious, a sort of weighty late 17C Gothic, as at Orléans equating the language of late medieval architecture with great church aesthetics. Elements of the earlier buildings were retained, as they had been in François I's church, a decision which is responsible for the north-western bell-tower, whose lower storey is all that survives of the monks' additions of 1132–50, and whose upper storeys were built in 1544. A single arcade springing also survives from the 12C work, at the point where the north nave arcade abutted the west tower. The most spectacular early medieval survival was only rediscovered in 1897, however, despite its having remained in use in the 16C church. This is the **crypt of St-Solenne**, fully dug out after a more extensive excavation in 1927, and which can be visited via a new stairway sunk into the south choir aisle. Sections of the lower walls of c 980 survive, recognisable by their thick layers of reddish mortar and finely cut ashlar, but the area was transformed during the 11C, when it was extended westwards and provided with two files of columns to create a vastly extended hall crypt. This last was probably motivated by Blois' growing popularity as a pilgrimage centre, as it was situated on one of the possible routes from Chartres to St-Martin at Tours. The earlier arrangements are perhaps more difficult to visualise, but it is these which make the crypt peculiarly significant, with a raised choir above and the shrine of St-Solenne housed in a short eastern crypt below, both high altar and shrine being visible from the nave.

South of the cathedral, the ground falls steeply towards the river, and a left turn by the best preserved of Blois' 15C timber houses, the **Maison**

des Acrobates, brings you down the most interesting of the streets in this quarter, the **Rue Pierre-de-Blois**, passing a succession of mostly 16C townhouses. At No. 13 the **Hôtel de Villebrême** links a late 15C south façade with a later *corps de logis* via a bridge, the western armature being supported by two wooden corbels which juxtapose a female head with an acrobat. Lower down the street No. 6 sports a 16C portal and wooden door, beautifully arranged to parade two coats of arms, one to either side of the knocker, while No. 3 saw the birth of Jean de Morvilliers, bishop of Orléans and chancellor to François II from 1568 to 1570. The finest house, without doubt, is the rambling medieval mansion at No. 1, whose 12C stone core still retains a single window high up to the right of the façade. It was rebuilt for Jacques Viart, chancellor of the county of Blois, some time after 1525, its splendid antique portal bearing the device *Usu Vetera Nova* (The old becomes new with use) above the main arch.

At the bottom of the Rue Pierre-de-Blois a left turn brings you to the attractive **Place Ave-Maria**, with the river quays beyond. The Place also gives onto the most unreconstructed of all Blois' late medieval streets, the **Rue du Puits-Châtel**, a street which, in addition, reveals two of the finest 16C townhouses to grace the Blésois. The first is an early 16C *hôtel particulier* (No. 5), superbly provided with an open gallery to connect the stair tower with the living accommodation, and carrying the initials L and A above the main doorway—Louis XII and Anne de Bretagne, presumably. No. 7 advertises its royal connections with more of a fanfare. The house became known as the **Hôtel Sardini** after the Italian banker Scipio Sardini took up residence during the late 16C, but it probably dates from c 1510, more sumptuously decorated than its neighbour and bearing a plaque depicting the porcupine of Louis XII.

From the Place Ave-Maria the easiest route to the château is to cut west across the Rue Denis Papin to the Place Louis XII, but there is a more revealing approach, albeit one demanding more effort, from the north. The **Rue Denis Papin** is the old main road from Chartres to Bourges, and to straighten its path for pedestrians Eugène Riffault, mayor of Blois from 1852 to 1870, put in train a series of civil projects which culminated in a monumental stairway, **l'Escalier Denis Papin**, linking the lower town with the new commercial precincts to the north. The statue towards the top was erected in 1880, a somewhat tardy homage to Papin who was born at Chitenay, just to the south, in 1647, and who has become more generally renowned as the first man to recognise the potential of steam for producing energy.

From the top of the steps the **Rue St-Honoré** runs west, taking you past the clumsily rebuilt **Hôtel d'Alluye**, originally begun shortly before 1505 for Florimond Robertet, a successful lawyer and treasurer respectively to Charles VIII, Louis XII and François I. Everything above first storey level on the street façade was rebuilt in 1885, but the inner court was less radically affected and remains, with its vases, garlands and terracotta medallions, one of the earliest examples of full-blown Italianate decoration in the Loire valley. (The building now belongs to the Societé d'Assurances Mutuelles, though permission to visit the courtyard is usually forthcoming during office hours.)

From here a combination of the Rues Chemonton and du Prêche brings you to the **Place Victor-Hugo**, and the tiered arcading of François I's Façade des Loges. The Place Victor-Hugo has been carved out of the 16C castle gardens to the north of the château, with the delicate **Pavillon de la Reine Anne de Bretagne**, now housing the Office de Tourisme, beyond the dour flanks of the neo-classical church of St-Vincent. But it is the château which dominates the scene, with the **Façade des Loges** offering a first glimpse of the full impact of Italian design on educated French taste during the first half of the 16C. This façade is the outer elevation of the north-west wing of the château, added for François I between 1515 and 1524, and clearly indebted to Bramante's Loggia at the Vatican, a design which was only completed in 1519.

The **CHÂTEAU DE BLOIS** was the first royal residence to which François I turned his attention after his accession in 1515, and the irregularities of both the site and the existing buildings clearly caused his masons some difficulties. Before considering the broader masses of the building it is worth examining these outer 'galleries'. The whole of this elevation is built out in front of three 13C towers, that to the left still clearly visible. But whereas the medieval château walls adhered to the high ground at the top of the bluff, François took the bold decision to pitch the façade forward by 6 metres, to the outermost points of the towers. He was therefore required to build a vast new substructure, creating the basement storey which slopes away towards the left. A three-storeyed loggia was raised above this, consisting of two sets of arcaded openings surmounted by a trabeated attic storey. These arrangements are startlingly close to those of the Vatican, but though it is evident that François' masons had access to drawings or descriptions of the Roman loggia, few interpretations could be further removed in spirit. In the first place the arcaded storeys do not work as galleries. You cannot move along them as in a corridor, and they are in effect simply deep recesses. More disturbingly, the vertical accents seem to be handled in an entirely ad hoc fashion. Some bays are separated by single pilasters, some by paired orders, and several by pilasters framing a niche. One might see the handling of this elevation as summing up early 16C French attitudes to architectural design. Rather than see Bramante's work as an invitation to greater lightness, symmetry and mathematical regularity of form, it was seen as a new way of putting on a good show, of laying decorative forms across an essentially thick wall.

Why this might be so is revealed when you follow the Rue de la Voûte-du-Château into the **Place-du-Château**. Men such as François I were brought up surrounded by the full pomp of French late medieval architecture, and even the most cursory of glances at the exterior elevations of Louis XII's east wing reveals the capacity of great Flamboyant architecture to flatter royal ambition. The Renaissance architecture of Rome must have seemed impossibly austere by comparison. Louis' eastern wing was in fact built a mere 20 years earlier, between 1498 and 1501, and though the diapered brickwork has been harshly restored it remains one of the finest secular façades of late 15C France, still capable of ravishing the eye with its shifts of colour, texture and ornament.

A passage beneath the equestrian portrait of Louis XII (a copy of 1857) brings you, via the inevitable large ticket hall, into the vast irregular spaces of Blois' **Cour d'Honneur** and face to face with its extraordinary range of effects. For it is only here that you get a measure of the scale of the château de Blois, and the extent of its architectural accomplishment. The main courtyard occupies the western spur of a sharp, rocky outcrop which shelves steeply to the north, south and west, a site which clearly commended itself to the early counts of Blois. The early medieval arrangements are uncertain, but the castle was comprehensively rebuilt during the early 13C, in all likelihood by Thibaud VI, Comte de Blois from 1205 to 1218. Elements of this 13C castle survive, the most visible being a south-western angle tower called the Tour du Foix, and the magnificent baronial chamber, known as the Salle des Etats-Généraux, in the north-eastern corner.

These 13C dispositions obviously had an impact on the subsequent development of the château, becoming embedded within it, but it is the later work which assails the eye, and the later work which has overtaken Blois. This takes the form of three wings arranged around an unequal U-shaped court, each sharply differentiated and each known by the name of its patron: the earliest, the Aile Louis-XII, consisting of the eastern range and recognisable by its decorative brickwork; the Aile François-I running along the north-western side and dominated by a majestic spiral staircase; and the Aile Gaston-d'Orléans closing the court to the west, and bringing a classically ordered elevation to a wholly unclassical space.

The **Aile Louis-XII** is virtually the sole remnant of a far grander programme of works which Louis XII lavished on Blois. Beginning in 1498 Louis had three new wings constructed, enclosing the central court along the east, south-east, and west sides. The west range, and most of that to the south-east, were demolished in the 17C to make way for Gaston d'Orléans' work, and what survives is the *corps de logis* and the truncated chapel of St-Calais. The existing block was begun first, and seems to have been completed by 1501, drawing on a rich tradition of late medieval manorial architecture while, unusually at such a date, renouncing towers and crenellations in favour of relatively flat surfaces and large window openings. The mouldings are kept consistently simple, and instead the decorative possibilities of contrasted brick and stonework are exploited to the hilt. The effect is heightened by confining the carved decoration to what might be described as the architectonic grid—jambs, stringcourses, balconies, doorways and the lavish framing of the dormer windows. One is conscious of the introduction of classically inspired Italian Renaissance motifs, namely the richly carved half-columns used around the main entrance, but the overall impression is one of late gothic invention, the main lines encrusted with leering headstops, windswept foliage and exquisitely carved reliefs of Louis XII's personal emblem, the porcupine.

The **Chapelle St-Calais** reinforces this impression, with a lierne vault over the apse bay and high bosses bearing royal devices. The nave has gone, the present west front being 19C, and all that is left is a choir which Louis would have entered from his private apartment to witness the Mass from the wooden gallery above the south door. The fittings which so inspired contemporary chroniclers have also disappeared, and the present stained glass is the work of Max Ingrand and dates from 1957. The chapel was not consecrated until 1508, but as the documentary evidence for Louis XII's work at Blois is incomplete it is difficult to gain much of a sense of the range of *chantiers* at work over the period. The master mason Colin Biart crops up in several texts, and is probably the best candidate to have been put forward as the designer of the east wing, if not also of the chapel.

The next area to receive attention was the **Aile François-I**, closing off the château to the north-west. The documents show that François made funds available for work at Blois within six months of his accession in 1515, and by 1524 the wing was more or less complete, the south-westernmost bays having been demolished to make way for the Gaston-d'Orléans wing. The shifts between the architectural language here and in the Aile Louis-XII are considerable, and most dramatic in the Façade des Loges, but once again it is the decorative exuberance of French late medieval practice that has won out.

It might be argued that the articulation of the court elevation according to a pattern of pilasters, architraves and recessed panels is ultimately Italian in derivation, as is the deployment of candelabra and putti around the gables of the dormer windows. This is undoubtedly true, but while these elements do contribute a certain crispness to the architectural rhythms they are not allowed to take control, and both the distribution of ornament across the façade and the handling of the larger volumes betray an attachment to indigenous building traditions. Not only is the pitch of the roof steep, it forms an important part of the overall design. And the greatest decorative congestion is to be found above the dormer windows, and around the balustrade separating the roof space from the main parapet of the building. Furthermore, the staircase has been thrust forward to project into the courtyard, a not uncommon arrangement in late medieval townhouses, and its lavish sculptural embellishment is rooted in structures such as the mid-15C Palace of Jacques Coeur in Bourges. Before the demolition of the south-west bays this polygonal staircase stood towards the centre of François' wing, and though much of the carving is mid-19C you remain in a good position to judge its formal temperament. Capable of exacting tremendous dynamism from the varied angles of its ramps and balconies, it is one of the truly great expositions of architectural drama of the early 16C.

The last area to be resolved was the **Aile Gaston-d'Orléans**, begun in 1635 for Gaston, Duke of Orléans and abandoned in 1638 after his creditors pulled the rug on the project, sensing that the birth of an heir to Louis XIII (the future Louis XIV) put paid to any hopes that Gaston could solve his financial problems by ascending to the throne. The project was nothing if not ambitious, and foresaw the demolition of the existing château to make way for a vast new quadrangular structure, consisting of a *corps de logis* with projecting pavilions, two wings at right angles to the main block, and an eastern screened entrance opening onto a forecourt, the latter to have extended across the existing

Place-du-Château. The architect was François Mansart, and it is clear from the projections that Mansart intended the new château to be a more sharply defined and expanded version of Salomon de Brosse's 1615 Palais de Luxembourg in Paris. In the event, no more than the central block was built—the present south-west wing of the château— and even here the interior was left as little more than a shell in 1638. Nonetheless the existing façade is among the most restrained and serene classical elevations to have been built in France, a wonderfully coherent restatement of Renaissance thinking, the orders rising through Doric to Ionic to Corinthian, and the broader masses handled with a deceptive simplicity.

The internal arrangements of the château obviously reflect the larger architectural decisions, but are, perhaps inevitably, even more piece-meal. Mansart's superb lobby in the Aile Gaston-d'Orléans remains incomplete for instance, and you can see the ground sketches for carvings which were never cut into some of the panels. Even the stairs were not added until 1932, and in the absence of Mansart's original plan are based on those he designed for the château at Maisons-Laffitte. The great reception room to the left is used to house temporary exhibitions, but as the first floor accommodates Blois' excellent library and cannot be visited except by arrangement, it is the interior of the Aile François-I that occupies most visitors' attention.

Félix Duban's essential restoration project of 1845–69 is at its most strident here, and, with a few notable exceptions, most of the decoration is 19C pastiche. The living accommodation was on the first and second floors, the principal early 16C survivals being found in the first room you enter on the first floor, where the carving embellishing both the fireplace and doorway is original, and in the **Cabinet de Travail**. The latter is decorated with 237 gilded wooden panels in shallow relief, the designs concealing a number of hidden compartments which were opened by pedals concealed in the skirting-boards, and whose variety constitutes a virtual pattern-book of Renaissance ornament. The second floor has been given over to a reenactment of the assassination of Henri, Duc de Guise on the morning of 23 December 1588, after de Guise, as Lieutenant-General of France and head of the Catholic League in Paris, had forced Henri III to call a meeting of the Etats-Généraux in Blois. The event was bloody, and the rearrangement of the rooms at this south-western angle of the Aile François-I makes it impossible to follow precisely the movements of one of the most celebrated and infamous scenes in French history, but it is well explained, and duly elaborated with reported exchanges after the event between Henri III and his mother, Catherine de Medici.

The **Salle des Etats-Généraux** lies just to the east, a superb example of early 13C castle halls whose internal decoration dates from 1861–68, and is again the work of Félix Duban. The interior now acts as a foil for a number of 17C tapestries, at their best in the scenes from the life of Constantine: The Invention of the True Cross; Triumphal Entry of Constantine to Rome; Marriage of Constantine; all woven in Paris to cartoons by Rubens in the early 17C. There are also two scenes from the life of Louis XIV, part of a larger cycle woven from designs provided by Charles Lebrun between 1663 and 1675, at the then newly established Gobelins factory. But these are by far the most arresting works of fine art on display in the château, and the **Musée des Beaux-Arts**, housed in the adjoining Aile Louis-XII, cannot be described as a major collection. The finest paintings are probably the fragmentary 16C fresco rescued from the château de Beauregard and based on Leonardo da Vinci's Last Supper in Milan, and Hyacinthe Rigaud's portrait of Louis XIV of c 1695, though even this lacks the intensity of the celebrated portrait of 1701 now in the Louvre.

To the south of the Place-du-Château a shallow flight of steps, les Petits-Degrés-du-Château, lead down to the **Quartier St-Nicolas** and the old commercial precincts along the banks of the Loire. Unfortunately, most of the area was destroyed in 1940 and has been rebuilt in workaday fashion, but the Rues St-Lubin and des Trois-Marchands were handsomely restored and offer the most picturesque route to the only major building which escaped comparatively lightly, the great medieval church of **ST-NICOLAS**.

The dedication to St-Nicolas only dates from 1791, in memory of a neighbouring parish church which had been destroyed during the Revolution. Prior to this the church was known as St-Laumer, and served a congregation of Benedictine monks driven from the monastery of Corbion, in the Perche, by the Norse raids of the mid-9C. The monks were eventually given a site between the *castrum* and the river in 924, and shortly afterwards translated the relics of St-Laumer into a new choir. This 10C abbey was badly damaged by a fire in 1114, resulting in a complete rebuilding programme which saw the present building take shape. The foundation stone was laid on 25 April 1138, the choir, transepts and eastern bay of the nave being complete for the consecration ceremony in 1186. The three western bays of the nave and twin-towered west front would seem to have followed during the early years of the 13C.

As St-Laumer is by no means a vast church this was a leisurely programme, undertaken at a time when architectural fashions were changing rapidly, which, combined with the results of a cavalier 19C restoration, can make interpretation of the building hazardous. With the exception of the 14C axial chapel and 1950s Max Ingrand glass, the whole of the church east of the easternmost bay of the **nave** is 12C, fully vaulted, spacious, and provided with ample chapel space. Most of the work up to the stringcourse separating the main arcade from the triforium probably dates from 1138–50, and was given an excellent set of now heavily recut capitals. The upper elevation is very much more tentative, and may well have been begun after a lengthy pause in the building programme, dating from c 1175–86. These areas introduce several more playful elements into the church—for example, the rhythm of bays as your eye moves from the arcade upwards in the apse is 7–8–5—but, most importantly, the decision to employ high rib vaults was taken. These are handled in distinctive fashion, as their springing point is appreciably higher than the sills of the clerestory windows, creating what is known as a 'giant' clerestory, and the ribs are sharply broken at the keystones and divided into slightly domical compartments.

The western bays of the nave are quite different, and not simply because every grinning corbel or historiated capital has been evicted from the building. The bays are a direct reflection of the nave of Chartres cathedral, then in building, and the appearance in Blois of two of its defining motifs—the *pilier cantonée* and composed window, separated by a triforium passage hollowed out of the wall—marks the arrival of this influential elevation in the Loire valley. There are variations on the theme: the bays at Blois are proportionally wider than those at Chartres, and there are five, rather than four, arches to the triforium and a thick margin of wall around the clerestory windows. But it is Chartres which lies behind this elevation, and probably Chartres which inspired the conservative twin-towered west front here also, its sculpture now reduced to the mutilated remains of the left portal, and an excellent early 14C cycle surviving in the angels and prophets of the central archivolts.

A stroll along the **Rue St-Laumer** reveals the north flank of the abbey, notable for the somewhat hesitant handling of the flying buttresses, and brings you out just to the north of **Les Jacobins**, the heavily restored hulk of a Dominican convent originally founded in 1273. All that now survives are the early 16C south and west walks of the cloister, their upper storeys housing two small museums, devoted to religious art and natural history respectively. Continuing west brings you into the spacious Place Louis-XII, the most animated of the squares of the lower town, and the result of the 1832 decision to pull down the medieval terraces at the western end of the Rue Lubin. In fact all that survived the devastation of 1940 was the one medieval remnant of the precinct, the **Fontaine Louis-XII**, improved by the king in 1511 and subsequently replaced by a copy. The Place parallels the north bank of the Loire, reached along the Rue Emile-Laurens, bringing you on to Jacques Gabriel's splendid 18C bridge and over the river.

The town which grew up on the **south bank of the Loire** is less interesting than Blois itself, but it retains something of the atmosphere of the medieval faubourg de Vienne, the old sailors and fisherman's quarter that once existed here. The area is now known as the **Quartier de Vienne**, though it suffered badly during the bombardments of 1940 and 1944, and the riverside terraces are almost wholly postwar. The streets to the south of the Quai Villebois-Mareuil retain a pleasant mixture of 16C–19C buildings, and the views across the river towards both the château and the cathedral are quite splendid. The old faubourg also includes, along the Rue Munier, a grand parish church and its 16C rectangular cemetery.

The church, dedicated to **St-Saturnin**, became the focus of an important local pilgrimage to the statue of Notre-Dame des Aydes, and was rebuilt at the instigation of Anne de Bretagne during the early 16C. The project was abandoned on the queen's death in 1514, but was revived in the early 17C when the church was completed in a deliberately historicising style. The two western bays of the nave were rebuilt at the same time, emphasising a peculiar disparity thrown up when the two western bays of an unfinished 13C church were retained in Anne de Bretagne's building. Apart from the drama inherent in this sudden shift into a taller church, St-Saturnin is more proficient than exciting, qualities which are reversed in the so-called **Cloître St-Saturnin**.

Despite its arrangement as four walks enclosing a quadrangle, the *cloître* was never intended as a cloister, but was built as the parish cemetery. These galleried cemeteries were once quite common in France, as in the great late medieval charnel house of the Aitre St-Maclou in Rouen, but few survived and it is rare to find one with its relationship to the church still intact. This explains the major oddity of the 'cloître'; its entrance door is arranged not in the centre of the east walk, but directly opposite the west portal of St-Saturnin, easing the passage of the funeral cortège out of the church and into the graveyard. The deeds of purchase suggest it was built between 1515 and 1520, subtly arranged so as to mimic the appearance of a rectangle, and given four timber-roofed walks. The graves have long been cleared and the walks now shelter a motley collection of mostly 16C and 17C stonework rescued from local houses destroyed during the Second World War. Note the excellent set of Romanesque capitals, thought to have come from a building destroyed in the Revolution, the ancient abbey of Bourgmoyen.

North-east of Blois

The flat, cereal-growing lands to the north-east of Blois lie well to the south of the Beauce proper, but so resemble the great plains around Chartres that the whole area has become known as the Petit-Beauce. With the exception of the Forêt de Marchenoir, and the odd remnant of ancestral parkland, the region has lost virtually all of its wooded cover, along with the greater part of its once dense pattern of seigneurial manors. In consequence the best way of exploring the Petit-Beauce is to strike out along the N152, and follow the north bank of the Loire. This brings you past the Marquise de Pompadour's superb 18C **Château de Ménars** (6km, closed to the public), stepped above a broad terrace when seen from south of the river, but here elusive behind its tall green gates. You can usually see just enough of Jacques-Ange Gabriel's principal façade of 1760–64 to make it worth stopping.

The situation is only a little more encouraging to the west, where a trio of sharply differentiated parish churches are generally kept locked, but are all worth visiting for their exteriors and situation alone (enquiries at the nearest house for Cour-sur-Loire, or the *presbytère* at 4 Rue du 8-Mai for Suèvres, will usually elicit a key). The first you encounter is **St-Vincent** at **Cour-sur-Loire**, superbly set back above the river and rebuilt to the north of a 12C bell-tower on the orders of Jacques Hurault, treasurer to Louis XII, some time after 1492. The two churches at (5km) **Suèvres** are by their nature very different, **St-Christophe** in the Place de la Mairie possibly the earlier foundation. This boasts a considerable quantity of re-used Roman brick, set in cross or herringbone courses in the west wall, all of which may be as early as the 7C or 8C. The nave was refurbished during the 12C, and the bell-tower is 13C, but the spacious timber porch is a far later addition, acquired during the 16C when the fashion for extending covered market halls around the western nave angles of parish churches became immensely popular along the middle-Loire.

The reason for the widespread re-use of Roman material at St-Christophe becomes evident as you delve deeper into the village along the Rue Bouteau. The street plan of this area is that of the Gallo-Roman town of *Sobodrium*, admittedly as expanded after the Hundred Years War and entirely rebuilt, but still provided with an old town gate at the southern end of the main town-river axis. Just beyond this gate you pass the old laundry precincts, with the second of Suèvres' parish churches, **St-Lubin**, in the distance. This is curious, with a delightful early 12C crossing-tower now serving as the western angle of a church which has lost its nave. The choir would seem earlier than this, but was provided with a south aisle in the mid-16C by the seigneurs of the château de Forges, hence the corroded heraldic crest above the entrance.

Beyond Suèvres the N152 runs fast and straight to (5km) **Mer**, now something of a service town for the nuclear power station at St-Laurent-les-Eaux, but with a fine late 19C corn market above the central square and an ambitious Flamboyant bell-tower, added to the west of the parish church of **St-Hilaire** between 1507 and 1512.

Striking north from Mer, along the D15 (badly signposted; it is the road to the right at the bottom of the market square), you rise above the flood-plains of the Loire and cut into the heart of the Petit-Beauce, crossing the wheat fields to one of the few remaining seigneurial houses at (9km) **Talcy**. The greater part of the present **château** dates from after 1517, when the Florentine banker, Bernardo Salviati, bought the house (though not the seigneurie) and was given permission to expand the earlier donjon with 'walls, towers, battlements, embrasures, drawbridges, outworks, ramparts, and other provisions for its defence'. Salviati then set about demolishing the 13C enceinte walls, adding machicolations to the later 15C square keep, and flanked this with two new wings. That to the west was demolished in the 18C, when the present rectangular casement windows were inserted into the keep, but the east wing survived, its north elevation provided with an elegant four-bay loggia. The adjoining two-storey wing was probably added towards the end of the 16C, bonding the castle into the church tower, and providing its Catholic residents with a direct entrée into the church at tribune level.

The rooms were mostly refurnished during the 18C, though a fine set of late 15C millefiori tapestries found their way into Salviati's Salle des Gardes, and the kitchen and scullery retain most of their early 16C decoration. The best of the furniture is to be found upstairs, where the old logis of the keep was transformed into a *Grand Salon*, and furnished with what for once survives as a more or less complete Louis XV interior. But the château is probably best known for its literary associations, for it was here in 1545 that the 21-year-old Pierre de Ronsard first met Cassandre Salviati, *'une beauté de 15 ans'*, and fell in love, writing the sonnets which make up the *Amours de Cassandre* over the following decade. Talcy's vineyards fell victim to the 19C phylloxera epidemic, and its mighty 16C grape press is no longer used, nor does its delightful courtyard well draw water. But the old flower gardens remain, in the shade of a particularly fine 16C *colombier*, and still provide a soothing postscript to any visit.

North-west of Talcy a well-signposted combination of the D15, D15A and D917 brings you to (9km) **Marchenoir**, a handsome and spacious market town which burgeons with life every Tuesday afternoon, but which otherwise finds little to disturb its tranquil airs. The centre, in so far as there is one, can be found in the small market square to the west of the church, but Marchenoir has effectively merged with **St-Léonard-en-Beauce**, and, although smaller, St-Léonard is the livelier place outside market days.

St-Léonard also accommodates the finer **church**, with a largely 13C nave to which a north aisle was added during the 19C, and a single 12C choir bay expanded to the east in the 15C. The church became the focus of a pilgrimage cult during the 1480s (inspiring the Comte de Dunois to vault the choir), and which doubtless lies behind the decision to employ Jehan de Beauce to design a bell-tower in 1520. Jehan is one of the best-known ecclesiastical architects of early 16C France, responsible for the great north-west spire of Chartres cathedral and, probably, the west front of La Trinité, Vendôme. The documentation explicitly links both Jehan and, as of 1524, his brother-in-law and cathedral architect at Tours, François Martin, with St-Léonard-en-Beauce. However, it cannot be said that late Gothic invention is the hall-mark of St-Léonard's belfry, fine though it is, and it remains a matter of some curiosity as to what brief two such distinguished architects were given.

From Marchenoir the least monotonous route through the wheatfields and back to Blois is via the rambling D50. This has the advantage of passing a number of accomplished minor parish churches, initially signalled by the arresting disproportions of the church of (10km) **Villexanton**. As in many of the churches in the Sologne and Orléanais, Villexanton was provided with a splendid exterior wooden gallery during the early 16C, acting as a covered market hall rather than a galilee, and which is roughly contemporary with the choir. The rest of the church would appear 12C, although the use of semi-dressed rubble and *petit-appareil* was ubiquitous in these parts well into the 18C.

At (3km) **La Chapelle-St-Martin** an early 12C bell-tower surmounted by a crude 14C octagonal spire is the point of interest, the latter reminiscent of the spires favoured in the Cher valley; but, again, potentially discordant elements are handled quite blithely and with great panache. Finally, at (4km) **Mulsans**, one of the earlier Romanesque parish churches in the region was transformed c 1500 by the addition of perhaps the most majestic of all the wooden galleries of the Petit-Beauce, superbly supported by octagonal posts throughout. And beyond, the D50 widens to weave a last 14km to Blois.

West of Blois

The situation to the west of Blois is very different, as the major centres of population congregate along the banks of the rivers Loire and Cisse. The paucity of river crossings makes it more sensible to explore first one side and then the other. With this in mind the following description advances along the south bank to Tours, returning to Blois via Vouvray and the north bank.

The first centre of significance you reach is (20km) **CHAUMONT**, the *Calvus Mons* of old, and the steepest of the few rocky outcrops along this middle section of the river. A wooden donjon was established on the site of the present **château** by Eudes I, Comte de Blois, during the late 10C, which had certainly been replaced with a stone fortification by the late 14C, when the younger branch of the Amboise family moved upstream to Chaumont. This castle was demolished on the orders of Louis XI in punishment for Pierre d'Amboise's participation in the rebellion of the *Ligue du Bien Public*, but the old warhorse soon returned to favour and was allowed to refortify the site in 1470. Pierre died in 1473, by which time he had completed the now vanished north range, along with the whole of the west wing as far as the south-western Tour d'Amboise. Completing the castle was the business of his grandson, Charles II d'Amboise, who inherited the estate in 1481 and delayed work while his political star was in the ascendant. Work on the château restarted in 1498, and seems to have been supervised by Charles' uncle, Georges d'Amboise, the brilliant cardinal-archbishop of Rouen then embarking on his influential remodelling of the château de Gaillon.

Between 1498 and 1510 the south and west ranges were added, and the diagonal entrance towers inscribed with the interlaced Cs of Charles and the arms of Georges beneath a cardinal's hat. The curious emblem of the smouldering rocks is a pun on Chaumont—*chaud mont*—and a throwback to a much earlier medieval device. Once within this diagonally canted entrance-block the castle reveals itself to be quite domestically orientated. You lose sight of the dramatic cylindrical towers, lending a powerful expression to the castle angles, and a gentler prospect opens up over the Loire. The *cour d'honneur* is approximately square, and the sense of regularity would have been more keenly felt prior to 1739, when Bertin de Vaugien demolished the north wing, and opened the court to the river.

The later history of Chaumont is one of neglect and reclamation. It was empty for much of the early 19C, after which two major restoration projects were unleashed on the building, that commissioned by Prince Amedée de Broglie from Paul-Ernest Sanson in 1878 being the more visible. The effect of this is made clear from the few photographs dotted about the interior, for the octagonal spiral staircase had been truncated at first floor level, and there was originally no balustrade work on the east wing. But Sanson was not insensitive, and the inventiveness on display in the dining-room, where the rich Gothic fantasies of the chimneypiece are his work, marks him out as one of the better Neo-Gothicists of the late 19C.

The first floor rooms had survived in better condition and were more easily restored, the great **Council Chamber** being much the finest, now splendidly hung with Flemish 16C tapestries depicting Roman deities. Although these tapestries were not woven for Chaumont, they do reflect an interest of one of the château's brief residents. In 1560 Catherine de Medici bought Chaumont, with the intention of forcing Diane de Poitiers to accept the château in exchange for Chenonceau. She barely stayed here, but the first floor chamber in the north-east tower is known as the **Astrologer's Room**, after the cabbalistic triangle and three circles above the chimney breast—a device of Ruggieri, Catherine's renowned astrologer. Before leaving it is also worth visiting Sanson's delightful **stables**, set to face the south of the château and buried within its ample grounds. Félibien records that in the 17C, at least, Chaumont was without either gardens or park. The rolling and mature parkland through which you now walk is entirely a creation of Achille Duchêne, commissioned by de Broglie during the late 19C to create a landscape in the manner of an English stately home.

Below Chaumont the D751 courts the narrow wooded ledge separating the Loire from the low cliffs to the south, offering occasional glimpses of the islands and sandbars which litter the river bed, before gliding over the border with Touraine and into (15km) **AMBOISE**. It is an impressive sight, the town sliding down to meet the river beneath the wreckage of a once vast castle, menacing the land from a promontory revealed by the tributary valley of the Manse. Neolithic culture found the site attractive, as did the Gallo-Roman peoples of the Loire, both of whom occupied the plateau to the east of the existing château, a site known as the *Oppidum des Châtelliers*. According to a late 11C chronicler Foulques Nerra also took advantage of the site, building a castle in the town and, in 1030, reconstructing a collegiate church dedicated to St-Florentin on the high ground. This church was joined to a second castle in 1115, when Hugues d'Amboise raised a stone keep above what are now the gardens of the château, having first demolished Foulques' earlier and lower donjon.

But it was the 15C which witnessed the development of the structures visible today. In 1431 Charles VII arrested Louis d'Amboise on a charge of treason, and seized both town and castle. As a royal property, within a day's easy ride of his favoured residence at Plessis-lès-Tours, Louis XI rebuilt the town walls and set about expanding the château, installing his wife, Charlotte de Savoie, and the royal children here. The future Charles VIII was born in this château in 1470 and, impressed by the local climate and the proximity of the great hunting forests to the south, launched a vast new building programme in 1491. The high point came with the accession of François I in 1515. **Leonardo da Vinci** was installed at the Manoir du Clos-Lucé, 230,000 livres were spent in a mere three years on building work at the château, and a tremendous succession of balls, feasts and royal celebrations were organised to mark the royal progress—François' engagement to Claude de France, his departure for Italy, and the birth of the Dauphin.

It was not to last for long. In 1519 Leonardo died, to be followed in 1524 by Claude de France. Furthermore, the new wing at Blois was also pretty much complete by 1524, and, with Chambord growing apace, François left Amboise for his new palaces to the east. Without a substantial mercantile community to sustain it the town went into decline. There was a brief and bloody hiccup in 1560, when the Protestant La Renaudie frightened Charles IX into leaving Blois for the more formidable defences of Amboise, but the decline was otherwise steady and uninterrupted. After Napoleon granted the château to Roger Ducos three-quarters of the buildings were demolished, to save the expense of upkeep, and even the arrival of the railway in 1845 brought little in the way of new industry.

Town Tour. The effect of royal patronage on Amboise is readily apparent, and beyond the cafés and souvenir shops of the Rues Victor-Hugo and National the town can seem little more than a sprawling annexe to the château. To leave it here would be unfair, as the town is not without buildings of interest: the splendid 14C **Porte l'Horloge** for instance, provided with a belfry in 1495, or the handsome **Hôtel-de-Ville** just to the north, originally built as a townhouse in 1500 by the architects Jacques Coquereau and Pierre Nepveu for Pierre Morin, mayor of Tours. The old parish church of Notre-Dame-en-Grève lies immediately opposite this, rededicated to **St-Florentin** after the earlier collegiate foundation was demolished by Roger Ducos. The church was built at the instigation of Louis XI between 1477 and 1484 as a simple parochial hall with a polygonal apse, but was so comprehensively denatured by the restoration of 1876 that any further judgements are impossible. Both the vaults and the aisles date from the late 19C, their harsh stonework enlivened only by the dense colours of an extremely fine cycle of modern stained glass, though the late 16C bell tower survived to toll a sprightlier note, diagonally sandwiched into the north-west angle. An even more unexpected note is struck to the west, where the friendship between Michel Debré, mayor of Amboise, and the surrealist artist Max Ernst led to Ernst's building **La Fontaine de Max Ernst** along the Quai du Général-de-Gaulle in 1968, charmingly decorated with bronze masks and a turtle. Buried deeper in the town, along the Rue Joyeuse, the **Musée de la Poste** accommodates a specialist collection in an early 16C townhouse, originally built for Fra Giocondo, and still set above two delightful garden terraces laid out in the early 16C by the great Italian designer Pacello da Mercogliano.

But it is the **CHÂTEAU D'AMBOISE** which is the town's compelling interest, reached along a ramp which rises from the Rue du Château to bring you onto a spacious plateau, terraced towards the Loire and shelving gently upwards through wooded walks to the south-west. There is not a great amount of building to fill so vast a space, and Jacques du Cerceau's engraving of 1579 makes clear the extent of Ducos' early 19C demolition. The Romanesque collegiate church of St-Florentin has gone, along with the gardens and conventual quarters which hugged the south-east corner of the plateau. And Charles VIII's huge new quarters towards the north and west are no more, leaving only the retaining walls, a couple of towers, the chapelle St-Hubert and the Logis du Roi.

The main building programme was launched by Charles VIII in 1491, and the accounts attest to the involvement of a virtual roll-call of late 15C royal masons, citing Colin Biart, Guillaume Senault, Pierre Trinqueau, and Jacques Sourdeau among the better known. This situation began to change as a result Charles VIII's extraordinarily successful march through Italy during 1494–96. He returned in triumph with over 20 Italian scholars and artists in his retinue, including the architects Fra Giocondo and Domenico da Cortona, the sculptor Guido Mazzoni, and the garden designer Pacello di Mercogliano, all of whom were put to work at Amboise. The extent of the contribution made by these Italian artists is difficult to gauge. Much of the work had already been done, and anyway the greater part of it is now lost, though the fact that they were engaged on other major projects in early 16C France suggests they were highly regarded. Furthermore, there was a sudden change of patron, for over the Easter of 1498 Charles cracked his head on a door lintel and, late in the evening of 7 April, died. His successor, Louis XII, was more interested in Blois, but completed the drum towers and added the lower storeys of the so-called Aile Louis XII-François I, a wing which was subsequently heightened by two storeys by François I between 1515 and 1519.

The **compulsory guided tours** begin with the **Chapelle St-Hubert**, begun in 1491 as a private castle chapel and seemingly complete by 1493. It is a simple design, a sleek cruciform structure with a relatively plain interior elevation and a splendid external lintel juxtaposing an image of St Christopher with the vision of St-Hubert. This latter is the work of Corneille de Nesves, one of two Netherlandish artists reported as working on the chapel, the other being Casin d'Utrecht, and certainly testament to the breadth of European talent Charles VIII brought to Amboise. But the chapel is now best known for housing the remains of Leonardo da Vinci, moved to the north transept after 1869 from his original burial place in the gardens to the north-west.

From here attention switches to the **Logis du Roi**, the main block belonging to the 1491–98 campaign and facing north towards the river, with that at right angles to it added in two stages between 1498 and 1519. This latter is known as the Aile Louis XII-François I, the shallow decorative panels of its upper storeys contrasting with the sharper window mouldings below, but the external treatment accorded both wings is relatively subdued. The interiors have certainly been more sensitively furnished than is the case with most royal châteaux, and you are usually swept straight into the Salle des Gardes of Charles VIII's northern logis. This now accommodates an excellent collection of late 15C and early 16C furniture, rippling with linenfold and with blind tracery applied across the panels of what are essentially simple cabinets and chests. The guardroom is the main lower chamber and gives onto an open gallery, a sentry walk overlooking the Loire. This sentry walk also gives access to the **Tour des Minimes**, the massive cylindrical tower which pins the northern elevations above the cliff, and acts as a major vehicle of circulation in its own right. Its title derives from the 16C Couvent des Minimes founded at its foot, but its function was quite spectacular—a magnificent spiral ramp intended to enable convoys of mounted cavalrymen to ascend from the Loire to the main courts.

The internal arrangements of the **Aile Louis XII-François I** are a little more hybrid, the lower rooms refurnished with mostly 15C and 16C chests and tapestries, and the upper floor arranged to reflect the return of Amboise to the Orléans family in the mid-19C, hence the fashionable Winterhalter portaits. The tour usually ends by bringing you back through the **Salle des Etats** in the Charles VIII wing, entirely refashioned by Ruprich-Robert in the late 19C, and perhaps the most elegant Neo-Gothic hall in western France. Beyond here, there is a choice of exits, the more stimulating being the **Tour Hurtault**. This parallels the

Tour des Minimes on the townside, and like the Minimes was given a spiral ramp, but here the vaulting was left largely unrestored and retains a superb run of late 15C figured corbels.

Beneath the Tour Hurtault, the Rue Victor-Hugo curves beneath the escarpment of the valley of the Manse to the **Manoir du Clos-Lucé**. The original manor house was built in 1477 for Etienne le Loup, warden of the forests of Amboise and Montrichard, and came into the royal gift after it was purchased by Charles VIII as a retreat from the court for his wife, Anne de Bretagne. The small stone chapel attached to the main house was built for Anne in the 1490s, and subsequently decorated with frescoes by one of Leonardo da Vinci's fellow-travellers, Francesco da Melzi, but it is for Leonardo himself that the manoir is most celebrated. For it was here that François I accommodated Leonardo in late 1516, and here that he died on 2 May 1519. It was with this in mind that the Saint-Bris family restored Clos-Lucé, stripping back the rooms to a notional early 16C state, and installing Renaissance furnishings and tapestries throughout. On the whole this has been well done, and both the ground floor reception room and the first floor study have been sensitively treated, while the exhibition of models based on Leonardo's drawings in the basement is excellent. But there is an element of commercial hard-sell in all this single-mindedness, a flavour which might be caught in the 'Leonardo da Vinci Boutique and Tea-Room' and 'Renaissance Garden'.

Amboise is also a good base for an **excursion** to the Duc de Choiseul's extraordinary **Pagode de Chanteloup**, half-hidden along a forest drive to the right of the road to Bléré (about 3km from the centre of Amboise, the easiest route being to follow the signs marked 'Pagode' from the Place St-Denis). As a former, and unusually popular, minister of state to Louis XV, de Choiseul was exiled to his estates on the Loire in 1770, renouncing the château d'Amboise in favour of a new palace at Chanteloup. This was modelled on Versailles, a vast and brilliant complex intended to house a court of opposition, and its destruction between 1823 and 1825 has deprived us of one of the most ambitious residences of late 18C France. An unexpected outbuilding has survived, however, for in 1773 de Choiseul commissioned the architect Louis-Denis Le Camus to build a 44 metre high pagoda in the grounds, ostensibly to celebrate the loyalty of his friends. With a circular, open colonnade at the base supporting six telescoping storeys, Camus' tower is based on William Chamber's 1762 Pagoda at Kew, but, although there is an occasional gesture towards Anglo-Chinese ornament, the overwhelming bulk of the decorative detailing is purely French. And as an additional incentive to persuade his guests to survey the Amboise domains, de Choiseul had each storey delicately spun with a wrought iron balcony, to offer one of the grandest panoramas of the entire Loire valley.

Between Amboise and Tours the D751 continues to follow the narrow shore separating the Loire from its southern cliffs, before the escarpment falls away to the west of Lussault and the road clambers above a man-made embankment. The return of the cliffs heralds the one significant town along this stretch of river, **Montlouis-sur-Loire**, the earlier medieval centre clustered defensively atop the escarpment to the south of the parish church. This **church** has been extensively restored, with an ample 16C nave giving onto a shallow 12C choir and south-eastern bell tower. The rise up to this church, indeed the whole of the cliff-face to the west, is riddled with caves, easily hollowed out of the soft *tuffeau* and used by the local viticulteurs as cellarage space. The fresh white wine made here, tending to be slightly sweeter than the Vouvray that is its closest equivalent, is among the better Loire wines to boast its own label, *Appellation d'Origine Contrôlée Montlouis*. Like all such wines in France it enjoys a considerable local reputation, pressed from the Chenin Blanc vines which cover the south facing plateau between here and the river Cher, and a sampling of the better years admirably justifies the time it might take to arrange a tasting.

Montlouis' better known neighbour, **Vouvray**, lies above the north bank of the Loire, but with the ferries now retired the only option is to travel via Tours and cross the river by the Pont Mirabeau (around 15km in total, for Tours see Route 4). The town itself, and the slightly smaller village of Rochecorbon to the west, abound with *dégustation-vente* signs, and tastings are easier to come by here than anywhere in the Loire valley—ask for a list of addresses at the Syndicat d'Initiative on the Rue Gambetta, or visit the **Ecomusée du Pays de Vouvray** along the Rue Victor-Herault, where the exposition of local viticulture forms an excellent background to any drinking you might do.

Beyond the Ecomusée, a right turn brings you onto the Route du Vernou, or D46, which winds through the smaller vineyards to (4km) **Vernou-sur-Brenne**, a more attractive town than Vouvray and one whose parish church supports an unusual early 12C west front. The chief interest here lies with the carving, and what may be a representation of the combat between Roland and the giant Ferragut on the right-hand capital. Otherwise, the more substantial vineyards are to be found above the valley towns, on the south facing côtes.

The terrain to the east of Vernou is marked by an unusual feature, however, as the valley of the Cisse parallels that of the Loire for the best part of 40km, creating a narrow peninsula of land rarely more than 2km wide. Most of the villages gather to the north of the Cisse, where the shallow bed is less prone to fragment. Thus, rather than take the N152 along the Loire, you might follow the D1 through the meadows and riverside towns of the Cisse. None of these settlements are particularly large, and their numerous 17C and 18C *manoirs* remain solidly locked behind gated walls, but it is a gentle, open landscape, excellent for leisurely walking, and is graced by a number of quietly expressive churches.

The parish church of St-Adrien at (12km) **Pocé-sur-Cisse** is fairly typical. It is an unassuming 16C building, somewhat over-restored, but none the less housing a fine set of 15C misericords beneath its choir stalls. The best is St-Saturnin at **Limeray**, with a Romanesque bell tower subsequently incorporated into the building, and a very fine octagonal rib vault over the early 13C sanctuary bay. The interior also acts as a sculpture gallery, since one of Limeray's 19C priests collected a considerable quantity of statuary which he placed on plinths against the aisleless walls. There is much late medieval material in the nave, a good collection of 18C figures around the apse, and a very fine 16C alabaster St Barbara in the belfry bay.

Just to the east of Limeray, the old poultry-breeding village of (2km) **Cangey** has retained a few panels of late 16C and early 17C stained glass in the three apse bays of the parish church. While over the border with the Blésois at (4km) **Monteaux** the handsome 16C château which stands at the entrance to the village has been transformed into the grandest of all the wine houses in the area.

The road becomes the D58 as you cross the border with the Blésois, traversing a low plain, now mostly ploughed and planted with maize and sunflowers, before a long main street brings you into the centre of (6km) **Onzain**. The town is most celebrated for the Renaissance south portal of its parish church of SS-Gervais-et-Protais, situated to the west of a handsome town square, its restoration recently complete. The portal is thought to date from c 1530, capping the statuary niches with mock dormer windows from which prying figures leer, and laying tiny cherubim across the capitals. This is not the only carving of merit as the church interior houses four statues of c 1660 by the Blois sculptor, Gaston Imbert, saved from a high altar dismantled during the 19C.

East of Onzain the D58 continues to mimic the path of the Cisse, now little more than a narrow stream, crossing the river at Chouzy-sur-Cisse before channelling you on to the N152 for a last 9km on top of the Loire embankment, and into Blois.

2

Romorantin-Lanthenay and the Sologne

ROAD (160km): Romorantin-Lanthenay D59/D20, 11km Château du Moulin; D20, 5km Mur-de-Sologne; D122/D7, 22km Fougères-sur-Bièvre; D38, 11km Château de Beauregard; D77/D765, 8km Cour-Cheverny; D102, 6km Tour-en-Sologne (for Villesavin); D112, 10km Chambord; D112, 8km Bracieux; D923, 21km Neung-sur-Beuvron; D925/D63, 13km St-Viâtre; D93, 8km Nouan-le-Fuzelier; N20, 12km Salbris; D724, 9km Selles-St-Denis; 16km Romorantin-Lanthenay.

The *pays de Sologne* is an area of low-lying marshland, caught between the valleys of the Loire and Cher and drained by the smaller rivers Sauldre, Beuvron and Casson. It is a melancholy landscape, a maze of overgrown coppices, pasture and heath interspersed with hundreds of tiny lakes, where earlier attempts at drainage have drawn the surface water into self-contained pools. The climate was notoriously humid and susceptible to outbreaks of plague—a fact which persuaded François I to switch his intended château from Romorantin to Chambord—but it does not seem to have deterred the 16C and 17C aristocracy, attracted by its hunting forests, from investing heavily in the area. The fowlers, woodworkers and highwaymen of the Middle Ages have obviously gone, but the big aristocratic houses of the Renaissance remain, and the Sologne boasts the most prolific concentration of châteaux of the entire Loire valley. The great houses to the north, Chambord, Cheverny, Beauregard, are easily reached from Blois; but Romorantin-Lanthenay is the only town of any size in the Sologne, and as both its early capital, and modern administrative centre, remains the best place to stay if you aim to spend several days exploring the region.

Romorantin-Lanthenay

History. The town acquired its double-barrelled title in the early 12C, when the counts of Blois established a donjon to protect the bridge over the river Sauldre, and the old parish of Lanthenay lost its southern reaches to the settlement that grew around the castle walls. The latter was known as *Riuus Morantini*, and the conjunction of a river crossing, an early wooden tower above the present Ile de la Motte and a stone castle at the eastern end of the Ile Marin, is largely responsible for the character of the town. The earlier castle was abandoned in the late 13C, but not before the counts of Blois had built a new keep above the north bank of the river, in the present Place de la Tour, and encircled the town with an enceinte wall. This keep, along with much of the town, was destroyed by the Black Prince in 1356, but, with the Valois-Angoulême family taking control at the end of the Hundred Years War, recovery and expansion were rapid.

It was here that François d'Angoulême, the future François I, spent his childhood, and here that Anne de Bretagne gave birth to his future wife, Claude de France, in 1499. The Valois-Angoulême château had been built in the south-west angle of the medieval enceinte, and a new wing was added to this in 1512 for Louise de Savoie, François I's mother. But, by 1517, François had decided this was all too modest, and commissioned Leonardo da Vinci to design a château which he intended as his principal residence. Leonardo's plans were ambitious, and he proposed encircling the new château with a series of canals which would intersect with a larger canal linking Romorantin with the river Loire. The site chosen was to the north-west of the earlier château (parts of which survive in the Sous-Préfecture), and the structure was to have two main blocks, one to either side of the river, connected by tiers of open galleries, the latter doubling up as viewing platforms for the envisaged *spectacles nautiques*. The town of Villefranche-sur-Cher was also to be dismantled, and its timber-framed houses moved, panel by panel, into a new enceinte at Romorantin.

It was not to be, and the project was abandoned in 1518, after an outbreak of plague persuaded François to move his new château north to Chambord. Following the death of his mother in 1531, François became even less enamoured of the town, and it was left to the weavers and drapers of the 17C to revive its fortunes. Their success is evident in the splendid mill buildings which straddle the various channels of

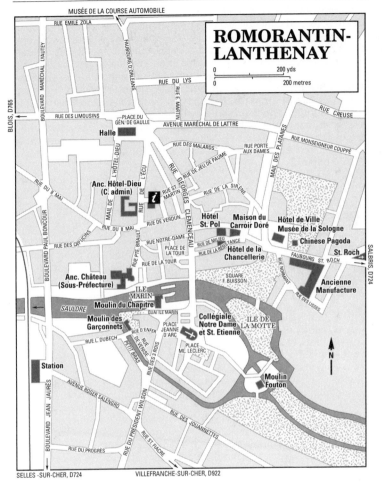

ROMORANTIN-LANTHENAY

the Sauldre, and, with a few notable exceptions, the fabric of what remains an attractive town is largely 17C–19C.

Town Tour. The largest of the river islands is the **Ile Marin**, home to the earliest building still to stand in Romorantin, the neglected collegiate church of **Notre-Dame-et-St-Etienne**. On the basis of the engaging arcaded decoration enlivening the crossing tower, it is presumed that the church was founded in the late 11C by the then counts of Blois. But no records survive prior to the early 12C, when the parish of Romorantin was split off from that of Lanthenay and given the use of the nave of the collegiate church. With the exception of the crossing tower and heavily reworked transept, most of the church dates from c 1200–50.

When work began on a new **choir** around 1200 the intention was to create a clear distinction between the choir and the nave. The main apse was given windows at two levels, to the west of which were one and a half straight bays, both given aisles which originally terminated square to the east. The vaults of this choir are domed-up Angevin rib vaults, supported to the east by statues of the evangelists in an arrangement which invites comparison with St-Martin at Angers or the abbey of La Couture at Le Mans, though the present statues are vapid late 19C substitutes. The main south aisle bay was also given some figurative sculpture, strictly the work of the original masons rather than professional sculptors, where you can still make out an Annunciation, Visitation and Adoration of the Magi, with the Ascent of a Soul on the capital opposite.

The three-bay **nave** was then started c 1220, entirely aisleless and with domed-up octopartite rib vaults which, along with the Cher valley churches of Mennetou and St-Loup, are among the easternmost examples of this quintessentially western French style. The aisles were added after 1445, at the insistence of a growing parish population, but the clumsy ambulatory and radiating chapels of the choir were the result of a 17C restoration campaign, aimed at making good some of the damage suffered during the Wars of Religion. This damage denuded the church of its medieval fittings, and, apart from an excellent organ of 1603, little can be said for their replacements.

South of the church, the narrower of the two main river courses is bordered by a pleasant riverside walk, inevitably known as the **Rue de Venise**, which runs west from the 16C Moulin des Garçonnets and the Rue d'Enfer. To the north, the major channel is spanned by an 18C bridge, giving rise to a number of views of the old downstream mills, the decaying **Moulin des Chapitres** above the left bank and the gloriously ivy-clad **Moulin de la Ville** to the right. Behind the Moulin de la Ville you can also make out the 15C east tower of the Valois-Angoulême *ancien château*, substantially refurbished during the mid-16C and now absorbed within the **SousPréfecture** (interiors open only to those on official business). A more picturesque route across the river can be had by heading along the riverside walk to the north-east of the church, and taking the footbridge over to the **Ile de la Motte**, its flattened terrace now supporting a large children's playground. From here a second footbridge connects with the north bank, bringing you through the delightful gardens of the **Square Ferdinand Buisson** and on to Romorantin's main street, the Rue Georges Clemenceau.

What survives of the medieval town is off to the right, along the Rue de la Résistance, where in quick succession you pass the early 16C **Hôtel de la Chancellerie** and the late 15C **Hôtel St-Pol**, the latter said to be the house before which François I was injured leading an attack on the bean-king of Romorantin on 6 January 1521. (It was a French tradition to eat a cake containing a bean, the *Galette du Roi*, on the feast of Epiphany, the finder of the bean being king for the day. Leading the attack on the Hôtel St-Pol, François was hit by a flying log, and to dress a serious head wound his surgeon shaved his scalp, prompting the king to grow a beard in compensation and so set the early 16C courtly fashion for full beards.) East of here, the junction with the Rue de la Pierre is occupied by the **Maison du Carroir Doré**, a superb townhouse of c 1480 with carved wooden posts sporting images of St George and the Annunciation, the figures of Gabriel and the Virgin flanked by two pelicans symbolising Christ's Passion (a fairly common late medieval juxtaposition, and one doubtless behind the idea that babies are announced by storks or pelicans). The house also accommodates the **Musée d'Archaeologie**, a local collection whose finest exhibits are to be found amongst the Gallo-Roman funerary material discovered at Gièvres.

The **Hôtel-de-Ville** is further east again, a handsome late 19C *hôtel particulier* subsequently donated to the town, whose grounds are embellised with a tiled **Pagode Chinoise**. The hôtel-de-ville itself is altogether less sensuous, and the second floor is given over to the **Musée de la Sologne**, a small display of the once staple craft industries of the Sologne. The one other museum of note is along the Faubourg d'Orléans, where the specialist engineering company, Matra, has established a **Musée de la Course Automobile**. For anyone with an interest in motor racing its library may already be well known, though the museum is equally aimed at the general visitor, and there is much beauty to be found among its blue-bodied Grand Prix racers.

Rural Sologne

An exploration of the rural Sologne might begin with **Lassay-sur-Croisne**, reached along a combination of the D59 and D20 (10km from Romorantin to Lassay). The parish church of **St-Hilaire** at Lassay serves as a useful prologue for a visit to the adjacent château du Moulin, of interest for the seigneurial chapel which Philippe du Moulin added in 1494, and embellished with the colossal wall painting of St Christopher which looms above his now shattered tomb. St Christopher is seen striding across a gulley which separates the church at Lassay from du Moulin's château, shown in a conventionalised but entirely 15C vein.

The **Château du Moulin** itself is about 1km from the village. It is the most picturesque of the smaller moated châteaux of the Blésois and you reach it by following the signs which direct you along a track to the west of Lassay. The house was begun shortly before 1490 by Philippe du Moulin, a local seigneur who grew in wealth and prestige after he saved the life of Charles VIII at the battle of Fornova in 1495, and in gratitude was offered the hand in marriage of the extremely wealthy Charlotte d'Argouges. The mason recorded as supervising the work in 1501 was Jacques de Persigny of Romorantin, but, though the workmanship may have been local, the overall design is one which might be paralleled throughout northern and western France.

The château consists of a square, moated terrace, originally enclosed by ranges and angle-towers, and supporting a freestanding *corps de logis* in the central court. The outer barbican, which offered the first line of defence and is visible in the painting at Lassay, has gone, as have all but one of the angle-towers, but these defensive precautions were subordinate to a desire to evoke an essentially picturesque chivalric fortress. Innumerable details serve to reinforce the point—the curious blind battlements to the left of the entrance block for instance, or the faintly absurd machicolations of the surviving angle-tower—all suggest that Philippe du Moulin's main purpose was to surround himself with seigneurial pomp while providing commodious accommodation. The splendid interiors he created are on show in the **corps de logis**, and, though much of the detail, and all the fireplaces, date from a sensitive restoration initiated after de Marcheville purchased the château in 1900, the lightness of these rooms remains striking. They now display 17C Flemish tapestries and mostly 17C and 18C French furniture, with the odd survivor from the earlier building, in particular the three stained glass panels in the chapel and a superb iron chandelier.

The simplest way to cut over towards the **western Sologne** from Lassay is to continue along the D20 to the pleasant roadside village of (5km) **Mur-de-Sologne**, handsomely shaded by a 13C church tower which, like its fellow west front, incorporates a considerable quantity of 11C masonry. From Mur, the D122 strikes due west to (14km) **Contres**, through a landscape whose marshes have been drained and the soil given over to potatoes, asparagus, maize and sunflowers. This change in character becomes even more marked west of Contres, for despite the survival of much of that dense and prolific Sologne woodland, the local farmers have largely abandoned pollarding in favour of maize and oats. The D7 is the best route through the area, bringing you to a village which exemplifies this shift towards tradeable efficiency, (8km) **Fougères-sur-Bièvre**, where a brand new woodworking factory occupies the high ground above the stunning roofscape of the **CHÂTEAU DE FOUGÈRES**.

Unusually for a Loire château, Fougères was wholly untouched by the 19C mania for restoration, and, having served as a spinning-mill, it was purchased by the State in 1932, and is in the process of being restored. It survives as a stripped-down late 15C château, and, most unusually, visitors are left to wander at will. The château was begun some time between 1475 and 1483 by Pierre de Refuge, treasurer to Louis XI, who obtained the king's permission to replace an earlier castle destroyed by the English during the Hundred Years War. Pierre died in 1497 and it is usually assumed that the château was complete by that date, a once fully moated rectangular complex arranged around an inner court.

The similarities with the Château du Moulin are striking. Despite the fact that Fougères was never built with a full set of angle-towers, both the main entrance block and the desire to group the vertical elements with an eye to creating a broken silhouette belong to the same school of thought. The square north tower has been seen as belonging to the earlier château, incorporated in the later building under Pierre de Refuge, but its architectural detailing is comparable to that of the indisputably late 15C work and its walls are too slender to belong to a presumably 13C keep. The internal rooms have lost any furnishings they once had, but the great joy of Fougères is that you can walk unhindered through its major roofspaces, and for anyone with an interest in architectural carpentry the revelation of the timberwork in its west and east wings is worth a journey in itself.

From Fougères, the D38 winds north through the spruce little villages of Chitenay and Cellettes towards the Forêt de Russy, beneath whose southern rim rise the imperious chimneystacks of the (11km) **Château de Beauregard**. Arriving from the south (the château is signposted from the village of Cellettes) brings you around the rear elevation of what is in reality a modest retreat from court, a *château de plaisance*. The house was built for Jean du Thier, an intimate of Henri II, and seems to have been swiftly constructed between 1550 and 1553. Du Thier is believed to have commissioned the painted wooden panelling of the first floor **Cabinet des Grelots** from the Italian Mannerists, Scibec de Carpi and Nicolò dell'Abate, both then working at Fontainebleau, but on the whole it is the later decoration which dominates the house. In 1617 Beauregard passed into the hands of Paul Ardier, *controleur général des gabelles*, who shortly afterwards acquired a consignment of Delft tiles depicting an entire army on the march—drummer-boys, cavalrymen, lancers, officers and all—and had them laid across the floor of the great first floor **Galerie des Illustres** (Portrait Gallery). Even more surprisingly, the 327 17C portraits which gave the room its name survive intact.

The idea of constructing a gallery of illustrious faces has its roots in the portraits of great men with which 15C Italian rulers liked to embellish their studies—the *studiolo* of Federigo da Montefeltro at Urbino being a good example—but actual portrait galleries on this sort of scale are a largely 17C phenomenon. Recent research suggests the paintings were executed in the studio of the local artist, Jean Mosnier, between 1676 and 1682, all ostensibly copied from contemporary portraits, and in certain cases offering a loose record of portraits known to have existed and now lost. They extend from early 14C figures, such as the Lucchese despot, Castruccio Castracani, Edward III of England and Philippe VI of France, to the mid-17C portrayals of Louis XIII and Charles I of England.

If you want to explore the **northern Sologne**, the D77 and D765 offer the best route through the woodland to the south of the river Beuvron, bringing you out into the spacious market town of (7km) **Cour-Cheverny**. As with several of the smaller towns to the south-west, Cour-Cheverny has been transformed by the proximity of a major château, and though less obviously dependent on the revenues generated by a stream of visitors than, say, Chenonceaux, it is no less amply provided with hotels and restaurants.

The 17C **CHÂTEAU DE CHEVERNY** lies 1km south of the town, imposing symmetry on its great sweep of lawns from an entrance façade designed with an almost neurotic respect for order. The present château was the result of Henri Hurault's confinement to Cheverny, a punishment for murdering his first wife and her lover after he discovered them *in flagrante*—after killing the lover he forced his wife to choose between poison and the sword. He married Marguerite Gaullard shortly afterwards, and in 1625 demolished the medieval castle at Cheverny, commissioning Jacques Bougier of Blois (also known as Boyer de Blois) to plan its replacement. Henri died in 1632, some two years before Cheverny was completed, but his was the controlling influence on a design whose precision and rigour are reflected even in outbuildings such as the orangerie, built the best part of a century later. As at Azay-le-Rideau, the main entrance block is emptied of all except a vaulted stair-ramp, but here at Cheverny, designed a good 100 years later, what impresses is the way in which the façade is controlled through its horizontal elements. Not only is the stone sunk with continuous channels, but the pediments create a series of emphatic lateral accents, modulated across each storey line and running to a particularly fine set of swan pediments at first floor level.

The **interiors**, though subjected to a fair amount of restoration work in the 19C, are overwhelmingly 17C, an exception being made for those private apartments occupying the western half of the first floor. The finest interior, the so-called **Salle des Gardes**, retains Jean Mosnier's original early 17C paintwork, thickening out the ceiling and shutters with arabesques, garlands and coats of arms. The wainscot was also painted with allegorical scenes bearing Latin riddles, such as the campanula's 'though I am small I am the colour of the sky', and relating the floral emblems to mythological subjects—a favourite 17C game, but one which rarely survives in a domestic interior.

The **Long Gallery** on the ground floor also houses a number of fine portraits, including three small works by François Clouet depicting Anne de Thou, comtesse de Cheverny during the mid-16C, and Philippe and Jacques Hurault, along with a self-portrait by the prolific early 18C portraitist Hyacinthe Rigaud. The best of the paintings are in the main **drawing room**, where Titian's portrait of the young Cosimo de Medici has been paired with the more arresting image of Jeanne d'Aragon, the latter probably painted in Raphael's studio c 1515. Towards the end of the recommended itinerary, the finest of the 17C tapestries have been hung in one of the smaller reception rooms, consisting of a superb set of peasant genre scenes, woven in Flanders to the designs of David Teniers.

North-east of Cour-Cheverny, the D102 passes another of the Sologne's formidable crop of châteaux, though in this case it is little more than a satellite of the far grander royal retreat to the north of the forêt de Boulogne at Chambord.

The **Château de Villesavin** (7km) lies just to the north of the village of Tour-en-Sologne, on the opposite bank of the river Beuvron, and your first impression is of a thicket of pyramidal roofs and dormer windows which seem as if floated down from Chambord. The connection is direct, for the château was built for Jean le Breton, François I's commissioner of works at Chambord. But, unlike its grander neighbour, Villesavin is a low and rangy house, conceived as a series of wings around three courts.

Jean le Breton acquired the site in 1527, and the date, 1536, inscribed on one of the dormers suggests work proceeded quickly. Architecturally, the compositions are marshalled from above, the roof being sprung from a cornice above the ground floor and broken by a sequence of rectangular chimneys and dormer windows. The interior was refurbished in the early 19C, and, with the exception of an impressive collection of pewter, offers scant interest, though a decaying early 17C fresco cycle of the Passion of Christ enlivens the chapel. A superb 16C **marble fountain** still acts as the centrepiece of the *cour d'honneur*, said to have been a gift from the sculptors then working at Chambord. It is a magnificent object, though the tale told of its origins might be classed as 'a likely story', for both its detail and its splendour suggests it was carved in northern Italy for Chambord itself, and was subsequently snatched for Villesavin.

From Villesavin the older tracks across the forest are well-signposted to (10km) the **CHÂTEAU DE CHAMBORD**, François I's great early 16C hunting lodge set between the northern edge of the forêt de Boulogne and the parkland to the south of the river Loire. Arriving from this direction little prepares you for the sublime power of Chambord's principal elevations. Even if you approach from the north, you are channelled over the river Casson and brought into the main court through Mansart's unremarkable late 17C south wing, via what amounts to a tradesman's entrance. Nonetheless, it is worth persisting with these back-door arrangements, braving the crowds and the sprawling car-parks, to reach one of the great rural palaces of Europe.

Chambord is widely regarded as a key statement of French Renaissance architecture, a building whose domestic arrangements and concern for symmetry owe little to the châteaux of the previous generation, and might be said to mark a break with the past. This view does need qualifying, for you may notice much that is late medieval in spirit, particularly in the groundplan and the treatment of the roofs. There is also the question of whether the château fulfilled a particular set of expectations, for as is often the case with architecture on this sort of scale, it is clear that the thinking of both the patron and the architects changed as the building progressed.

The known facts are that following an outbreak of plague in 1518, François I abandoned work on the château Leonardo da Vinci was designing at Romorantin, and instead decided to build to the north of an old feudal castle of the counts of Blois at Chambord. Plans for the château de Chambord were drawn up in 1519, work beginning immediately under the master mason, Jacques Sourdeau. Sourdeau died in 1522, to be replaced by Pierre Nepveu of Amboise, but François I's imprisonment in Pavia between 1524 and 1526 brought work to a halt. By the time it recommenced, François had appointed Jean le Breton, with whom he had shared his captivity, to act as Commissioner of Works. The 21 years between 1526 and François' death in 1547 was probably the period which saw most of the early 16C work at Chambord completed. Pierre Nepveu remained master mason until 1537, when the roof of the *corps de logis* was in the course of being built, after which the masons were supervised by Jacques Coqueau of Blois. The east wing was underway by 1539, with the leadwork on the main roofs gilded in 1541, suggesting that the *corps de logis* was being furnished and decorated by this date. Finally, a start was made on the west wing in 1550, after François' death, but though Jacques Coqueau remained master mason until 1569 this last 16C phase seems to have been abandoned before the *cour d'honneur* had been completed, since an engraving by Jacques du Cerceau published in 1579 describes the courtyard arrangements as proposals. In the event, the present low ranges which enclose the court were built to the designs of Jules-Hardouin Mansart between 1683 and 1685.

In all this there is no mention of an architect, and most debates about Chambord have centred on the identity of the first designer. There are two major candidates, both of them Italian: **Leonardo da Vinci**, the designer of François' projected château at Romorantin, who died at Amboise in the same year as Chambord was begun, 1519; and **Domenico da Cortona**, a rather shadowy figure, said to have first come to France with Giuliano da Sangallo in 1495 and best known as a woodcarver. Domenico da Cortona was certainly responsible for building a wooden model of Chambord in 1519 or 1520, sadly now destroyed, but known from a surviving late 17C drawing and description by Félibien. This model is of particular interest, since it demonstrates that the general plan of Chambord was settled at the outset, but that a number of telling details were changed in the course of construction.

As with the present **corps de logis**, the model shows a square central block with four cylindrical angle-towers, its overall shape reminiscent of a late medieval château such as Saumur. Its internal arrangements were quite unprecedented in France, however, for each floor is divided into four equal arms by corridors which lead off the central staircase, forming a Greek cross. The space allotted to each corner is thus identical, and is partitioned into one reception hall, two smaller rooms, and a closet. In other words, the *logis* is divided into a series of self-contained apartments. This arangement became the fundamental principal of French domestic planning for the next four centuries, but its origins were Italian and were first developed by Giuliano da Sangallo, Domenico da Cortona's master, for Lorenzo de' Medici in the villa at Poggio a Caiano. It is for this reason that Domenico is seen as more than just the model-maker, and is presumed to be the initial designer, but the question of whether other architects were consulted remains to be asked.

The case for Leonardo's involvement, at least in an advisory capacity, is, as ever, elusive, but is circumstantially strong. One of the major differences between Domenico's model and the present *logis* is the **staircase**. Domenico foresaw a straight ramp, whereas Chambord was built with a double-spiral staircase, so that anyone walking up cannot collide with anyone coming down. Domenico da Cortona may have been a skilled and proficient designer, but the brilliant spatial geometry of this staircase would have been beyond the capabilities of all but a tiny group of early 16C architects, and one suspects Domenico was not quite in this class. Leonardo was, and is known to have experimented with helix and double-spiral designs. The problem is that the dates do not add up, and unless one assumes that Leonardo exerted a posthumous influence on Chambord one has to look elsewhere. The obvious places to turn are Blois, where the François I wing was given a superb external stairwell before 1524, and Italy. The stairwell at Blois shares an interest in the sculptural possibilities of interlocking steps and balustrades with Chambord, but is a single spiral. Italy is more promising, for the other great double spiral to be built in early 16C Europe is at Orvieto, where in 1528 Antonio Sangallo the Younger used the form in the Pozzo di San Patrizio. Sangallo the Younger had been employed by Donato Bramante as a draughtsman in Rome, and the designers of the François I wing at Blois certainly had access to drawings of Bramante's Vatican Loggia. This circle of Bramante seems the most likely source for what is justifiably seen as one of the master-pieces of European Renaissance architecture.

Otherwise, it is the French masons who win out. Domenico da Cortona's model showed the ground floor of the *corps de logis* was to be enclosed by an arcaded loggia, with the windows of the first and second storeys surmounted by blind, semi-circular arches. These fea-tures were dropped in favour of the grid-like pilasters and stringcourses found in contemporary French buildings, such as Blois or Azay-le-Rideau.

The great synthesis is the **roof**. Domenico's model had lost its roof by the time Félibien drew it, but it is inconceivable that this inventive forest of turrets, lanterns and chimneystacks could have been worked up to such a flamboyant pitch by anyone other than a French designer, and also inconceivable that the flattening of the surface decoration would have been possible without the early 16C fashion for Italian architectural sculpture. The most obvious Italian feature is the use of decorative stone inlays, but—as in medieval England, where marble inlays were imitated with polished purbeck marble—at Chambord, slate has been used. The mixing of French and Italian elements has become complete, combining with extraordinary virtuosity to create an architectural language which embodies something quite new, some-thing that can perhaps be described as Grand Mannerism. For a walk across these **roof terraces** is one of the great architectural experiences of northern Europe, akin to stepping into an ideal cityscape by Piero della Francesca or Francesco di Giorgio, but here fantastically reor-dered to reflect the irregular and asymmetrical.

The **appartements** are less exciting, their interiors having been mostly stripped in the 19C and the resulting space given over to short thematic expositions, of hunting on the second floor, for instance, or the life of the unhappily-named Dauphin, the grandson of Charles X and Pretender to the French throne during the late 19C. The **Apparte-ments de François I** are in the east wing, now sparsely furnished with later furniture or copies of 16C portraits, but by far the most interesting work relates to the 18C occupation of Chambord, and is concentrated in the northern rooms of the first floor.

Louis XIV's reaction to the château was to turn the principle of central planning on its head. The four equal apartments created by a Greek cross flew in the face of Louis' desire for quarters which were both visibly more spacious than those of his courtiers, and lay at the heart of the château. Accordingly, the first floor was redesigned to merge the north-west and north-east apartments with the north aisle, creating a single royal *logis* and giving Louis more than twice the space of anyone else. These rooms were subsequently occupied by the Maréchal de Saxe, after Louis XV presented him with Chambord in 1746, and much of the refurbishment is due to de Saxe. This includes a striking fireplace carved from Pyrenean marble and a splendid 18C ceramic stove now islanded in one of the vestibules.

But it is the treatment of the principal elevations which remains the most exhilarating feature of Chambord, and before leaving it is worth crossing the bridge over the Cosson to take in that superb north front, enclosed by water since the early 20C when Achille Duchêne finally diverted the river.

South-east of Chambord, along the D112 and beyond the river Beuvron, lies the *Sologne des Etangs*, the wide, marshy flats, dotted with lakes, coppices and scrubby pasture, which stretch for 40km or more from Bracieux to Salbris. Much of the area has been drained, obliterating most of the mosquito spawning-grounds that made the region the sparsely populated, fever-ridden backwater of 19C literature, but it remains a harsh living, and the thin sprinkling of small villages and isolated farms reflects this. Unlike Romorantin to the south, the few towns in the area never really grew between the 16C and the 20C. You can see this most clearly at **Bracieux**, an attractive market town on the southern banks of the Beuvron. It is now much favoured by French holidaymakers, who flock to the campsites along the river, drawn by the tennis, boating and fishing, and has acquired a superficially chic atmosphere, as Parisian buyers have started to invest in second homes in the area. But even when admiring the handsome 16C covered market hall, whose splendid upper storey now houses summer exhibitions, or its fine collection of 17C and 18C houses, you are conscious that Bracieux never made the most of its location to become one of the key market towns of the Sologne.

A more obviously neglected air clings to those villages further from Blois and the Loire, the majority of the settlements mired within a haunting landscape of woods and lakes which unfolds to either side of the D923 as you press east. At 5km is **Neuvy**, a once considerable medieval market town but now shrunk to a sprawling hamlet some way east of the parish church. The latter is one of the more handsome churches of the northern Sologne, with a bare and essentially 11C nave whose exterior was faced with lozenge-patterned brickwork c 1520, at the same time as the new choir, lateral chapels and eastern bay were added.

To the east, the D923 stays north of the river Beuvron, sweeping through pockets of dense woodland, now interspersed with coniferous plantations, as far as the old roadside town of (16km) **Neung-sur-Beuvron**. From here, the more interesting route east is first to head south, along the D925/D121, and then turn left onto the D63 to (13km) St-Viâtre, crossing a landscape more typical of the Sologne before it was drained and agriculturally 'improved', a maze of rough pasture, mossy woods and scrubland, whose companion lakes and marshes lie off to the south.

St-Viâtre was known throughout the Middle Ages as *Tremblevy* or *Tremblevit*, in honour of the 6C anchorite, Viaster, who died here and was 'buried in the trunk of an aspen (*tremble*) which he himself had hollowed out for a coffin'. The narrow 11C ambulatory crypt in which his relics were enshrined still survives beneath the 19C altar in the **parish church**, but it is for a very different and entirely unexpected object that the village is now most celebrated. François I gave the seigneurie of Tremblevy to Wolfgang Eberhard, Count of Lupfen, when in Milan in 1515, and Eberhard seems to have celebrated the acquisition by commissioning the four great wooden panels now housed in the south transept. As a native of Stülinghen, on the German-Swiss border, it was perhaps natural that he turned to a Rhenish artist to produce this **retable**, but it still comes as a surprise to find the work of a German 16C painter in an area otherwise noted for its interest in early 16C Italian forms. The panels are painted on both sides, and have been hinged on a bracket to allow you to inspect both the Passion cycle, which was probably visible when the retable was closed, and the cycle of the life of St-Viâtre, which was the principal subject. The transepts are probably slightly later, perhaps commissioned by Eberhard's wife, Jeanne Cléret, as that to the north bears her coat of arms alongside Eberhard's on the main vault boss, while its counterpart to the south pairs Jeanne's arms with those of her second husband, Ludovic le Groing, whom she married in 1534.

To the east of St-Viâtre the D93 crosses the motorway, bringing you into the long-established roadside village of (8km) **Nouan-le-Fuzelier**. The central square is enlivened by a fine, stocky tower-porch, added to the parish church of **St-Martin** c 1500, and decorated with the brick lozenges then much in vogue in this area. However, the incessant howl of traffic can overwhelm Nouan's modest charms, and the promising café terraces along the main street offer scant consolation. The reason for this abused air, the N20, sweeps south from Nouan with scarcely a bend to bisect the busy market town of (12km) **Salbris**, another unremarkable centre overshadowed by its early 16C parish church, dedicated to **St-Georges**. The church houses a good 17C stone retable, but as Salbris is not a town to inspire a lingering visit, you are advised instead to head west, along the D724 to (7km) La Ferté-Imbault and Selles-St-Denis.

La Ferté-Imbault is perhaps the most prosperous of all the villages of the southern Sologne, beautifully situated along the banks of the river Sauldre, whose weirs and races once turned its mills. The 10C fortress from which it took its name was destroyed during the Hundred Years War, and the present château (firmly closed to visitors) was begun in the first quarter of the 16C for Jean d'Estampes, its western façade of stone and brick visible from the village. A better vantage point can be had from the north bank of the river, where a small 17C chapel incorporates the sole surviving fragment of the collegiate church of St-Thaurin, a delicate 12C portal which presumably dates from shortly after its foundation in 1164. Behind the chapel, beyond a curve in the river, the heavily restored surfaces of the château come into view, the outer defensive works and pavilions dating from the 1630s, when Jacques d'Estampes attempted to make good some of the damage sustained in the Wars of Religion.

Selles-St-Denis (2km) rises above the opposite bank of the Sauldre just to the west of La Ferté, an attractive village and worth a stop for the 15C wall paintings in the parish church of **St-Genoulph**. The church stands at the heart of the village, substantially as it was built in the 15C, though the lower wall of the nave is clearly earlier, and quite possibly pre-Romanesque. The **wall paintings** are towards the top of the nave walls, opening with a marriage scene (of the parents of St-Genoulph) in the north-western angle, and then running east along the north wall, west along the south, and north along the west, before culminating in two scenes of burial and glorification to either side of the west window.

The paintings are wholly devoted to the life of St-Genoulph, an Early Christian bishop of Cahors, whose remains were interred at the monastery of Estrée-St-Genoulph (Indre) and seem to have been translated to Selles-St-Denis in the late 8C. The pilgrimage became locally popular, and the paintings reflect this, stressing healing, miracle-working and intercession, each scene represented with admirable sharpness and economy. The drapery is angular and stylised and the architectural volumes almost abstracted, any spatial development relying on the vanishing lines of a tiled floor. It is an extremely effective late 15C pictorial cycle, a fine example of simple, vernacular preaching art which deserves to become more widely known. The church also contains a wooden tie-beamed roof which reflects the late medieval rood arrangements, and the east window frames four panels of 17C glass. The glass seems to have been given by Jacques d'Estampes, Marquis de la Ferté-Imbault, shortly after 1661, who carries a crest emblazoned with the devices of a Knight of the Order of St Michael.

West of here the D724 clings to the northern flanks of the **Sauldre valley**, offering glimpses of the asparagus and maize whose cultivation has depleted much of the older woodland in these parts, and occasionally throwing off a glorious view of wooded parkland as you once more approach (16km) Romorantin-Lanthenay.

3

The Cher Valley: Mennetou to Tours

ROAD (107km): Mennetou-sur-Cher D100, 3km St-Loup; D51/D35, 24km Selles-sur-Cher; D17, 17km St-Aignan; N76/D176, 8km Thesée-la-Romaine (D176/D21, 5km Château de Gué-Péan); D176, 10km Montrichard (D764, 12km Château de Montpoupon; D764, 7km Pontlevoy); D176, 9km Chenonceaux; D40/D31, 8km Bléré; D40, 8km St-Martin-le-Beau; D83/N76, 11km Véretz; N76, 9km Tours.

The above itinerary charts the progress of the river Cher from the point where it flows into the Blésois, just above Mennetou-sur-Cher, downstream as far as the industrial suburbs of Tours. It is a flat landscape, the river cutting a shallow valley through the limestone plateau, but both its depth and speed of flow made it a significant frontier, acting as a boundary between the ancient dioceses of Bourges, Orléans and Tours, as well as marking the transition between the old counties of Berri, Blois and Touraine. With the exception of the area around the Roman road station at Thésée-la-Romaine, the lower valley was sparsely populated during the Gallo-Roman period and became the haunt of hermits in the 5C and 6C, a distinction which fostered the growth of a number of shrines in the later Middle Ages. The churches which house these cults are the most significant cultural monuments you encounter above Thésée, which may make the earlier stages of the route seem a little repetitive. Sadly, it is also the case that several of these buildings fell victim to some of the most insensitive restoration programmes of the 19C, which means that if medieval ecclesiastical architecture is not a passion, you are better off heading straight for Montrichard.

The area downstream of Thésée developed a very much more prosperous secular culture, reflected in châteaux such as Gué-Péan, Chenonceau and Montpoupon. With these in mind, the itinerary includes a number of detours, but as the more interesting towns and villages are quite evenly disposed above both banks of the river, there is anyway a fair amount of switching back and forth.

Mennetou-sur-Cher is a pleasant town in which to begin an exploration of the middle and lower valley of the Cher. Situated at the point where the modern *département* of Loir-et-Cher borders the medieval duchy of Berri, the town grew up around an important monastery (*Monastelum* to *Monesto*, finally corrupted to *Mennetou*) founded by Ingertrude, daughter of Clothair I, in 586. This monastery and its successors have long gone, but the foundation inspired Hervé II, lord of Vierzon, to construct a castle to the west of the monastic precincts in 1212, and encircle the town with a rectangular wall. The present town is substantially contained within this enceinte—a check on the confusion of crumbling medieval terraces and 18C gardens—and three of the gates, along with two towers, have survived.

The great gate which now opens on to the N76, the **Porte d'En-Bas**, originally acted as a water-gate, for prior to the 16C the waters of the Cher lapped against the southern walls of the town. The Porte d'En-Bas was modified in the 15C, as can be seen by the splendid late medieval fireplace which decorates the first floor. It leads into the Place des Armes with the **Grande Rue** beyond. The latter forms the major longitudinal axis of the town, connecting the Porte d'En-Haut with the **Porte Bonne Nouvelle**, the old eastern gate which protected the monastery itself. The earlier abbey was refounded as a convent in the 13C and what survives is tucked into the angle of the Bonne Nouvelle, a handsome late medieval *logis* which obviously accommodated the prioresses in some style. There are also a number of fine houses along the Grande Rue, the best a rare and excellent 13C mansion now housing the town library, to which an engagingly messy west elevation was added in the late 16C.

The great barn-like church of **St-Urbain** was always the parish church, its largely early 13C spaces illuminated with Flamboyant traceried windows during the early 16C, though the lower walls of the bell-tower belong to an 11C building on the site. The church has managed to retain a few fittings, including a 14C statue of St Barbara and a good 17C altar retable. But the great pleasure of Mennetou lies in just wandering its streets, for there is simthing compelling about the way in which many of the medieval buildings have been re-used or incorporated into later structures. Before returning to the Porte d'En-

Bas it is worth taking a close look at the houses which occupy the spaces between it and the church; everywhere you look you will see elements of Hervé's 13C castle.town, connecting the Porte d'En-Haut with the **Porte Bonne Nouvelle**, the old eastern gate which protected the monastery itself. The earlier abbey was refounded as a convent in the 13C and what survives is tucked into the angle of the Bonne Nouvelle, a handsome late medieval *logis* which obviously accommodated the prioresses in some style. There are also a number of fine houses along the Grande Rue, the best a rare and excellent 13C mansion now housing the town library, to which an engagingly messy west elevation was added in the late 16C.

The great barn-like church of **St-Urbain** was always the parish church, its largely early 13C spaces illuminated with Flamboyant traceried windows during the early 16C, though the lower walls of the bell-tower belong to an 11C building on the site. The church has managed to retain a few fittings, including a 14C statue of St Barbara and a good 17C altar retable. But the great pleasure of Mennetou lies in just wandering its streets, for there is something compelling about the way in which many of the medieval buildings have been re-used or incorporated into later structures. Before returning to the Porte d'En-Bas it is worth taking a close look at the houses which occupy the spaces between it and the church; everywhere you look you will see elements of Hervé's 13C castle.

A picturesque way of advancing **west from Mennetou** is to cross the Cher by the bridge near the riverside **Plage de Mennetou**, an artificial beach where you can swim, and pick up the D100 to (3km) **St-Loup**. Here, banked against the northern slopes of the rise and surveying the river valley, rises a parish church which serves as a landmark across the wider region (if locked the key is kept in the house opposite the south door). The **church** was built between c 1180 and 1223, with a fully vaulted and aisleless three-bay nave, square sanctuary bay and a low three-celled apse. The latter carries a fading set of wall paintings depicting a Christ in Majesty and a Lady of Sorrows, which must be contemporary with the church. There are also remains of late medieval frescoes in the nave, along with a fine 16C sculptural group showing the Coronation of the Virgin. But the most surprising object is a particularly grand wooden housing for the celebrant's throne, dating from 1540–45 and embellished with reliefs of St George and St Martin, a Veronica Head, the Beheading of John the Baptist and Christ Healing a Cripple.

Beyond St-Loup, the D51 tracks the southern slopes of the Cher valley, dropping to meet the low meadows and coppices which fringe the river banks before swinging through (6km) St-Julien-sur-Cher and (3km) La Chapelle-Montmartin. West of here the road briefly changes designation to the D35 as it cuts through the northern corner of the *département* of Indre, bisects the old roadside town of (7km) Chabris, and strikes out across the flood plains to rejoin the river at the medieval frontier town of (8km) **SELLES-SUR-CHER**.

Built above the south bank of the river, where the Sologne, Touraine and Berri come together, the town grew up around the hermitage of St-Eusice, whose prayers Childebert considered responsible for his victories against the Visigoths in Spain. By way of thanks, the king built a monastery above the hermit's tomb in the mid-6C. This early settlement fell prey to the Norse raids of 853 and 873, and was reconstructed and fortified in the 10C by Thibaud le Tricheur, Count of Blois, who seems to have added a donjon on the site of the present château. With the exception of those parts of the 13C castle incorporated into the later building, none of the medieval fortifications has survived. Yet, despite its 18C expansion, the shape of Selles reflects the medieval enceinte, and the principal thoroughfares still lie between the castle and the abbey.

This abbey, dedicated to **St-Eusice**, forms the centrepiece of the town and lies in its main square, directly opposite an attractive range of hotels and cafés. Monastic life did not endure for long at St-Eusice—in fact the very term monastic does not do justice to the irregular congregation of *clerici* who made up the community—and after the Norse had driven out this band of priests during the 9C the abbey lapsed, the ruins only recolonised by a group of itinerant 'clercs' c 1020. This sort of loose institutional arrangement came under attack throughout Europe during the Gregorian Reform of the late 11C, and St-Eusice was no exception. By 1140 the 'clercs' had decided to seek the protection of the powerful abbey of Marmoutier, but, fearing he would lose authority over the church, the archbishop of Bourges imposed a college of Augustinian canons regular in 1145, and it was in this guise that the church functioned until the French Revolution.

The later history of the building was one of disaster and dereliction. In 1533 the spire was destroyed by lightning, and in 1562 Coligny led his victorious Protestant troops south from the battlefield at Dreux, crossing the Cher at Selles and sacking St-Eusice after plundering its treasury. Little more than the outer wall of the ambulatory and radiating chapels survived from the choir, though the nave was pretty much unscathed. The building was patched back together in 1613, and in 1882 the architect A. de Baudot was commissioned to restore the crumbling structure and set to work in the choir. The result is that these eastern parts are an improved replica of what de Baudot felt they should once have looked like, and their machine-cut 'correctness' is even more chilling than that of St-Aignan. The aisles and main arcade of the nave fared better, giving you an opportunity to assess the wider merits of the building.

It seems likely that what remains of the Romanesque church predates the arrival of Augustinian canons, and that the major part of the west front, south aisle wall and ambulatory chapels date from the late 11C and early 12C. The **west front** incorporates some marble columns from an earlier structure, perhaps Childeric's 6C church, but, excepting the south aisle wall, the rest of the nave dates from c 1300, with a rather fine **north door** carrying stems of wild roses between the mouldings.

The church is justifiably best known for the splendid **frieze sculpture** which enlivens the exterior walls of the apse ambulatory. The two main cycles are attached to the axial chapel, with a series of panels relating the Life of St-Eusice above the windows and a New Testament cycle below. The latter subverts the scriptural order of the scenes, and appears to have done so for reasons of narrative emphasis, depicting from left to right, the Passion of Christ, Annunciation, Nativity, Resurrection of Lazarus. The upper register is more finely carved and probably dates from c 1075, while that below is cruder, more vivid and essentially undatable. It has certainly lost none of its power to thrill, and the fiery demon shaking Judas in the Last Supper is one of the most dramatic compositions of early Romanesque sculpture. The northern radiating chapel and ambulatory wall has also acquired a heterogeneous collection of reliefs, with what may be a hunting scene, or even elements of the Labours of the Months, beneath the roofline, and a Visitation jammed into the angle with the transept. This is an unusual and important example of Romanesque frieze sculpture; unusual in that it is the only example of narrative relief sculpture in the Loire Valley, important in that it attaches a reliquary saint's life to the exterior of the choir.

The rest of the town is as bitty as St-Eusice, the most attractive area being down towards the river, where the **château** rises proud of a magnificent terrace and on a still day carries a marvellous reflection across to the north bank. The earliest part of the present fabric belongs to a 13C château begun by Richard de Courtenay, replacing a castle destroyed by Richard Coeur-de-Lion. The interiors were refurbished after 1604, when Philippe de Béthune, brother of the Duc de Sully, pulled down most of the eastern walls and erected two elegant pavilions, joined by an arcaded wall. To the west, de Béthune introduced a third element to the medieval structure and had the **Pavilion Doré** built, furnishing it with gilded fireplaces, coffered ceilings and frescoed walls. A few of the early 17C portable items have also survived, most splendidly the great canopied bed in the room Marie Sobieska, exiled Queen of Poland, occupied during the 18C, and much of the furniture in the delightful Games Room.

To the **west of Selles** the Cher is joined by the narrow river Fouzon, whose ambling course through the limestone is finally thrown north by the beds of flint around Meusnes. It is a dusty landscape, the forests having been cleared to make way for cereals and the quarries long closed. Even the roadside towns have an exhausted and depopulated air. However, the central square at (7km) **Meusnes** is enhanced by one of the finest early Romanesque churches still standing in the old county of Blois.

The church now serves a parish, but when the documents first mention it in 1206 it functioned as a priory, dedicated to **St-Pierre** and subservient to the abbey of Beaulieu-lès-Loches. All earlier documentation is lost, though the use of *petit appareil*, strengthened with fully dressed stone around the crossing tower and outer angles, suggests a date in the first half of the 11C. The most notable feature is the handling of the crossing, for the arch which gives on to the nave is lower than the arches of the transeptal axis and supports a triple arcade, punched through the wall as a flying screen in what amounts to a throwback to Carolingian practice. The simple clarity and assurance with which these internal spaces are handled mark out St-Pierre as a significant 11C building. It is also worth visiting for its fine 16C and 17C statues. Apart from the café, the one other area of interest lies to the north of the church, where the Marie accommodates the **Musée de la Pierre à Fusil**, a small museum devoted to a local gunflint industry which, at its peak, produced 30 million flints a year, keeping Napoleon's armies fully supplied.

Below Meusnes the D17 adopts the high ground to the south of the river, before sweeping downwards to meet the Cher at the superbly situated hill town of (10km) **ST-AIGNAN-SUR-CHER**. The old town was the site of an important seigneurie, one of a number of fiefs created by the 10C counts of Blois to protect their southern flanks from the expansionist ambitions of the counts of Anjou. Eudes I de Blois raised the first wooden donjon on the high promontory at the centre of the present town during the 980s, but his vassal, Geoffroy de Donzy, was defeated in battle by Foulques Nerra of Anjou, and languished in Foulques' great donjon at Loches until his death c 1030. Geoffroy was returned for burial to St-Aignan, and with Foulques Nerra's mortal remains interred a mere 40km to the south-west, at Beaulieu-lès-Loches, St-Aignan was absorbed into greater Anjou.

All that now remains of the medieval castle are a 13C polygonal tower and elements of a late 14C tower, the rest having been replaced by a splendid Renaissance **château** reached along a monumental flight of steps which ascend from the Place de l'Eglise. The château remains in private hands and you might see no more than the *cour d'honneur*, but the climb is worth it for the views over the town, and the chance to examine the early 16C eastern elevations of a particularly fine building (the west wing is largely late 19C).

Returning down this flight of steps brings you through a 13C western tower-porch and into the collegiate church of **St-Aignan**. This is an undated structure, though a church dedicated to Aignan, the celebrated mid-5C bishop of Orléans, existed by the late 10C. The status it enjoyed when Eudes constructed his donjon *ecclesia ab heremitis olim habitata* (a church where for a long time hermits dwelt), is uncertain, one can only say that by the 12C St-Aignan served both a chapter of secular canons and a parish, but it lay within the diocese of Bourges, and the determination of the archbishops to extract two papal bulls confirming their authority during the 12C suggests it was an independent-minded chapter. Sadly, a vicious restoration between 1858 and 1870 entirely reconstructed the choir and completed the western tower-porch, and was so wholesale in its effects that it is difficult to advance more than a general chronology of the building.

It seems likely that the choir dates from the final quarter of the 12C and the nave from c 1200, the capitals of the latter surviving in a reasonable state though the superficially attractive 'Romanesque' capitals of the choir are free interpretations on the part of the restorers, who seem to have drawn on the vocabulary of the 11C porch sculpture of St-Benoît-sur-Loire. The **crypt** was spared this process, as in the 19C it was rented out as a cellar to a local wine merchant, and its decaying interior has more to offer than the rest of the church. This is primarily due to the cycle of **wall paintings** which survive here, that of the axial chapel devoted to scenes from the **Life of Christ**, with a Raising of Lazarus and a fragmentary rendering of a table at which a meal was taken, both beneath a medallion of the Agnus Dei and two Evangelist Symbols. The southern radiating chapel elaborates four scenes from the **Life of St-Gilles**, again beneath an Agnus Dei, showing St-Gilles handing his cloak to a semi-naked beggar, healing a man bitten by a snake, and saving a ship from disaster through prayer. The fourth scene is illegible.

Both of these cycles appear to be late 12C, that to the south markedly richer and deeper in tone, with a colour range which bears comparison to the Romanesque painting of Catalonia and south-western France. They are clearly the work of two different painters, but the fact that the St-Gilles Master painted the geometric designs on the intrados of the entrance arch to the axial chapel makes it possible they worked simultaneously. The St-Gilles Master seems to have landed the plum commission, however, and was responsible for the superb **Christ in Majesty** of the central apse semi-dome, a Christ seen handing keys and a scroll to figures of St Peter and St James the Less. The saints are in turn petitioned by three cripples, one of whom displays a coin in his right hand while leaning on a walking stick.

An early 16C Last Judgement embellishes the vault and western bay, but as the central composition this late 12C Christ in Majesty came to act as a devotional focus for a pair of early 15C frescoes, showing Louis II de Chalon, lord of St-Aignan from 1398 to 1424, between his mother, Marie de Parthenay, and his Aragonese second wife Jeanne de Perellos. The sin for which Louis and Jeanne are asking forgiveness caused a scandal at the Burgundian court in 1420 when the two eloped, leaving Louis' first wife, Marie de la Trémouille, an abandoned woman. Recent speculation has also suggested that the once fine 15C tomb embedded in the exterior north wall of the nave may be that of Jeanne de Perellos, as an adulteress memorialised on the outside of the church.

The more interesting route **west from St-Aignan** lies along the north bank of the Cher, taking the N76 at the crossroads beyond the main river bridge and then the D176 to (8km) **Thésée-la-Romaine**. Thésée acquired its suffix in honour of the impressive **Gallo-Roman site** at **Les Maselles**, 1km along the D176 to the west of the town. There is a small archaeological museum in the Mairie at Thésée, elucidating the Gallo-Roman background and displaying some of the finds, but the site at Les Maselles is much more exciting. It functioned as *Tasciaca*, an important road station rebuilt under the emperor Hadrian in the early 2C AD to serve the route from Roman Bourges to Tours. The principal survival is the market hall, a large rectangular shell, 40m by 13m, superbly constructed of squared *petit appareil* with intermediate brick banding, which stands to a height of around 3m. To the south are the remnants of subsidiary buildings, storerooms and accommodation blocks mostly, the footings suggesting they were similarly coursed of brick and squared stone.

A little further west, a right turn on to the D21 brings you into the village of (3km) **Monthou-sur-Cher**, passing a number of *caves* hollowed out of the soft *tuffeau* where the local vignerons press and store their wine. Just beyond the village, along a winding forest track and above a gentle, flat-bottomed valley, rise the towers and courtyard of one of the finest of the lesser known châteaux of the Loire, the **Château de Gué-Péan**. The house itself is arranged around a *cour d'honneur*, and fastened at the angles by four cylindrical towers. Although the early documentation of the château has been lost, it seems likely that the two entrance towers and flanking pavilions were built for François Alamand, controller of the *Gabelles* (Salt Tax), some time before his death in 1550. The architectural detailing of the two L-shaped pavilions, with half-columns at ground storey level and delicately fluted columns above, certainly suggests a date of c 1540. The entrance is flanked by two semi-circular artillery platforms, but the angle towers are not defensive and are there to give a show of ancient seigneurial pedigree, that to the left capped by a superb bell-shaped roof. The rear blocks were replaced in the 17C in a rather severe idiom, and it is to the interiors that one turns for evidence of the château's later splendour. The rooms here were mostly furnished in the 18C, and splendidly hung with tapestries and paintings by Hyacinthe Rigaud and Jean Honoré Fragonard, the surviving fireplace in the **grand salon** having been designed by Germain Pilon. As the châtelain now lets rooms to over-night guests, one can only hope it becomes better known.

West of here the D176 again offers the best route downstream, bringing you into the handsome market town of (11km) **MONTRICHARD**, its main street pinned between the rocky fastness of the castle and the river Cher.

History. The site was first developed by Foulques Nerra, who raised a wooden donjon above the promontory to the north of the river c 1010 in order to command the point where the Roman road from Tours to Bourges crossed the medieval route from Blois to Poitiers. This was replaced by the present ruinous stone keep between 1110 and 1130, but it was Richard Coeur-de-Lion who in the 1190s expanded the castle and built the first town walls, giving rise to the popular legend that he lent his name to the town (a name that in fact goes back to the early 11C). The town became a direct fief of the French crown in 1461, when Louis XI took it from the lords of Amboise to act as a base for his pilgrimages to the miracle-working shrine of the Virgin at Nantheuil. Louis also married his daughter, the terribly deformed 12-year-old Jeanne de France, to Louis d'Orléans in the castle chapel in 1476, intending the inevitably childless marriage to extinguish the Orléans branch of the Valois line. The plan backfired when Louis'.son, Charles VIII, died childless at Amboise and Louis d'Orléans was crowned Louis XII, repudiating Jeanne and marrying the king's widow, Anne de Bretagne, in accordance with Charles' will. The town's later history was uneventful and, despite some clumsy redevelopment, it remains an industrious market town with a fine residue of medieval buildings.

Town Tour. The shape of the **Rue National** makes this immediately apparent, connecting the splendid Monday and Friday vegetable market, at the junction with the Rue du Pont, with the western market squares of the Places l'Hôtel-de-Ville and du Commerce. The finest buildings are also to be found here, with two late 15C half-timbered houses at the corner of the Rues National and du Pont, reminiscent in their diagonally-set brick panels of their contemporaries in Tours. The easternmost is known as the **Maison de l'Ave Maria** and houses the Tourist Office. Walking west, the 16C Fontaine Ste-Catherine gives on to an adjacent 16C house, beyond which a pleasant rise of 15C–18C townhouses leads to the Place du Commerce, whose northern tower is all that survives of the medieval town barbican.

To reach the **Château de Montrichard** you should ascend the Grand Degrès Ste-Croix, turning left just before you reach the church. The main defences are arranged across a series of western facing terraces, with an outer curtain wall dating from c 1250 giving way to the upper bailey walls and keep. The whole complex was partially dismantled on the orders of Henri IV in 1589, but what remains is impressive, and centres around an early 12C square **keep**, whose truncated upper storey offers a breathtaking panorama of the lower valley of the Cher. The 16C Governor's Lodge has been converted to house the **Musée Tivoli**, with sections devoted to local geology, archaeology and folklore.

The original castle chapel, dedicated to **Ste-Croix**, was situated in the southern lee of the promontory, being made over to the town as a parish church after 1589. It was crudely over-restored during the mid-19C when, in an uncharacteristically sensitive touch, it was given a charming narthex-porch. Of the late 12C chapel only the west wall and nave south arcade piers survive, the north aisle and choir dating from the early 16C.

Although Louis XI would now recognise little of Ste-Croix, he would be less surprised by the object of his interest in acquiring Montrichard, the pilgrimage church of **Notre-Dame-de-Nantheuil**. This lies between the town centre and the railway station, on the old road to Amboise, a small cruciform building which remains a place of veneration and attracts a great procession each Whit Monday. The focus of this pilgrimage is a miracle-working statue of the Virgin and Child, for which Louis provided a first storey chapel to the west of the north transept after 1461. Access is either via a flight of steps from the exterior of the building, or from within the church, neither of which prepares you for a dull chamber in which a post-medieval image of the Virgin is now enshrined. The rest of the structure is, in its way, one of the more exciting smaller churches of the Loire, with a late 12C choir and transept whose northern chapel supports a stunning Romanesque capital, and an early 13C nave. This nave is a fairly simple four-bay vessel, with domed-up octopartite rib vaults sprung from corbels set into the wall. The easternmost vault is the only 13C survivor, the three western vaults respecting the earlier forms but replaced after 1461, when Louis XI renewed the church and added the north and west doors, splendidly decorated with Flamboyant finials and angels who carry Louis' once painted arms.

Montrichard is also an excellent base for **two excursions** to the north and south of the Cher.

The first excursion, south along the D764, brings you through the remnants of the old hunting forests which gather on the high ground between the valleys of the Cher and Indrois. It was these forests that initially inspired the building of the (12km) **Château de Montpoupon** on a natural limestone ledge overlooking the confluence of three small valleys. The château is first mentioned in 1208, and one can see elements of the 13C enceinte walls and western angle towers incorporated into the later structure, but what now survives is a late 15C central block, substantially refurbished in the 18C, and a handsome 16C **postern gate**. This latter houses a small upper chapel in which the surviving painted stonework of a freestanding late medieval chapel is displayed. You can also visit part of the *corps de logis* and the outbuildings, the former housing some good 16C–18C furniture, while the latter are mostly devoted to a museum of the local hunt, which here means deer and wild boar.

The second excursion, north-east along the D764, brings you to the ample estates of (7km) the **Abbaye de Pontlevoy**. The monastery was originally founded in 1034 by Geudoin de Saumur, a then virtually landless vassal of the counts of Blois (he was defeated by Foulques Nerra at the battle of Pontlevoy in 1016 and lost Saumur in 1026) in fulfilment of a vow he made after surviving a shipwreck on his return from a pilgrimage to the Holy Land. The church was largely destroyed by an English army in 1424, and though rebuilt it had fallen into desuetude before Cardinal Richelieu was made abbot, an appointment which led to the introduction of the Congregation of St-Maur to the monastery during the 1630s, and the secondary foundation of a college. This college was subsequently expanded by Louis XVI and enjoyed a brief life as an *Ecole Royale Militaire* until its dissolution in 1793.

The remaining buildings are in consequence a mixture of styles and dates, but an educational use has been found for one part of the complex, the northern wing, which now acts as a training school for lorry drivers. All tours are guided and begin with the surviving rump of the church, a fairly routine and largely 15C choir whose clerestory was entirely replaced during the late 19C restoration, though the 17C fittings survived in good order, with a fine set of choir stalls of 1642 and a good altar of 1651 by Charpentier. The most impressive of the conventual buildings lie to the south, where the west walk of the **cloister** and **refectory wing** were built to a beautifully restrained and modular design shortly after 1701, the refectory retaining a superb three-tiered 18C **ceramic stove** closely related to that of the Maréchal de Saxe at Chambord. The rest of the complex is given over to a quartet of small museums, concerned respectively with road haulage, chocolate, aviation, and an early 20C photographic history of Pontlevoy, in all of which you will receive enthusiastic and extremely extensive guidance.

West of Montrichard the D176 stays north of the Cher, following the railway line through the eastern Touraingeaux vineyards to the village of (9km) **Chenonceaux**. The principal activity of the village is now providing food and accommodation for the multitudes who descend on the château. But the place has charm, and retains some handsome 15C–18C houses and a modest 12C parish church.

It is easy to appreciate why the **CHÂTEAU DE CHENONCEAU** (only the village takes the -x) is regarded as one of the great 16C buildings of France.

History. The complex began to take on its present shape in 1512 when Thomas Bohier, a financier and collector of taxes under Louis XII and François I, bought the earlier seigneurial castle from Pierre Marques. He demolished all but a circular keep tower from the early 15C castle, and under the probable direction of the Amboise mason Pierre Nepveu (usually known as Le Trinqueau) began building in 1515. His choice of site is revealing, for, rather than adopting the old castle bailey to the north of the river, Bohier decided to raise the château above the piles of an old water mill on the river itself, subjecting the elevations to the shifting attentions of low, water-borne light, and creating a palatial residence whose principal defence lies in having been floated off above the bed of the river Cher. The early northern block seems to have been complete by 1521, the year of Bohier's return from Milan, and, given his long absences abroad, it is generally believed that Bohier's wife, the Tours born Catherine Briçonnet, oversaw the building operations. The Italianate contributions are the driving force in the design of this northern wing, and the building is arranged as a rectangle with a single central corridor, an alternating ramp replacing the usual French spiral stair. Even the round angle-towers, whose roofs form such an important element of the design, have become shrunken into turrets and assimilated into the relatively flat overall treatment of the exterior elevations.

Bohier and his wife had little time to enjoy Chenonceau, dying in 1524 and 1526 respectively, and the discovery that Thomas Bohier owed considerable sums to the crown exchequer compelled his son, Antoine, to convey the château to François I in 1535. The subsequent 16C history of Chenonceau is a startling tale of ownership shuttled between royal mistresses and widows, and half-realised schemes of stunning grandeur.

On his accession in 1547 Henri II gave Chenonceau to Diane de Poitiers, widow of Louis de Brézé and lover to both François I and Henri II. Diane commissioned Philibert de l'Orme to build a 60m **bridge** linking the south elevation of the château with the opposite bank of the river, and laid out the larger of the two garden terraces. It seems likely that de l'Orme also designed a covered gallery for this bridge, but it was never built, as on Henri II's death in 1559 his widow, Catherine de Medici, forced her great rival out of Chenonceau and began to make serious provision for the expansion of the château. A second garden was laid to the west, and between 1570 and 1576 the architect Jean Bullant was brought in to erect a two-storey gallery over Philibert de l'Orme's earlier bridge. This is one of the most exciting structures of late 16C France, richly articulated with an almost Mannerist love of complexity, the pediments at second storey level oversailing the windows to link up with the intermediate panels in a graceful alternating system reminiscent of Daniele da Volterra's work at the Vatican. As an engraving of 1607 by Jacques du Cerceau makes clear, Catherine de Medici's ideas for Chenonceau also extended to a second rectangular wing, matching Bohier's earlier north wing but on the opposite, southern, bank of the Cher.

Catherine's death in 1589 marked the end of this expansive phase and she bequeathed Chenonceau to her daughter-in-law, Louise de Lorraine, better known as *La Reine Blanche* after she went into permanent mourning for her husband, Henri III, assassinated by the monk Jacques Clément in 1589. It was the royal custom to wear white when mourning, a habit reflected in the château's most disturbing room, the small upper **Chambre Louise de Lorraine**, whose harrowing and lugubrious scheme of tears, knotted cords and monograms in white on black was designed for her meditations on grief.

Louise de Lorraine's bedroom is one of a series of rooms which have either retained their 16C decoration, or have been accurately and sensitively restored to their 16C apearance. It is this décor which is considered by historians of the period to be the château's most significant asset, offering a rare glimpse of a fully painted and tapestry-hung Renaissance residence. Even more remarkably, visitors are allowed to wander at will. The following brief description is intended merely to highlight the more important features and adopts the itinerary you will find recommended when in the building.

The Tour. Entry is via a drawbridge to the south of the **Tour des Marques**, the surviving rump of the early 15C castle, bringing you directly into the central hall. To the left the **Salle des Gardes** and **Chapelle** house a number of very fine 16C Flemish tapestries and a group of minor religious paintings respectively. The **Salle Diane de Poitiers** is known to have been used as a reception area by Diane, and is graced by a thickly carved fireplace by Jean Goujon bearing a modern portrait of Catherine de Medici, and further 16C tapestries. The **Salle Verte** off to the left was Catherine's study, its splendid ceiling quite unrestored, though Jacob Jordaen's Drunkenness of Xylene and the 17C Venetian Solomon and Sheba are more recent acquisitions.

From here you are directed to the **gallerie**, a superlative rectangular hall from which Catherine de Medici's court watched mock naval battles on the Cher below, and where she held several of the banquets for which her later life was famous. The **Salle François I** to the west of the hall carries Thomas Bohier's hopeful motto—*S'il vient à point me souviendre* (If it is built right remember me)—on the fireplace, and houses Primaticcio's portrait of Diane de Poitiers as a huntress on a wall of 19C canvas painted to imitate the original 16C Cordoban leather. The adjoining **Salle Louis XIV** was clearly refurbished by François I, the fireplace emblazoned with his salamander and the ermine of Claude de France, and also carries perhaps the most famous of all portraits of Louis XIV, superbly realised by Pierre Mignard and hung in its original frame.

The first floor opens with the **Chambre Gabrielle d'Estrées**, named after a mistress of Henri IV and the finest interior at Chenonceau, restored in 1970 to replicate the early 16C painted ceiling and with a marvellous canopied bed of c 1520. The ceiling of the adjoining **Chambre des Cinq Reines** was cannibalised from the panelling of two late 16C outbuildings during the 19C, and is also hung with a full complement of Flemish 16C tapestries. On the opposite side of the hall the **Chambres Catherine de Medici** and **Vendôme** have suffered the greatest alterations of any the interiors, and one is left to reflect on the theatrically mournful attic bedroom wherein Louise de Lorraine remained inconsolable.

From Chenonceaux you might take the D40 to La Croix-en-Touraine, where a left turn will bring you back over the Cher and into the attractive riverside resort of (7km) **Bléré**. The town is understandably popular with French holidaymakers, drawn to the boating and fishing to be had from the terraces and campsites above the south bank of the river, and there are some pleasant streets which gather around the Place Charles Bidault. The Place also plays host to the eclectic parish church of **St-Christophe**, which draws together a Romanesque apse, 15C south aisle and 16C stump of masonry at the crossing tower. Most of the rest was rebuilt in the 19C, with an octagonal belfry and spire overshadowing the pavement cafés to the north. The town's most intriguing monument is some way to the south-east, where a tiny funerary chapel rises above the gardens of the Place de la République, erected on the orders of Jean de Seigne in 1526 to house the remains of his father, Guillaume, *Receveur-Général* of the King's Artillery.

From Bléré it is worth retracing the bridge over the Cher, turning left by the Romanesque parish church of (1km) **La Croix-en-Touraine**, and taking the D140 as far as (7km) **St-Martin-le-Beau**. The main interest is provided by the parish church of **St-Martin**, whose sumptuously decorated late 12C portal and apse belong to a building practically replaced during the first two decades of the 16C, when the aisles were built, that to the north housing an extremely fine early 16C Pietà. The village gained its designation after the church was founded here in thanksgiving for the defeat of the Vikings near Tours in 903. This was dedicated to St-Martin-de-Bello, and, though nothing is known to survive from the original building, the belfry of the present church is certainly earlier than the apse or portal, perhaps dating from the mid-11C.

The more interesting route west to Tours involves crossing the Cher via the D83, looping to the right of the Château de Nitray and picking up the N76. This brings you within sight of two of the more important monuments of the Basse-Cher: (6km) the **Château de Leugny**, reconstructed for Ambroise Ribaud in 1779 in a style which owes everything to the Petit Trianon at Versailles, and the 16C church at (5km) **Véretz**. The latter is an unusual structure, a Renaissance seigneurial church which was built c 1540 for Jean de la Barre at the same time as the château which looms above it. Jean de la Barre incorporated the base of a 12C bell-tower from an earlier church, but the most interesting element is to be found inside—an impressively baronial oratory decorated with terracotta medallions set between pilasters, the mural paintings added by Jacob Bunel in the late 16C.

From Véretz the N76 skirts the southern bank of the Cher, shrugs off the industrial suburbs of (5km) St-Avertin, and brings you into the southern reaches of (4km) Tours.

4

Tours

History. Recent archaeological discoveries suggest that Tours was founded during the early 1C AD, its original title, *Caesarodunum*, born of the resolve of the emperor Augustus to create a series of new administrative centres in Gaul, each of which would respect the territorial boundaries of the existing tribal domains. In this case that meant the land of the *Turones*, and the siting of the new city on the left bank of the Loire, upstream of its confluence with the Cher, was sufficiently removed from the Gaulish *oppidum* at Amboise to encourage the Romanisation of the area. Two mid-1C inscriptions, mentioning *Civitas Turonorum Libera* (The Free City of the Turons), imply the policy was successful, and under the title *Turones* the city flourished, extending over the best part of 60 hectares to the south of the Loire by 150. This early city was quite open, with an amphitheatre to the north-east of the present cathedral, and a large residential district underpinning the present Rues Colbert, du Commerce, des Halles and de la Scellerie. But Tours, along with the larger administative centres of western and central France, fell prey to the Barbarian raids of the late 3C and 4C, and retreated to a small fortified enceinte to the south and east of the later medieval château, the Gallo-Roman walls readily visible beneath the north elevation of the Logis du Gouverneur.

External threat was not the only factor which affected the development of the city, however, for Tours had developed a substantial early Christian community. Even before the accession of Constantine as emperor, Gatien (died 304) was described as bishop, and under Lidoire a cathedral was begun in 337. More spectacularly, the city attracted one **Martin**, a legionary convert who joined Hilary, bishop of Poitiers, in founding the first monastery in Gaul at Ligugé (Poitou) in 360. He seems to have moved north into the Touraine in the late 360s and, having been created bishop of Tours c 372, used the city as a base from which to launch a series of missionary journeys. Martin died at Candes on 8 November 397, but not before founding one of the most significant monasteries of the early Middle Ages at Marmoutier, 2km north-east of Tours' Gallo-Roman enceinte. His body was removed from Candes by monks from Marmoutier three days later, and the story goes that as they approached Tours from along the Loire, the winter trees turned to leaf, birds sang, and a carpet of flowers settled along the banks. He was interred in an established Christian cemetery about 1km west of the walled city, and by the mid-430s miracles were being reported at the site. These seem to have been the pretext for St-Brice's decision to build a modest chapel above the grave, which was swiftly replaced under Bishop Perpet by a sumptuous funerary basilica—'large and magnificent, where one might count 8 doors, 52 windows and 120 columns'—St-Martin being translated to a new marble sarcophagus on 4 July 470.

The effect of this basilica on both the shape and the significance of Tours was dramatic. In 496 Clovis, king of the Franks, visited the shrine and promised to be baptised if he defeated the Alamanni. His Catholic baptism later that year in Reims gave him the excuse to move against Alaric II, the Arian king of the Visigoths, whose army he defeated at the battle of Vouillé in 507. These victories were associated with St-Martin, and seem to mark the beginning of a peculiar relationship between the Merovingian monarchy and St-Martin at Tours, in which the saint was seen as the special protector and patron of the Franks. Not only did Clovis display the insignia of the proconsulship the Emperor Anastasius I had bestowed on him in 508 in the basilica, but his widow, the Burgundian Clotilde (subsequently St-Clotilde), retired to St-Martin's after Clovis' death in 511.

The development of a pilgrimage to the shrine encouraged the growth of a secondary town, and a steady flow of illustrious pilgrims lent a political importance to early medieval Tours that was out of all proportion to that enjoyed by its Gallo-Roman predecessor. One of these pilgrims, a sickly young nobleman from the Auvergne named **Gregory**, settled in Tours in 563 after a visit to the tomb of St-Martin had resulted in his being cured. Born of an old Gallo-Roman senatorial family which had already produced a number of bishops, most notably St-Nizier of Lyons, Gregory was himself elected bishop of Tours in 573, in succession to a cousin of his mother's, and unleashed a wholesale reform of the cultural life of the city. A Benedictine abbey dedicated to St-Julien was founded among the vines which separated the area around St-Martin's from the *Cité*; royal permission was obtained for the establishment of two mints, one in the *Cité* and one attached to St-Martin; and monks were encouraged to settle at the basilica of St-Martin itself. Most famously, Gregory set himself to write his *Historia Francorum* (History of the Franks), an untidy and magnificently detailed account of Frankish affairs up to 591, which as a source for early medieval history compares in importance to Bede's History of the English Church.

The Carolingian monarchy was equally anxious to maintain strong links with St-Martin, and the abbacy became something of a royal sinecure in the late 8C and 9C. The most celebrated of these royal appointees was the great Anglo-Saxon churchman, **Alcuin of York**, installed as abbot by Charlemagne in 796. Ostensibly a place of retirement from the court at Aachen, where Alcuin had served as tutor and librarian, the new abbot created a school within the precincts, concentrating on two distinct cycles of instruction, the first elementary and the second based on the liberal arts. The preferred method of teaching was through dialogue, with Boethius, Augustine, and the Latin grammarians the staple fare, its formal grouping of subjects and argumentative rigour having a profound effect on the later development of the great medieval schools and universities. Alcuin also revived the monastic scriptorium, initially concerned with the production of good 'clean' texts, but subsequently blossoming into one of the greatest of all Carolingian 'schools of illumination', producing a majestic run of de-luxe bibles for the likes of Charles the Bald and the emperor Lothair.

Such brilliance was not to last. The first of the Norse raiding parties to reach Tours sacked the abbey in 853, and was followed by waves of Christian refugees fleeing up the Loire, and a debilitating series of raids aimed at the *Cité*. The area around St-Martin was almost totally destroyed by a fire in 903, resulting in a hasty reconstruction of the church, the reconstitution of the abbey as a college of secular canons, and the erection of a timber palissade. The latter was designed to protect both the canons and the townspeople, and, though the first version was only completed by 918, it seems to have been swiftly replaced by a stone wall. The area it enclosed became known as the *Châteauneuf*, or *Martinopolis*, and—as in London, with its two distinct quarters on the same bank of the river, the City and Westminster—Tours enjoyed a bipolar existence. The subsequent medieval history of Tours was concerned with building against these two enceintes, eventually filling the whole of the area which separated them. Nevertheless, the effect of these twin walled enclosures can still be felt today.

The first expansionary move came in 1034 under Eudes, Comte de Touraine, who constructed the *Bourg des Arcis* to the west of the *Cité*, facing a new bridge over the river Loire. The annexation of Touraine by the counts of Anjou in 1044 stimulated the extension of this bourg, and by the mid-12C it was joined to the *Cité* by the construction of a new embracing wall. The earliest moves further west seem to have been made by the new mendicant orders, with the Franciscans establishing a convent in 1222 between les Arcis and the one substantial foundation to have endured the Norse raids, the abbey of St-Julien; and the Dominicans building where the theatre now stands, in 1224. The major initiatives came with the Hundred Years War. Following the defeat of Jean le Bon at Poitiers in 1356, a huge new city wall was built, connecting *Châteauneuf* with the *Cité* and *les Arcis*, a colossal undertaking which was only completed c 1400 but, when finished, enclosed a city of around 58 hectares. Not only was this effective, but it was instrumental in persuading Louis XI, in 1461, to elevate Tours into the capital of France. This was not a status it enjoyed for long—indeed on Louis' death in 1483 the court moved to Amboise—but Tours retained its royal favour well into the 1520s, and with exalted patronage came the transformation of the urban fabric. Louis XI's contribution was to build a château at Plessis-lès-Tours, but it was the mercantile community which had the greatest impact, and a rash of new and splendid townhouses were constructed to the north of St-Martin and along the Rue du Commerce. In addition, the arrival of silk-weavers from Lyons enriched an already booming economy and enabled Tours to withstand the evaporation of royal interest in the city. By 1500 the population had reached 17,500 and was further expanded by the construction of the *Faubourg la Riche* during the 1540s, fanning out beside the old coaching road linking *Châteauneuf* with Plessis-lès-Tours.

The 17C and 18C were, by contrast, years of decline, despite the efforts of Richelieu and Colbert to revive the foundering weaving industry. The population dropped sharply, to be overtaken by those of Angers and Orléans, and the port stagnated. Even the big municipal projects of the early 19C, the *bibliothèque* of 1829 or *palais de justice* of 1843, failed to rekindle the sort of energy which had so invigorated

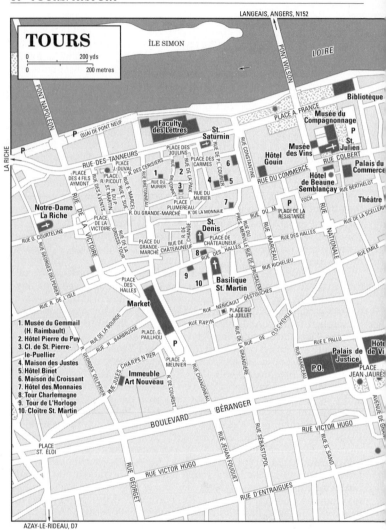

TOURS

ÎLE SIMON

LANGEAIS, ANGERS, N152

LOIRE

1. Musée du Gemmail (H. Raimbault)
2. Hôtel Pierre du Puy
3. Cl. de St. Pierre-le-Puellier
4. Maison des Justes
5. Hôtel Binet
6. Maison du Croissant
7. Hôtel des Monnaies
8. Tour Charlemagne
9. Tour de L'Horloge
10. Cloître St. Martin

AZAY-LE-RIDEAU, D7

the early 16C, and it was left to the arrival of the railway in 1845 to revive the city. The main station was built at St-Pierre-des-Corps, a good 3km south-east of the earlier centres, and the topography of Tours began to change with it. A new administative centre developed around the Place Jean-Jaurès, which briefly housed the French government after the fall of Paris in October, 1870, provoking the building of vast residential estates between the old city and the Cher during the late 19C. The industrialisation of Tours was also concentrated to the south and east, leaving the city with a fairly dismal hinterland beneath the left bank of the river Cher. This area was badly damaged by the

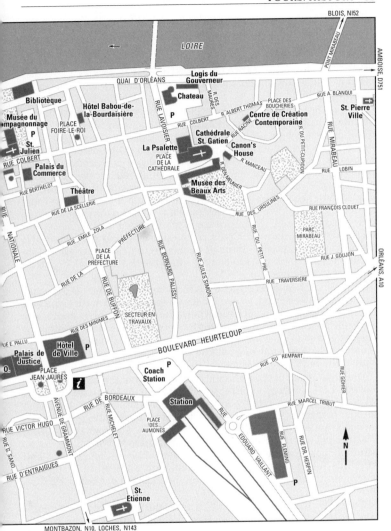

bombardments of August 1944, when the Allied armies were attempting to push south over the Loire, an engagement which caused a considerable amount of damage in the older centres along the Loire also. Coupled with the havoc caused by an aerial attack in June 1940, Tours suffered badly in the Second World War, and the predominantly late medieval river frontages have entirely disappeared, though the restoration undertaken in the 1950s was sensitive to the overall shape of the city. This initial restoration was augmented in the 1970s by an ambitious scheme to revive the then decaying quarters around the Place Plumerau and Faubourg la Riche, which has certainly returned commerce to the area, and perhaps completed the renewal of what remains one of the great cities of western France.

Town Tour. The best place to begin an exploration of Tours' dual identity is the **CATHÉDRALE DE ST-GATIEN**, whose expanded interior spaces now straddle what was the southern wall of the Gallo-Roman enceinte.

The earliest church to have occupied the site was begun under St-Lidoire in 337, and was substantially expanded by St-Martin in 371 to serve the growing early Christian community as a diocesan cathedral. Despite the cathedral's current dedication to St-Gatien, founding bishop of Tours in the late 3C, the 4C church was placed under the protection of St-Maurice, and remained so until rededicated in 1498 in a determined attempt to point out the then metropolitan see's ancient credentials. St-Lidoire's early church was rebuilt by Gregory of Tours during the late 6C, an important wooden-roofed structure about which little is known, and which in turn was destroyed in the course of a dispute between Henry II, Count of Touraine and King of England, and Joscelyn, archbishop of Tours. It seems Henry caused considerable damage to the town and some four years later, in 1170, work began on a new cathedral.

Elements of this latter structure do survive, most visibly at the outer angles of the west front, where the lower stages of the north tower and the huge and thickly-walled south elevation of the south-western tower are substantially late 12C. The north tower is the more revealing, and houses at first floor level a superb square chamber, the *chambre des métaux*, which was one of a number of rooms given over to the masons during the later Middle Ages.

The greater part of the cathedral is later, work beginning in, or shortly before, 1241 under the master mason Etienne de Mortagne. It seems likely that the initial intention was to preserve the 12C nave, hence the shift in alignment as one moves east through the crossing, but, in the event, the nave was also renewed and a somewhat faltering programme extended work well into the 15C. De Mortagne's mid-13C **choir** is perhaps the least compromised of these campaigns, and certainly the most confidently handled, with a majestically spacious ambulatory and a proportional system reminiscent of Chartres Cathedral.

Unusually, the choir arcade makes use of the *pilier cantonée* throughout, treating the capitals in an identical way to those of the nave at Chartres, but, unlike its great neighbour, overlays this with a glazed triforium. The distinctive **tracery** here, and in the clerestory, whereby trilobes are piled above each other at the head of the arch, may represent an updating of the original design, and is indebted to Louis IX's Sainte Chapelle, an undoubtedly prestigious and contemporary reference. In fact Louis took a personal interest in the progress of the choir, pressing for work to be speeded up before his departure on crusade in 1248. His subsequent captivity would have prevented any resumption of work before 1254, and these upper storeys probably date from this period. It is a variant of the Gothic architecture of the Ile-de-France, and though later than the choir of Le Mans Cathedral (or the Benedictine abbeys of St-Martin at Tours and St-Laumer at Blois for that matter), Tours Cathedral does more or less mark the final rejection of the indigenous hall church traditions of western France in favour of an architecture imported from the north and east.

The choir was not completed until 1279 but the high **glass** seems to date from between 1255 and 1270, and it is the depth of colour evident here which first strikes one on entering the cathedral. The triforium glass belongs to the earlier part of this glazing campaign, with panels of grisaille in the straight bays (mostly modern) and apostles processing around the apse towards a Virgin and Child, which probably dates from c 1255. The **clerestory windows** are more ambitious, and can be dated by their donors or subjects. That depicting St-Maurice in the bay immediately north of the axial window, for instance, was given by Geoffroy de Freslon, bishop of Le Mans between 1258 and 1269, who was probably motivated by the translation of the relics of St-Maurice here in 1267. The subject matter is certainly wide-ranging, with a Passion of Christ in the axial window accompanied by an Infancy and Tree of Jesse to the south. These are augmented by a window depicting the book of Genesis, from the Creation to Lamech chastised for killing Cain, and a tremendous run of windows concerned with the lives of the saints—Peter, Stephen, Nicholas, Martin and Julian among them. Most of these frame the various scenes in superimposed medallions, unusual in a clerestory cycle, and are evidently indebted to the formulas developed in the upper chapel windows of the Sainte Chapelle.

There are important exceptions, however, most notably in the two windows which face each other across the easternmost straight bay of the choir. These are not what are usually described as 'full-colour' windows, but are arranged so as to separate the tiered figures by horizontal bands of lightly painted grisaille. That to the south is devoted to bishops of Tours, while its northern counterpart was given by the canons of Loches after the château de Loches had been formally incorporated into the French royal domain in 1259. The castle is depicted towards the bottom right, and acts as a point of departure for the canons who progress through two levels to offer themselves to the Virgin and Child.

The advantage of including **grisaille glass** in such a window is that it admits far more light into the building, and enables you to see the architectural detailing around the triforium and clerestory more clearly. There was a general tendency towards the use of lighter glass throughout France and England at the end of the 13C, but here the most striking aspect is the alternation of full-colour and grisaille in bands, to create what is the earliest known example of a 'band window' to survive in Europe.

The glass in the radiating chapels is both very different and considerably earlier, probably dating from c 1245, with that in the axial chapel grouping an Infancy of Christ and scenes of the Passion and Resurrection to either side of a typological window. The windows in the two intermediate chapels are roughly contemporary interlopers: that of St-Férréol to the south having been brought from the abbey of St-Julian; while the account of the life and posthumous miracles of St-James was saved from destruction during the demolition of the abbey of

St-Martin, serving as a reminder of Tours' strategic position astride the great pilgrimage road from Paris to Santiago de Compostela.

The **transepts** and first two bays of the nave were the next areas to receive attention, though it was not until the opening years of the 14C that the mason, Simon du Mans, was engaged by the chapter with a brief to demolish the 12C nave. However, he was required to incorporate a considerable body of earlier masonry in the south transept, and the problems of alignment caused by mounting the nave piers on the 12C foundations created serious structural difficulties in the north transept. Faced with the possibility of imminent collapse in 1329, the superstructure of the north transept had to be bolstered by the addition of two huge flying buttresses and stiffened with a central column which cuts the rose window in two. Given this setback, it comes as no surprise to learn that work in the western four bays of the **nave** proceeded cautiously, and the main arcade and aisle chapels were not completed until c 1350. There the matter rested, at least until c 1425, when the architect Jean de Dammartin was brought in to complete the nave and west front. This work was liberally financed by Charles VII and Jean V, Duc de Bretagne, and opened with the upper superstructure of the four western bays of the nave, hence the shift from the simple tracery patterns of the two eastern bays to the wonderfully inventive Flamboyant tracery to the west. These new bays were linked to the earlier western block by a peculiar half-bay c 1430, but work was already underway as early as 1427 on transforming the 12C façade, cloaking the principal elevation with a thick overlay of late Gothic detail. The statuary has sadly gone, and what figures one can make out are mid-19C replacements; but, even bearing this in mind, it is hardly the triumph of delicate fretwork which the main portals indicate may have been the intention. The lantern above the north tower was not finished until 1507, a precocious extravagance so dazzlingly encrusted with Italianate ornament that it served as a template for its mid-16C counterpart to the south.

With the exception of the glass, the cathedral has retained little of its medieval imagery. The one major **tomb** to have survived came originally from the choir of the abbey of St-Martin. This is now situated in a chapel off the south transept, and was commissioned in 1499 by Anne de Bretagne to commemorate the two children she had by Charles VIII, Charles and Charles-Orlans. As with the tomb of her father, François II de Bretagne, in Nantes Cathedral, Anne turned to the Florentine sculptor Girolamo da Fiesole, and here, too, she seems to have had second thoughts about entrusting the entire work to the one man. In consequence, the sarcophagus, with its strange scenes from the life of Samson and Hercules, is the work of da Fiesole, while the effigies seem to have come from the shop of the local sculptor Michel Colombe. It is a moving work, the mutilated fragments of its once eloquent inscription having been mounted against the eastern wall, and the effigies epitomising something of the ease and calm that Colombe brought to essentially late Gothic forms.

The earlier conventual buildings have been much diminished, though a door off the north aisle of the nave gives entry to the **Cloître de la Psalette**, so called because its library found a later use as accommodation for the choir school. The complex has lost the chapter house and south walk of the cloister, but what remains is impressive. The north and east ranges are the latest, dating from 1508–24, and connect up with a west walk of c 1460. A glorious spiral staircase, designed by Bastien François and built in 1524, gives access to the upper storey, and allows the visitor into the early 16C scriptorium and adjacent mid-15C library. Denuded of its books and choristers, the library now houses a small group of routine wall paintings of c 1300 from the choir of Beaumont-Village.

South of the cathedral, the **Musée des Beaux-Arts** has been accommo-dated in the Archbishop's Palace, a composite building with a 17C west wing joined to the medieval 'Salle de Synode' by an 18C central block. Entry is via the 17C west wing, bringing you up the main staircase to the first floor suites. These early rooms are principally given over to 17C and 18C French painting and sculpture. The Gallerie de Diane (Room 3) has been restored to its original 18C decorative scheme and houses Jean-Antoine Houdon's bronze statue of Diana the Huntress of 1776. The Salon Louis-XV (Room 5) includes mid-18C mythological painting, with two luminous works by **François Boucher**, *Sylvie fuyant le loup* and *Amintas revient à la vie dans les bras de Sylvie*, both of 1756. The later rooms on this floor are given over to the work of lesser-known artists, with the vivid social satire implicit in the painting of **Abraham Bosse** (1602–76) the undoubted highlight.

Bosse was a native of Tours who, having encountered the work of the brilliant Mannerist engraver Jacques Callot, determined to make a career as a printer and engraver. A broad selection of his prints is well displayed on the museum walls, but to modern eyes the wit of Bosse's carefully contrived situations, achieved by combining extreme artifici-ality with closely observed detail, is perhaps less accessible in his engravings than in the paintings. The latter were in fact derived from the printed works, and the series devoted to the Five Senses in Room 10 certainly testifies to the popularity of the engravings of c 1635.

The ground floor galleries are the province of medieval and Renais-sance painting, and open with a collection of **Italian Trecento panel paintings** in which a diptych of the Annunciation and Adoration of the Magi by Nardo Ceccarelli of c 1340, and the predella panel depicting the funeral of St Benedict by Spinello Aretino are outstanding. The star of the entire museum is to be found in Room 14, where two small panels by **Andrea Mantegna**, the **Agony in the Garden** and the **Resurrection**, have been arranged alongside each other. These originally belonged to the high altarpiece of the church of San Zeno in Verona, commis-sioned by the Papal Pronuncio, Gregorio Correr, and executed by Mantegna between 1457 and 1459. They formed the outer scenes of a three-part predella of which the central image of the Crucifixion is now in the Louvre, the whole lower composition originally situated beneath a Virgin and Child flanked by two panels of standing saints. The altarpiece was removed from San Zeno in 1797, on the advice of Baron Gros, and broken up, but, though the three major panels were returned to Verona in 1815, the predella remained split between Paris and Tours. It is unfortunate that the altarpiece should have been dismembered in this way, for the scenes are now read in isolation, losing sight of the pathos of Christ's gaze in the Garden of Gethsemane, diagonally tilted towards the Crucifixion and the heavenly court above. But they remain extremely powerful works, strongly drawn, austere, and possessed of a quite extraordinary emotional range.

The second floor galleries concentrate on **French 19C and 20C painting** and **ceramics**, with a fine pair of rooms given over to *Orientalisme* and *Réalisme* respectively. The former houses **Eugène Delacroix**'s *Comédiens, ou Bouffons Arabes* of 1848 and Louis Bellanger's memorable 1836 portrayal of *Honoré de Balzac in a dressing-gown*, while the latter displays Joseph Landais' occasionally gruesome ceramics. Finally, a suite of rooms has been put aside towards the western end of the first floor to provide a European context for the museum's holdings of 17C French painting. Here you might find the early 17C Genoese artist, Bernardo Strozzi, portraying St Bartholomew, David Tenier's portrait of a young drinker, or Rembrandt's youthful Flight into Egypt of 1627. Perhaps the finest work on display is **Rubens'** *Virgin presenting the Christ Child to Alexandre Goubeau and his wife Anne Antoni*, an astonishingly vivid realisation of an improbable scene. It was commissioned by the Guild of Masons for their chapel in Notre-Dame at Antwerp in 1615, and delivered by Rubens with all his usual panache and heightened colour.

To the east of the museum the **Place Gregoire-de-Tours** provides an excellent view of the east end of the cathedral, as well as giving onto the gable-end of the 12C **Salle du Synode**. The latter formed the medieval archbishop's palace and, although extensively refurbished during the 18C when it gained the majority of its windows, still retains the rectangular, two storey shape of a great archiepiscopal hall. One of its more illustrious 16C residents, Martin de Beaune, was responsible for adding the first floor balcony in 1522, providing a platform from which the sentences of the diocesan court were proclaimed.

The area to the east of here was mostly given over to cathedral officials during the later Middle Ages, hence the rather drastically restored 14C **Logis de la Justice des Bains** on the Rue Racine, and the splendid 15C canon's residence on the corner of the Rue Manceau. But the finest houses are close to the cloister, along the **Rue de la Psalette**, with a delightful 18C *hôtel particulier* at No. 8 designed by Pierre Meusnier, and an excellent 17C complex at No. 3, whose reliance on the foundations of the Gallo-Roman wall is revealed in its cellars.

At the bottom, beyond the Rue Thomas, the remaining towers of the **Château de Tours** mark the north-west angle of the Gallo-Roman town, and the site of the long vanished medieval bridge over the river Loire. The castle has not fared well, and of Philippe le Hardi's late 13C fortress just the two towers remain, though the plan of the irregular rectangular keep can be made out in the foundation walls to the west. The surviving north-eastern tower is known as the **Tour de Guise**, in honour of the young Duc de Guise, who was imprisoned here from 1588–91 after the murder of his father in the château de Blois. This is connected to the south-eastern tower by a long, three storey range, the Pavilion de Mars, built c 1785 and which now houses the **Musée Grévin**. This is a historical waxworks collection, evoking the more spectacular episodes from the history of Touraine in a series of 30 tableaux, and at its best in the more generalised Valois balls and workshop scenes. The adjacent **Logis du Gouverneur** takes a more high-minded approach to the visualisation of historical moment, and has made over the second floor to a collection of paintings, prints and models illustrating the changing patterns of life in Tours (open afternoons only from April–October, closed Tuesdays). It is also a handsome building in its own right, a long, late 15C gabled range whose northern elevation rises above the Gallo-Roman wall, its narrow tiled courses enlivening the greater sweep of squared facing stone.

There is a choice of routes from the castle westwards, though the **Rue Colbert** is the most interesting, a superbly modulated street of mostly 18C houses and shops. Halfway along, the **Place Foire-le-Roi** opens to the right, home between the 13C and the late 19C to Tours' smaller markets and fairs. Shortly before 1474 the monks of St-Julien acquired the western side of the square, and were responsible for the central terrace of houses, all originally half-timbered and now boasting façades refaced in stone. One late 15C façade has survived intact to the north, and admirably exemplifies that local tendency to derive colour and texture from a diagonally-set timber lattice. The grandest townhouse lies on the opposite flank, the **Hôtel Babou de la Bourdaisière**, built c 1520 for Philibert Babou, superintendent of finances, and attributed to the masons Martin and Bastien François. The building has been divided into two distinct residences, but you can still peer into the main courtyard to admire the projecting wings and broken silhouettes of the principal façade.

A brief stroll west along the Rue Colbert brings you to the lesser of Tours' great Benedictine foundations, the abbey of **St-Julien**. The first monastery to grace the site was founded in the late 6C by Gregory of Tours, and colonised by monks from the Auvergne who brought with them relics of St-Julien of Brioude. This was destroyed during the Norse raids of the late 9C, and subsequently rebuilt between 937 and 943, acquiring a western tower-porch under Abbot Bernard c 970. This church was in turn reconstructed between c 1040 and 1084, with Bernard's tower also being subject to a general refurbishment. Elements from the earlier structure were incorporated into the upper chamber of the present west tower but, given Guérin's drastic late 19C restoration, it is difficult to separate the 10C from the 11C work. Guérin entirely renewed the lower storey—facing stone, capitals and all—leaving only a pair of sirens on the exterior north-east angle, and, though the shape remains Romanesque, most of the detail of this important monument has been lost.

With the exception of a bit of 10C walling to the east of the existing conventual precincts, the rest of the church is 13C. It seems that the **nave** collapsed after a storm in 1224, and work on a new building got underway in 1243, the structure being completed in 1259. This consists of a double-aisled and square-ended choir, narrow transepts, and a five bay nave. Unusually for a French 13C building, the east end is treated as a pretext for a very grand eight-light traceried window, framed by a substantial margin of wall in the manner of contemporary English east fronts. It seems likely that this eastern bay of the choir was the last area to be completed, as parts of the Romanesque choir were retained for services while work on the western two choir bays, transepts and nave proceeded.

The rest of the design is an accomplished, if conservative, piece of work, ringing the changes with the tracery and indulging a bizarre predilection for laying the quatrefoils diagonally. With the exception of the two early 16C chapels, little was changed prior to the Revolution, and after a series of changes of use the building was restored as a church between 1846 and 1859. The original glass and fittings had gone by that stage, to be replaced by a modern glazing cycle which is at its best in Le Chevallier's splendidly realised east window of 1960.

Leaving St-Julien by the west tower brings you round into the conventual precincts. A lavish 9-bay chapter house of c 1200 survives to the east, while the late 12C cellar range has been appropriately given over to the Musée des Vins de Touraine.

The 16C dormitory above the chapter house is now a museum dedicated to the rarely celebrated achievements of trade guilds. This is known as the **Musée du Compagnonnage** (accessible from the Rue Nationale), after the various associations of *compagnons* (or companions, derived from *cum pane*, an equal with whom one would share bread) which evolved from late medieval guilds. The collection is principally concerned with their history between the 18C and present day, organising the displays in cabinets or areas devoted to specific trades–carpentry, cooperage, baking etc. The most impressive items are the presentation pieces, either given by apprentices petitioning for admission into a trade guild, or made by the *compagnons* themselves to mark some particular event.

The old western precincts of St-Julien were demolished when the **Rue Nationale** was built in the 18C, driving a north–south axis through the town to connect with the Pont Wilson and so divert the earlier Paris–Spain coaching road through Tours rather than Amboise. It is not a particularly attractive street but it does disguise one stunning ruin, reached through a passageway by No. 28. There you will find the remnants of the Renaissance **Hôtel de Beaune-Semblançay**, shattered by the bombardments of 1940 and 1944 and consolidated within a rebuilt courtyard. The remains are in three parts: a freestanding two storey wall, originally forming the south elevation of the 'galerie' of 1518; a very beautiful **fountain** of 1508, sculpted from imported Italian marble by Martin and Bastien François; and an exquisite **Sainte Chapelle**, supported by an open loggia and dating from 1517–18. The complex was once considerably larger, and was developed out of the mid-15C townhouse of Jean de Beaune. The western angle sustained a two storey stone mansion, begun in 1507 after Jean's son, Jacques de Beaune, was made Général des Finances for Languedoc, and the Sainte Chapelle was only added in 1517, after Jean was offered the adjacent Dunois mansion by Louise de Savoie, mother of François I. These royal connections were short-lived, however, for in 1525 Jacques de Beaune was arrested, tried for embezzlement, and hanged in Montfauçon.

To the west of the Rue Nationale, the **Rue du Commerce** links the early medieval quarter around the cathedral and château, with the later mercantile precincts of the **Place Plumereau** and **Grand Marché**. That this area was favoured with 15C bourgeois patronage becomes apparent the moment you reach the **Hôtel Goüin**. A medieval house had in fact already been built on the site when Jean de Xaincoings, Charles VII's treasurer, decided to rebuild in 1440. Xaincoings was responsible for the shape of the main block, but the richly carved façade which greets you on entering the courtyard is due to René Gardette, a wealthy mid-16C silk merchant, who, like most of his contemporaries, developed a penchant for grafting Italianate ornament onto essentially late medieval design. It is perhaps the most picturesque of all the 16C townhouses in Tours, with its shallow relief carving on the main elevations contrasting with the larger projecting volumes; and was mercifully undamaged by the bombardment of 1940 which gutted the interiors.

It was subsequently sensitively restored and is now an **archaeological museum**, housing the collections of the Societé Archéologique de Touraine. These open in the cellars with a modest selection of prehistoric and Gallo-Roman material, and extend chronologically upwards to the main areas of interest. An impressive collection of late medieval work is displayed on the ground floor, with a moving 15C painted **wooden image of the Virgin**, and a superb early 16C **statue of St Barbara**. The most significant exhibits are to be found on the first floor, where the *Cabinet de Physique et Chimie de Chenonceau* has been assembled. This is a laboratory of **scientific instruments**, made in 1743 for Charles Dupin de Francueil to the designs of Abbé Nollet, and brought together at his château de Chenonceau by his secretary, the youthful Jean-Jacques Rousseau.

The Rue du Commerce leads directly to the **Place Plumereau**, the social heart of present-day Tours, but the more interesting route is to loop north, just after you enter the pedestrianised zone, along the Rue Courrier. This takes you past the crisp 16C detailing of the **Maison des Justes** (No. 17), so-called after the sculptors responsible, the Italian brothers Giusti, to the rather dull outlines of the 16C church of St-Saturnin. A left turn here, along the **Rue-** and then **Place-des-Carmes**, allows you to snake south-westwards through a glorious mixture of medieval and 18C houses, winding streets, and tranquil squares. The area may have been over-restored, with buildings often returned to a putative original façade and rents driven sky-high, but its revealing juxtaposition of architectural surface and urban space is one of the triumphs of 1970s municipal regeneration.

Taking one possible route, along the Rue Lamproie to the Square Henri de Segogne, you pass three good 17C and 18C *hôtels particuliers*. If you then cross the Rue de la Paix into the **Place St-Pierre-le-Puellier**, the extraordinary resourcefulness of Touraine vernacular architecture becomes apparent. The houses here have simply been built in or over the remains of a 12C church, the canons' residences to the north variously reconstructed between the 15C and 18C, while the foundations of the old claustral range to the west of the Briçonnet have been reworked as a modern garden. The great set-piece remains the **Place Plumereau**, originally the hat-sellers market at the heart of the late medieval artisans' quarter, and now ablaze with restaurants and café terraces. The Place has become the social hub of Tours, and is a pleasant place to while away an hour or two, gazing at the late 15C terrace of timber houses to the south, or watching the locals promenade and talk.

The area immediately south of the Place Plumereau is very different in character, a reflection of its originally enclosed status within the early medieval walled *burg*. The narrow streets encountered here were squeezed within an enceinte wall after 903, a state of affairs which lasted until the early 15C, when the north and east angles were demolished so that the old precinct might be brought within a single, expanded city wall. You can see the shape of the old rectangular *burg* in the later streets and squares which colonised the demolished walls; the Rue NéricaultDestouches to the south, Place du Grand-Marché to the west, Rues de la Rôtisserie and du Petit-Soleil to the north, and Rues du Président-Merville and de Jerusalem to the east. Before it was walled, this area was often referred to as *Martinopolis*, in recognition of the great abbey which stood at its centre, but, with the establishment of a defensive enclosure between 903 and 918, it became known as the *Burg Châteauneuf*, and was adopted as a residence by the counts of Touraine. This dual role is reflected in the **Place Châteauneuf**, with the 14C château of the counts of Touraine to the north (closed to the public) and the mighty **Tour Charlemagne** to the south.

This last structure was the north transept tower of the **COLLEGIATE CHURCH OF ST-MARTIN**, the monks Gregory of Tours had encouraged to settle in the late 6C having been replaced by secular canons in the wake of the Norse raids of the late 9C and early 10C. A number of churches have stood on the site, beginning with St-Brice's early 5C chapel, but the most important of the pre-Romanesque structures was undoubtedly Perpet's basilica of 466–470, described by Gregory of Tours as the finest in Gaul. This was 53m long, dwarfed by the great Early Christian basilicas of Rome or Constantinople admittedly, but impressively large by French standards. More significantly it boasted two towers, in addition to its marble columns and many doors—a 'secure' western entrance tower and what, from the early medieval descriptions, sounds like a lantern tower above the transepts, with a bell hung from a roof turret above. Both were to prove influential features.

Perpet's basilica was extensively modified in the late 6C, and largely rebuilt after the fire of 903, only to fall to an even mightier conflagration in 997, an event which persuaded the collegiate treasurer, Hervé, to clear the site and build anew. Building seems to have proceeded quickly, for in 1014 the relics of St-Martin were translated into a new shrine, and the church was consecrated. This 11C church is regarded by most architectural historians to have been one of the most important early Romanesque buildings in France, incorporating a fully developed apse-ambulatory with five radiating chapels, aisled transepts, and an 11 bay nave. It was also nearly twice the length of Perpet's 6C church, but, like the earlier building, wooden-roofed and so prone to fire.

Recorded fires litter the documents—1096, 1123, 1202—and, as it is plain that a number of important modifications were made to Hervé's church, the sequential dating of St-Martin has become a matter of considerable controversy.

The problems are not simply concerned with the adoption of an apseambulatory (for few would doubt that this type of design belongs to the 997–1014 church and has its origins in the region), but stem from the realisation that the elevation of the transepts of St-Martin relates it to a select group of buildings along the pilgrimage roads to Compostela. These are St-Foi at Conques, St-Martial at Limoges, St-Sernin at Toulouse, and the cathedral of Santiago de Compostela itself. These buildings are all fully vaulted, with ample tribunes, two-storey elevations and a particular cadence of vaulting types—high barrel vaults with transverse arches, quadrant vaulting in the tribunes, and groin vaults in the aisles. This pattern was followed at St-Martin when the transepts were vaulted, and, if early, would make Tours the prototype. However, the scarring apparent on the south face of the Tour Charlemagne makes it likely that the vaults were built after the 1096 fire, and that St-Martin's was thus looking to an established set of forms, most probably those of St-Sernin, Toulouse.

The 1123 fire does not seem to have caused much damage, or, if it did, it was swiftly repaired, for Aimery Picaud, writing in the 1130s, could say 'over it [the shrine of St-Martin] a great and splendid basilica, in the likeness of the church of St James, has been built'. Nevertheless, the nave was reconstructed in the late 12C and given a high rib vault and twin-towered west façade. The last of the major medieval fires, in 1202, precipitated the rebuilding of the choir, a design which probably went up between c 1210 and c 1230 and was explicitly modelled on the great double-ambulatoried choir of Bourges Cathedral.

Nearly all of this church was lost after the Revolution, when what was by then a badly run-down building briefly functioned as a parish church. The final blow came in 1802, when the lack of any constructive response to a vault collapse of 1798 persuaded the municipal authorities to demolish the nave, most of the transepts and choir, to make way for two new streets, the Rues des Halles and Descartes.

What remains of the old church can be easily described. The lower stages of the impressive **Tour Charlemagne** appear to belong to Hervé's early 11C church. This seems to have been extensively altered after the fire of 1096, and the magnificent chamber on the first floor (access by appointment only) was probably vaulted at this date. The extent of the subsequent alterations is more readily apparent from the south, where the 19C retaining wall collapsed in 1927, revealing the splendid capital which still sits over the aisle return pier. Arguments over the dating of this capital continue to rage, but it seems likely that it, too, dates from after 1096, repeating a central figure on all four faces, flanked by lions—Daniel in the Lions' Den, perhaps?

Further west, the **Tour de l'Horloge** rises above the southern face of the Rue des Halles. It is a good spot from which to appreciate the size of St-Martin, which stretched another 20m east of the Tour Charlemagne. The *Horloge* originally formed the south-west tower of the main façade, dating from c 1175–80, and at its north-western angle carries the scars of a portal screen, a delicate frieze of rosettes running up the surviving chamfer.

A left turn here, on to the Rue Rapin, brings you to the **Musée Martinien** (restricted opening hours; telephone 47.21.66.52), where a collection of religious artefacts connected with St-Martin, along with a few fragments from the church, are accommodated in the 13C cloister chapel of St-Jean. You can also get into the cloister from the museum (if closed the cloister is accessible from No. 5 Rue Descartes on afternoons between 15 July and 15 September). Elements of the mid-13C west walk are still visible, but the only walk that remains standing is to the east, where Bastien François' carefully carved friezes and vaults date from the first quarter of the 16C.

The largest monument still to grace the site is, unfortunately, the least appealing. Although the **Nouvelle Basilique St-Martin** was built in a spirit of high-minded religiosity, its heavy-handed revivalism suffers by comparison with medieval St-Martin. The inspiration behind the building was the rediscovery, during archaeological excavations in 1860, of the **tomb of St-Martin**. Despite the problems caused by the axis of the Rue des Halles, the site of this tomb was enshrined within a tall, Romanising basilica between 1887 and 1924, under the architect Victor Laloux, and now acts as a centre for the revived cult of the saint.

The best route west to Petit-St-Martin, and the downstream settlements at La Riche, is parallel to the river along the **Rue du Grand-Marché**. The latter is an attractive street, although the roads off to the north offer more individually stimulating buildings. The **Rue Briçonnet**, for instance, has elements of an early 13C house at No. 31, a substantially 14C complex at No. 29, a crumbling 18C *hôtel particulier* at No. 21, and an important late 15C gabled mansion at No. 16. This last is known as the **Maison dite de Tristan l'hermite**, after a grand chamberlain of Louis XI who mysteriously disappeared in 1475. It was in fact built for Pierre du Puy in 1495, whose device—*Prie Dieu Pur*—an anagram of his name, appears above a courtyard window. The house incorporates contemporary Flemish motifs, doubtless motivated by the strong mercantile links which existed at this date, orchestrating the carved stone dressings and brickwork beneath a lavishly stepped gable.

The **Rue du Murier** is equally attractive, curving gently west past the leafy courtyard of the Hôtel Raimbault, built over a 12C cellar range in 1835. The mansion now houses the **Musée du Gémail**, a specialist museum of mostly laminated, and thus unleaded, stained glass (or *gémail*). The Rue eventually winds down to the Rue Bretonneau, on the far side of which the Rue du Grand-Marché continues the westwards march, past the rather self-conscious craft zone of Petit-St-Martin and into the Place de la Victoire.

The curious spectacle to the west of this Place is the parish church of **Notre-Dame-la-Riche**, the immense width of its hall choir crammed against the congested roofs of a later nave. An oratory was first built on the site by St-Lidoire in the mid-4C, in order to house the remains of Tours' founding bishop, St-Gatien. This was known as Notre-Dame-la-Pauvre, and the church only gained its current dedication in the 12C, when it was rebuilt to serve the expanding parish of La Riche. Parts of the crypt of this 12C church survive to the west of the Rue Alleron, but the present building is entirely 15C and 16C and dates from two distinct campaigns. The choir belongs to the mid-15C church, an ample and spacious hall church whose aisles are the same width as the central vessel, and which was celebrated by contemporaries for its great cycle of wall paintings by Jean Fouquet. These were sadly destroyed, along with much of the glass, by Huguenots in 1562, the damage being sufficiently severe to necessitate the rebuilding of the nave. The late 16C replacement shoehorned double aisles into the same space as is occupied by the choir's single aisles, covering them with the transverse gables that are such a feature of the exterior. The high vault and clerestory of the nave are almost entirely an invention of Gustave Guérin's catastrophic 1860 restoration, but the most interesting aspect of the building is its **stained glass**.

This is concentrated in the choir, where the late medieval standing figures of St-Martin and St-Etienne date from c 1460, but the opportunity was taken late last century to group the early 16C fragments together to form scenes wherever possible. These mostly date from c 1525, among which you can make out St-Catherine of Alexandria, a Doubting Thomas, St-Anne and the Virgin, the Virgin and Child, and a bewildering array of fragments from an obviously once magnificent Passion and Resurrection cycle. A very fine group of painted terracotta statues has also been gathered at the west end of the north nave aisle, depicting the Marriage of the Virgin, and originally commissioned from Marc-Antoine Charpentier in 1650 for the convent of the Minims at Plessis-lès-Tours.

West of Tours

The easiest way to reach (3km) La Riche is to follow the south bank of the Loire, along the Rue des Tanneurs. The chief interest in what was a favoured royal residence, but has now become an industrial suburb, lies in the **Château of Plessis-lès-Tours** and the priory of St-Cosme. Both are well-signposted, and the ruined outlines of **St-Cosme**, sunk in the old flood plains of the Loire, are encountered first.

The **priory** was founded on the site of a small 10C chapel (dedicated to SS. Cosmas and Damian) between 1014 and 1018 by Hervé de Buzançay, treasurer of the collegiate church of St-Martin at Tours, and was placed under the protection of the abbey of Marmoutier. It was this foundation which sheltered the great 'heretic' Bérenger between 1075 and his death in 1083, but, in the face of a lax 11C regime, the chapter of St-Martin reclaimed the priory, and replaced the monks with five canons who wished to live under the Augustinian rule. It is unlikely that any of the present buildings in a meticulously restored site predate this refoundation.

Of the **church** itself only the south transept and apse-ambulatory survive to any great extent. The apse, with its handsomely vaulted radiating chapels and ambulatory bays, can be dated c 1100, and appears indebted to the architectural forms of neighbouring Poitou.

The internal elevation of the choir and south transept were clearly remodelled in the 15C, though, as was so often the case, much of the Romanesque stonework was retained and simply recut.

The **conventual buildings** lie to the north of the church, where elements of the west walk of the cloister survive to give entry to the **refectory**. This is quite majestic, a great rectangular hall of c 1130–40. It houses a stunning **pulpit**, sumptuously decorated with chevron and diaper ornament, sirens and monsters. A small two-storey *hostellerie* was added to the east of the refectory in the early 14C, the ground floor serving as a kitchen and the first floor reserved for guests, a space which has now been taken over as a library by the *Societé des Amis de Ronsard*.

This introduces the priory's most celebrated occupant, for in March 1565, at the height of his fame as a poet, **Pierre de Ronsard** was commended as Prior of St-Cosme, succeeding his brother, Charles. He spent much of his later life at the priory, writing the whole of his poetic history of France, the *Franciade*, here and entertaining Catherine de Medici, François d'Alençon, and Cassandre Salviati in the prior's lodging.

The 15C lodge, which is the first building you come to on entering the grounds, provides a preliminary audio-visual display on monasteries and the life of Ronsard. The lodging Ronsard would have known was without partition walls or an internal staircase, with just one large room on each floor, access being by an external spiral stair. The upper room is where, according to tradition, Ronsard died on 27 December 1585. He was certainly buried in the church, and his grave was discovered during an archaeological dig in 1933. He has been reburied in the same, now roofless, spot, a rose bush planted above the gravestone in recognition of the family device, *Ronce Ardent* (a burning bramble), and of his lines: 'I do not want marble broken for the pride of seeing my grave more beautiful. But I want shade from a tree. A tree always clad in green'.

The **Château de Plessis-lès-Tours** is about 1km south of St-Cosme, a less evocative site but no less important. The building is best known as Louis XI's favourite residence, indeed the house to which he came to die in 1483.

Louis first acquired the site in 1463 when he bought the earlier manor of Montils-lès-Tours. He demolished the old house and began work on a new château c 1474, a building which was extended by Charles VIII c 1490, when the chapel was added, and refurbished between 1505 and 1510 to make good the damage caused by a violent storm in 1504. The greater part of what was a colossal complex, grouping three wings around a U-shaped court, was demolished in the 18C, and only the south wing now remains. Even here the nature of the work at Plessis makes it difficult to assess whether this wing belongs to the late 15C or early 16C campaigns. Nevertheless it is an imposing structure, the exterior best seen from the south, where the vertical accents imparted by the steep dormer windows are strongest. The interior has been savagely restored, with little more than the linenfold panelling of the room in which Louis is said to have died surviving to give a hint of the splendour of its decorative forms—a sad reflection on the reign of a neglected monarch.

5

The Indre and Indrois: Nouans and Loches to Azay-le-Rideau

ROAD (Loches to Azay-le-Rideau, 52km: Nouans to Azay-le-Rideau, 76km) Loches; N143, 4km Chambourg; D17, 4km Azay-sur-Indre: Nouans-les-Fontaines; D760, 8km Montrésor; D10, 24km Azay-sur-Indre: Azay-sur-Indre; D17, 8km Courçay; D10, 4km Cormery; D17, 10km Montbazon; 16km Saché; 6km Azay-le-Rideau.

The river Indre rises deep in the Berry, to the south-east of La Châtre, flowing north-west into the Touraine near Bridoré, before cutting east of the forêt de Verneuil to pass beneath the rocky eminence of Loches. It is a relatively shallow river, rarely more than two or three feet deep, and—before it picks up the waters of its principal tributary, the Indrois—remains fairly narrow. The landscape through which it flows is marked by a low, dusty plain, now mostly given over to cereals, and the river has carved a broad, gently shelving valley through the limestone, occasionally cutting steep cliffs where it comes up against the harder rock formations around Loches and Montbazon. The itineraries described below are arranged to enable you to explore what is the major river course of the southern Touraine, with an initial section devoted to Loches and the Indre as far as its confluence with the Indrois at Azay-sur-Indre, and a second section dealing with the Indrois itself. The final section deals with the lower valley down to Azay-le-Rideau.

Loches

The significance of the town can hardly be overlooked, particularly if you wander over the bridge to the right bank of the Indre and gaze at the succession of walls which girdle the steep bluff above the river, punctuated by the rising accents of the Logis Royal, St-Ours, and the Donjon.

The rocky promontory was mentioned as supporting a 'castellum' by Gregory of Tours in the late 6C, but it was Charles the Bald's gift of the manor to a retainer and its mid-10C acquisition through marriage by Foulques le Roux, count of Anjou, that led to the town's development as a great feudal fastness. The first of the fortified castles seems to have been built by Foulques Nerra, probably during the 1030s, and was integrated into the town defences by the construction of an enceinte wall in the 12C.

This bonding of the town with its seigneurial overlord bestowed considerable importance on Loches, particularly during the late 12C and early 13C struggles for control of the Touraine, waged between the Plantagenet counts of Anjou and the Capetian kings of France. The town eventually fell to Philip Augustus in 1205, after a 12-month siege, and was made over to the son of Philip's captain, Dreux de Mello, but having been repurchased by Louis IX in 1249 it remained in royal hands until the Revolution. It is in this latter guise, as a favoured 15C and 16C royal residence, that Loches is best known, and as a largely intact late medieval walled town that it merits leisurely exploration.

Town Tour. The modern town centres on the **Place de la Marne**, across the river from the station, from where you might follow the **Rue de la République** as far as the Porte Picois. This stretch, together with the Place-du-Marché-aux-Légumes, forms the main shopping area of Loches, attractively furnished with café tables and restaurants which gather in the shade of the 16C belfry tower of St-Antoine.

The **Porte Picois** allows you to break through the second enceinte, a mid-15C extension of the town with which the Porte is contemporary, and thus arrive in the late medieval centre. To the right, crammed against the angles of the wall, is the **Hôtel-de-Ville**, built between 1535 and 1543, where the constrictions on space necessitated the breaching of the main façade by a corner stair-tower. From here the **Rue du Château** climbs as far as the earlier, inner town, interrupted by the occasional fanfare from a *hôtel particulier*, as at No. 8, built c 1550 by a pupil of Philibert de l'Orme and known as **La Chancellerie**, on account of its twin Latin inscriptions advocating the rule of Justice nourished by Prudence. The **Maison du Centaur** (No. 10) is another grand residence, splendidly articulated with a 17C relief depicting the centaur, Nessos, wounded by a poisoned arrow from Hercules' bow, for having been so bold as to lift Déjanire, the wife of Hercules, across his flanks.

At the top of the Rue du Château the **Porte Royale** offers the sole entry to the old inner enceinte. As with the western portion of the wall visible here, the Porte was originally built by Henry II in the later 12C, and subsequently modified by Philip Augustus after 1205, and again during the 15C. The latter period is responsible for the upper ramparts of the walls, along with the inner elevation of the gate. Most of the townhouses within this huge inner enclosure were reconstructed during the 17C and 18C, creating quiet and handsome prospects along the streets which connect the Logis Royal to the north with the old castle at the southernmost extremity. A left turn inside the Porte Royale brings you past the **Musée Lansyer**, a small museum dedicated to the work of a local late 19C pupil of Courbet, and on to the collegiate church of **ST-OURS DE LOCHES**.

The church did not acquire its current dedication to St-Ours, the 6C evangelist of the southern Touraine, until 1792, when the relics of the saint were translated here from a now destroyed earlier church beneath the town. Prior to this it was known as Notre-Dame-de-Loches, and had been founded as a college of secular canons by Geoffroy Grisegonelle, count of Anjou, c 980. The earliest documentary records date from 1151–68, when Prior Thomas Pactius replaced the wooden-roofed nave with 'two *dubes* [hollow stone pyramids] resting on pillars and arches raised for that purpose'. During the same period the choir, transept and western narthex porch were built, and work was begun on a south aisle, subsequently substantially modified and completed c 1200. The north aisle was not added until the 14C, but it is still the case that by c 1165 the building had taken on the distinguishing characteristics that are so celebrated by writers on architectural history.

Nothing survives of the late 10C church except a small crypt beneath the south transept chapel, and interpretation of the current structure is complicated by the results of an insensitive restoration of 1838. Two major building campaigns can be identified, the first datable on stylistic grounds to the late 11C and confined to the earlier western tower-

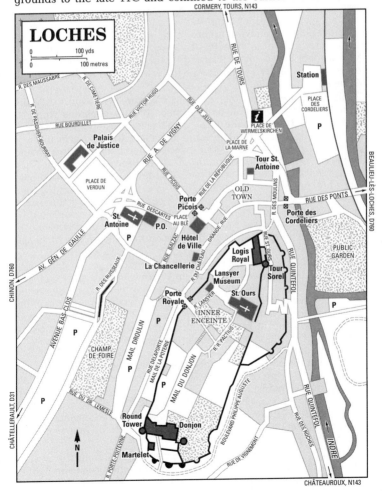

porch. This is now sandwiched between Pactius' outer narthex and the two bay nave, being reinforced externally by strip-buttresses which divide the tower into three distinct bays. The first floor of this tower originally gave on to a wooden-roofed nave and acted as a western tribune, magnificently covered by a domical 'cloister-vault' comparable to those of the Tour Charlemagne at Tours, or the western tower of St-Paul at Cormery. These essentially local Romanesque solutions were oddly incorporated into Thomas Pactius' wide-ranging late 12C building. The impact of this later campaign on the shape of the church is best assessed from the south, along the Rue Pactius, where you can see four stone pyramids soaring above the parapet lines and isolating the various elements of the building. Pactius had served as chaplain to Foulques le Jeune, count of Anjou, and was clearly aware of the possibilities of the pyramidal roofs of Fontevraud, as well as the new vaulting technologies of Angers Cathedral. Hence the superlative **vault** and pointed relieving arches of the majestic narthex porch. The experts are inclined to view this as a significant monument, the first evidence that the so-called 'Plantagenet style' (or what Anglo-American historians prefer to call 'Angevin Gothic'), had a future outside Maine and Anjou.

Visitors who are more interested in sculpture will want to see the **inner portal**. This probably dates from c 1165, the voussoirs arranged radially to carry a fantastic array of harpies, mermen, acrobats and monsters. The spandrels have come to act as a sort of graveyard for a few surviving early Gothic statues, shoehorned between the arch and the vault, and retaining remnants of late medieval polychromy. They were probably put there during the later Middle Ages but their provenance remains a mystery, as does their date, the guesses ranging from c 1160 to c 1200 for the various groups. They are arranged in three tiers, each stylistically distinct, with the figure of St Peter accompanied by an abbot or bishop at the base, two badly weathered piers showing an Annunciation and Visitation above, and an Adoration of the Magi and Nativity at the top.

By contrast, the principal delight of the **interior** lies in staring upwards into the hollow cones of Pactius' extraordinary nave roof. The rest of the interior was sadly mutilated, either by Revolution or restoration, and few fittings survive, though a mid-17C Assumption of the Virgin by David Tenier the Younger, and a damaged late 12C wall painting depicting St-Brice (recently removed from the crypt to the south choir chapel) offer some pictorial interest.

Evidence of the popularity of Loches with the French royal family can be seen to the north of St-Ours, where the ascending verticals of the **LOGIS ROYAL** proclaim Valois ambition in matters of family advertisement. The logis was built on the site of a 12C residence of the counts of Anjou, and, as it lies at the northern edge of the earlier walled town, it needed to act as a strong-point within the walls, as well as provide comfortable accommodation.

It is easy to appreciate the exterior elevations from the eastern terrace, where the 13C southern tower, the so-called **Tour Sorel**, forms an angle with the later elevations, and is all that remains of the 13C town improvements. To the right, two sharply differentiated two-storey blocks unfold: the late 14C main residence, strengthened by half-towers and giving onto a sentry-walk beneath the roof; and a more self-consciously palatial northern wing, added between 1491 and 1514.

The logis is perhaps best known as the residence in which Charles VII and his favoured mistress, Agnès Sorel, spent much of their time together, and where Joan of Arc was received by the future Charles VII in June 1429. Joan's famous petition: 'Noble Dauphin, do not listen to these counsels, so numerous and so long. Rather you should come quickly to Reims, to claim the crown which is your right' was delivered in the great hall of the **Vieux Logis** (the late 14C wing). This room is one of the most splendid 14C halls in France, warm, relaxed, and now beautifully hung with 17C pastoral tapestries, combining spaciousness with intimacy to an unusual degree.

Beyond here you step into the later wing, where the alabaster effigy from the **Tomb of Agnès Sorel** has been preserved in the Salle Charles VIII. This originally graced the collegiate church of Notre-Dame (St-Ours) and has been carefully restored after it was smashed during the Revolution, alone serving to give one a sense of the beauty and gentleness for which Agnès was celebrated. She died at the age of 28 in 1450, and presumably the effigy dates from shortly afterwards. Her enduring fame might be gauged from the numerous portraits dotted about the room, most notably where Jean Fouquet represents her as the Virgin in a Virgin and Child, bearing a breast in the manner she pioneered at court. Most of the paintings in the Logis are in fact copies, the one major exception being in the room to the north of Agnès' tomb, where a triptych of 1485 from the Chartreuse du Liget has been reassembled, the work perhaps of itinerant Flemish painters. This northern wing was built for Charles VIII and Anne de Bretagne, which accounts for its most decisive architectural element, the delightful **oratoire** in the north-western angle, whose stonework has been decorated with the knotted cords and trailing ermine of Anne de Bretagne's device.

Any serious defence of the town was conducted from the mighty **donjon** above the southern cliffs of the promontory, on the site of Foulques Nerra's early 11C castle. The title 'donjon' is confusingly applied to the entire complex, but current opinion is inclining towards the view that the great rectangular keep at its heart would indeed have been known to Foulques Nerra, and perhaps dates from c 1030. This forms the centrepiece of an impressively cogent system of fortifications, rising through three main storeys to a height of 37m, and provided with a subsidiary stair-tower to the north. A secondary ditch was dug to the south in the second half of the 12C, when Henry II (Plantagenet) encircled the whole of the southern perimeter with a steep enceinte wall. The only buildings to retain their roofs belong to the late 15C, when a second, circular, keep was raised to the west, known as the Tour Neuve, and the sinister **martelet** was excavated out of the old quarry workings at the south-western angle of the ridge.

The martelet is particularly interesting, consisting of three superposed cells used to house the castle's impressive roster of noble prisoners. One of these, Ludovico Sforza, Duke of Milan, was imprisoned here from 1500 until his death in 1508 and decorated his cell with a vast and faded wall painting, emblazoning the walls with stars and the legend, understandable in the circumstances, *'celui qui n'est pas contan'*. Two of his contemporaries, the bishops of Autun and Le Puy, simultaneously carved a small Crucifixion in the wall of the cell beneath, praying for release from the charge of involvement in Charles de Bourbon's rebellion of 1503.

There is also a substantial body of graffiti in the **Tour Neuve**, particularly in the upper room of a tower which saw Louis XI's adviser, Cardinal La Balue, languish for 11 years after betraying Louis to Charles le Téméraire of Burgundy. Philippe de Commynes, Louis' governor of the château de Chinon, describes late 15C prisoners being incarcerated here in 'cages of wood and iron, with terrible locks, no more than 8 feet long and the height of a man plus a foot'.

One km east of the 15C Porte des Cordeliers, on the opposite bank of the river Indre, the early medieval 'burg' of **BEAULIEU-LÈS-LOCHES** retains a character quite distinct from that of its grander neighbour. This is largely a matter of site, for, unlike Loches, Beaulieu sits above flat meadowland, in the shade of its now semi-ruinous abbey, a building which still acts as the focal point of an attractive village. Foulques Nerra was responsible for the first **Abbaye de la Trinité** in 1004—the chronicler Raoul Glabar asserted that he was sufficiently anxious that monks should offer prayers night and day for the repose of his soul that he founded a Benedictine monastery on the site. Foulques was subsequently buried in the church in 1040 and the abbey began to prosper, acquiring its magnificent northern bell-tower in the early 12C. The Hundred Years War was harsh to Beaulieu, and in 1366 the town was largely destroyed by fire, with the abbey specifically targeted for a second fire in 1412. The damage was considerable, and the choir was rebuilt during the later 15C in a sort of stripped-down Flamboyant, simply recutting the Romanesque masonry wherever possible. From here it was mostly downhill. Guignières' 1699 engraving makes it clear that the western bays of the nave had already been abandoned by that date, and the partial fall of the crossing tower in 1791 persuaded the townspeople to demolish all but the north wall of the western nave, in order to extend the main market square.

The visitor is now confronted by a rather dull and abbreviated church, standing amidst the ruins of a once significant Romanesque abbey. These ruins come in two parts: a section of the old nave north wall, which connects the remodelled 15C nave with the bell-tower; and two out of three Romanesque ambulatory chapels, accessible along a track to the north of the bell-tower, which were simply abandoned when the new 15C choir was built. The dating of both these elements is uncertain. Documentary records speak of Foulques Nerra's son, Geoffroy Martel, rebuilding the abbey between 1040 and 1052, but the scarred capitals of the northern radiating chapel and exterior billet-moulding make it unlikely that these eastern fragments were built much before the very end of the 11C.

The **nave** must have been splendid. When Foulques Nerra's church was consecrated in May 1007, it stood for no more than a single day, at the end of which fire broke out in the roof timbers. It is unlikely that any of the existing nave wall dates from this first church, but it is clear from the vault departures above the capitals that at some subsequent date the nave received a transverse-ribbed barrel vault over narrow aisles. This writer, for one, is inclined to see this as a later remodelling of a nave Geoffroy began in the mid-11C, to create something similar to a fully vaulted Poitevin hall church.

Whatever the solution to the nave, it remains the case that the extraordinary display of mutilated **sculpture** on the exterior of the **north transept gable** has as many explanations as it has critics. (To get the best view of this powerful relief sculpture it is worth wandering into the allotment to the south of the early 13C bell-tower of the parish church of St-Laurent.) It appears early 12C and depicts knights on horseback, three fragmentary combats, lions, horses and other quadrupeds, and thickets of foliage arranged in such a way as to suggest a forest. Theories range from St-Hubert, St-Eustace, or St-Gilles hunting, to the coronation of Foulques Réchin as King of Jerusalem in 1130.

To the **north of Loches**, the N143 offers a fast route to (22km) Cormery, though a right turn on to the D17 at (6km) **Chambourg** provides an altogether gentler route, along the left bank of the Indre to its confluence with the Indrois at (4km) Azay-sur-Indre (see below).

The valley of the Indrois

The valley of the Indrois is more intensely rural than that of the Indre, steeper sloped and gently wooded, with apple and cherry orchards surviving on the higher ground where all has not yet been given over to cereal growing. The village of **Nouans-les-Fontaines** lies a few kilometres east of the valley proper, just above the banks of the Tourmente, still the best place from which to embark on an exploration of the Indrois.

Nouans caused a great stir in art-historical circles in 1931, when Paul Vitry cleaned a grimy and darkened panel painting from the parish church and revealed a magisterial **altarpiece**, which few doubt to be the work of the great 15C French court painter, **Jean Fouquet** (c 1420–81). The painting is still displayed within an otherwise unremarkable aisleless 13C church, and depicts the moment when Nicodemus and Joseph of Aramathea, having taken the body of Christ from the Cross, lay him in a shroud before the Virgin and St John. To the right a donor is commended by the figure of St James the Pilgrim, though the area to the left was presumably lost when the panel was cut out of its frame. At any rate it has been cut down. It is one of the finest 15C French panel paintings to have survived, and much the greatest to remain in a church, though the question of how it came to Nouans remains unanswered.

The composition has a precedent in an early 15C book of hours by the Boucicault Master, but its attribution to Jean Fouquet seems a solid one, and it probably dates from c 1470. Most scholarly work on the panel has understandably been concerned with the identity of the donor. Jean Bernard, bishop of Tours, is the most popular candidate, but he is usually seen commended by John the Evangelist, and the resemblance does not compare closely with other known representations. The most intriguing recent theory claims Jacques Couer (1400–56) as donor, the brilliant 15C merchant from the Berry, and that the panel formed the central field of the great lost triptych which stood in the chapel of the Hôtel Jacques Couer in Bourges. The arguments against this provenance are formidable, and most scholars are reduced to searching the 15C annals for likely candidates named Jacques (the probable reason for a commendatory James, or StJacques). It is testimony to the beauty and power of the work that these questions are pursued with such tenacity.

From Nouans the D760 picks up the Indrois just below the 12C bell-tower of (4km) **Coulangé**, before sweeping into (2km) **Villeloin**. Here, along a narrow road to the right of the Mairie, survives the 15C gatehouse of a small Benedictine abbey, handsomely banked above the river and giving on to an earlier medieval enceinte wall. A few fragments of the 15C conventual buildings have also been picturesquely set into a later house, and, rising from a terrace above the northern walls, the late medieval abbot's *logis* has been incorporated in a splendid 18C *hôtel particulier*.

Villeloin is a mere 2km east of **MONTRÉSOR**, and the views of the town as you approach from this direction are quite stunning, for not only is it the major settlement of the Indrois valley but it is also one of the most attractive, and this in an area noted for the beauty of its towns and villages.

The strategic potential of the site was first recognised by Roger le Petit-Diable, an ally of Foulques Nerra, who built the first castle to occupy the steep bluff above the river c 1000. This was rebuilt by Henry II and expanded during the 15C, but it was not until Ymbert de Bastarnay bought the manor of Montrésor in 1493 that the town began to take on the shape visible today. Ymbert built a new castle within the earlier enceinte walls, expanded the residential quarters to the west, and opened Montrésor to commerce with northern and central France. As counsellor successively to Louis XI, Charles VIII, Louis XII, and François I, he also imported metropolitan models, the results of which can be seen in the first of the larger buildings you encounter when approaching from the west, the collegiate church known as **La Collégiale**.

This was begun by Ymbert in 1519, and was completed in 1541 to a relatively simple design—aisleless, with tall three-light windows and a narrow transept—but its conception was worthy of the Valois Dukes of Burgundy. It was to serve Ymbert as a family mausoleum. This made the church a prime target during the Revolution, and unfortunately resulted in the smashing of the Bastarnay tomb and the loss of most of the glass. Bastarnay's magnificent tomb originally stood in the crossing, the marble effigies of Ymbert, his wife, Georgette de Montchenu, and son, François, laid above a black marble slab and supported by saints, prophets, and apostles in niches. The wreckage was brought together and restored in 1875, after the Polish emigré, Count Xavier Branicki, acquired Montrésor, but the loss of much of the detail makes it difficult to judge the usual attribution to Jean Goujon. Just two of the early 16C windows came through, at the west and east ends of the building respectively, the latter very fine indeed, and depicting Christ before Pilate, the Road to Calvary, and Crucifixion. This, and the surviving wooden doors and choir stalls, suffice to give one a sense of what has been lost, but it was the 19C which was responsible for the church's most unexpected attribute. After the 1875 restoration Branicki gave four fairly routine 16C Italian pantings, now hanging in the nave, and a superbly vivid early 17C Annunciation, painted by Philippe de Champaigne and now in the north choir chapel.

Xavier Branicki had an even more dramatic effect on the **Château**, just to the west of the church. This was a hybrid structure when he acquired it in 1849, with a late 12C northern curtain wall, ruined gatehouse of 1395 and a late 15C enceinte stacked above the river. The centrepiece was Ymbert de Bastarnay's early 16C residence, a spacious two-storey pavilion pinned between two decorative round towers, with four handsome dormer windows breaking a sharply pitched roof. Branicki's restoration left the complex more disparate than ever, and the interior rooms are now livid with 19C wood-panelling, hessians and wallpapers, with access to the first floor provided by an internal wooden spiral stair. The majority of the furnishings relate to Polish 18C history, or the Branicki family, but there is some good 16C furniture, and an eclectic collection of paintings mostly purchased by Xavier Branicki from the collection of Cardinal Flesch. These include Veronese's *Christ and the Woman taken in Adultery*, four small 15C Tuscan panel paintings, a number of 17C bas-reliefs by Pierre Vanneau, and a collection of work by the 19C German portraitist, Winterhalter.

The town may be dominated by these two buildings but it is not without vernacular interest, and the 17C timber **Halle aux Laines** on the Rue du Marché still houses a thriving market. The **Rue Branicki** also connects the upper town with the river, pitching steeply towards the old farmhouses which front the Indrois and the locally favoured fishing spots.

Montrésor is a good base for an **excursion** to the **Chartreuse du Liget**, some 5km along the D760, established in the fôret de Loches in 1178 by Henry II and yet another of the religious houses Henry was said to have founded in expiation for the murder of Thomas Becket. It was the custom for Carthusians to separate the conventual areas given over to the monks from those of the lay-brothers by up to a mile. Hence the first precinct you encounter is the 'maison basse', or **Couroirie**, where the lay-brothers lived and worked, consisting of a modest late 12C church to the east of a predominantly 15C range of workshops and living quarters. (This estate is in private hands and cannot be visited, but the exteriors are visible from the road.)

The **monastery** proper is on higher ground to the east. This is now entered by the one breach in an impressively intact precinct wall, an 18C portal which carries a bas-relief of St-Bruno, founder of the Carthusian order. The main pavilions and abbot's lodge were all rebuilt in the 17C or 18C and are now privately owned, so to visit the complex you should obtain permission (always given on payment of 3 francs) at the lowest door on the left. The roofless west end and western choir areas of the late 12C church are still standing, as is the west walk of an enormous 17C cloister, the latter originally giving on to the monks' cells.

More remarkably, a tiny circular chapel, **St-Jean du Liget**, survives in the woods about 1km west of the main monastery. Its origins are enigmatic, for though it was in the possession of the monks when one first hears of it, it could plausibly pre-date the Carthusian foundation. The architecture has been so heavily restored that it is impossible to give an accurate date beyond 12C, but the internal cycle of **wall paintings** appears to belong to the 1180s and is a rare survival. Painted in earth colours on a light ground, the murals depict the Nativity, Presentation in the Temple, Descent from the Cross, Three Maries at the Sepulchre, Dormition of the Virgin, and Tree of Jesse, with saints and bishops in the window embrasures.

The valley road **north-west of Montrésor** is the D10, curling above the river and flanked by stands of alder and willow, bringing you to the dam at (3km) **Chemillé-sur-Indrois**. This has created a shallow lake, popular with French holidaymakers, where you can hire boats, swim, or play tennis. Beyond Chemillé the road winds to the north of the Indrois, only regaining the river at the little market town of (7km) **Genillé**, its central square to the north of a late 15C château. Several of the parish churches hereabouts have retained their 15C benefactions, and at Genillé a very fine marble water-stoup of 1494 has been preserved beneath the western gallery. A lively vaulting boss, in which a bishop offers a permanent benediction above the altar, also survives in the one 13C choir bay.

7km downstream at **St-Quentin-sur-Indrois**, an accomplished church with a good 16C choir has preserved a remarkable tooled leather **plaque**, recording the establishment of a fund for masses to be said for the souls of Adam Fumée, doctor to Louis XI, and his wife, Thomine Ruzé, both of whom died in 1496. The road then sweeps downhill from St-Quentin, throwing off splendid views of the Indrois valley above the point where the river flows into the Indre at (7km) **Azay-sur-Indre**.

The Indre Valley

Below the confluence of the two rivers the D17 offers much the most attractive route downstream, riding above the woodland, gardens and watermeadows which cling to the Indre's left bank. At (3km) **Reignac-sur-Indre**, the modern church has incongruously preserved elements of a 9C western tower to the north of a largely 19C château. And at (5km) **Courçay** the parish church glories in an enormous bowl of a Romanesque font, and a 12C rubble tower and spire whose rugged forms seem to have been something of a local speciality.

If you take the D10 north-west from Courçay you first become aware of the approaches to (4km) **CORMERY** as you pass **Notre-Dame-de-Fougeray**, built by Cormery's monks to serve as a parish church outside the earlier town walls. Badly decayed, it was put together in a single mid-12C campaign as an aisleless and fully vaulted transeptal church, with some fine capitals above the crossing piers, and four statues of the evangelists set in the triforium arcade of the apse. The cemetery opposite also hosts a curious column set above a medieval altar table, which may once have acted as a *croix hosannière*—a place where wreaths were fixed to honour the dead during the great *fêtes des morts*, namely Palm Sunday and All Saints Day.

The once great Benedictine abbey of **St-Paul-de-Cormery** lies a little further to the west, reached along the Rue de l'Abbaye, which brings you underneath the old western tower-porch, across the N143, and into Cormery's central square. The town's particular peculiarity is that many of its houses have grown up within the earlier abbey precincts, and the Rue de l'Abbaye itself was built along the axis of the former nave after the monastic buildings were sold off in the half-century following the Revolution. What remains provides a fascinating insight into the structure of a once important abbey, and to join an excellent tour you should apply to the Syndicat d'Initiative on the corner of the Rue de l'Abbaye and the central square.

The tour starts in the **Logis Boyer**, a mid-17C house built above the late 12C cellar range to the north of the abbey, and just beyond the compound windows of a magnificent 13C refectory preserved within a terrace of private houses. From here it is a short walk to the western tower-porch, the **Tour St-Paul**, where you are brought face to face with the early history of the abbey.

The attractions of the site were first recognised in 791 when Ithier, abbot of St-Martin at Tours, established a 'cella' on the southern banks of the river Indre to act as a religious retreat. The cell seems to have flourished, and success persuaded Ithier's immediate successors as abbots of Tours to take a personal interest in its affairs, with Pope Leo I joining the great Anglo-Saxon schoolman, Alcuin, in confirming its foundation as a monastery colonised by Benedictine monks from Aniane. This constitution of 800 stipulated that the monks should live under the Benedictine rule, but it also insisted that they should be subordinate to the authority of St-Martin at Tours. With that authority, Alcuin's successor at Tours, Fridugise, undertook the construction of a new monastic church c 831. This church was destroyed during the Norse raids of 853, but elements of its successor survive in the eastern wall of the tower, where the blocked triple opening originally gave on to the late Carolingian nave. The western face, and indeed most of the rest of the tower, date from a good thirty years after the consecration of a new choir in 1054, perhaps c 1080–90, and the first floor chamber still boasts a superb domical **cloister-vault**, a significant example of a type of rib vault used elsewhere in the region. South-east of here fragments of the 14C southern walk of the cloister and 13C **chapter house** survive, the latter startlingly treated to a basilisk prancing above a grinning head. And just to the west of the 16C abbot's lodging the late 15C **Lady Chapel** has been transformed into a barn, its splendid vaulting bosses carrying images of St-Paul and the arms of Abbot Jean du Puy, its patron. Before leaving, as you pass beneath the tower arch, you should look upwards and to your left, where the 15C figure of a fishwife once served to remind visitors that they were passing out of the world of celestial hierarchies and into an altogether more salacious market place.

The easiest way to follow the **Indre downstream from Cormery** is to cut west along the D17, past the striking parish church at (4km) **Esvres**, whose rough-hewn masonry sports two re-used Merovingian sepulchral plaques, and whose 12C bell-tower and spire echoes that of Courçay. Another of these belfry spires is to be found at (4km) **Veigné**, where a weir has been thrown across the Indre, creating an excellent watersports centre. 2km west, the prosperous market town of **Montbazon** is still dominated by the startling outline of Foulques Nerra's early 11C rectangular keep, louring above the cliffs to the south of the town and now acting as the base for a hideous mid-19C statue of the Virgin and Child. The **castle** is deteriorating badly and, as it is in private hands, cannot be visited. This is a particular disappointment as it is one of only three of Foulques Nerra's fortresses that has not been either destroyed or rebuilt, making it one of the earliest motted castles to survive in Europe.

Below Montbazon the D17 passes through a number of towns and villages that serve as dormitories for Tours, some 12km to the north, sweeping around the **Château d'Artannes** (10km), the 15C residence of the archbishops of Tours, and the handsome 18C watermills at (2km) **Pont-de-Ruan**. The parish church of **St-Brice** here carries an over-restored though beautifully vaulted 13C choir and austere 12C western portal. The village of (2km) **SACHÉ** has a delightful parish church, **St-Martin-de-Vertou**, banked against the hillside which rises from the river, its beguiling juxtaposition of shapes and volumes extending to a 13C belfry and an engaging run of transverse gables above the 16C north aisle. To the west of the tiny church porch, the **Place Alexandre Calder** celebrates a recent famous resident, the American sculptor Alexander Calder (1898–1976), one of whose vast metal mobiles lends colour and movement, and something of the atmosphere of a railway platform, to the square.

But Saché is best known for the **Château de Saché**, and for **Balzac**. The château is a handsome, though unremarkable, early 16C building with an irregular cruciform plan, set amidst lawns to the west of an earlier moat. It became the property of Mr de Margonne, a close friend of Honoré de Balzac, early in the 19C, and between 1829 and 1837 Balzac spent several months each year here—'a melancholy place full of harmonies'. The first floor is arranged as it was during the early 19C, retaining its astonishing painted wallpaper designs of 1803, while the second floor serves as a sort of epiphany to Balzac. Given the great man's prodigious work-rate it comes as no surprise to discover that not only were such novels as *Le Lys dans la Vallée* set at Saché, but that *Louis Lambert, La Recherche de l'Absolu* and most of *Père Goriot* were also written here. Dozens of volumes of Balzac's works, lithographs, paintings and photographs have been arranged across a suite of rooms as testimony to the author's mid-19C reputation, but it is Balzac's study and bedroom which is the most interesting. This may have been restored, but the arrangements would still be recognisable to the author as the place where he worked for up to 14 hours at a stretch, sustained by no more than bread, butter, and up to 40 cups of coffee.

Below Saché the D17 sticks to the south of the river, threading through orchards and woodland where once stands of mulberries fed the silk-worms that provided the raw thread for the mills of Tours. You regain the river at (6km) **AZAY-LE-RIDEAU**, a significant Gallo-Roman settlement and important river crossing on the road from Tours to Chinon. Its château is among the most popular in Touraine, and can be uncomfortably crowded in July and August, but the lower town is largely unruffled by this, and the old centre, along the Rue Gambetta and in the Place du 11 Novembre, is an excellent place to get a feeling for Azay as a whole.

The town takes its suffix from Rideau d'Azay, one of its late 12C seigneurs, who first raised a castle above the northern end of the earlier medieval bridge over the Indre. This, and the town, were destroyed in 1417, when one of the guards of the Burgundian garrison then occupying the town insulted Charles VII as he passed through Azay on his way to Tours. In retaliation Charles successfully laid siege to the castle and razed the town, its title briefly changing from Azay-le-Rideau to Azay-le-Brûlé. Recovery was slow and largely due to the Tours financier Gilles Berthelot, who acquired the seigneurie on his marriage to Philippa Lesbahy. It was Gilles who was responsible for the great château astride the river. He also encouraged the construction of a number of new terraces and townhouses along the Rue Balzac and even became involved with the parish church of **St-Symphorien**.

After pressure from the parish Gilles agreed to finance the replacement of the two western bays of the north aisle, work beginning in 1519 on what is an extremely straightforward addition. But as even the briefest inspection of the church makes plain, St-Symphorien is the only building in Azay to conserve elements which pre-date the 1417 fire, and the most arresting of these elements are most peculiar. Looking at the **west front** you might notice that the right-hand block is made up of a picturesque confusion of sculpted panels, billet-moulded stringcourses and decorative stonework. There is a plain portal and a 13C window which breaks through a frieze of arcaded figures, above which the upper wall has framed a curious gable, the majority of whose stones are diagonally set. A number of carved panels have been brought together above the window, centred on a representation of Christ holding a book, who is in turn flanked by six figures, all set beneath arcades, and whose weathered features would appear to be female to the left, male to the right. The fact that the window is 13C, and breaks the lower frieze of figures, suggests that the arrangement was in place by then, but there can be no presumption that these figurative panels were originally carved for the west front of the building. Furthermore, the billet-moulding which is used to divide the front into a series of fields looks early 12C, and sits uncomfortably above corbels in its lowest register.

It is an extremely unusual arrangement, though not beyond comparison, and the parallels are mostly local, at Cravant, Rivière, Bourgeuil, St-Mexme de Chinon, and St-Paul de Cormery. None of these is precise, and it is more a question of shared elements, with Chinon offering the closest formal connections and Cormery boasting the most promising institutional links. All the above are probably mid to late

11C, in which respect the gift of the church to the abbey of Cormery by Geoffroy de l'Ile-Bouchard between 1026 and 1040 assumes a considerable importance. At the date of the gift, St-Symphorien was reported to be ruinous and abandoned, and may thus have been rebuilt towards the end of the 11C, sections of this late 11C façade subsequently trapped in a 13C church. Whatever the case, it remains a tantalising spectacle, and the original placement and meaning of the sculpture an unsolved mystery. The rest of the building is much less interesting, with a largely 13C nave and slightly earlier north aisle, to which Gilles added his two western bays in 1519.

At the **CHÂTEAU OF AZAY-LE-RIDEAU** it is the rigour and regularity of the design which first strikes you as you approach from the north. Along with Chambord and Chenonceau, Azay is one of the most influential châteaux of the first half of the reign of François I, and might even be considered one of the fundamental Renaissance buildings of France. In this respect it is interesting to note that, like Chenonceau, Azay was commissioned by a wealthy bourgeois, Gilles Berthelot, who began work on the site of a ruined feudal castle in 1518, sinking a series of pools to the south of the Indre where previously a moat had stood. He was never actually to move in, for in 1527 François I confiscated Azay and made over both the town and the largely completed château to the Captain of his Guard, Antoine Raffin. It was not until after 1791, when the Montmorency-Biencourt family acquired the château, that Azay-le-Rideau took on its present appearance and the two angle towers to either side of the *cour d'honneur* were built.

Nevertheless, for the most part, the château is an early 16C building, and evidence that at that time a more systematic understanding of the principles of Italian Renaissance design was making itself felt in France. The quality most frequently commented on by historians of French late 15C and early 16C architecture is the way in which Italianate motifs—pilaster orders, brackets, candelabra, and swags of fruit—were grafted on to buildings whose spatial dynamics were late Gothic. What seems to have inspired educated French patrons to investigate Italian forms, particularly during Milan's French dependency between 1500 and 1525, was their admiration for the luxurious way of life of the Italian courts. Italian dress, Italian gardens, Italian etiquette, Italian ornament were all readily embraced, but Neo-Platonic philosophy, Antique sculpture, Florentine painting, architectural 'gravitas' were barely recognised. This ability to invest late medieval forms with Lombard ornament produced a number of astonishingly successful buildings, for example the châteaux at Blois and Amboise. But designs such as Chenonceau and Azay-le-Rideau mark a turning point, the beginning, and only just the beginning, of an interest in creating flatter, more controlled elevations.

At Azay, for instance, the dormer windows are major elements in the design, and the superposed classical orders of the main entrance bay are broken by late medieval statuary niches, but the horizontal stringcourses which run across the elevation and the overall flatness of treatment tend to isolate the vertical accents so that they become little more than picturesque flourishes. Most significantly, the great staircase is not housed in an external tower but is brought within the main block, and is no longer a spiral stair but a ramp. Even here the temptation to embellish the stairway with a pendant coffered vault proved irresistible. So, once again, you are witness to a plundering of Italian ideas to create a hybrid and unmistakably French building, albeit one more ordered than any of those of the previous generation.

The purchase of the château by the State in 1905 led to a major refurbishment, and the transformation of several of the rooms into museum galleries. Visitors are confined to the ground and first floors, with the kitchen and main service quarters in the west wing, and the spacious **Chambre Jaune** to the south of the ground floor, the latter hung with an excellent 16C portrait of Mary of Austria. To the left of the main staircase on the first floor, two smaller bedrooms, the so-called **Appartements Royaux**, are furnished with 16C portraits of the de Guise and Valois families, and a very fine 16C Spanish cabinet. To the right, the **Salle des Fêtes** is given over to 16C Flemish tapestries; the four grandest, woven in Audenarde, depict the reconciliation of Jacob and Esau and scenes from the life of Solomon. The best of the tapestries are around the corner, where two 18C Beauvais hunting scenes, full of movement and colour, declaim the life and freshness of the chase.

6

Le Grand-Pressigny to Chinon via Ste-Maure-de-Touraine and Richelieu

ROUTE 6A (80km): Le Grand-Pressigny D60/D100, 11km Ferrière-Larçon; D50, 21km Le Louroux; C1/D101, 11km Ste-Catherine-de-Fierbois; N10, 6km Ste-Maure-de-Touraine; D59, 7km St-Epain; D21, 5km Crissay-sur-Manse (2km Roches-Tranchelion); D21, 11km Cravant-les-Coteaux; 8km Chinon. **ROUTE 6B** (78km): Le Grand-Pressigny D42, 12km Descartes; D5/D107, 17km MarignyMarmande (D110, 4km Bois-Aubry); D20, 16km Richelieu; D749, 6km Champigny-sur-Verde; D113, 10km L'Ile-Bouchard; D760, 3km Tavant; D760/D749, 14km Chinon.

The area between Le Grand-Pressigny and Chinon consists of a vast chalk plateau, drained by the rivers Creuse and Vienne. The rivers come together near the hamlet of Sauvage, effectively dividing the plateau into two, with the great plain of Ste-Maure stretching far away to the north until it too is broken by the valley of the Cher. These plains were once densely forested, but, although pockets of woodland survive, the greater part has been cleared and given over to cereal production. The area has always been sparsely populated, and the market towns are as likely to be grouped around the smaller streams as in the protection of the major valleys, for which reason the itinerary has been divided into two distinct sections. The first section deals with the plateau de Ste-Maure, before heading west along the valley of the Manse to Chinon; while the second cuts across the wheat fields to Richelieu, approaching Chinon along the south bank of the Vienne.

Le Grand-Pressigny

As befits an established frontier town surveying the borders of the Poitou from within the old county of Touraine, Le Grand-Pressigny hosts a substantial **château**. The earliest structure on the site, the rectangular donjon overlooking the plateau towards the east, is late 12C, and the first seigneur whose name has survived is Guillaume de Pressigny, *chevalier banneret de Touraine* (crested knight of Touraine) in 1204. Given the advantages of Grand-Pressigny's situation, at the lip of a plateau above the confluence of the rivers Claise and Aigronne, one might have expected the feudal lords of Touraine to have built a castle earlier, but it seems that the great Poitevin fortress at La Roche-Posay provoked few emulators just across the border. Two of the walls of the donjon collapsed in 1988—to the great surprise of those who saw it happen—and much of the rest of the château had already fallen into ruin after the Revolution. But what does survive is impressive.

The vast dry moat to the north and the curtain wall date from the early 13C, presumably erected shortly after King John ceded control of Touraine to Philip Augustus in 1205. Extensive modifications during the 15C saw sections of these curtain walls given machicolations and a sentry-walk, a new seigneurial residence constructed and the existing barbican reconfigured. Finally, between 1550 and 1580 Honorat de Savoie, Maréchal and Grand Amiral de France in 1572, built the present **corps de logis**. This Italianate two-storey wing divides the old castle bailey into two sections—the *grand cour d'honneur*, which greets you on entering, and the earlier eastern sections, in which the lower walls of the 15C seigneurial residence and chapel are exposed.

Honorat's mid-16C *logis* now houses the **Musée de la Préhistoire**, a small but important collection of Neolithic and Bronze Age material. The area around Grand-Pressigny was extensively occupied during the Neolithic period, the settlers drawn by the deposits of flint to be found in the valley of the Claise. These flints are large, formed in the yellow chalk strata of the late Turonian age and, given their rich buttery lustre, are known as *livres de buerre*. They are capable of providing cutting and scraping tools of anything up to 38cm in length, useful for harvesting grasses or cereals, or cutting reeds for thatch, and the unique quality of these Claise valley flints led to their widespread export, examples having turned up as far afield as Belgium and Switzerland. The exhibits are not in themselves unusual, but are superbly displayed on the upper floor accompanied by geological charts, photographs and videos.

The actual **town** of Grand-Pressigny is small, spilling down from the château in a maze of twisting streets and tiled roofs to the pleasant square between the church and the Mairie. The **parish church** is fairly typical of the smaller foundations in the area. It has a Romanesque apse, ramshackle nave and 16C belfry, the one ostentatious note being the late Gothic mouldings around the north door. It is best seen on a Thursday morning when the market stalls gather beneath its eaves, and the terraces of the cafés across the street expand to supply the needs of the working population of this profoundly rural area.

A. Via Ste-Maure-de-Touraine

North-east of Le Grand-Pressigny, the D60 sweeps through the corn-fields to cross the narrow Brignon valley at (7km) Paulmy, where a right turn on to the D100 will bring you into (4km) **Ferrière-Larçon**. The chief interest here is the parish church of **St-Mandet** and its Roman-esque nave, 13C hall choir and octagonal spire make a picturesque silhouette. The earliest part of the structure stands beneath the belfry, where the piers of an 11C crossing survived to be incorporated into a Gothic rebuild. An aisleless nave was added c 1130, its **west portal** embellished with simple foliage above which a couple of lion capitals animate the originally single window opening. This relatively simple Romanesque church was then crowned with a late 12C belfry and engulfed by a mid-13C **choir**.

The latter is remarkable, an irregular three bay hall-choir with a beautifully vaulted trio of apses. However, this ambitious programme was clearly too costly for the parish to support, and it eventually foundered in the south aisle, where the springers never received their intended vaults and the tracery of the west window sails disturbingly above the roof. It is, none the less, an intriguing structure, a localised response to the great Angevin hall-choirs north-west of here.

To the north, the D50 races across the plateau de Ste-Maure, dipping to thread a path through the dull roadside town of (7km) Ligueil, before rejoining the open windy heights. It is worth continuing as far as (14km) **Le Louroux**, a gloriously unselfconscious fortified medieval village whose structural arrangements and rectangular enceinte have sur-vived virtually intact. The finest view is from the narrow side road to (the C4) St-Bauld, a vantage point from which you can make out the whole of one long side-wall, framed by two semi-circular angle-towers and fronted by a moat. A broken-down medieval bridge crosses the moat, breaching the wall to provide access to the 15C *seigneurie* lodged against the eastern enceinte wall. The village is first mentioned as a possession of the abbey of Marmoutier in the late 10C, whose abbots remained lords until the French Revolution, and, though it is impossible to disinter a precise date for walls that were frequently repaired or built against, this type of rectangular walled village was a relatively well known form in 10C northern Europe.

Although none of the buildings inside the walls is as early as the 10C, all are basically medieval. The earliest is the 12C western **bell-tower** of the church, attached to a largely 13C nave and modest 17C choir and situated along the southern edge of the enceinte. The buildings to the north and east are now occupied by a farm, but include the 15C **residence** of the abbot's châtelain, its outer elevation sumptuously refurbished with brick and tall dormer windows in the 18C, and a quite magnificent late medieval grange, dividing the village into two un-equal courts.

Le Louroux is a mere 26km south of Tours reached by the D50. But if you intend heading west, towards the valley of the Vienne, you should take the C1, signposted 'Vers Ste-Maure-de-Touraine', switching right onto the D101 at the (7km) crossroads beyond the hamlet of Le Valet. The advantage of this route is that it takes you to (4km) **Ste-Catherine-de-Fierbois**, now a quiet village but once an important overnight halt on the pilgrimage road from Chartres to Santiago de Compostela, and a place redolent with memories of Joan of Arc. Legend has it that a chapel dedicated to Catherine of Alexandria was established in a forest clearing here, and that after his great victory over a Moorish army on the plains between Tours and Poitiers in 732 Charles Martel was moved to offer his sword in thanksgiving to Ste-Catherine. The documents are largely silent before 1375, when a blind paralytic, Jean de Godefroy, vowed that he would restore the abandoned chapel if he regained his health, and, once cured, redeemed his pledge. Hundreds of miracles reputedly ensued and by 1400 a tradition had grown up whereby knights returning from battle would offer a sword to the shrine as an ex-voto. Indeed, both its situation and sudden fame prompted Jean II le Meingre, better known as the Maréchal de Boucicault, to found a hospice dedicated to St-Jacques-de-Compostelle in 1415, fragments of which are incorporated into the present Mairie.

Its later reputation derives from **Joan of Arc**'s staying the night of 5 March 1429 in Boucicault's hospice, immediately prior to her first meeting with Charles VII at Chinon. According to the deposition of her trial of 1431, when Charles gave her command of an army at Blois she refused the sword he offered and instead despatched soldiers to fetch her a sword from SteCatherine-de-Fierbois. 'The best is found behind the altar of Ste-Catherine which I much love. You will find it easily, it is marked with five crosses.' From this grew the legend that Joan fought with the sword of Charles Martel—a powerful connection to make in late medieval France. But although it was almost certainly some late 14C seigneur's sword which Joan of Arc wielded, the weapon definitely came from Ste-Catherine.

It was this which inspired the building of the present **Church of Ste-Catherine**, probably undertaken by Hélie de Bourdeilles, archbishop of Tours, after 1468. Before his elevation the Franciscan de Bourdeilles was entrusted by Charles VII with examining the official verdict of heresy passed on Joan of Arc, an investigation which rehabilitated her reputation and, to medieval eyes, her soul. Her innocence was formally recognised by the Papacy in 1456, but de Bourdeilles' career took him elsewhere before his appointment to the diocese of Tours gave him the opportunity to rebuild a significant sanctuary.

The church is now little more than an architectural shell, its late medieval imagery smashed during the Wars of Religion, or lost through subsequent neglect. But it is still a handsome late Gothic building, with a two-bay chancel and nave separated by a narrow transept. The architectural detailing is quite spare, a few lean mouldings running seamlessly from the walls into the vault, and the tracery of the apse subject to a beautifully symmetrical reversal. The whole building probably went up quite slowly, since one of the high bosses carries the arms of both France and Brittany, testimony to royal involvement certainly, but either Charles VIII or Louis XII, and not Charles VII.

The vast featureless plain around here, the **Plateau de Ste-Maure**, takes its title from its largest town, **STE-MAURE-DE-TOURAINE**, a long established roadside coaching stop some 6km south of Ste-Catherine along the N10. It is very much a town of two parts, a great collection of hotels and restaurants flanking the old Paris–Bordeaux road as it sweeps down from the north, and a more ancient centre lying above a rise to the east of the main road. The old town is much the more interesting and seems to have developed in the early 11C, when the first donjon was thrown up on one of the few hills to offer broad views over the plateau. The present **Château de Ste-Maure** occupies the same site, though is now reduced to a plain two-storey *logis*, graced by a south-east angle-tower and a polygonal spiral staircase. The interior has been refurbished to house a museum of local history, best visited for its account of the making of the famous native goat's cheese, a cheese which has been recently awarded its own *appellation d'origine contrôlée*.

To the south-west of the château, and just beyond the shell of the main castle gate, the parish church of **Ste-Maure** was rebuilt in 1866 in a dimly-understood neo-Romanesque style, retaining nothing of the original save its colossal 11C and 12C crypts (open Thursday morning only). From here the Rue 11 Novembre curves above the surrounding cornfields and woodland to connect the château with Ste-Maure's great market squares, the Places 11 Novembre and du Maréchal-Leclerc. This pair of squares is in reality one single market place, divided into two unequal parts by a superb stone-built trading hall, known simply as **Les Halles**, which was commissioned in 1672 by the then seigneur Anne de Rohan. Best seen on a Friday, when the market stalls teem beneath the mutilated Rohan arms of its south door, the *halles* consist of a single tall 'nave' surrounded by low aisles on three sides. The raised central 'nave' is now used for conferences and exhibitions and is rarely open, but the splendid roof timbers of the aisles still shelter the fish and meat stalls of a Friday morning.

The rest of the town extends along the slope between the market squares and the main road, and is a very much more varied and interesting place than it might at first appear. It certainly repays strolling along the **Rue du Dr-Patry**, past the 16C half-timbering of *La Belle Image*, skirting the best of the Renaissance stone houses at No. 2 Rue Auguste-Chevallier to end among the picturesque courtyards along the back of the Ruelle Auguste-Chevallier.

West of Ste-Maure, the **Valley of the Manse** sustains a string of attractive villages whose parish churches rank among the more notable in an area renowned for the quality of its ecclesiastical architecture. At (7km) **St-Epain** the highlight of a somewhat over-restored church is an excellent 13C bell-tower, rising above a late 12C nave, early 16C north aisle and good set of ten 16C choir stalls. The church is also part of a larger composition, forming an angle with the medieval priest's houses and 15C village gate, a not uncommon arrangement in smaller walled settlements but an unusual survival none the less.

At (5km) **Crissay-sur-Manse** the church of **St-Maurice** is early 16C, with some good Flamboyant tracery and a very fine Renaissance piscina in the chancel. The village itself has a superb concentration of 15C and 16C houses built by officials serving at the court of the powerful Turpin-de-Crissé family. The huge square keep at the top of the village is probably early 12C, while the ruined *corps de logis* beneath was launched in the 15C and completed some time in the 1520s by Jacques I Turpin-de-Crissé, the seigneur responsible for seeing the church consecrated in 1527. To the south and east of here are a good dozen substantial late medieval mansions, the finest grouped around the communal well, with **La Maison de Justice** dating from c 1480, and the so-called **Maison Renaissance** and **Grand Maison** belonging to the early 16C. The population is less than a sixth of what it was during the 17C, many of the houses now acting as second homes, but it remains a beguilingly lovely place, and where on a mid-August evening you can watch a performance in the tiny theatre set up in the last remaining vigneron's *cave*.

Crissay is also just 2km south of the ruined collegiate church at **Roches-Tranchelion**, easily reached along a track just to the right of an old fortified farmhouse, but tricky to find in the first place (either take the road to the left of the Maison Renaissance in Crissay, or the second right as you head west along the D21 and then look out for signs). Like Crissay, the church dates from the early 16C, with an aisleless polygonal choir, transepts and a two bay nave, all roofless and perched on the edge of a sheer cliff. Most of the building stands to parapet level and the north transept stair-tower survives in large part—the graffiti covered walls are a pattern book of 19C and 20C calligraphy. [The *Monuments Historiques* record two 16C inscriptions '*Lancelot de la Touche bâtit une belle et notable église*' and '*V Tounner couvreulx demorant à Cryssé mil cinq cent XXII en Septembre le VIII*'. This writer did not manage to spot either among the later graffiti, but the latter, if genuine, would have an impact on the dating of the church. The major donations towards the building were recorded as made by the des Tousche family in 1522.]

The interior is quite plain but the **west front** forms a well-controlled display of early 16C Italianate decoration. The upper panels are inlaid with medallion portraits, a profile head even having escaped on to a capital to the north, and there are pilasters set with lozenges and circles and a single great arch encompassing a statue of God the Father adored by seraphim.

Another of these settlements to the north of the D21 valley road, (2km) **Avon-les-Roches**, boasts a parish church with an excellent pair of Romanesque portals. The church was extensively altered during the 13C, leaving an early 12C belfry, north doorway and a west porch of c 1150 as hostages to the earlier build. A 19C restoration blocked the north door and moved its portal to the south of the porch, while the porch itself lost the original arrangement of open arches which would have seen the north wall mimic the south. It sounds more complicated than it is, but even in this disordered state it remains an evocative composition, a sort of miniaturised version of the porch at Loches, with two archivolt figures (said to be St Peter and St Luke) which again suggest the involvement of sculptors from the Saintonge.

West of Avon-les-Roches the D21 plunges through the vineyards, skirting yet another village, (9km) **Cravant-les-Coteaux**, whose centre lies off to the north. Prior to the construction of a new church in 1863, the de facto centre was in what became known as **Cravant-le-Vieux-Bourg**, 1km along the D44, but the decision to remove parochial services to the roadside village led to the eventual preservation of Cravant's Romanesque church of **St-Léger** as a small lapidary museum. This is best known for the exterior treatment of its nave, a dazzling exhibition of geometrically varied stonework whose inventive rhythms put even those of nearby Rivière in the shade. The nave is often described as Carolingian, these exercises in pattern-making equated with the use of herringbone coursing, but the close relationship between Cravant and both St-Mexme at Chinon and Azay-le-Rideau argues for a date in the mid-11C.

When first built the nave terminated in a simple apse, and the existing 12C extension involved demolishing the earlier eastern wall to construct a new choir. The one other alteration was made in the early 15C when the local seigneur and intimate of Charles VII, Charles de la Trémoïlle, added a chapel to the south and commissioned a fairly crude wall painting for its western wall, featuring himself and his three daughters offering prayers to the Virgin and Child. The interior is in a poor state, but the lapidary museum houses the 13C cloister columns from nearby Croulay and a few good late 16C foliate capitals. The rest is the usual jumble of ammonites, agricultural tools and cobwebs, but one feels an effort is being made. And to the west the D21 wends a delightful 8km through the vines to the altogether more decisive aspects of Chinon.

B. Via Richelieu and L'Ile-Bouchard

West of Le Grand-Pressigny, the D42 follows the rapidly broadening valley of the Claise, fostering the flood meadows as far as (7km) **Abilly**. A prehistoric archaeological site has been consolidated on the eastern edge of the village, exposing four successive eras of occupation, from the Paleolithic to the Gallo-Roman, all reasonably identifiable beneath the encompassing hangar, though the promised expository material will make for a better display.

5km downstream, just beyond the confluence of the rivers Claise and Creuse, the market town of **Descartes** recalls the eponymous 17C philosopher René, born in Châtellerault in 1590 but rushed by his mother to the village of La Haye for baptism, before spending most of his childhood in Descartes. The town is now a scrappy collection of 19C terraces and through-roads, though the heavily restored house where René Descartes was raised, No. 29 Rue Descartes, acts as a small museum (open 14–18 only, closed Tues) with a few engravings and personal mementoes, relics of a career spent mostly at Dutch Universities and which saw his seminal *Discourse on the Method* published in 1637.

West of Descartes, there are a number of routes to Richelieu, the most direct being to follow the D5 along the left bank of the river Creuse and, after you cross the (10km) bridge over the Vienne at the meeting of the two rivers, pick up the D107 to (7km) **Marigny-Marmande**. Of no particular interest in itself, Marigny-Marmande is a significant rural market and road junction, from whence the D20 will take you straight to (16km) Richelieu.

If moved by great churches fallen on hard times, you might make a slight **detour** via **Bois-Aubry**, 3km north along the D110 to the right of which a well-signposted lane leads to the remains of the (1km) abbey of **St-Michel-de-Bois-Aubry**. Initially founded as a chapel by Robert the Hermit, c 1080, Bois-Aubry was created a dependent priory of the abbey of Tiron in 1118 in response to the petition of a group of Robert's disciples. Tiron was the mother-house of a small monastic order, Cistercian in all but name, which would have been attracted by Bois-Aubry's remoteness, but, in the event, Tiron had little to do with the abbey's architectural and sculptural forms. These are rooted in a further shift in status, for in 1138 the archbishop of Tours made the priory an autonomous Benedictine abbey, from which decision came most of the buildings you might still see on the site. That these can be visited is due to the purchase of Bois-Aubry by a small community of Orthodox monks in 1978, but the monks are currently unable to find the resources necessary to revive the ruins as a monastic complex. As the intended restorations may or may not take place, the following account must be considered provisional.

The **monastic church** has lost its two westernmost bays but it is clear from the lower portions of the nave, where the unmoulded arches of several blocked window openings can be seen, that the earliest surviving fabric probably dates from Bois-Aubry's days as a priory, i.e. 1118–38. This church was subsequently heightened c 1160 and its nave divided into four square bays, whose clustered wall-shafts and capitals rise to support a high ribbed vault (the two surviving bays of nave vaulting were replaced c 1250). To the east, the choir and transepts were extensively refurbished in the early 14C, while the obviously once splendid *jubé* (screen)—originally separating the monks' choir from the western areas of the church and now jammed against the west wall of the truncated nave—dates from c 1470.

The **conventual buildings** to the south are mostly late 12C, with the recently restored chapter house the earliest, its capitals reminiscent of mid-12C sculpture in and around Le Mans. Of the rest, the dormitory is still roofed, one wall of the refectory stands and the old warming-house and library in the west range retains a good 16C fireplace. But the finest structure is the **bell tower**, sunk against the north wall of the transept and majestically rising through four stages to culminate in a superb octagonal spire. Its upper stages and buttressing are 15C, while the lower chamber houses the most exciting find of the 1980s restorations: a splendid tomb effigy, clearly indebted to the forms of the Plantagenet tombs at Fontevraud, and perhaps the late 12C tomb of Bois-Aubry's principal abbot-builder, Clément.

West of Bois-Aubry, a combination of the D110, D58 and D757 will bring you through the cornfields and into (17km) **RICHELIEU**. Approaching the town from this direction takes you through the 19C Porte de la Clôture du Parc and into the Place des Religeuses, but in order to get a measure of 17C Richelieu it is worth first turning left at the Porte du Gare, and following the enceinte wall round as far as the **Place du Cardinal**.

When Cardinal Armand Jean du Plessis de Richelieu regained control of the family estate of *Richeloc* or *Richelieu* in 1624, virtually nothing stood on the site of the present town. A castle had been established on the right bank of the river Mâble in the late 12C and was rebuilt during the late 15C, but a decline in the du Plessis family fortunes seems to have left the château in a poor state of repair, and nothing in Cardinal Richelieu's rapid and brilliant rise prior to 1624 suggests he took any serious interest in it. What precisely altered his outlook is unclear; wealth, status, seigneurial responsibilities must all have played a role, but in 1631 the Cardinal determined to build a new château and simultaneously embarked on the creation of a new town. On 17 May 1631, by letters patent, Louis XIII authorised the establishment of a borough 'enclosed by walls and ditches, with market halls, lodgings, banks, shops and other commodities', and in August the old fief of Richelieu was raised to the rank of duchy. The town was laid out to the north of this new château, above the left bank of the Mâble, the old du Plessis stronghold being retained until c 1638 when work on Richelieu's great palace was well advanced, and parochial responsibilities were transferred from Les Sablons to Notre-Dame-de-Richelieu.

Little, apart from the grounds and a few fragmentary structures, remains of the Cardinal's **Château de Richelieu**, the greater part having been demolished in 1805. What does survive is now administered by the Sorbonne, the last Duc de Richelieu having given the estates to the University of Paris in 1930. The château was designed by Louis XIII's architect, Jacques Le Mercier, along an east–west axis, i.e. at right angles to the town, with two outer or *basse cours* leading to the great inner *cour d'honneur*. The only part of the château proper still standing, the **dôme**, lay at the centre of the south wing of the middle court, a significant position but hardly one which calls for the sort of architectural ornament with which the main residential wing was embellished. There is a small exhibition of engravings and models in the *dôme*, which amply bears out the opinion of contemporaries that Richelieu's château was among the greatest buildings of the reign of Louis XIII. Richelieu furnished his house with two statues by Michelangelo, originally destined for the tomb of Pope Julius II, placed either side of the principal door (the 'Dying Slaves'), and a phenomenal array of paintings by Mantegna, Perugino, Lorenzo Costa, Poussin, Titian, Rubens and Van Dyck. These were seized by the Revolutionary Directoire after the château was confiscated in 1792, and eventually distributed between the Louvre, Versailles, Orléans and Tours. To the east of the *dôme*, the platform which once supported the *logis d'honneur* retains its original moats and bridge and, beyond what were the formal *parterres*, an orangery and wine cellar escaped demolition. Sadly this is all that remains of one of the most important houses to grace 17C France.

The **town**, by contrast, survives in large part, with relatively few 19C or 20C buildings rising within the enceinte to dilute its 17C forms. The creation of a new town in the early 17C has obvious parallels elsewhere in France—Sully's 1605 foundation of Henrichemont (Cher), for instance, or, more spectacularly, Charles de Gonzague's Charleville-Mézières (Ardennes) of 1608—and Richelieu built on these precedents with considerable entrepreneurial flair. To manage the project the Cardinal assembled a committee variously consisting of the architects Jacques, Pierre and François Le Mercier; the Parisian financiers Jean Thiriot and Jean Bourbet; the *chef de projet* Henri de Sourdis, bishop of Maillezais; and the property dealer Alphonse de Loppez—the all-powerful intermediary between the Cardinal, the builders and the buyers.

The **enceinte** was planned as a rectangle some 690m by 390m, enclosed by a wall whose exterior was protected by ditches and a counterscarp and pierced by three gates: the Porte de Chinon to the north, Porte du Château to the south, and Porte de Loudun to the west. The ditches and counterscarp now mostly accommodate vegetable gardens. Further gates have at various times been cut through the wall, or again blocked up, but the circuit of these walls is largely intact and determines the organisation of the town as a whole.

Richelieu was planned around a symmetrical grid with two large squares, the Places du Marché and des Religieuses, to the north and south of the main gates. These were connected by the Grande Rue which acted as the town's main thoroughfare, forming an intersection with the Rue Traversière to divide Richelieu into four equal rectangles. Subsidiary streets were run behind the Grande Rue connecting with the secondary cross axes to either side of the main squares. The grid is also governed by a system of modular measurements, whose principal unit is ten square *toises* (1 *toise* is approximately equal to 2 metres). The houses along the Grande Rue all occupy 10-*toise* plots. The longest terrace is the length of seven of these 10-*toise* units. The depth of the blocks between the axial streets is four units, and an angle terrace in the main squares represents two units. The advertised prices were equally precise. An *hôtel* on the Grande Rue was 10,000 *livres*, one of the smaller properties on a main square 8000 *livres*, and the huge mansions opposite the north and south gates 16,000 *livres*. The historian Paul Fénelon has pointed out that none of the Cardinal's contemporaries at court bothered to purchase houses in Richelieu, and that most were eventually rented out to traders with little use for their *grandes salles* and high ceilings. Nonetheless, by 1709 the town had a population of more than 3000, which is some 800 more than are listed on the current electoral roll.

Entering the town by the **Porte du Château** brings you straight into the **Place du Marché**, the most lively of the two main squares and the best place from which to survey the town. It also affords a first glimpse of the finest of the 17C terraces built before the Cardinal's death in 1642, either side of the **Grande Rue**. Each house has been given two windows to either side of a courtyard arch, creating a consistent rhythm along the entire street. This rhythm is also echoed in the dormers, or at least in those houses where the original roof and dormer windows survive. But apart from the roofscape and the odd modern shop window, the street elevation is essentially that of the early 17C. The commitment to symmetry is impressive, and best exemplified by standing in front of any door or window along the street (there are two exceptions) and turning round to face an exactly equal and opposite door or window.

The major buildings are grouped around the Place du Marché, with Pierre Le Mercier's superb timber market **halle** of c 1637 to the east, host to the Monday and Friday markets, and the parish church of **Notre-Dame-deRichelieu** to the west.

The church was one of the earlier structures to be planned, the foundation stone being laid in 1632 and the first baptism celebrated in the completed eastern bays in 1637. It was designed by Pierre Le Mercier as an occidented basilica, meaning the sanctuary and altar are at the west and the processional entrance is an east front, with a short choir, contained transepts and a four bay nave. As in the rest of the town, the commitment to rectangular forms is paramount, so that the aisle walls are contained within a single outline from the entrance right through to a pair of eastern chapels. The latter support some dismal 19C paintings by Pauthe de Béziers, and, except for the altar and tabernacles in the north chapel and the clerestory glass, all the 17C fittings have been lost. Even the huge altarpiece showing the Assumption of the Virgin is a copy of Charles Lamy's mid-18C retable. The architectural frame has been better treated, however, and Pierre Le Mercier's geometric sensibilities and deployment of very simple, shallowly carved detailing have conspired to create something akin to Cardinal Richelieu's ideal of 'austere majesty'.

Pierre Le Mercier died in 1639 and is buried in the south transept, but his portrait—the architect seen musing on the plans with the church acting as a backdrop—can be seen in the small **Musée Municipal** on the first floor of the Hôtel-de-Ville. This museum also houses a good stock of 17C engravings of Richelieu's château by Jean Marot and Gabriel Pérelle, and a few remnants of the château's internal furnishings.

The first village you come across after leaving Richelieu by the Chinon gate (6km along the D749) is **CHAMPIGNY-SUR-VEUDE**, founded initially as a Gallo-Roman settlement and revived in the late 11C, when the counts of Anjou established a castle above the river. Nothing is known of this early fortress, as in 1477 Louis I de Bourbon inherited the seigneurie and began building the present **château** after his return from Charles VIII's Italian campaigns, eradicating all traces of any earlier structures. Construction was a long-winded affair, and the *communs* were only completed shortly before the death of Louis II de Bourbon in 1582. The tangled alliances of the Bourbon family led to the seigneurie passing by marriage into the hands of Gaston d'Orléans, Louis XIII's brother, and, after his exile from Louis' court in 1634, Cardinal Richelieu constrained him to exchange Champigny for Bois-le-Vicomte. It was said that the Cardinal was jealous of the splendour of Champigny, and that he was looking for a means of supplying stone for his new buildings at Richelieu, but, though his demolition of the *logis d'honneur* bears out the former rumour, his sparing of the *communs* and chapel throws some doubt on the latter. The rest would have gone during the Revolution but for de Quinson's intervention in 1791, and the wily *Receveur-Général* had the *communs* refurbished and restored the chapel.

The core of the **communs** is late 16C, the ornament largely confined to de Quinson's dormer windows, with a grand platform the sole reminder of the late 15C *logis d'honneur*. The **chapel** survives in splendid form however, and, unlike the *communs*, can be visited. Architecturally this is a good, freestanding, aisleless castle chapel, of the type destined to acquire a portion of the True Cross and become known as a Sainte Chapelle, and in its general form is not dissimilar to that of the château at Ussé. It was laid out in 1507, though the handling of the wall shafts, buttressing and vaults suggests little work was done before the 1530s, and the aggressively neo-classical porch certainly post-dates the consecration of 1545. Ornament is confined to the vertical supports—the internal wall shafts, for instance, support a rich repertoire of lozenges, shaft-rings and scroll-work, whose canopies were almost certainly intended to shelter statues of the 12 apostles.

This leaves the walls largely free for glass, and the glass which fills the windows here is not only amongst the finest early 16C **stained glass** to survive in Europe, it is also one of the few cycles to survive in its entirety. The windows were commissioned in 1538 by Claude, Cardinal de Givry, to celebrate the marriage of his niece, Jacquette de Longwy, to Louis II de Bourbon. The identity of the master glazier is unknown, but the stylistic consistency of so large a cycle is striking, and suggests it is the work of a single shop. Each window is treated in three registers, with scenes from the Passion and Resurrection at the very head of each frame, episodes from the Life of St-Louis beneath, and, at the base, illustrious members of the Valois and Bourbon families matched with portraits of Cardinal de Givry and Jacquette de Longwy. These lower registers are clearly identified with French inscriptions—an understandable precaution where dynastic pedigree and earthly fame are at stake, more unusual when it comes to the Life of St-Louis. And it is this commitment to a clearly ordered arrangement of images which lies behind the brilliance and clarity of the glass, creating one of the most tightly controlled and legible pictorial sequences of Renaissance France.

North-east of Champigny, the D113 climbs through fields of maize and sunflowers, cresting a ridge beyond the Lémeré crossroads to reveal the soft contours of the valley of the Vienne, and bringing you to the river by the quiet market town of (10km) **L'Ile-Bouchard**.

The river island is first mentioned as L'Ile-Bouchard in 1189, though a local seigneur by the name of Bouchard probably raised a donjon here at the end of the 10C, facilitating control of what was an important medieval river crossing. The later castle, which came to dominate the island, was destroyed in the 17C, leaving a large market square (the Place Bouchard), the Mairie and a couple of cafés to occupy the site.

By the 12C, however, the town had developed subsidiary settlements to either side of the river, and a total of four parishes were founded to serve a population considerably in excess of today's. The parish of St-Pierre on the island was suppressed in 1465, but something survives of the churches of the remaining three, with the ruined apse of the **Prieuré de St-Léonard** in the southern town the most interesting of the trio.

Although it was awarded parochial responsibilities in the mid-12C, St-Léonard seems to have been founded as a Benedictine priory, a daughter-house of Déols, some time before 1108. Little more is known about the church, and virtually all that now stands is a semi-roofless apse ambulatory, shorn of its axial chapel. This must once have been splendid, and is certainly ambitious, with columnar piers and a blind triforium reminiscent of the soaring proportions of the choir at Fontevraud. The ability of the builders to raise the church obviously outstripped their ability to buttress it efficiently, hence the later blocking of the arcade which so diminishes the impact of the **historiated capitals** around the apse. These are usually dated on stylistic grounds to c 1150, the four major capitals carved on all faces and the subjects here described from north to south, left to right: 1. Annunciation; Visitation; Angel ordering Joseph to return to Bethlehem; Nativity; Annunciation to the Shepherds; Adoration of the Magi. 2. Baptism; Massacre of the Innocents; Presentation in the Temple; Flight into Egypt. 3. Crucifixion; Last Supper; Betrayal? 4. Triumphal Entry into Jerusalem; Noli Me Tangere; Temptation; Arrest of Christ.

North of here, **St-Maurice** boasts a good hexagonal belfry and spire of 1480, and a superb freestanding early 16C choir stall with an Annunciation and Flight into Egypt carved on the side panels, and a Christ among the Doctors on the misericord. The arm rests are also shaped out of representations of the sculptors at work, both the quality and form of the piece suggesting that it was made for the prior of a significant abbey or collegiate foundation.

The last of the group of churches lies above the north bank of the Vienne, at the bottom of the sinuous **Avenue de la Liberté**. **St-Gilles** is the earliest documented foundation, the Archbishop of Tours having blessed the laying of the first three stones of the apse in 1067. The greater part of the church is probably late 11C, the north aisle having been added as the population expanded c 1130, and the choir replaced in the 15C. An appalling late 19C 'restoration' has stripped the interior of whatever subtleties it might once have possessed, and one is left to muse on some good fragments of 16C glass in the choir, along with a late 11C belfry and west portal.

To the **west of L'Ile-Bouchard** the D760 crosses the flood plains of the Vienne, the silty meadows now planted with maize, leaving the vines to the chalk slopes above the north bank. At (3km) **TAVANT** the road passes between two important Romanesque churches; the one to the north, Ste-Marie, was founded as a priory of the great abbey of Marmoutier, with the southern church, St-Nicolas, the domain of the parish. The history of the two is entwined, for Ste-Marie was built after a fire destroyed the earlier church in 1070, while St-Nicolas seems to have followed c 1100 as a means of reserving the priory for the sole use of the Benedictine congregation. Little now survives of **Ste-Marie**—elements of an aisle wall are preserved in a private house by the Place Ste-Anne, along with the 15C bell tower, and the buildings you see off the beautiful Cour du Prieuré either incorporate or reuse the conventual quarters.

St-Nicolas survives in better shape, despite the loss of its aisles and the disconcerting truncation of its octagonal crossing tower. Though the church is best known for its **wall paintings**, the **sculpture** includes a finely-judged west portal and a set of crossing capitals which include a depiction of the Fall, amidst a popular stock of serpents and chimeras. The paintings are on two distinct levels. The choir is enhanced by a huge Christ in Majesty in the apse semi-dome, with a fragmentary narrative cycle covering the barrel vault to the west, opening with an Annunciation and extending as far as the Flight into Egypt. All this seems likely to date from c 1150, and bears no relationship to the celebrated cycle of paintings in the **crypt**.

This sense of division would have been keenly felt during the Middle Ages, for the only entrance to the crypt was originally via an exterior north door, and the area is in effect a quite separate, and possibly exclusively monastic, chapel. Despite this, the iconographical scheme seems to work from west to east. Presumably, after entering from the north, you turned right along the aisle, then round to face the altar flanked by two nimbused female figures holding elegant and stylised lilies of purity. It is certainly when standing here that the area comes into focus, for Tavant's is a tiny hall crypt, with eight monolithic columns dividing the space into three aisles and a set of groin vaults which were entirely plastered and painted at some point in the early 12C.

It has been said that 'for lightness of touch and sheer windswept delicacy of feeling these paintings have no equals in the Romanesque wall paintings of Europe', a sentiment which this writer would happily endorse. The exhilarating fluency and confidence with which the figures are outlined has also led some commentators to compare their style to late Anglo-Saxon manuscript illuminations, and that peculiar combination of vibrancy and isolation in the small-scale figures does have something of the quality of manuscript painting. One even suspects that manuscript illustrations were the source for a number of the allegorical themes. However, there is little agreement about Tavant's meaning. The subjects can change quite suddenly, and, although there is a movement from Old to New Testament themes as you move eastwards, it is not emphatic and is embroiled in a marvellously rich series of personifications, as if a type of moral discourse were taking place. The breadth of these figures is astonishing, ranging from the Shame of Adam and Eve, David Harping, and Saul Enthroned, to a Deposition of Christ, Harrowing of Hell, and Christ in Majesty. And amidst these Biblical scenes a tumbling descant of contemporary or classical voices is heard—a pilgrim carrying a staff and palm, a knight doing battle with a devil, Sagittarius, an Orant, and Luxuria, the harrowing personification of lust thrusting a lance into her own bosom.

Below Tavant, the D760 swings south of the old riverside settlements, relieving the delightful Rivière of any traffic congestion and, joining the D749, crosses the Vienne to reveal a view of stunning majesty— Henry II's mighty château above the town of (14km) Chinon.

Chinon

History. Chinon's situation, with the old town caught between the limestone crags of the Landes du Ruchard and the Vienne, is the key to its historical significance, a position which combined security from attack with the guarantee of trade along one of the major watercourses of western France, a position wherein one might cultivate a strategic outlook.

The earliest town-dwellers were Gallo-Roman, who established an *oppidum*, known as *Caino*, on the plateau above the river. This original settlement was subsequently encircled by a wall, in all likelihood in the early 4C, but by c 400 had fallen to the Visigoths, who encouraged an already established secondary settlement closer to the banks of the river, beneath the present château. With this move came Christianity. Brice, St-Martin's successor as bishop of Tours (397–442), founded a church which he dedicated to St-Martin and—according to Gregory of Tours, writing in the late 6C—another of Martin's disciples, Maxime (later known as St-Mexme), established a monastery. Maxime was evidently considered a saint within his own lifetime, and was credited with repulsing a siege on the part of the renegade Roman general Aegidius and a Frankish army in 463—the power of his prayers provoking a violent storm which forced the attackers to flee. These two foundations were joined by a third in the 6C, after a Breton hermit, Jean, had adopted one of the *tuffeau* caves in the cliff-face to the east of Caino, inspiring Queen Radegonde to seek his advice on the collapse of her marriage to Clothaire and the possibility of establishing a nunnery near Poitiers.

The existence of three religious foundations at so early a date bestowed considerable importance on Chinon, an importance confirmed by the existence of a substantial Merovingian mint in the town by the late 6C. With the decay of Carolingian government, however, Chinon passed into the hands of the Counts of Blois, who in the mid-10C raised the first donjon at a point where the cliff is least precipitous. A few archaeological discoveries suggest this may have been the site of the Gallo-Roman *oppidum*, but it was emphatically the site on which the great medieval castle grew, and a position from which the Counts of Blois exchanged threats with the emerging county of Anjou. In the event Chinon followed Tours, and was swallowed into greater Anjou in 1044, Count Geoffroy Martel celebrating his advance by rebuilding the castle and consolidating its southern walls.

With Angevin patronage the town began to expand, tentatively at first, rapidly in the second half of the 12C under Henry II (Plantagenet). Henry recognised in Chinon a possible haven from which to control his vast feudal empire. It was midway between Aquitaine and the Channel, the climate was good, and there were few sqabbling local barons to contend with. Henry began to pour money into Chinon, building an enceinte wall to protect the lower town, financing the rebuilding of the parish church of St-Maurice, and expanding the château to create the largest 12C fortress in Europe. This mighty complex, Henry's beloved 'castle in the middle of France' stood at the very centre of Plantagenet political life, the favourite residence of its king, a frequent meeting place for his court and, on 6 July 1189, the place where the creator of the most dynamic empire of 12C Europe died. Chinon's heyday was brief, for Henry was only 56 when he died, worn out, betrayed by his sons and crying 'shame on a conquered king'.

Henry's death intensified the struggle for control of western France, and the pressure brought by Philip Augustus on first Richard Coeur-de-Lion and then John led to the forfeiture of all Plantagenet dominions in France in 1202, and the eventual bloody surrender of Touraine by Hubert de Burgh in 1205. With Chinon a fief of the French crown, the town lapsed into provinciality. Philippe le Bel turned the castle into a prison, throwing the last of the Templars into the Coudray Tower in 1308, and it was not until the Hundred Years War that the potential of the place was again recognised. In 1416 the future Charles VII moved into the château, and in 1427 transferred the apparatus of court and government to Chinon. Charles and his Queen, Marie d'Anjou, Yolande d'Aragon, titular Queen of Sicily, and the palace officers and royal guard were installed at the château, while the rest of the court officials were lodged in the town. It was here that Joan of Arc first met Charles VII in 1429, and from Chinon that she set out to raise the siege of Orléans. The impact this had on the town cannot be overstated, both in terms of the place it came to occupy in the telling of French history and in terms of the urban fabric. For the great townhouses built by courtiers in the early 15C provoked a wave of mercantile building in the late 15C and 16C, and with that the present-day structure of Chinon was laid down.

Château de Chinon. Although it is those magnificent curtain walls that dominate the scene when you approach Chinon from the south, unfolding westwards for over a quarter of a mile, the **Château de Chinon** is now but a shadow of its former self. By the early 17C the French monarchy had lost all interest in their former Loire valley residences, either making them over to relatives or mistresses, or selling them. Chinon was also hopelessly outmoded by then, the last structures having been added during the late 15C, and so in 1633 Louis XIII sold the château to Cardinal Richelieu. Richelieu seems to have been initially attracted to the idea of demolishing the château and re-using the site, but, in the event, he simply left it to languish and the buildings gradually disintegrated. Total collapse was only averted in 1855 when Prosper Merimée stepped in, and commissioned the Saumur architect Joly-Leterme to launch the first of the restorations. By this date most of the internal structures had vanished, and Joly-Leterme concentrated his efforts on saving the curtain walls, angle towers and Coudray Keep, but, even so, the thinking which lay behind the castle is readily apparent.

To speak of Chinon as one château is perhaps misleading, for it consists of three axially arranged forts, separated by their own internal walls and ditches and linked only by drawbridges. Embracing all three

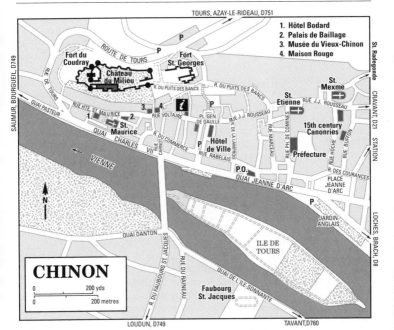

1. Hôtel Bodard
2. Palais de Baillage
3. Musée du Vieux-Chinon
4. Maison Rouge

is a vast curtain wall, approximately rectangular and enclosing an area of 400m by 70m. Henry II was responsible for the adoption of this arrangement and, as with his construction of the north-east curtain wall at Dover castle, it was to exert an almost mesmerising influence over the military architecture of the next two generations. For, although Henry's defences are sequential rather than concentric, they still provide a number of fall-back positions, requiring an attacker to breach a whole series of walls and rendering him liable to counter-attack when exposed within the ditches or baileys. The vulnerable eastern flank overlooking the plateau was secured by an advanced redoubt, called the **Fort St-Georges** after its collegiate chapel, which was separated from the middle castle by a deep gully and a system of angle towers and inner walls. The Château de Milieu occupied the central spaces and enclosed the main bailey, while the Fort du Coudray housed the major keep and prevented any attack from the town side.

Little survives of the Fort St-Georges and you now enter the château via a bridge which brings you straight into the **Château du Milieu**. The sheer size of this inner bailey can come as a shock, even after you have digested the fact that the curtain walls are almost half the length of the entire town, and with this sort of space comes flexibility. The few buildings which now stand against the southern wall occupy less than one tenth of the bailey, and the area originally provided accommodation for a standing garrison, as well as the mass of servants, laundry women, cooks, blacksmiths, pig keepers and assorted camp followers who formed the domestic core of castle life.

The most imposing survivor is the **Tour de l'Horloge**, a late 14C gate tower whose four floors now house the **Musée Jeanne d'Arc**. The famous story of the meeting between Joan of Arc and Charles VII in the castle on 8 March 1429 is well set out both here and in the Logis Royaux to the west. Briefly, Joan arrived in Chinon on 6 March 1429, in the company of six soldiers who had ridden with her from Domremy in the Champagne. She lodged in the town while waiting for an audience at the château, and when one was granted two days later, Charles VII attempted to disguise himself by swapping robes with a courtier. Indifferent to this ruse Joan addressed Charles directly, saying 'The King of Heaven sends word by me that you shall be annointed and crowned in the city of Reims. You are the heir to France and true son of the king'. Given that his father was mad and his mother had taken a number of lovers, Charles was famously plagued by doubts as to his own legitimacy, but he seems to have been wholly convinced by Joan, and on 20 April gave her command of an army. On 26 April she raised her standard at Blois, on 8 May relieved Orléans, and, having inflicted two serious defeats on the English in June, accompanied Charles to his coronation in Reims on 17 July. The rest of the exhibits in the small museum are concerned with Joan's subsequent arrest and trial at Rouen in 1431, enhanced by a few 19C engravings and a 13C jacket of chainmail uncovered from the battlefield at Lewes.

The most extensive of the remaining buildings within the Château du Milieu are the **Logis Royaux**. These are largely ruinous but house an audio-visual exhibition and two 16C Flemish tapestries in the early 15C west rooms, and expose a very grand late Gothic fireplace from the old great hall on what has become an outside wall. North of here the **Tour d'Argenton** was built towards the end of the 15C as a bulwark by Philippe de Commines, governor of the castle, superimposing vaulted chambers over three storeys and acting as a spur to protect the Coudray ditch. To reach the **Fort du Coudray** you need to cross this ditch, the present drawbridge bringing you out between the 12C Tour de Boissy and the **Coudray Keep**. The latter was raised by Philip Augustus after 1205, a superb cylindrical keep of a type the French monarchy favoured when reinforcing the major castles of newly won domains, as, for example, in the contemporary Talbot Tower at Falaise. The rooms themselves are also circular, connected by a stair vice built within the 3m thick walls, and have accommodated some celebrated names: Jacques de Molay, the last Grand Master of the Knights Templar was imprisoned here in 1308, along with Rimbaud de Carton and Geoffroy de Gonneville, commanders of Cyprus and Normandy respectively; and tradition maintains that Joan of Arc was given the upper chamber after her first meeting with Charles VII. Although it does not immediately strike one this way, the Coudray Keep is not all that different to Henry II's keep, built out above the south-west angle of the Coudray fort and now known as the **Tour du Moulin**. Keeps are places of last resort, strongpoints. They are not intended as a principal residence, or at least not in a large castle, and the emphasis in both these keeps is on enclosing vaulted chambers within thick walls, one room per floor. The difference is that Henry's keep is not circular—the internal rooms are in fact hexagonal—and that it overlooks the town.

The easiest way to get into the **town** from the château is to take the Rue Puy-des-Bancs, turning sharply right to descend the Rue Jeanne d'Arc. This brings you out by **Le Grand-Carroi** (great crossroads), where the medieval main street of Chinon, the **Rue St-Maurice**, intersected with a street leading down to the bridge over the river Vienne. It is also where you will find the greatest concentration of late medieval half-timbered houses, with Nos 28, 30 and 31 substantially mid-15C, No. 45 dating from c 1500, and the much celebrated, though heavily restored, **Maison Rouge** said to date from c 1400. The latter dating is locally important, for during the late Middle Ages the Maison Rouge was next to the Hostellerie du Grand-Carroi, which was where Joan of Arc stayed while waiting for an audience with Charles VII in 1429. The temptation is to try to visualise the streetscape she might have known, with No. 34 also alleged to be of c 1400. The *Societé des Amis du Vieux-Chinon* have taken matters a stage further by constructing a mock well alongside No. 34, in an attempt to recreate the well head Joan was said to use to help her dismount when at the *hostellerie*.

Whatever the relative dates, it is a splendid streetscape, the timber and inlaid brick of the taverns and mercantile housing creating deep splashes of colour when juxtaposed with the bleached *tuffeau* of the aristocratic *hôtels particuliers*. One of the best of the latter, No. 44, hosted Charles VII's assembly of the Estates General in October, 1428, and now houses the **Musée du Vieux-Chinon**. The delegates met in the great hall on the first floor, whose long walls and beamed ceiling survive from the early 15C structure, but which was considerably shortened some time after the present street façade was added in the early 16C. The collections are eclectic, with some good late medieval panelling and statuary placed alongside a plaster-cast of the important 11C Crucifixion plaque from St-Mexme (the original has been badly damaged by water from a faulty gutter in the last 20 years).

The so-called **Chape de St-Mexme** (cope of St-Mexme) is conserved on the second floor, a sumptuous 11C Arabic silk woven with a repeated design of affronted lions, which was probably made as a mantle for a horse, the trophy of some returning crusader? The rest of the second floor is given over to boat-building and navigation on the Loire and its tributaries, alongside a few engravings and models of pre-19C Chinon. Eugène Delacroix's rather routine portrayal of François Rabelais, an exhibit at the Salon of 1834, rounds up the collection in the great hall below.

Continuing west along the **Rue Haute St-Maurice** you will discover a tremendous range of fine vernacular building: the late 17C galleried stairway of the **Hôtel du Gouvernment** (No. 48); the 19C Neo-Gothic gables of the **Hostellerie Gargantua** (No. 73); the restrained late 15C carving of the stair-tower of **No. 62**; the 17C town gates bizarrely mounted beneath the 16C dormer windows of the **Hôtel Bodard** (No. 81); all of which bring vivacity and breadth to a marvellously varied street.

The largest of the buildings along the south flank of the Rue Haute St-Maurice is the parish church of **St-Maurice**, a foundation first mentioned in the 10C, and one whose fabric reflects the peaks of Chinon's medieval prosperity. The bell tower is late 11C, with a north aisle (originally the nave) of c 1180 the result of a donation from Henry II, and a south aisle built on the back of bourgeois patronage in 1543. The church Henry II knew was aisleless, and was treated to a good set of 'Angevin' vaults whose cardinal ribs are supported by tiny figures, while a crown of angels clasps the central bosses. The sculptural treatment is similar to that of the parish church at Fontevraud, also financed by Henry, and is plausibly the work of the same masons and stonecarvers, but the disfiguring cloak of late 19C paint and heavy restoration make detailed analysis hazardous.

The south aisle is simpler, aligned with the refurbished 14C south chapel, but with a tierceron vault and bosses which originally would have carried guild or confraternity devices. Otherwise the building has been stripped of its medieval fittings, a copy of a very beautiful Virgin and Child of 1518 by Cima da Conegliano can just be seen in the western tribune, the original despatched to the Louvre in 1812, and the choir houses a 17C Crucifixion. The rest is more recent—even the ostensibly late 15C spire was reconstructed at the end of the last century.

East of St-Maurice, the Rue du Palais curves right to avoid the 16C rear façade of the **Hostellerie Gargantua**, less dramatically restored than the front and in fact built as the principal elevation when the structure served as the Palais de Bailliage, the residence of the town bailiff. Further east, the 16C courts and houses off the **Rue de la Poterne** give way to the 18C artisans' terraces lining the **Rue du Commerce**, bringing you into the modern centre of Chinon around the **Place du Général de Gaulle**. Built in the late 19C, as an elongated rectangle at right angles to the medieval town axes, the Place runs north from Emile Hébert's 1882 statue of François Rabelais to the bank of pavement cafés gathered around the circular Font des Trois Grâces. The principal buildings are also late 19C, the **Hôtel-de-Ville** having replaced an earlier timber market hall and forcing the present Thursday markets to spill around the Place in the open air.

Continuing east, the **Rue Jean-Jacques Rousseau** passes the splendid Louis XII and François I pastiche of 1880 at No 59, and leads to the most important of Chinon's surviving medieval churches. The first church you come to is **St-Etienne** (open 15–19 in summer—if closed out of season the presbytery is just round the corner on the Rue Urbain-Grandier), an aisleless late Gothic barn of a church, built to replace a late 11C structure and retaining the lower storey of a Romanesque tower to act as the base of the present belfry. Work seems to have begun in the early 15C, with the nave in building during the Tours archiepis-copacy of Jean Bernard (1441–68), whose arms are emblazoned on the vault keystone of the third nave bay. The final phase benefited from the interest of Philippe de Commines, governor of the château, who was probably responsible for inviting the Tours architect Robert Mesnager to work on the building. Mesnager was presumably responsible for the **west front**, whose powerful twin portal is the one extravagance to enliven the church. This incorporates the arms of Chinon, above those of Philippe de Commines and Guibert, archbishop of Tours, which, along with the fragmentary late 12C wall painting from St-

The river Cher near
Selles-sur-Cher

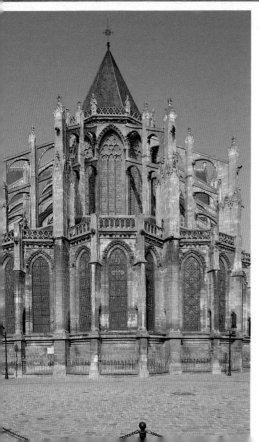

Tours: exterior of
cathedral apse

Loches: Tour Sorel and late 14th century wing of the Logis Royal

St-Epain: town gate, priest's house and church

Asnières-sur-Vègre

Meeting of the rivers Loire and Vienne at Candes-St-Martin

Lavardin: interior of the late 11th century church of St-Genest looking east

Vendôme: early 16th century misericord from La Trinité illustrating grapepicking (September)

Le Lude: porcupine, early 16th century, the device of Louis XII, from the north wall of the château

St-Denis-d'Anjou: 16th century wall painting depicting the Feast of Herod and Vision of St-Hubert

*Plessis-Bourré:
Jean Bourré's late
15th century château
seen from the south-
east*

*Angers: Maison
d'Adam*

Montreuil-Bellay: gardens, walls and château

Pontigné: early 13th century wall painting from St-Denis showing the Raising of Lazarus

St-Florent-le-Vieil: David d'Angers' 1825 tomb of the Marquis de Bonchamps

St-Aubin-de-Luigné: early 16th century house of Jean de Pontoise, now the Mairie

Mexme now positioned along the north wall, constitute the best of the medieval work in a building much altered by 19C intervention.

From St-Etienne you need only turn the corner to find yourself staring at the eroded surfaces of one of the great Romanesque compositions of the Loire valley, the west front of **St-Mexme**, though unfortunately St-Mexme's post-Revolutionary history has left most of the buildings in a pitiable state. After parish services were transferred to St-Etienne the church was briefly used as a munitions store, but the crossing tower collapsed in 1817, taking most of the choir with it, and in 1825 the town acquired what was left. A school was installed in the nave and, after the purchase of a parcel of land to the north in 1858, the north aisle wall was demolished, the major damage to the footings being caused by the construction of the boys' latrines. The removal of the school in 1983 led to the demolition of the 19C buildings, and a major archaeological investigation of the site was launched. This is continuing, and though ostensibly it means the nave and interior of the west front are closed to the public, if you observe the proprieties the archaeologists are usually happy to let you look at the nave.

According to Gregory of Tours, the church was first founded as a monastery during the mid-5C by Maxime (the name became contracted to Mexme, pronounced *même*, during the Middle Ages), a disciple of St-Martin of Tours. By the 10C, the state of the monastery seems to have become precarious, and at some time between c 990 and 1006 the church was reconstituted as a collegiate foundation, almost certainly at the instigation of Archambaud de Seuilly, archbishop of Tours. Everything that survives dates from after this institutional change, and the current excavations are in part aimed at establishing a chronology for a building which developed rapidly between the early 11C and late 12C.

There seem to have been three main phases of construction. Firstly, a church with a triapsidal east end, contained transepts, and a simple cliff wall at the west end was laid out in the first half of the 11C, its most remarkable feature being a tiny hall crypt which supported the deep axial chapel. Twin towers and a two storey tribune porch were then added to the existing cliff wall at the west end c 1070, and an imposing single arch punched through the former façade so as to give a sight of the nave from the western tribune, pretty much as at Jumièges. Attention then switched to the east at the very beginning of the 12C, when the old choir was demolished and a much larger apse ambulatory was built, salient transepts raised and the nave extended two bays eastwards. Secondary alterations include the unusual placement of a funerary chapel off the eastern end of the nave north aisle in the late 12C, and the rebuilding of the south and west walls of the south tower during the 15C.

The **west front** is the most complete survivor, its central façade treated to a similar display of decorative stonework as so enthrals at Cravant-le-Vieux-Bourg. Despite the insertion of a 13C window, the upper area also contains a fantastic array of relief sculpture, arranged in tiers but now sadly weathered beyond recognition. The original design has been the subject of much academic debate, though the suggestion that the set of roundels originally carried signs of the zodiac has to be discounted, and all one can say with certainty is that representations of Christ and the Apostles are involved. Another very famous sculptural relief is to be found within the porch, and stood in the high gable of the early 11C cliff façade. This depicts a Crucified Christ below emblems of the sun and moon, with figures of Longinus and St John beneath the cross-arms, the former oddly given only one leg. It is an extremely moving image, archaic in both its motifs and its technique, and, although it seems early 11C, may not necessarily have been carved for the gable in which it is placed (the recent water damage is such that you are better looking at the plaster cast in the Musée du Vieux-Chinon).

The **nave** is more straightforward, a now roofless skeleton with unmoulded square piers and a clerestory whose windows are out of synchronisation with the nave bays at the west, and are inclined to catch up as you move east to create a secondary rhythm. The 11C collegiate church of St-Jean-Baptiste at Château-Gontier employs a similar trick and has much else in common besides.

At the north-west angle of St-Mexme, a narrow track snakes up the cliff-face, passing a number of old cave-dwellings before coming to one of the most curious Early Christian shrines in western France—a rare complex of rooms and passages cut out of the *tuffeau* and known as the **Chapelle de Ste-Radegonde** (open Easter to late September, 10–12, 14–18, the walk from St-Mexme taking about 15 minutes). At its heart, a steep flight of steps leads down to a well, an arrangement which almost certainly acted as the focus for a Gallo-Roman cult. As several Early Christian church councils called for the destruction of pagan sanctuaries—or, where these could not be destroyed, their christianisation—a Breton hermit by the name of Jean came to occupy the cave above the well.

There are dozens of 'holy wells' in Europe with similar origins, but what makes the sanctuary here extraordinary is not only its situation, within the cliff-face, but that the wife of Clothair, the saintly Queen Radegonde, sought Jean's protection after fleeing from her husband c 550. The stay witnessed Radegonde's decision to found a nunnery, the influential convent of Ste-Croix, outside Poitiers, and, after Jean was buried in a tiny niche cut into the rock, a pilgrimage grew up. Such was its success that in the 12C the cave was extended southwards as a means of enlarging the chapel space, and a fragmentary wall painting of c 1200 survives on its rear wall. The faded pigments show what appears to be a royal hunt, in which the figures of King John, Isabelle of Angoulême and Eleanor of Aquitaine are fondly imagined, to the west of which the earlier passage used by pilgrims to the well still survives.

There seems to have been a revival of interest in the cult in the 17C, when a priest was appointed to the chapel whose quarters, hollowed out of the rock next door, can also be reached along this well-passage. The priest's lodgings, and an adjacent farmhouse, are now a museum of 18C and 19C vernacular life, their marvellous jumble of tools and domestic ware often animated by the supremely well-informed enthusiasm of a visiting German guide who spends her school holidays here.

And, as an insight into the conditions of life in a *maison troglodyte* (a cave house), these visits cannot be bettered.

Back to the south of St-Mexme, the Rues Hoche and du Buffon lead past a couple of extremely fine 15C canonries to the largest of Chinon's squares, the **Place Jeanne d'Arc**. Most of this quarter was planned in the mid-19C, Jules Roulleau's colossal 1885 equestrian statue of Joan of Arc a relative newcomer to the scene. But the great coup was the planting of a **Jardin Anglais**, a broad tree-lined garden set between the eastern town and the river. The great avenue of limes remains a popular promenade, where you might take the shade of a summer afternoon, lay out a picnic, stroll, play boule, and amble back to the centre along the river quays.

7

The Loire Valley: Tours to Angers via the North Bank

ROAD (116km): Tours N152, 6km Vallières; D276/D76, 4km Luynes; D76, 3km St-Etienne-de-Chigny; N152, 10km Langeais; N152/D35, 13km Ingrandes; D51, 8km Bourgueil; D749, 5km Port-Boulet; N152, 19km Pont-de-Saumur; D952, 7km Boumois; 10km Les Rosiers; 11km St-Mathurin; 20km Angers.

As it flows from Tours towards Angers the river Loire describes a gentle southwards arc, pushing through the limestone to throw up steep cliffs above its southern flank. Initially, both banks share the same underlying geology, but once you pass Langeais the limestone plateau gives way to an area of low-lying marshland, drained by the river Authion, which has created a vast and featureless plain known as the Vallée d'Anjou. As a consequence, flood-free, defensible sites were hard to come by along the north bank, and most of the abbeys, châteaux and trading settlements which sprang up in the wake of the Roman withdrawal from Gaul favoured the southern shore. Nonetheless, the Roman road west of Tours adopted the northern route, and consistent attempts were made both to found and protect smaller downstream towns and villages. Although the Loire flood defences were finally consolidated in the 19C, the underlying system of high earth embankments, or *levées*, was first established by Henry II (Plantagenet) to protect Bourgueil in 1160, and the whole of this northern shore had been portected against inundation by the 15C. The flattish tops of these *levées* are ideal for primary roads, and for most, though not all, of the 108km to Angers the N152/D952 runs along the crest of these earthworks, offering an unrivalled opportunity to watch the slow broadening of the Loire as it swells with the additional waters of the Cher, Indre and Vienne. The ecology of this stretch of the river is quite distinct, and its culture grows out of that ecology, for which reason the above

itinerary is largely confined to the riverside settlements. The Vallée
d'Anjou is described along with Baugé and eastern Anjou in Route 11.
But few visitors are likely to explore first one bank and then the other,
and, with eight bridges now constructed between Tours and Angers,
the following description might be used in conjunction with that of the
south bank in Route 8.

The simplest route along the **north bank from Tours** is to leave the city
as if you were going to the priory of St-Cosme and pick up the N152,
the main northern route to Angers. This immediately brings you on to
the Loire embankment, rising above the north-western suburbs of
Tours to offer a glimpse of the marshy wastes to the south, where the
river Cher briefly parallels the course of the Loire. It is worth slipping
away from the river occasionally, and an initial right turn on to the D276,
and its continuation the D76, at (6km) Vallières brings you beneath the
decorative brick panelling of the late 15C **Manoir de Chatigny**, en
route to (4km) Luynes.

Luynes owes its name to Charles d'Albret, who took the title Duc de
Luynes and conferred it on the town in 1619. Prior to this, it was known
as Maillé, a medieval corruption of Malliacum, and it is for its significant Gallo-Roman and medieval remains that the town is best known.
The Gallo-Roman settlement lay on higher ground than that occupied
by the present town centre, with the **château** built on the site of an
important Roman citadel. This is still owned by descendants of the 17C
duc de Luynes and may not be visited, but its impressive main façade
is visible from the small cemetery on the western edge of the town
(easily missed, but signposted, *vue sur château*, as a left turn off the
Rue Paul-Louis-Courier). The cylindrical towers originally formed part
of the 13C curtain wall, but a complex series of building programmes
saw the central towers modified to become part of the *corps de logis* in
the 15C, with the strange assortment of windows inserted between the
15C and late 17C.

The medieval town grew up beneath the southern flank of this castle,
the stone steps ascending from the Place des Halles to the château
tempting, but chained and gated. The market place itself offers a
straightforward 15C wooden market hall, with just beyond, at No. 4
Rue Paul-Louis-Courier, a very fine timber-framed townhouse of c
1430. Recently restored, it has four vividly carved post-figures, signi-
fying St-Jacques, St-Geneviève, the Pietà, and St-Christophe.

Although a series of excavations in the early 1980s uncovered part of
a large 2C bathhouse, and a section of the Roman road from Tours to
Angers, these have been refilled, and the one substantial Gallo-Roman
survival that can be seen lies some 2km north-east of the town, along
a twisting lane signposted 'Vers **Aqueduc**'. A total of 44 closely spaced
piers survive, those to the centre still carrying their arches of stone and
brick, axially aligned to carry water to the citadel of Malliacum and
built, with a heavy mortar, of roughly finished local *tuffeau*. The effect
of these piers on the landscape can be quite extraordinary, haunting
even, particularly if seen in harsh midsummer light when the frag-
mented run of sun-bleached pylons rises proud above the corn.

West of Luynes, the D76 descends rapidly to (3km) **St-Etienne-de-Chigny**, a smallish village whose name is now extended to two quite distinct settlements—the collection of mostly 17C and 18C troglodyte dwellings at the Pont-de-Bresme, and the old centre of le Vieux-Bourg, 1km off to the right along the D126. **Le Vieux-Bourg** is the more interesting, its principal monument the eponymous church of **St-Etienne**, built in less than two years after Jean Binet gave monies towards the replacement of a 13C church in 1542. Not only is this all of a piece, its inner walls encrusted with Binet's devices together with those of his wife, Jeanne de la Lande, but the magnificent timber roof is wholly intact. Binet even chose to appear with his wife in the great east window, the couple commended by the Virgin and St John, who themselves stand at the base of a dramatically attenuated Crucifixion. Almost certainly the work of glaziers from Tours, the glass endorses a mid-16C tendency one finds elsewhere in northern France: the adoption of motifs from popular German woodcuts and engravings, here seen in a receding landscape similar to those which appear in the work of Albrecht Dürer. The western arrangements also survive in good order, with an unusual mid-16C font paired with the piscina, occupying what was intended as a western baptismal bay. At some future date this was bizarrely joined by a second font, mounted to the right of the door and now serving as a water stoup, which arranges Christ with nine apostles and seems to date from c 1200, its provenance a mystery.

Below St-Etienne-de-Chigny the road soon picks up the Loire embankment, or N152, tracing the 5km downstream to **Cinq-Mars-la-Pile**. The town owes its strange suffix to an even stranger brick tower, visible as you approach Cinq-Mars from the east. On closer inspection **La Pile** turns out to be built of Roman brick, 5 metres square at the base and rising 29.40 metres to a parapet which carries four subsidiary turrets. These turrets are additions, but just beneath them the upper register carries a total of 12 mosaic panels, the patterns of eight of which can still be made out. The sophistication of these panels is considerable, and the precision of their geometry is further emphasised by that of the tower as a whole. 29.40 metres is exactly 100 Roman feet. Both its date and function have excited varied comment, though comparison with a number of surviving funerary towers in south-western France suggests it was probably erected as a memorial, the subsidiary tombs and inscriptions lost, and both its form and decoration look late 2C. Local tradition maintains it acted as a lighthouse, and, though access to the top would have to have been via an outer wooden staircase, it could certainly have acted as a beacon, four leagues west of Roman Tours, and overlooking both road and river.

The town is less intriguing, with a dull central square to the west of the Romanesque parish church of **St-Médard**. This was grimly reworked by the restorers of 1888, but the nave was probably early 11C, with the transepts and choir having been added in time for a consecration ceremony in 1091, and the crossing capped with an octagonal stone spire in the 15C.

The **château** was also subject to a programme of 19C improvements, in this case during the 1840s, but, perhaps because its forms were already fractured and piecemeal, the effect was less radical. What survives falls into two main areas: the old *logis des gardes*, a mostly 19C wing now rented out as *chambres d'hôtes* and to which two low 14C towers still cling; and the inner castle proper. The latter was partially dismantled in 1642, after Henri d'Effiat, marquis de Cinq-Mars and an intimate of Louis XIII, was beheaded for his part in Gaston d'Orléans' attempt to overthrow Cardinal Richelieu—*rasé à hauteur d'infamie*. Since then it has grown a little wilder, spawned a lavender garden to the west, and found its towers topped with 19C battlements. But it remains an impressive ruin. The splendid walled moat was sunk in the early 16C, at the same time as a set of new apartments were constructed linking the then four cylindrical towers. Only the two towers survive from this final complement of buildings, that to the east being 12C while the ashlar-faced western tower is thought to be early 13C. These towers also received a 15C refurbishment, which saw the main chambers covered with octopartite rib vaults; and in the 16C new windows and fireplaces finally brought them to something like their present internal shape.

The next town you reach is **LANGEAIS**, 5km downstream from Cinq-Mars and with important fortifications. The **Château de Langeais** is not only an architectural complex of the first rank, but its two main building periods each produced monuments which were to have a profound impact on the strategic or aesthetic thinking of the subsequent generation. The site is less imposing than those of the châteaux of Loches, Saumur or Chinon—a natural ramp climbing gently from east to west—but it gives on to a steep bluff, and it was towards the west that Foulques Nerra chose to build the first castle some time around 994. The remains of this castle, the **Vieux Donjon**, are visible the moment you step into the main enceinte, though, as it stands some two thirds of the way up the slope, it is easy to miss strolling up the hill to inspect its tantalising shell, and this would be a loss.

What you see are two walls of a **rectangular hall**, a little patched-up but still largely constructed of small pieces of squared and coursed stone, with a mixture of brick and stone used around the window arches—a technique known as *opus incertum*. One can make out the rectangular frame of the hall, its division into two main sections by strong buttresses, and its extension over two storeys. Entry was originally via a doorway set relatively high in the ground storey. The two lower entrances are later—possibly 12C—insertions, and the subsidiary structure to the left is all that remains of a projecting tower, perhaps one of a pair which might originally have had wooden balconies. The traditional interpretation is that this hall was built by Foulques Nerra, and, as the buttresses are bonded into the *petit appareil* which constitutes the main finishing of the walls, that most of what survives is from the first phase of building. Foulques Nerra did not hold Langeais without interruption. He was reported as laying siege to the place in 1038—though when he lost Langeais is not recorded—and it seems likely that the construction of the hall pre-dates this action. If so, this would make Langeais one of the very few early 11C castle buildings to survive in France—a counterpart to Foulques' other standing enterprises at Montbazon and Loches, and a parallel to the great early castles to the north, at Ivry-la-Bataille and Ste-Suzanne.

Remarkably, when the citizens of Tours negotiated the return of Langeais to French control in 1428 it was on the understanding that everything should be demolished except the *grosse tour*. This was understood as applying to Foulques Nerra's castle hall, which possibly stood alone until 1465, when Louis XI determined to build anew. Louis appointed Jean Bourré as his clerk of works, and chose to build at the bottom of the promontory. The new work was probably finished in 1490, and certainly by 6 December 1491, when the great hall witnessed the marriage of Charles VIII and Anne de Bretagne— an event of which much is made in a huge waxworks tableau. The political implications of this match were serious, however, and rooted in the thinking of a generation brought up towards the end of the Hundred Years War. Anne was heir to the determinedly independent duchy of Brittany; therefore, if her domains could be assimilated into the French body-politic it would mark the demise of the last major fiefdom within France. Charles VIII was so determined to follow this policy that his will included the instruction that if he were to pre-decease Anne without issue, she was to marry his successor—hence her marriage to Louis XII in 1498.

The **new château** consists of two wings, that to the south at an oblique angle to the main block, with access between storeys provided by three polygonal stair-towers deployed across the inner court elevation. The outer face of the château is dominated by three cylindrical towers which, in a new departure, are treated as if they are a part of the main elevation, meaning that they are not only given windows, but that the sentry walk runs without interruption beneath the roof parapet of the towers and the gutteral walls alike. This has the effect of drawing your eye across the surface of each tower, lessening their autonomy as motifs and lending a sinuous, elastic quality to the design as a whole. To increase the complexity of the roofscape, in what was to become an influential treatment, each tower is given an additional storey, 'set-back' from the circumference of the main drum, as if forming part of an extendable telescope.

The elevations that overlook the inner court are, on the whole, less forbidding, arranging the windows vertically under simple drip-moulds, with steep, crocketed gables lending a picturesque drama to the roofscape. And, as with Jean Bourré's own château at Plessis-Bourré, the division of the elevation into vertical bays is quite eccentric, particularly around the portcullis, where paired gables surmount an odd number of window openings which continue downwards to different levels.

With the exception of a two-storey chapel in the south wing, which is the result of an early 19C intervention, the arrangement of rooms in the interior is exactly that of the late 15C, though few of the furnishings and decorations are original. However, the furnishings do give you some sense of late 15C décor, as between 1886 and 1904 the château's then owner, Jacques Siegfried, laboured to restore the interiors to a pre-16C condition, and filled the rooms with late medieval furniture and tapestries. The provenance and iconography of this work is admirably explained by multilingual captions in each room. If pressed for time, it is worth making your way to the **Salle des Gardes**, to see one of the finest 15C fireplaces to survive in France. And above this, in the **Salle Anne de Bretagne**, seven early 16C tapestries from a series of 'Nine Valiant Knights' are spread across the walls, depicting Godefroy de Bouillon, Julius Caesar, Alexander the Great, King Arthur, Hector, Joshua, and King David; probably the work of weavers from the western Anjou or Maine.

The rest of the **town** is, by comparison, disappointing. The earliest parish church traces its foundation back to the late 4C and the personal intervention of St Martin of Tours, but what survives on the site as the church of **St-Jean-Baptiste** is disconcertingly eclectic. The western tower-porch dates from the late 11C, its upper stages heightened in the mid-12C when the lateral buttresses were altered, and the octagonal stone spire finally raised c 1450. It is a handsome structure, and the surviving photographs and engravings of the original late 10C nave suggest that this was even more so, but a startlingly inappropriate intervention of 1869 replaced the earlier nave with the present tran-sept. Everything else was polished up at the same time, and all that survived of the mid-12C east end were the three eastern apses and a single impost block in the south aisle—depicting two confronted lions and probably a leftover from an 11C choir. Prior to the rebuilding the nave boasted rough, cylindrical piers, unmoulded clerestory windows, and the same type of masonry as is found in Foulques Nerra's magnifi-cent hall just up the road.

Langeais' second parish church has survived in better shape, despite the loss of its roofs in a fire of 1861, and can be found along the D57, just before the road climbs out of the town and up onto the plateau. Originally dedicated to **St-Laurent**, the building has been recently restored to house the **Musée de l'Artisinat**, with exhibitions of the work of local artisans. As far as the fabric is concerned, the nave appears early 11C, and was originally framed by a simple rectangular sanctuary and a western porch, the present west entrance and triapsidal east end dating from c 1100. The latter is in a poor state of repair, but is beautifully constructed of large blocks of ashlar with—as at Cinq-Mars—the transept gables embellished by diagonally-set stones, or *opus reticulatum*.

Beneath Langeais, the N152 parallels the railway line, before dipping to the south of (9km) **St-Patrice** to continue along the Loire embank-ment. It is worth turning right on to the D35 here, which takes a direct route through the vineyards to the old wine-making town of Bourgeuil. A slight detour along the back road is even more rewarding, and, if you pick up the D51 at (4km) **Ingrandes**, it will take you past the handsome 18C **Manoir La Philberdière** and on through Lossay to the splendid agricultural village of (3km) **Restigné**. The market square envelops an attractively arcaded **Mairie** of 1840, with an adjoining square to the west, grassed and sporting a hexagonal bandstand, the whole area originally all part of one large *prairie*. In the middle of this greater area stands the parish church of **St-Martin**. This is one of the more tantalising of the smaller Romanesque buildings to survive in

Touraine, its originally aisleless **nave** probably belonging to the mid-11C, with a north aisle added in the mid-12C, and a new T-section timber roof dating from the early 16C, the latter with the usual 'crocodile' masks appearing to swallow the beams. The west wall of this nave still reveals its original moulded gable, the interior decorated with the diagonally planted stonework, or *opus reticulatum*, which formed such a strong early Romanesque tradition locally, as at Azay-le-Rideau, Bourgeuil, Langeais etc.

But it is the **south door** which is the most extraordinary feature of the building, now set beneath an ample 16C timber porch. The portal has obviously been subjected to a number of changes and reconstructions, but the geometric patterning of the main arch is similar to that at Le Lion d'Angers and, along with its hood-moulding, seems contemporary with the nave, i.e. mid-11C. The four sculptural plaques and peculiar tympanum are quite different, however, with crude foliate designs in the tympanum, and a lion, two affronted serpents and a Daniel in the Lion's Den serving as a lintel, all boasting late Carolingian parallels and either reused or incorporated from an earlier door in the same position. A very good square-ended **choir** was added c 1230, with an excellent 'Angevin' vault embellished with bosses depicting Christ, a bishop, the Lamb of God and a superbly coiffed woman, among innumerable angels and minor players.

Bourgeuil lies another 5km along the D51, a pleasant small market town famous in the 16C for the variety of its fruit orchards, but now almost wholly dependent on the production of wine for a living. Its speciality is a fullbodied red wine, *Appellation Bourgeuil Contrôlée*, the most rounded of all Loire reds, which, having been fermented from the Cabernet Franc grape, is aged for a good three or four years before drinking. A Benedictine abbey was founded in the town in 990, a few remnants of which outlasted the Revolution and still stand at the eastern end of the Rue de Tours. The 17C abbot's lodge now serves as an old people's home, attended by a congregation of nuns who have taken over the 13C cellar range (which may not be visited). The remaining buildings have been acquired by the town and now serve as the **Musée de l'Abbaye** (open Fri–Mon, 14–18 only), but sadly they do not amount to much. The south walk of a late medieval cloister survives, along with an 18C refectory in which a cinema and theatre have been installed, the rest of the southern range accommodating a miscellaneous collection of embroidered coiffes, agricultural implements, and general local bric-a-brac.

A little further west, the **Mairie** dates from 1828 and backs on to a handsome covered market hall, while the parish church of **St-Germain** rises opposite. Like Restigné, this retains a western gable of *opus reticulatum*, which probably dates from a church begun shortly after a fire destroyed most of the town in 1061, but, as the rest of the nave was virtually rebuilt in the 19C, the precise sequence of building work is unclear. The choir has come off best, an ample and rather elegant 9-bay hall church, ultimately derived from St-Serge at Angers and provided with an excellent complement of figured vault bosses.

The best way to regain the Loire from Bourgeuil is to take the D749 south, and about 500 metres before you come to the bridge at (5km) Port-Boulet cut right, on to the back road to Chouzé-sur-Loire. This takes you past the most picturesque of the smaller châteaux along this stretch of the river, the **Château des Réaux**, said to have been built c 1495 for Guillaume Briçonnet, Charles VIII's Minister of Finances, but more likely built for his son, Jean, some time between 1514 and 1559, with the north wing added after 1714. The design is a well-established one—a pair of cylindrical towers framing the main entrance, both decorated with panels of alternating brick and stonework to contrast with the shallow pilasters of the window embrasures, but a satisfying twist has been given to the south tower, where the panels have been arranged to form a series of chevrons, pointing you round the building.

Below the bridge connecting the north bank with the nuclear power-erstation at Avoine-Chinon, the N152 soon reaches (3km) **Chouzé-sur-Loire**, an old fishing village fallen on hard times, but still able to sustain an attractive sweep of river wharves along the Quai des Sarrasins. West of here you catch some splendid views of the river and the great châteaux along the south bank: of Montsoreau from the delightful picnic area 500 metres off to the left of the N152 shortly before you pass (6km) the Pont de Varennes; and, most spectacularly, of Saumur, seen in the foreshortening light from anything up to 6km away.

The village of (6km) **Villebernier** has a fine parish church, well cared for and with a good Romanesque belfry and south portal. But it is Saumur which really dominates this particular stretch of the river. If you are heading instead for Angers, the N147 cutting up to the north-west of the Loire offers the quickest route, though the traffic can be heavy. The old road along the north bank here changes designation to the D952, though, it must be said, there is much less of interest between Saumur and Angers on this side than along the south bank.

Some 7km west of the Saumur bridge, the **Château de Boumois** houses an excellent collection of armour, and an extremely mannered mid-16C Virgin and Child by the Florentine painter, Francesco Salviati. The 17C *colombier* just to the left of the gates also retains the type of revolving ladders which were always in use in such structures, but as usual it is the building which is the star. This was built on the site of a 14C castle for René de Thory, work beginning c 1490 and continuing intermittently until c 1540, when the chapel was completed. It is a conventional design, an essentially quadrangular plan with cylindrical reinforcements and a graceful octagonal stair-tower, but, for once, the superb heraldic carving over the stair portal survives unrestored.

West of Boumois you pass a string of attractive villages: (2km) **St-Martin-de-la-Place**, centred on a splendidly conservative belfry of 1630; (3km) **St-Clément-des-Levées**, sloping down to meet a glorious river quay from which you can see the massive donjon at Trèves, and just make out Cunault, thickly wooded and glimpsed across a great sand-bar; and (4km) **Les Rosiers**, its pair of central squares overlooked by another fine belfry, this one dated to 1538 and sunk against the north flank of the church. But beyond here the settlements become sparser and duller. The delightful manor house which René of Anjou built for his wife, Jeanne de Laval, at (6km) **La Ménitré** in 1450 still stands, known as the **Grenier aux Rentes**; but it is firmly locked and now owned by the big Vilmorin agricultural company. If tempted by the sight of its exteriors, it lies about 200 metres east of the church, along the Rue du Manoir.

4km further west, in **St-Mathurin-sur-Loire**, the reasons for the relative sparseness of settlements along this stretch of the Loire are set out in the **Observatoire de la Vallée d'Anjou**, housed in the old railway station to the rear of the village. Here you will discover that although the system of *levées* that form the Loire embankment was largely complete by the 15C, the old northern flood-plains downstream of Saumur remained vulnerable to flooding from the river Authion. Indeed, until the completion of the big pumping station at Ponts-de-Cé in 1985, they were subject to frequent inundations. The principal exhibits and audio-visual displays are much concerned with this, dealing with the archaeology and ecology of the rivers Loire and Authion with exemplary clarity. Given the current debates about the banning of sand extraction along the Loire, and the huge new dams planned to straddle the river and its tributaries upstream of here, all designed to arrest the potentially catastrophic speeding up of the river flow, the museum has found a valuable role. This distinctive and fragile ecology is also what accompanies you for the last, picturesque 20km along the D952 into Angers.

8

The Loire Valley: Tours to Angers via the South Bank

ROAD (116km): Tours D7, 16km Villandry; 20km Ussé; 20km Candes-St-Martin; 1km Montsoreau (D947, 4km Fontevraud); D947, 11km Saumur; D751, 12km Cunault; 3km Gennes; D132, 5km Le Thoureil; 15km St-Jean-des-Mauvrets; D751/N160, 7km Ponts-de-Cé; N160, 6km Angers.

In many ways the south bank of the Loire is the reverse image of the north. Whereas it is the area east of Angers which is most susceptible to flooding above the northern shore, it is the area west of Tours whichsuffers to the south. On the north bank the protective cliffs are concentrated between Tours and Langeais, a stretch where the south is afforded little shelter, and that rim of limestone heights which forms such a dramatic backdrop to towns such as Saumur and Montsoreau only begins to climb steeply once you head west from Candes-St-Martin. The patterns of settlement reflect this, becoming denser after the last of the great southern rivers, the Vienne, has joined the Loire. Before you move beyond Touraine it is the more fertile tributaries to the south which are better suited to supporting the larger towns, as at Azay-le-Rideau and Chinon, both of which are treated in this volume as belonging to their respective valleys (see Routes 5 and 6). Nevertheless the underlying ecology, geology and historical culture of each bank is inseparably entwined, and, as mentioned in the previous section, with eight bridges now constructed between Tours and Angers the following description should be used alongside that to the north bank (Route 7).

The obvious route west of Tours, the D7, avoids the narrow tongue of moorland and marsh separating the Loire from the Cher and dips south to track the lesser river, where the shallow *tuffeau* crags provide some protection against flooding. In the immediate environs of Tours it is a dull landscape, the tedium relieved by a succession of scrappy roadside towns which occasionally, as at (13km) **Savonnières**, shelter a mediocre parish church and a handful of rundown 16C houses. The church of **SS-Gervais-et-Protais** at Savonnières manages to rise above the general run, despite the hamfisted restoration of the interior, and the late 12C south portal at least retains a semblance of its original form. Beneath the decaying stonework you can still make out an angel emerging from the keystone and, among the affronted griffons, dragons and warriors of the outer order, a pair of basilisks holding a toad by its hind legs. Even the hood-moulding has been given a graceful long-tailed dove with the ears of a hind.

At the meeting of the rivers Loire and Cher, just below the important medieval seigneurie of Coulombiers, is the village of **Villandry**, with its early 16C château. In 1189 Henry II (Plantagenet), Richard Coeur-de-Lion, and Philip Augustus agreed a short-lived truce here, the *Paix de Coulombiers,* which might have prevented Philip's successful-absorption of Anjou, Maine and Normandy into the French royal domain had Henry not died two days later.

The **CHATEAU DE VILLANDRY** owes its main outlines to Jean le Breton, a Touraine financier and president of the Chambres des Comptes de Blois under François I. He acquired the 12C castle in 1532 and, as with his smaller château at Villesavin, probably started work immediately. Parts of the 12C donjon were retained to act as the present south-western tower, and three wings were laid around a U-shaped *cour d'honneur,* the two lateral arms opening into a fastidiously carved arcade at pavement level. The ornamental repertoire—in particular the use of roundels within the pilaster orders and triangles to articulate the transverse faces of the piers—derives from Chambord. As Jean le Breton acted as Commissioner for Works at Chambord, one assumes that the links are direct. This courtyard, with its suite of rooms arranged across three storeys, forms the core of the château. This is largely due to Dr Joachim Carvallo, a Spanish scientist, who bought Villandry in 1906 with the aim of restoring it to its early 16C state.

When Carvallo arrived the château looked very different, as confirmed by a set of photographs of 1900 displayed in the interior. It had been extensively remodelled in the late 1750s by its then owner, the Marquis de Castellane, who added two (surviving) Neo-Classical outhouses to either side of the château, filled in the moats and laid a balustrade around the old donjon. He also refurbished the interiors and inserted tall casement windows in all the main façades. Carvallo set himself to reverse most of these changes, removing the 18C windows and reopening the moats, though he was not averse to compromising the 16C aesthetic when it suited the demands of his own collections, hence the superb 13C mudejar ceiling he bought from Toledo to grace the east wing. But it was the creation of the **gardens** that absorbed most of Carvallo's time, and, to quote Marcus Binney, these are indeed '*éclatant*—positively dazzling'.

Villandry is known to have had an extensive garden terrace in the 16C but, lacking a visual record, Carvallo was forced to base his new garden on Jacques du Cerceau's engravings of the great 16C gardens at Bury and Fontainebleau. French 16C garden design not only favours symmetry, arranging the plants in formal *parterres* or geometric borders, it also organises the terraces according to a strict hierarchy. Carvallo was determined that these principles should be adhered to at Villandry, and stated his intentions very simply in Prosper Péan's *Jardins de France* in 1924: 'Our ancestors had a different conception of life from ours, [where] the various elements of domestic order each had its place. The 19th century, imbued with the principles of an absurd egalitarianism contrary to nature and good sense, completely upsets this domestic order. A garden therefore should be on several levels—the *jardin-potager*, the *jardin-d'ornament*, and the *jardin-d'eau*'. This type of extremely formalised design is not to everyone's taste, nor is its implicit creation of a morality in nature, but Carvallo was acute in his choice of models and on a quiet day, when you are less conscious of the crowds, the capacity of the gardens to guide and change one's 'humours' can be intensely satisfying.

The **Jardin-d'Eau** occupies the highest terrace, retaining the great 18C basin which de Castallane had established above the canal, and provides the irrigation for the lower terraces. The **Jardin-d'Ornament** is laid out to the north-east, between the south elevation of the château and a striking belvedere from which you can survey the gardens as a whole. It consists of four boxwood parterres, cunningly arranged to suggest a square but in fact trapezoidal, each of which employs a complex geometry to symbolise the Renaissance view of the four states states of human love—fickle, tender, tragic, and foolish. At the bottom lies the **Jardin-Potager**, a vast chequerboard of colour, texture and shape, wafted by the aromatic vapours of the herb garden and set in the lee of Villandry's parish church. The origins of the 'Potager' lie in the monastic kitchen gardens of the Middle Ages, which were interspersed with beds of roses and divided between vegetables and herbs. By the 16C, Italian garden designers such as Pacello da Mercogliano had encouraged an interest in the decorative potential of the vegetable garden, which here inspired Carvallo to arrange the plants according to colour, juxtaposing blue leeks with red cabbage, beetroot with bright green carrot tops. The effect is surprisingly delicate, delicious even, and changes with the spring and summer plantings, the one constant being the proud thickets of standard roses.

The **parish church** in the village retains an aisleless 11C nave whose proportions and use of small squared stones are reminiscent of contemporary buildings in the Maine. The transepts, crossing and choir date from the mid-12C, enlivened by some well-carved capitals along the half-columns of the crossing and a splendidly varied display of geometric ornament above the abaci and stringcourses. But the cold hands of the 19C restorers are otherwise everywhere apparent.

Below Villandry, the D7 speeds through a couple of dull villages before meeting the old crossroads at (8km) **Lignières-de-Touraine**. A modest parish church, dedicated to **St-Martin**, rises in a crook of this junction, its heavily restored choir carrying a number of early 13C vault paintings concerned with the Temptations of Adam and Eve and of Christ in the Desert. The intrados of the choir arch also received a now abbreviated cycle of the Labours of the Month which, along with a fine 13C wooden nave roof, just about warrants the visit. West of here the road crosses the river Indre, loops past a number of handsome 15C and 16C farmhouses, and pulls you alongside the staggering roofscapes of the **CHÂTEAU D'USSÉ**.

Seen from a distance, Ussé is the most thrillingly picturesque of all the Loire Valley châteaux, its silhouette changing rapidly as you move from east to west, when the purposefully fractured elements of its roofs are brought fully into play. Seen close to, it can be disappointing, the east elevation in particular having a rather harsh and crudely worked character. This may well be due to the extensive restoration the château underwent when owned by the Comtesse de la Rochejacquelin between 1829 and 1883. It remains in private hands, and you will certainly pay the price for keeping it so, for as well as being one of the most popular tourist attractions in Touraine it is one of the most expensive (FF52 per adult in 1994).

Work started under Jean V de Bueil shortly before 1477, when the large cylindrical tower at the south-west angle was raised above the foundations of an earlier, probably 12C, tower. As at Chaumont, the intention was to build a rectangular complex, with large drum towers at the outer angles and an enclosed inner court. By 1485, the south wing and the first two bays of the wing to the east were complete, when the château was sold to Jacques d'Espinay, chamberlain to the future Louis XII. The north end of the east wing followed, suitably heightened and elaborated, and the north and west wings were built under Jacques' son, Charles, before 1523, the essentially late Gothic detailing of the father's work giving way to an austere and specifically Italianate ornamental language. When Ussé was begun, Louis XI's new château at Langeais was in building, and a number of its innovations are reflected here. The most obvious is the plan to continue the sentry-walk around the towers to form a continuous passage across the outer walls. And above this the angle towers are given that same miniaturised upper storey that so animates the exterior elevations of Langeais. Where Ussé differs from its royal counterparts, and in fact comes even closer to Chaumont, is the effect the various 17C alterations had on the nature of its accommodation.

In 1659 the château passed into the hands of Bertine de Valentinay, who demolished the north wing and so opened the court to a view of the Loire valley, seen beyond a series of formal garden terraces. The original entrance block in the north-east corner was walled-up, an orangery built and, with the windows of the south wing enlarged, the château was transformed into a sunny and commodious residence.

Along with the 19C restorations, it is this work you are most conscious of when being taken round the interior, with the **Chambre du Roi** originally designed for Louis XIV, and the splendid main staircase also belonging to the mid-17C.

Although the landscape has changed, the most impressive structure in the grounds was very much a part of the château Charles d'Espinay would have known, built in accordance with the provisions of Jacques d'Espinay's will to serve a college of canons, and now usually referred to as the **Collégiale du Château**. A streamlined aisleless box, with a polygonal apse and a pendant vault above the altar space, the chapel was finally completed in 1538, three years after the death of Charles' wife, Lucrèce de Pons, hence the initials L and C so subtly entwined above the western door. Together with the early 16C choir stalls, it is this western entrance which was accorded the most lavish treatment, glorying in a superb display of floral candelabra, memento mori, and busts of the apostles.

Ussé lies at the northern edge of the **Forêt de Chinon**, an old royal hunting forest whose oak and beech now cover just 15 square miles of gently rolling country. Its paths and tracks are accessible from St-Benoît-le-Forêt, just to the south, or from what is known as *le vieux église*, Ussé's old church at **Rigny-Ussé**, whose internal peculiarities and ramshackle outline commend themselves to any serious medievalist with the patience to root out the key (which can be tricky).

West of Ussé the D7 unfolds above the south bank of the Indre, slipping to the north of (4km) **Huismes**, whose late 12C and 13C parish church may be over-restored, but still has a good set of capitals where the tower bay gives way to the apse.

This stretch of the Indre, where it parallels the river Loire for a last 10km or so, is particularly beautiful, the soft, reedy banks sustaining a number of 16C manors and farmhouses beneath a wilderness of poplar, ash, and alder. After this, the confluence of the Indre with the Loire is a disappointment, marked by the industrial sheds and concrete chambers (7km) of the Avoine-Chinon nuclear power-station rising suddenly out of the greenwoods, the massive pressurised water reactor of Chinon B capable of producing over 5 per cent of France's total electricity supply.

8km downstream of its confluence with the Indre, the Loire is joined by another major river, the Vienne, the great reach of water gloriously overlooked by the slate-blue roofs of **CANDES-ST-MARTIN**. The village developed around the site of a large Roman villa, and by the 4C boasted a sizeable Gallo-Roman port. Its strategic situation was sufficient to attract the great late 4C evangelist and bishop of Tours, St-Martin, to Candes, where he built himself a house and a chapel dedicated to St-Maurice and where, on the 8 November 397, he died. His body was removed to Tours, but, though his house and chapel are rather dubiously recorded as standing in the 12C, Candes does not seem to have become a significant pilgrimage centre until the later Middle Ages.

The great church which forms the heart of the village certainly incorporates the site of the little chapel of St-Maurice, although its status, the **Collegiate Church of St-Martin**, and its form date from c 1175. The damage caused to the church during the French Revolution and the uncertain nature of the mid-19C restoration make it difficult to know precisely how the church may have looked by the end of the Middle Ages, but both its general design and the survival of a considerable quantity of painted sculpture make it a building of quite exceptional interest.

Work began to the east c 1175, the old chapel of St-Maurice lying just north of the main apse, and had reached the western crossing piers when building ground to a halt, probably as a result of Philip Augustus' campaign to oust King John of England from his Angevin strongholds. When work restarted on the **nave** c 1215 the design was radically altered, and, rather than a conventional low-aisled building, the new architect planned a four-bay hall church, the aisles rising to the full height of the central vessel. This new architect is known as the Candes Master, and he must have received his training in Anjou, the design of his vaults being indebted to those of St-Serge at Angers and Le-Puy-Notre-Dame. But the axis of the nave is significantly different from that of the choir and seems to have caused the masons all manner of problems, giving rise to almost wilfully eccentric bay divisions. Even more unusual is the startling array of **painted statues** which support the majority of the aisle responds, or interpose themselves beneath the clustered shafts to west and east. Some of these may have been moved around, but they were probably never intended to be read as part of a single programme. They include an excellent Massacre of the Innocents at the east end of the north aisle and a very good Moses, along with a few saints or apostles holding the instruments of martyrdom, along the west wall.

As the processional route to the church was from the river, the main entrance is via a superb **north porch**. The main galilee area is covered by a virtuoso set of Angevin vaults sprung from a single free-standing pier, while the outer façade carries a disordered arrangement of life-size statues, running across two registers and confounding the apostles with figures of St-Etienne, St-Denis, John the Baptist and others. The main portal is the most puzzling of all, for the justifiably famous socles, with their inventive arrangement of foliage, chimeras and human heads, are of a different stone from that of the larger jamb figures, indeed a different stone from anything else in the building, save the north porch entrance. They probably belong to an earlier scheme, conceived when the porch conformed to a narrower rectangle, but retained when it was subsequently broadened and a more extensive figurative programme mapped out. Although the masks are quite archaic, the two crowned heads being comparable to the portrayals of Henry II (Plantagenet) and Eleanor of Aquitaine in the nearby parish church of Fontevraud, the naturalism of the foliage makes a date of c 1225 likely. The larger jamb figures are certainly later, say c 1250, and include part of a once rather fine Presentation in the Temple, Abraham sacrificing Isaac, and the Four Evangelists, but again they have been much shuffled about.

The last of the major medieval alterations dates from the 15C, when the west front and north porch were provided with machicolations in the hope of deterring any attack from further down the Loire.

The rest of the village is also extremely attractive, with the late 15C manor house just above the church built for the archbishops of Tours, and a number of fine 17C and 18C houses revetted against the steep slope of a bluff which, when climbed, reveals perhaps the most glorious of all views of the Loire.

Candes has now effectively merged with **MONTSOREAU**, though as you pass from one to the other you cross an ancient frontier, one which marked the division between the Andégaves and Turons in pre-Roman Gaul, and between Touraine and Anjou during the Middle Ages. Montsoreau takes its name from Sorel, who built the first castle here in 1089, but, as its name suggests, this was located on the cliffs above the river, whereas the present **château** lies right on its banks. In fact, until the construction of the Saumur to Chinon road in 1820 (now the D947/D751) the Loire lapped against the northern walls of the castle and fed its moats directly, doubtless facilitating the collection of levies on passing river traffic—the principal money-spinner for its seigneurial owners.

Just one wing of a château, originally built to a quadrangular plan, survives. This is the *corps de logis*, built between 1440 and 1455 for Jean des Chambes, counsellor to Charles VII and husband of Jeanne Chabot, the heiress to Montsoreau. An extremely fine octagonal stair-tower was added to the north-east angle of the courtyard c 1520, embellished with medallions and carved friezes, on one of which two monkeys can be seen working stone beneath a banderole which reads *Je le feray* (I will make it). The first floor houses the **Musée des Goums Marocains** (Museum of the Moroccan Regiments), a collection of maps, books, weapons and photographs relating the history of the various French Moroccan Regiments, an exhibition that cannot have been altered since it was removed from Rabat after Moroccan Independence in 1956.

But the castle is best known for its historical connections. The great-grandson of Montsoreau's builder, also called Jean des Chambes, was the notorious Angevin organiser of the 1568 St Bartholomew's Day Massacre of the Huguenots. Revenge eventually came in 1575 when he was assassinated, only to be succeeded by his brother Charles, husband of Françoise de Maridor, the celebrated 'Dame de Montsoreau'. Athough Alexandre Dumas rechristened her Diane de Maridor in his novel *La Dame de Montsoreau*, she is the same historical character responsible for the downfall of Bussy d'Amboise, governor of Anjou, who as her lover was ambushed by Charles des Chambes and died *se jeter dans un piège fatal* at La Coutancière.

Montsoreau also lies a mere 4km north of one of the great monasteries of medieval Europe, the fantastically wealthy and aristocratic **ABBAYE DE FONTEVRAUD**. Fontevraud owes its foundation, and its peculiar administrative status, to Robert d'Arbrissel, an itinerant preacher born c 1045 at Arbrissel in eastern Brittany. Having studied in Paris he assisted in the reform of parochial life in the diocese of Rennes, and then retired to La Roë (Mayenne) in 1095 where he established a community of regular canons. This brought him to the attention of Pope Urban II, in Angers during February 1096 to enlist support for his call for the First Crusade, who conferred on Robert the title 'sower of the divine word'. The response was immediate and d'Arbrissel took to the roads, a charismatic preacher who, to quote from Jacques Dalarun's recent biography (*L'impossible sainteté: La vie retrouvée de Robert d'Arbrissel. Paris, 1985*), 'had scarcely to open his mouth when a new crowd would form behind him, made up of all social ranks and both sexes, but always with women in greater numbers'. It was probably sheer popularity that persuaded Robert to settle and organise life on a communal basis. In early 1101, with the blessing of Pierre II, bishop of Poitiers, he established a religious community near a spring known as 'Fons Ebraldi'.

This community was mixed, a bizarre assortment of priests, beggars, noblewomen, lepers and prostitutes, all housed in mud huts and assembled in confusion. It was also not without critics. Marbode, bishop of Rennes, complained that d'Arbrissel went about in rags, with wind-blown hair and bare feet, and should never have been allowed to leave La Roë. He deprived poor priests of their tithes by persuading parishioners to leave and, above all, he slept with women. This latter charge was repeated by Geoffroy, abbot of Vendôme, in 1106, who accused him of asking 'to be crucified on their bed through a new martyrdom'. Robert d'Arbrissel's defence was that he should arouse his carnal desires the better to overcome them, and his first biographer, Baudri de Dol, maintained 'it was important that the women should live with the men, who would then be confronted with the closeness of a female presence'. By this date, however, Robert had already renounced direct control of the community and appointed Hersende de Montsoreau to act as prioress, with Pétronille de Chemillé as her assistant. The constitution of Fontevraud also began to change, and as of 1106 separate houses were laid out for the various members of the community. The main convent was known as the Grand-Moûtier and was reserved for 'virgins', meaning women who have led an exemplary life. The men were accommodated in the monastery of St-Jean-de-l'Habit, while the convent of La Madeleine was for 'repentant daughters' and married women. Finally, the Prieuré St-Lazare was set aside for the lepers.

As such, Fontevraud had evolved into an abbey with four communities on the same site, but the question of its rule was only resolved in 1115, when Robert d'Arbrissel promoted Pétronille de Chemillé to the rank of abbess and presented the statutes which confirmed male subordination to the women. From then on an abbess acted as head of the abbey and, as Fontevraud had been constituted as a reformed Benedictine order, legislated for all Fontevrist houses. It was under Pétronille, a widow, and her successor, Mathilde d'Anjou, a 'virgin', that Fontevraud began to acquire the characteristics for which it was best known during the Middle Ages, a conventual haven for nobly born widows and daughters. Mathilde had been married as a child to William Atheling, Henry I's (Beauclerc) son and heir, but his untimely death in 1120 brought her to the abbey. As sister of Geoffrey Plantagent, she was instrumental in persuading the counts of Anjou to take a more active interest in Fontevraud. Her nephew, Henry II (Plantagenet), stayed at Fontevraud before crossing the Channel with Eleanor of Aquitaine to be crowned at Westminster, London, in December 1154, a year after the first Fontevrist priory had been established in England. And Henry entrusted the education of two of his children to the abbey: Joan (born 1165) who stayed there until 1176, and John (subsequently King John, born 1166) who was unhappily removed at the age of five.

Henry II was eventually buried at Fontevraud, after his death at Chinon on 6 July 1189. The express stipulations of his will that he be buried at Grandmont were overruled by Richard Coeur-de-Lion. William Marshal maintained that Henry had confided on his deathbed a wish to be interred at Fontevraud, though the chronicler Benedict of Peterborough averred that, during the funeral, blood began to run from the old warhorse's nose, as if his corpse were expressing its disapproval. That the abbey became an Angevin mausoleum is due to Eleanor of Aquitaine. She retired to Fontevraud in 1194, finally taking the veil shortly before her death on 31 March 1204, but not before she had designed a necropolis to house the tombs of Richard Coeur-de-Lion and Joan, both of whom died in 1199, alongside that of their father. And she herself was buried here, to be followed by the tombs of Isabella of Angoulême (King John's widow, who had become a nun at Fontevraud, was buried in the nun's cemetery in 1246, and translated to the church in 1254) and Raymond VII, count of Toulouse, who came to join his mother, Joan, here in 1250. Even Henry III, John's son, bequeathed his heart for burial at Fontevraud.

In view of this it would seem ironic that the 13C and 14C should mark a low-point in Fontevraud's fortunes. John's loss of his north-western French possessions in 1204 deprived the abbey of a valuable protector, and the anti-Cathar crusades in Languedoc and Aquitaine enfeebled Fontevraud's south-western dependancies. There was no building work to speak of at the mother house, and virtually no new priories were founded, compared with 123 prior to 1189. The pressure on resources was such that in 1247 the Papacy took the unprecedented step of allowing nuns to inherit their parents' fortunes, even after they had made their profession. And, although Fontevraud was not directly sacked during the Hundred Years War, its neighbouring estates were decimated in 1357, 1369, and 1380, provoking widespread local famine.

The tide only turned with the 15C and the appointment in 1457 of Marie de Bretagne as abbess, authorised to draw up 'statutes which they [a Parisian council of four] will judge proper for the wellbeing of the great monastery and its priories'. Daughter houses too poor to sustain themselves were closed, properties were repossessed, separation between men and women, reported to have lapsed, was reinstated, and a new priory was established at Madeleine-lès-Orléans from which a spiritual reform might be undertaken. The renewal was continued under Renée de Bourbon, abbess from 1491 until 1534, who reintroduced strict enclosure, reformed the majority of the remaining priories, and reconstructed the conventual precincts. With Renée's death came *ad commendam* rule and a parade of Bourbon abbesses who passed the title from aunt to niece in a virtually unbroken succession until the abbey's dissolution in 1789. This is not to suggest that Fontevraud suffered materially under their patronage. Indeed, unlike most monasteries under *ad commendam* rule, Fontevraud prospered, acquiring the vast new infirmary block of St-Benoît, the new precincts around St-Lazare, and a splendid novices' house. But it largely ceased to be a place of austerity and contemplation.

The end came quickly. On 2 November 1789, all Church property in France was made over to the state, and by mid-1791 the monks had left, the last nuns following a year later. The furniture was sold off immediately but, despite the parcelling up of the grounds into 19 lots, Fontevraud found no purchasers and was intermittently looted and vandalised until, in 1804, Napoléon decided to transform the precincts into a prison. Charles-Marie Normand was engaged as architect and, in order to build a secure wall, squared the enclosure around the Grand-Moûtier, demolishing all structures in the way. A new wall was then constructed around this, and those buildings deemed useful— the cloister, novices' hall and elements of the conventual precincts—were converted. A number of alterations were made to Normand's prison, particularly early this century, but the Grand-Moûtier remained in use until 1963, and the last of the prisoners did not leave the Madeleine quarter until 1985. Work began on the demolition of the prison quarters of the Grand-Moûtier in 1963, since when a colossal restoration programme has transformed the site. The question of a new role for Fontevraud was resolved in 1975, with its establishment as an educational and cultural centre, the *Centre Cultural de l'Ouest*, which has acted as a spur to the main restoration programmes, and was also responsible for the extensive archaeological excavations. Fontevraud is now one of the most important arenas of medieval archaeology active in Europe.

Entrance to the site is via the 18C **upper gate**, bringing you past a collection of mostly 19C storerooms and workshops and down to the *Accueil des Visiteurs*, the abbey ticket-office and bookshop. Here you can join a guided tour, or roam free. Either way you step into the heart of the abbey precincts, a vast monastic 'city' stretching over the best part of 14 hectares—on a similar scale, though of a very different form, to the enclosures at Cluny.

The **abbey church** lies just to your left, its west front, like any number of Romanesque churches in the region, given a single portal beneath a large lancet window. Perceptions of the building have begun to change with the recent archaeological excavations, and not only has the site of the royal mausoleum been established, but the discovery of two abandoned schemes has demonstrated that the church's present form was arrived at more tentatively than previously thought. In the first place, an earlier church has been uncovered underlying the existing south transept. This was triapsidal and relatively small. Its southern apse forms the foundation for the present south transept chapel, but, for the moment, it is impossible to confirm whether a similarly modest nave was ever added. Secondly, the existing nave was only begun after a plan for a basilica with narrow aisles had been displaced, the lower part of the present walls seeming to belong to this early nave.

As such, the aspect most often commented upon in the present chuch—that sublime contrast between the bright and lofty choir and the low but spacious nave—cannot have been intended from the start. In reality the two areas belong to entirely different architectural traditions. The tall, squeezed proportions of the **choir**, the height concentrated in the slender columns around the apse hemicycle, derive from the great abbey of Cluny III. The detailed treatment, and particularly the absence of apse-chord markers (there is no strengthening of the piers to mark the transition between the straight and curved bays) are western French, but its overall frame, its spatial aesthetics, are those of Cluny. Given the discovery of an earlier church, the date at which this choir was begun has become uncertain, certainly after 1106 and perhaps as late as 1110. Whenever it was started, it was undoubtedly complete in time for Pope Calixtus II's consecration of the high altar in 1119.

The **nave** unfolds in very different terms. Whereas the choir is exhilarating, the nave seems almost stately. This is partly the result of its squarer proportions and partly due to the use of domes. The two are obviously related, and they tend to slow the architectural rhythms and compartmentalise the bays. The employment of such coverings over an aisleless nave represents a re-think at Fontevraud, and the thick and fleshy foliage of the capitals towards the top of the lower walls looks like the work of sculptors from southern Poitou. These capitals probably date from the 1120s, when the idea was to construct a narrow-aisled church, probably along the lines of Notre-Dame-la-Couture at Le Mans. But the arrival of active Plantagenet patronage transformed the situation, and the proposed aisles were replaced by a single unified space covered by four magnificent domes. This final scheme was likely to have been undertaken c 1150, and the fact that the domes rise above pendentives has persuaded most architectural historians to look to Henry II's marriage to Eleanor of Aquitaine in 1152, and the bringing of south-western France into the Plantagenet domains, as the likely pretext for the shift. The rationale is that these sort of domed naves have their roots in Aquitaine, at Angoulême cathedral or Souillac for instance. But there were analagous experiments taking place closer to home, and, though the eventual dispositions of Fontevraud were clearly modelled on Angoulême, the overall effect is not dissimilar to Angers Cathedral.

With four exceptions the church has been stripped of its moveable imagery, but these exceptions are very grand, consisting of the remnants of the **Plantagenet Royal Tombs**. Although the documentary accounts always pointed in this direction, excavations have proved beyond doubt that the royal tombs were originally adjacent to the north-western pier of the transept, where it gives onto the nave. Low on the west face of the same pier a mid-13C painting of Raymond VII, count of Toulouse, was also uncovered, though sadly Raymond's tomb had been badly damaged, and Joan's long gone. The four survivors are now displayed in the eastern bay of the nave—Henry II, Richard

Coeur-de-Lion, Eleanor of Aquitaine, and Isabelle of Angoulême. The shape of these tombs is quite extraordinary and utterly distinctive, each figure being laid across a simple bed which has been draped with an under-blanket. This forms the underlying structure for a treatment which subtly alters for each figure: Henry pale and firmly locked to his sceptre; Isabelle tense and prayerful; Richard seen in ferocious youth; and Eleanor broad-hipped and reading a book, no doubt poetry as usual.

The south door of the church brings you into the **cloister** and the heart of the Grand-Moûtier, the abbey church being principally reserved for the 'virgins' of this claustral precinct despite its theoretically serving all monastic communities on the site. The layout dates from the 12C but the forms you now encounter are 16C, and are among the finest examples of Renaissance conventual building to have survived in France. The south walk was begun first, under Renée de Bourbon in 1518, and is more medieval in form than the three remaining walks, all of which were built under Renée's niece, Louise de Bourbon, between 1549 and 1561. These actually take up one of the motifs of the interior of the church, the paired column, as a means of articulating the exterior of the bays, though here the columns are monolithic and the order is Ionic. Louise was also responsible for the **chapter house**, a sleek rectangular space superbly divided into six bays by two free-standing columns. The carving is equally fine, particularly the relief panels of the coffered arches which flicker with Louise and Renée de Bourbon's initials, memento mori, seraphim, saints and supplicants. The walls were eventually painted by Thomas Pot, a local painter, c 1560, an accomplished cycle which runs from Christ's Washing of Feet to an Assumption of the Virgin, though the prayerful figures of abbesses were mostly added later. The main conventual halls were also rebuilt at the same time, hence the exquisite mid-16C staircase at the south-east angle which leads to the upper dormitory, and the vast refectory of 1503, crowned by an excellent run of domed-up rib vaults.

The refectory was provided with a new kitchen in the 16C, but the famous **kitchen** lies immediately to the west. The handling of the minor details here suggests this is broadly contemporary with the surviving choir of the abbey church, say c 1115, but you should be cautious in reading too much into the external silhouette. Magne's restoration of 1904 was fairly cavalier with the exterior pinnacles and, as the photographs inside make clear, the only lantern standing in 1902 was that at the apex of the roof. None the less, it is a magnificent structure, one of a handful of Romanesque kitchens to survive in Europe; and in terms of geometry, one of the most exciting 12C buildings of France. At its heart lies an ability to spin polygons, the octagon of the roof being the octagon of the lower walls twisted through 22.5 degrees, so that a point becomes a side. Looking up into this roof can be a bewildering experience, the transitional magic being worked by an internal square, expressed by the four great arches from which the inner skin rises. The square itself is inscribed within the lower octagon to create a series of 157.5–22.5 angles, squinches laid to connect its faces, and, with that established, everthing else is plain sailing.

To the east of the Grand-Moûtier, **St-Benoît** acted as an infirmary block for the entire monastery. The first, very modest chapel was reported to be complete by 1109, but—like neighbouring St-Lazare—was replaced in the second half of the 12C by a new **Chapelle St-Benoît**. The apse and main sanctuary bay of this survive, extensively restored but boasting a good 'Angevin' vault over the main square bay and the same sort of interest in drawing pairs of windows together to create a squared double-bay effect that one sees in Le Mans. The nave was adapted to take an upper storey *logis* by Louise de Bourbon in the mid-16C, and came to serve as the *logis des grandes prieures*, but is now close to collapse and solely held together by scaffolding. The area to the south of the chapel was laid out around two courts, the Infirmary Yard and the *Cour St-Benoît*, though these have now merged, the rather austere wings which surround them dating from the 1580s and the abbacy of Eléonore de Bourbon.

To the north-west of the infirmary block lay La Madeleine, of which relatively little now stands other than its wash-houses, with the old monks' house of St-Jean-de-l'Habit on the far side of the precinct walls totally destroyed after 1796. But the **Prieuré St-Lazare** survives in part at the bottom of the hill to the south-east of St-Benoît. Built to accommodate the nuns who served the leper hospital, it now comes in two parts—a simple chapel to the north, built between 1150 and 1162 at the expense of Henry II, aisleless and unadorned, and an 18C conventual block, whose restrained spaces now house an excellent hotel and restaurant.

Until recently, it was thought that the **village of Fontevraud** simply grew up around the abbey and that there was no settlement here before 1101. However, the 1986–90 excavations at the east end of the abbey church revealed that this was built on the site of a cultivated field system, suggesting that Fontevraud was less 'of a solitude' than was previously imagined. Whether there is an earlier village or hamlet underlying the present village is still open to question, though there must have been one close by, served by the parish church at Roiffé some 7km to the south. Nevertheless, it was the abbey which spurred the growth of the village and when, in 1177, the parish of Fontevraud was finally detached from that of Roiffé, its church was financed by no less a person than Henry II.

This church was situated just to the east of the precinct walls and dedicated to **St-Michel**, the greater part of the present fabric dating from c 1180 when building work finally began. The western bay was refurbished in the late 15C, at roughly the same time as a chapel was added to the north, and the handsome wooden gallery offering shelter around the exterior of the building is 18C. But the rest is late 12C, with Angevin octopartite rib vaults, a square east end and a series of figurative imposts and vault bosses, the two to the south-east of the sanctuary bay said, quite plausibly, to represent Henry II and Eleanor of Aquitaine. The church was also a substantial beneficiary of the patronage of Fontevraud's abbesses, hence the late 17C stone retable against the east wall, the gilded high altarpiece of 1621, and the remarkable late 15C wooden Crucifixion in the north chapel.

An abbess, Louise de Bourbon, may equally have had a hand in the most bizarre object to survive in the church—a **Crucifixion scene**, painted c 1565 by Etienne Dumentier, quite crudely executed but functioning as a blatant parable of religious intolerance. The main players are contemporary figures, with Henri II of France holding the lance that pierces Christ's side surrounded by his three sons. At the foot of the cross Catherine de Medici is depicted as Mary Magdalene, and the two lamenting Maries to the left are her daughters-in-law, Elizabeth of Austria and Mary Stuart, with Protestantism and Catholicism shown as two warring soldiers massacring a figure thought to be Michel de l'Hôpital, the great preacher of religious tolerance.

With the exception of the beautifully vaulted early 13C funerary chapel of **Ste-Catherine**, which now serves as the tourist office, the rest of Fontevraud is 18C and 19C—small, pleasantly quiet out of season, and boasting a complement of restaurants and cafés out of all proportion to its native population.

West of Montsoreau

To the west of Montsoreau, the soft beds of chalky *tuffeau* rise almost sheer from the flood plains, forming cliffs that can reach upwards of 100 feet. Not only is this stone—an exceptionally pure, calcarious limestone with few fossils and a consistent texture—ideal for building, but, in this configuration, it is easily quarried out of the cliff-face. The crags and outcrops to the south of the river are fissured with innumerable caves left over from quarry working. An obvious use for such caves was to seal the front with a window wall, plaster and partition the internal space, and move a family in. These **'troglodyte' dwellings** can be found all the way along the Loire and its tributaries, from Trôo to Loches, but their most spectacular development is to be seen along the stretch of river between Montsoreau and Saumur, and following the D947 west every left glance will reveal a dozen or more. It is now rare to find them inhabited, but the local mushroom growers and vignerons have adopted them with alacrity, and they do make excellent *'caves'* for storing the local red *Champigny*. Around (1km) **La Maumenière** and (1km) **Le Manoir de la Vignole**, the caverns have been embellished with 18C classical ornament, and the old road cut into the cliff-face deepened to allow the construction of cliff houses on anything up to three levels.

A succession of attractive villages also lie between the cliffs and the river, generally centred around a handsome late medieval parish church. That at **Turquant** (3km beyond Montsoreau) is mostly late 15C, its chancel arch now propped up by scaffolding, but its simple internal spaces an obvious candidate for conservation. At (1km) **Parnay** the church actually stands on the cliff top, its delightful early 16C west portal enlivened by sculpted rosettes, and its Romanesque belfry capped with a 15C spire. The best of these villages is probably (2km) **Souzay**, with a number of 17C and 18C *hôtels particuliers* overlooking spacious rear gardens, and the streets gently climbing towards the 18C Manoir de Villeneuve. The church is more disappointing and rarely open, the Flamboyant vaults of a 15C nave giving on to a straightforward 16C bell-tower.

From here it is but 5km to Saumur, the road passing the Renaissance dome of Notre-Dame-des-Ardilliers, of which more below, and quietly entering the town along the Quai Mayaud.

Saumur

History. The origins of the town remain obscure. A few modest archaeological discoveries suggest there may have been a Roman settlement here but, if so, it was small and the documentary history cannot be pushed back further than 848, when Charles the Bald gave the Villa Lohannis to the displaced monks of St-Florent-le-Vieil. The monks were again run out by the Norse raiding parties of the 850s and it is only c 950 that one hears of Thibaud le Tricheur, Count of Blois, offering the monk Absalon protection for the relics of St-Florent within his castle enceinte. This castle was known as the *Vieux Tronc*, suggesting a cylindrical donjon, and it seems likely that both a monastery and a town grew up within its skirts, as, by 968, the settlement was referred to as 'Salmurus'. Some 12 years later this had been Latinised to 'Salvus Murus', safe wall, but the philologists suspect the Latin to be an artificial formation and the meaning of the 'Sal' of Salmurus remains unknown. The early settlement was an outpost for the counts of Blois and Touraine, but—having established donjons such as Langeais, Montbazon and Loches, all well within territory formerly controlled from Blois and Tours—Foulques Nerra, Count of Anjou, turned his attention to Saumur. The wall came under increasing attack, and in 1026 Foulques finally managed to destroy the town, throwing Eudes of Blois back on Tours and leaving it to his heir, Geoffroy Martel, to rebuild.

Once in Angevin hands the town began to grow, despite a second destruction in 1067 at the hands of Guy, Count of Poitiers. Geoffrey Plantagenet constructed a new château on the site of the present building, a parish church was built at Nantilly to serve the town, and the monks moved 2km downstream to St-Hilaire-St-Florent. The absorption of Anjou into the French royal domain in 1203 also reflected well on Saumur, with a second wall constructed at the foot of the bluff by Louis IX c 1230, effectively bringing the town down to meet the river, and a new set of works launched at the château by Charles d'Anjou in 1246. And in 1360, when Jean le Bon handed out royal appanages to his sons—creating Jean Duc de Berri, and Philippe Duc de Bourgogne—Anjou was given to Louis, a man already known to favour Saumur. Under Louis, the château was rebuilt as a ducal residence and a substantial mercantile community was drawn to the town, a favoured status which was continued under Louis' grandson, René d'Anjou.

But it was the Reformation which was to have the most marked effect on Saumur. In 1589 Henri III appointed Philippe Duplessis-Mornay, a distinguished Protestant theologian, diplomat and intimate of Henri of Navarre, governor of the town. The great *Académie Protestante de Saumur* he founded in 1599 made the town a second Geneva, bringing thousands of students from throughout Europe to sit at the feet of scholars such as the great Hebraicist, Louis Cappel, and the brilliant Scottish physician, Marc Duncan. By 1620, the population of the town burgeoned to over 10,000, but relations between Duplessis-Mornay and the predominantly Catholic population were always strained and, dubbed the 'Huguenot Pope', he was forced to retire by Louis XIII in 1621. The real setback came with the Revocation of the Edict of Nantes in 1684, when the Protestant temple was burned and the Huguenots flung out, the population slumping to 6500 within the ensuing decade.

It is sometimes said that Saumur never really recovered, but while it is true that it lost its mercantile base and its academic traditions were marginalised, renewal of a sort came with the creation of a military school in 1767. This had its roots in the *corps des carabiniers*, a mounted regiment stationed in the town in 1763, and by 1771 Saumur was the sole training establishment for cavalry officers in France. Variously suppressed and revived during the Revolution, the school re-emerged as the *Ecole de Cavalerie* in 1825 and, given the abolition of the equestrian academy of Versailles, its famous *Cadre Noir*, the black-jacketed instructors, became the great French repository of classical equestrianism. But with the development of modern armour its military role began to change, and since 1918 the school has functioned as the main training establishment for French mobile armoured divisions. Its staff were deployed in the defence of Saumur during the German attack on the Loire in the early summer of 1940, an event which sadly resulted in the destruction of much of Saumur's river frontage. The town was damaged again in 1944, though, in common with other towns along the Loire, Saumur never suffered from the intensity of aerial and artillery bombardment that so devasted Normandy and northern Maine. The effect of this historical development has been to create a number of identifiable wards, both within and attached to the town— Vieux Saumur, the 'Cité Equestre', Nantilly, Ardilliers. The following description treats each of these areas separately. As the château over-looks all it is probably the best place to start.

Town Tour. Although Thibaud le Tricheur's donjon probably occupied the present site of the **CHÂTEAU**, and Geoffrey Plantagent's early 12C castle certainly did, it was not until Louis IX gave Saumur to his brother, Charles of Anjou, in 1246 that the building took on its present quad-rangular appearance. The circular bases so clearly visible beneath the angle towers formed part of this mid-13C castle, and though the complex silhouettes of the late medieval château are not rooted in earlier precedent, the geometrical layout of the building is. It is this late medieval château for which Saumur is so justifiably famed.

When Louis was made Duke of Anjou in 1360, he seems to have preferred Saumur to Angers as a residence. He did not set about building immediately, but when he did, in the late 1360s, it was in rivalry to two of his brothers' new houses, Charles V's Louvre Palace in Paris, and Jean, Duc de Berri's château at Mehun-sur-Yèvre. Like his brothers' châteaux, Saumur forms the backdrop to one of the calendar illustrations in the *Très Riches Heures du duc de Berri*, and, despite the loss of its forest of girouettes, chimney-stacks and subsidi-ary turrets, its interest in the possibilities of the fantastical silhouette are still plainly visible.

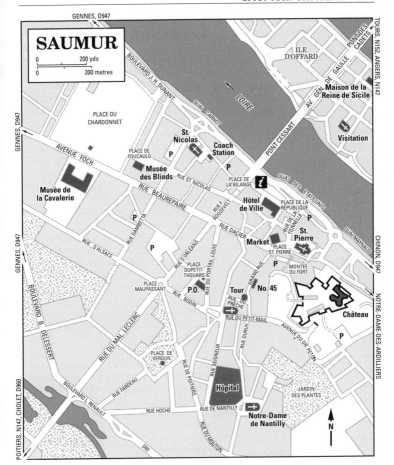

For a start, Louis got rid of the cylindrical shape of the earlier angle towers in favour of polygons, their faceted surfaces set between pilasters. Next, having demolished all but the lower section of the walls, he constructed a large *corps de logis* along the river side, enhanced the exterior with a picturesque *châtelet*, and built secondary wings to east and west to create an enclosed inner courtyard. There have been alterations since—René of Anjou refurbished the *corps de logis* and added the octagonal staircase at the north-eastern corner between 1454 and 1472, and, fearing the possiblity of Catholic attack, Philippe Duplessis-Mornay added the massive tapezoidal artillery platforms on the town side in the 1590s—but the essential detailing of the château remains late 14C. However, after Duplessis-Mornay left in 1621 the western range collapsed, and the depredations caused by the building's use as a prison during the 18C and a barracks in the 19C are all too apparent.

Having been made over to the town in 1906, the château is now used to accommodate two museums—the Musée d'Arts Decoratifs occupying the first floor of the east and north wings, and the Musée du Cheval on their respective second floors—both reached via the stairwell in the south-west angle tower. The collections of the **Musée d'Arts Decoratifs** are perhaps the more significant, and certainly the more eclectic. Except for the late medieval and Renaissance chests and a number of the tapestries, they were assembled by Charles Lair, Inspector of the French Archaeological Society, and left to his home town of Saumur in 1919. The rooms are arranged chronologically, with the medieval section including a good 13C Limoges enamelled crucifix, and three excellent fragmentary tapestries, woven in Tournai or Arras between 1450 and 1470. Beyond, in the **Salle de Parement**, most of the work is early 16C, with a particularly fine Tournai tapestry of c 1490 depicting the Siege of Jerusalem originally part of a larger cycle, and a number of proficient wooden statues which include an extremely beautiful St-Barbara of c 1520.

The post-medieval collections are heavily weighed towards faïence, juxtaposing the 17C Delft-ware with contemporary Chinese porcelain, and assembling the core of the collection in the **Chambre de la Reine**. Inevitably, it is the French 18C ware which is shown in the greatest depth, the dense colours of the work from Rouen set against the thinner dyes of Nevers. However, the highlight of the museum is arranged above these cabinets—a series of tapestries woven at the Gobelins factory c 1718 to the designs of Charles Lebrun, and depicting a group of children industriously gardening in a landscape worthy of Claude Lorrain.

The **Musée du Cheval** is concerned with the history of man's domestication of the horse. This opens with an account of equine physiology, contrasting the skeletons of a prehistoric animal found at Solutré, a Mongolian wild horse, and the celebrated 1899 English Derby winner, Flying Fox. The main displays fall into two parts: a room devoted to Greek, Roman and medieval images of horses alongside miscellaneous examples of stirrups, spurs, horseshoes etc; and a very much fuller collection of post-16C equestrian paraphernalia.

Beneath the château, the Rue des Remparts winds steeply down towards the **old town**, emerging on to the **Montée du Fort** and picking its way past a number of very fine 15C houses. Like most vernacular architecture in Saumur these are built of local *tuffeau*, but occasionally, as at No. 7, the odd half-timbered structure stands as a reminder of a type of house popular, even here in good quarrying country, during the late Middle Ages. The best of these is at the bottom of the hill, in the **Place St-Pierre**, where No. 3bis sports an attractive array of shallowly carved relief figures on the main uprights.

The 17C façade around the corner belongs to the church of **ST-PIERRE**, replacing a 13C west front destroyed by lightning in 1674, and superposing a fine Doric entrance with a peculiarly robust Ionic colonnade. The church was founded as an annexe to Notre-Dame-de-Nantilly in the late 12C, giving Nantilly a parochial presence within the walls of the old town. The choir and transepts seem to date from this period while the nave, wider and carrying a delicately ribbed set of Angevin vaults, followed in the first half of the 13C. Two chapels were subsequently opened off the north wall of the nave, that to the west in the 15C and to the east in 1549, the latter entered via an impressive coffered arch. Opposite these is the tomb of Béatrice de Boumois (died 1450), given a superb ogee wall-arch and a miniature vault whose boss supports her coat of arms. This general area of the nave is also an excellent place from which to gauge the full impact of St-Pierre's late 17C organ, which was beautifully restored between 1979 and 1984 and is often used on summer evenings for organ concerts. The instrument attracts organ scholars from central and western France, and of an afternoon it is not unusual to be treated to a free recital, or a sort of informal master class.

Notwithstanding the marvellous choir stalls of 1474–78 (only the misericords and seating survive from the late 15C guild-commissioned arrangement, the backs and canopy work being the work of the 1843 restorers) the church is best known for its 16C tapestries. These fall into two sets, the more impressive commissioned in 1524 by Jacques le Roy, abbot of St-Florent, to embellish the choir of the abbey. Following the almost total destruction of St-Hilaire-St-Florent during the Revolution, the tapestries were dispersed, and only brought back together at St-Pierre early this century, shorn of three of their original 19 scenes. They depict the **Life of St-Florent**, the first five hangings each narrating three episodes, with the final piece originally running to four. Though incomplete and rather bittily displayed in the nave and north transept, they remain among the finest early 16C wall-hangings to survive in France, their exquisite delicacy of colour rivalling even that of the much earlier Apocalypse tapestries in Angers.

The second cycle, devoted to the **Life of St-Pierre**, was commissioned for the church here from the Duval shop in Tours after 1535. It appears quite crude by comparison, the crowded compositions sinking close to confusion, though the disappearance of most of the warmer colours may well be responsible for this impression.

To the north-west of St-Pierre, the **Rue de la Tonnelle** originally acted as one of the main axes within the walled enceinte but is now reduced to a scrappy collection of 18C houses and modern shop fronts. It brings you out into the **Place de la République** and the major municipal buildings of present-day Saumur. The **Théâtre**, occupying the western corner of the place and built in a self-consciously heroic Neo-Classical style in 1886, now houses the **Maison du Tourisme**. The **Hôtel-de-Ville** was built in 1508 as an integral part of the main town walls so that, as at Montsoreau, the north façade was originally lapped by the waters of the river Loire. The stonework is now decaying but it remains an extremely fine building, with machicolated turrets at the angles and a splendid run of barley-sugar columns framing the windows of the inner courtyard. The last also gave the architect Joly-Leterme the decorative style he employed on the west wing in 1856.

With the exception of these two buildings, the Place de la République can seem somewhat spare, and the social and commercial heart of Saumur has moved to the other side of the theatre, to the **Place de la**

Bilange. The main shopping streets, the Rues St-Jean and Roosevelt, converge here, and the densest concentration of cafés and restaurants are to be found in the Place itself and along the adjacent Rue St-Nicolas. It is also within easy reach of the **Pont Cessart**, where much the finest of those famous views of town and castle are to be had, and the **Ile Offard**, the predominantly 18C quarter which grew up just to the north of the old town. This is not of itself an area of particular interest, but before the river islands were consolidated it was favoured by the 15C and 16C aristocracy as a peaceful haven on which to construct spacious manor houses. One excellent example does survive, the **Maison de la Reine de Sicile**, built in the early 15C for Yolande d'Aragon, widow of Louis II (King of Naples in addition to being Duke of Anjou) and mother to René d'Anjou. At that date there was a cluster of islands in the river, this one being known as the Ile d'Or, whose manorial crests and gables must have aped the skyline of Louis' castle and mocked the sober walls of the enceinte over the water.

The area to the west of the Place de la Bilange is largely given over to the **Cité Equestre et Militaire**, the quarter occupied by the old cavalry school when it was first established in 1767. The centrepiece is the immense Place du Chardonnet, the 18C parade ring where the *Carrousel* is staged. These displays of horsemanship on the part of the staff and students of the *Ecole d'Application de l'Armé Blindée et de la Cavalerie* (E.A.A.B.C.—the successor to the earlier cavalry school) have been held every July since 1828, and draw huge crowds, so if you intend watching a show it may well be worth booking ahead. The cavalry school is now principally a vehicle for the education of the officers of France's mobile armoured divisions, hence the collection of tanks and armoured personnel carriers housed in the **Musée des Blindes** in the Place Charles de Foucauld. Stepping west of here brings you straight into the **Place Chardonnet** itself, its earth walks and stamping grounds enveloped on three sides by late 18C stables and accommodation blocks. The fourth side is given over to the school building, completed in 1768 in a superbly restrained Neo-Classical style, and a section of whose first floor now houses the **Musée de la Cavalerie**. (Open 13–17 except Fridays. But be prepared—since the Ecole functions as a military establishment, at least one member of your party will need to leave a passport or driving licence at the desk.)

The museum was founded in 1936 as a result of a bequest by Barbet de Vaux, Vice-President of the *Féderation des Cuirassiers de France*, whose superb collection of 19C swords and armour form its heart. The rest of an extensive suite of corridors and rooms is given over to the personal effects of a number of *maréchaux de France*, and an account of the development of modern tank warfare, very good of its sort and all captioned with military precision.

In addition to the *Cité Equestre*, Saumur supported two other distinct quarters, at Nantilly and les Ardilliers, though these have now merged with the rest of Saumur to form the modern town. **Nantilly** seems to have become established some time after Guy de Poitiers sacked Saumur in 1067, when monks from St-Florent founded a priory, Notre-Dame-de-Nantilly, south of the castle and outside the town walls. Prior to the creation of St-Pierre as a dependancy within the town, all parochial services were held in Nantilly and a sort of *faubourg* grew up around the priory. This is most easily reached from the Place St-Pierre, where the **Grande-Rue** originally led out to Saumur's main southern gate, a 15C tower from the enceinte wall still standing just off the Rue du Prêche. The street also takes you past the finest 16C houses to survive in Saumur, with the residence of the abbots of Asnières at No. 4–6 Grande-Rue, and Duplessis-Mornay's late 16C townhouse at No. 45, No. 47bis originally acting as a lodging-house for students at the Protestant Academy. Once over the Rue du Petit-Mail you are out of 'Vieux Saumur' and in Nantilly, the great priory lying along the same axis at the bottom of the Rue Pascal.

Though it is known that **Notre-Dame-de-Nantilly** was a daughter-house and priory of St-Florent from an early date, the absence of any documentation makes interpretation of the Romanesque building difficult. All the existing fabric post-dates the destruction of Saumur in 1067, and the nave would seem earliest, dating from c 1100 and, in its general handling, related to the abbey of the Ronceray at Angers. Its amplitude is striking, a vast, aisleless space, over 12m wide, spanned by a barrel vault whose transverse arches have been slightly pointed. The arches above the windows of the north elevation endorse a local tradition—see also Le Lion d'Angers or Restigné—in cutting the voussoirs to a point, creating a zig-zag pattern in the mortar separating the two orders. To the east, the crossing and choir would seem mid-12C, though, with the exception of their southern apsidal chapel, the transepts were refurbished during the 14C. This southern chapel houses the statue of Notre-Dame-de-Nantilly itself, a 12C painted wooden **Virgin and Child**, which attracted a considerable local pilgrimage and inspired the great Marian devotee, Louis XI, to finance the building of a **south aisle** during the 1490s.

Louis' initial intention had been to found a college of canons, but this was spurned by the Benedictine monks of St-Florent, who feared the dilution of their monastic prerogatives, and so he introduced his college to Notre-Dame-du-Puy instead. The south aisle went ahead regardless, and, architecturally, it is this which is the most accomplished area of the church, its inventive tracery heads surmounted by a bewitching run of transverse gables and its vaults emblazoned with heraldic bosses. Louis also had a small oratory constructed in the westernmost bay, and as a sanctuary marker the **high vault** carries one of the finest late medieval images of the Archangel Michael and the Dragon to survive in western France, though its recent repainting was a great mistake. There are other objects of note to grace the aisle: the memorial tablet René d'Anjou composed on the death of his wet-nurse, Thyphaine, in 1458; and the remains of the crozier of Gilles, archbishop of Tyre, buried in the church in 1266, only for the figures of Adam and Eve to be ripped out of the head of the crozier in a particularly brutal theft in 1988.

But it is for its magnificent collection of 16C and 17C **tapestries** that the church is most celebrated. The following list simply identifies their subjects and provenances where known. The numbering system is that employed within Notre-Dame-de-Nantilly, No. 1 being at the south-western end of the nave aisle:

1. Adoration of the Shepherds and Magi, 1619, Grillemont
2. Adoration of the Shepherds, early 16C, Tournai
3. Capture of Jericho, late 16C, Flemish
4. Jacob blessing his Children?, late 16C, Flemish
5. Coronation of the Virgin, early 16C, Bruges?
6. Dormition of the Virgin, early 16C, Tours?
7. Childhood of the Virgin, 1529, Tours?
8. Crucifixion, mid-17C, Aubusson
9. Pentecost, mid-17C?, Aubusson
10. Angels Carrying the Instruments of the Passion, late 15C, Angers?
11. Calling of Peter, late 16C, Brussels?
12. Tree of Jesse, 1529, Tours? (from the same series as No. 7)

Nos 13–16 are pairs of hangings mounted from left to right along the north wall of the nave. The series is devoted to the life of the Virgin and was commisioned for Notre-Dame from the Aubusson shops in 1619. The subjects are:

13. Marriage and Annunciation
14. Visitation and Nativity
15. Presentation in the Temple and Holy Family with John the Baptist
16. Return from Egypt and Lament over the Entombment of Christ

Le Quartier de Fenet et Les Ardilliers occupies the land between the cliffs and the river to the east of the château. Again, it is easily reached from the Place St-Pierre, where the Rue Fournier, Rue Jean Jaurès and their continuations will eventually bring you to Notre-Dame-des-Ardilliers. Until early this century, the whole of this quarter functioned as a manufacturing centre for rosary beads, between 1000 and 1500 people being employed to work from the houses along the Rues Rabelais and Jean Jaurès, each artisan known as a *paternôtrier*. The industry grew out of the 16C pilgrimage to Ardilliers, and by the late 17C Saumur enjoyed the curious distinction of sharing a monopoly in the production of rosaries with Florence, and for a centre of Protestant study to be surrounded by *paternôtriers* is very odd indeed. This state of affairs has its origins in a small stone Pietà, discovered in 1454 covered in clay, or *ardille*. A local pilgrimage developed, and, anxious both to encourage the cult and antagonise the Huguenots of Saumur, the Jansenist bishop of Angers, Henri Arnauld, planted seven new religious communities in a ring around the town during the early 17C. One, the Oratoriens, was given charge of the Pietà, and in 1614 both the conventual buildings and the church of **Notre-Dame-des-Ardilliers** were begun.

  The present church reflects the efforts of four generations of architects and patrons, though it possesses a stylistic homogeneity that owes much to its eventual adoption of the great Venetian ex-voto church of Sta Maria della Salute as a model. The nave belongs to the Oratorien building of 1614 and was extended to the north under Cardinal

Richelieu after 1635, and to the south under the patronage of Abel Servien, Louis XIV's governor of Anjou, in 1652. The Pietà was eventually moved into Richelieu's new north chapel, but it is the dome, acting as a vast galilee or narthex to the west, which dominates the building, projected as early as 1655 though not completed until 1693. Badly damaged during 1940, it has been fussily reglazed by Max Ingrand, but the softer relief carving of the Evangelists and Doctors of the Church and, above all, the immense and simple geometry of the structure remain, thankfully, unscathed.

Beyond Saumur

Evidence of **prehistoric settlement** along the south bank of the Loire is fairly commonplace, there being around 30 Megalithic dolmens surviving between Saumur and Angers and a definite concentration to the south and west of Gennes. This is a relatively specialist area of interest and, although it falls outside the scope of this guide to identify remote standing stones and tomb-chambers, an exception must be made for the **Grand Dolmen de Bagneux**, 200m off to the left of the N147 as you pass through the Saumur suburb of (2km) Bagneux. This is the largest prehistoric covered tomb-chamber to survive in France, of the type known as a portal dolmen (sometimes described in English as a cromlech), and is thought to date from c 3000 BC. It now stands in a shady café garden, a few tables set beneath the flanks of a chamber with an internal length of no less than 18m. The largest of the capstones weighs about 40 tons, supported on flags dug 3m into the underlying soil and, like all the megaliths used, is of a tertiary sandstone thought to have been transported a good 500m from the slopes of the hill to the south. It certainly remains an imposing structure, and one whose form, with a portal arranged to the south-east and a tall rectangular chamber, was considered so definitive in the 18C that all such tombs became known as *dolmens angevines.*

To the **west of Saumur** the D751 forces its way through a dense succession of ancient settlements, squeezed between the cliffs and the south bank of the Loire. At (2km) **St-Hilaire-St-Florent**, the sad ruins of a 12C ambulatory and raised choir from the once great abbey of St-Florent lie across a park from a later parish church, itself early 13C, and strikingly fortified in 1418 before a western tower was added in 1865 to disturb its simple harmony. The late 12C narthex of St-Florent also survives to the west, enclosed within a modern building, impressive, beautifully sculpted, but accessible only via negotiation with the Mairie in Saumur.

Further west, the road passes (1km) the **Musée du Champignon**, testimony to the enterprise of local growers, who have successfully colonised old quarry workings in the cliffs to cultivate enough mushrooms to keep 75 per cent of the total French market supplied.

Beyond, at (5km) **Chênehutte-les-Tuffeaux**, a medieval settlement grew along the river while its eminent predecessor lay ruinous on the plateau. The Gallo-Roman *oppidum* at Chênehutte sits buried beneath a cornfield, but if you take the lane that climbs the cliffs to the rear of the church you can make out the earthen rampart that protected it from the south and west, and a weathered board illustrates the plan of the rectangular town, revealed after harvest during the dry summer of 1987. A Carolingian villa was subsequently established on the site and, to the west, the abbey of St-Florent built a small priory whose 16C prior's lodge has been converted into the luxurious 'Hôtel le Prieuré'. The parish church and medieval town were always on the river, where the early 12C belfry of Notre-Dame-des-Tuffeaux once acted as a river mark, aligning the local stone-carrying barges up the shallow channels here.

The next village (3km) is **Trèves**. Its strange title derives from early 11C realpolitik. After Geudoin de Saumur, a vassal of the counts of Blois, had been defeated by Foulques Nerra at the battle of Pontlevoy in 1016, he asked for a truce. No treaty seems to have been signed and, to poke fun at Geudoin, Foulques built a castle here which he called Trèves (truce)—a prelude, as it turned out, to his successful capture of Saumur in 1026 and the absorption of virtually all Geudoin's fiefs into the county of Anjou. This castle was dismantled by Foulques Rechin in 1068, after its owner, Geoffroy le Fort, had supported Rechin's disgraced brother at the battle of Brissac. But in 1089 Rechin reversed his policy, and gave Trèves to Geoffroy Fulcrade with instructions to rebuild immediately. After this the village began to grow, and, in 1106, Fulcrade's son, also named Geoffroy, founded a priory between the castle and the river.

What little survives of the **Château de Trèves** is due to Robert le Maczon, one of René d'Anjou's counsellors, who purchased the barony of Trèves for 4,000 livres in 1417. The following year, Robert was asked by the future Charles VII to build 'a strong place along the Loire' and was awarded the right to charge river tolls as a means of financing it. It was completed in 1435, by which time Trèves boasted a busy river port and three annual fairs free of royal taxes. Robert's château was originally quadrangular, its four wings arranged on a raised platform around an enclosed inner courtyard, with a colossal cylindrical donjon situated at the south-western angle. A few fragments of 15C walling came through after the lower wings were demolished in 1747, but it is the donjon itself which is the principal relic, surviving to toll a mournful note over a village once twice its present size.

Robert le Maczon's mutilated tomb can be found in the south transept of the tiny priory church of **St-Aubin de Trèves**, a building whose picturesque juxtaposition of arches and roofs reveals a sequence of alterations. The church is mostly 12C, begun in 1106 as a daughter-house of the abbey of St-Aubin at Angers. But, though the lowest stage of the bell-tower and the smaller blocked window openings of the nave date from this first campaign, it is clear that the building has been heightened. Big strip-buttresses reinforced with half-columns were inserted into the nave c 1130 and, at some later date, arches were punched through the three western bays to give on to broad aisles, their openings having been subsequently blocked up. A further complication is that the pavement is a good metre above the original floor level, the land around having been raised to protect the village from flooding. Despite all this, it is a splendid spot, its warm and sympathetic interior still housing, in addition to Robert, an excellent 12C font.

West of Trèves, the road twists above a great sweep of sandy shallows, formed by an island in the river, before bringing you (1km) to the north of the most accomplished of all Romanesque buildings to rise above the south bank of the Loire—the great priory church of **NOTRE-DAME-DECUNAULT**.

The surrounding area was converted to Christianity during the 5C by St-Maxenceul, a disciple of St-Martin, who seems to have been buried in what was then a wooded solitude. This spot is referred to in a mid-9C charter as the *monasterium quod vocatur Cunaldus* (the monastery known as Cunault), and was granted to the monks of St-Philibert at Noirmoutier by Charles the Bald in 847. It thus played a role in that startling odyssey that saw the relics of St-Philibert removed from the threat of Viking raids first to Déas and then, between 858 and 862, here to Cunault, before the Norse ships began to harry the shores of the Loire as far east as Orléans and the monks again decamped, eventually to settle in Tournus (Burgundy). They added the remains of St-Maxenceul to those of St-Philibert, and an optimistic charter of 875 lists Cunault as a priory and daughter-house of the Benedictine abbey of Tournus. The date at which monks returned is unknown, but a community was in residence once more by the early 10C, having brought with them the relics of St-Maxenceul and, quite plausibly, what was to become the great pilgrimage draw of Cunault's high middle age—the wedding ring of the Virgin Mary.

By 1058 we hear of a *cella sanctae Marie*, or Lady Chapel, on the site, and ten years later Foulques Rechin compensated the monks for the liberties snatched by the castle at Trèves by awarding them the revenues of a market and port. The latter were removed in 1091, when both market and port returned to Trèves to assist Geoffroy Fulcrade in the rebuilding of the castle, and Cunault was offered rights to cultivate vines on their estates at 'Lisis' in their stead. The revenues of the previous 23 years would have been substantial, however, and the influx of merchants and traders brought an upsurge of pilgrims in their wake. This expansion in both wealth and prestige is likely to have triggered the surviving building campaigns at Cunault, though the restoration which Prosper Merimée persuaded the Saumur architect, Joly-Leterme, to undertake between 1842 and 1866 demands great care be taken in the matter of details.

The volumes and silhouette of the building are memorable, with a richly decorated **belfry** rising midway along the north aisle, and a tall and spacious hall church interior rising through two flights of steps to a magnificent apse-ambulatory. The belfry is certainly the earliest part of the building, and both incorporates an earlier structure and reflects an earlier plan. The rough stonework and distinctive pair of windows in the lowest section of the north wall suggest they originally formed part of the church mentioned in 1058, perhaps its north transept front. To this were clamped those piers and responds which launch the belfry, their arches springing from a level appreciably lower than any others in the church to climb above the earliest of the figurative capitals to survive, a marvellous Annunciation on the left-hand side of the external wall. Above this, the belfry rises through three storeys, the arches and stringcourses elaborated with a tour-de-force of geometric ornament, and with warriors and monsters shoehorned into plaques between the supporting corbels. It seems likely that this was begun before 1091, when the market was still being held just to the north, and was intended to be quasi-freestanding, rising above the north transept and thus clear of the main body of the church. By the time the upper storeys were completed, c 1100, the market had returned to Trèves but the large-scale architectural expansion of the priory was just beginning, and it was this second Romanesque phase which was to engulf the belfry and create the building which is so justifiably celebrated today.

The chronology of this, the major 12C campaign, is conjectural, but it is evident from the complex shifts of sculptural and architectural style that work proceeded from east to west, and that the first area to be laid out was the outer wall of the **choir**. The respond capitals here sport shallowly carved leaves with a simple central vein, animals in profile, and occasional figurative groupings—as in the Flagellation capital to the east of the southern radiating chapel—which are treated to an almost frieze-like development. The architecture is equally distinctive, the opening to the now vanished axial chapel cut with triangular-headed archivolts similar to those at Notre-Dame-de-Nantilly while— as in the Saintonge and supremely at St-Eutrope de Saintes—the subsidiary radiating chapels form a very shallow angle with the aisle wall and are sumptuously decorated with external blind arcading.

All this suggests a date c 1110, and it seems likely that the main elevation of the choir was raised shortly afterwards, with the unequal transepts dating from c 1140 and the two eastern bays of the nave following on slowly from there. The crisis of 1164 at Tournus is likely to have brought building to a temporary halt, and the three western bays of the nave and west front date from c 1180–1200. Although this lengthy and far from continuous building programme adheres to a consistent spatial form, that of the hall church, and maintains a wide central nave, relatively narrow aisles and tall windows, it is prone to sudden changes of handling and style. You can see this in the pier profiles, which in the nave adopt, and then reject, the paired half columns of the apse hemicycle, or in the vaulting, where the western three bays have been given domed-up octopartite rib vaults. The capitals were most susceptible to this sort of continual updating, and here they announce the changes of workshop.

These **capitals** are among the most varied to survive in any Romanesque church of western France, with the thicker and fleshier ornament of the choir giving way to more geometrically controlled drill-work as you move west. The foliage capitals are interspersed with what to modern eyes seems a disorderly bunch of exquisite narrative or figurative scenes. A second Annunciation appears above the north-easternmost apse hemicycle pier, for instance, this time accompanied by David harping and a sulking Jesse, desultory amidst the foliage to the south. And among a tremendous collection of combat scenes one might single out that on the western face of the north apse-chord marker, and the two warriors slugging it out across the third pier from the west in the north nave arcade. There are two other capitals which also deserve mention, islanded a third of the way up two half-columns just before you ascend the steps towards the altar. They represent St-Philibert implored by a native to rid the region of a dragon, and a choir of monks chanting. Before the lower sections of these piers were replaced in the 19C restoration it is likely they had been stripped to receive the backs of the choir stalls, and that these capitals rose above them, added perhaps at the same date as St-Maxenceul was translated to a new shrine in the early 13C.

The **Shrine of St-Maxenceul** is preserved in the southern radiating chapel, a painted wooden reliquary chest featuring 12 arcaded apostles beneath a steep gable which relates the Ascension and Pentecost, the apostles effectively witness to both. There are other relics of the later middle ages, though none as compelling as the 12C work, with a good 16C Pietà in a niche off the north choir aisle and a few, mostly faded, 15C paintings still clinging to the nave walls, of which a St Christopher and Transfiguration are the most complete.

Cunault's older Gallo-Roman neighbour, **Gennes**, lies 3km further west along the D751. Despite the existence of a sizeable Roman town on the plateau at Chênehutte, the 1837 discovery of an amphitheatre just to the south of the modern centre of Gennes revealed a hitherto unexpected density of Gallo-Roman settlement along this stretch of the Loire. The excavations of 1985–93 have shown this to be a good 2C or 3C elliptical demi-amphitheatre of a type favoured in provincial northern Gaul, as at Chenevières (Loiret), with a capacity to seat around 5000. Current opinion tends to see Gennes as less a town and more a rural religious centre however, with a nymphaeum and bath house constructed around a spring known as 'Avort' and possibly a temple of Mercury on the hill above which St-Eusèbe now stands.

The small **Musée Archaeologique** on the Rue de l'Ancienne Mairie offers a background to the current excavations, along with finds from elsewhere in the town, most notably a rare Merovingian belt buckle from the necropolis at St-Vétérin, but there is no substitute for a visit to the **Amphitheatre** itself. This lies in the woods to the west of the Avenue de l'Amphithéâtre, the large oval arena beneath a natural scarp which originally supported an elliptical cavea. Some of the lower walls of this cavea and part of a dressing room survive, constructed from alternating courses of stone and brick, a technique known as *opus mixtum*. Except for an area to the south, reserved for patrician visitors, the seating was of wood, the one other element of interest being the drainage channels, laid for water rather than blood, and beautifully tiled to act as a gulley between arena and cavea.

This initial importance seems to have been sustained during the early Middle Ages, for Gennes developed as a two parish town, its brace of churches overlooking the centre from the higher ground to east and west. **St-Vétérin** occupies the lower rise to the east, the mixture of brick and small squared stones at the base of the belfry suggesting a church was standing here by the late 10C. Above this rises an early 12C bell-tower, sunk against the west wall of a slightly later transept and choir and, in its situation, very different to that of St-Eusèbe, so clearly visible on top of the hill on the far side of the town. Despite the discovery of a bronze statuette of Mercury on the hillside here, it seems likely that **St-Eusèbe** was the later of the two foundations, though the loss of its roof timbers in the early 19C has left the nave little more than a shell. The eastern walls of this nave are the earliest part of the surviving structure, made up of beautifully alternated courses of stone and brick and likely to date from the early 11C. The deeply projecting eastern apse and choir are 12C, while the 13C belfry is here treated as a crossing tower and rises to support an originally 15C octagonal spire, rebuilt after its destruction in 1944. The south wall of the nave now also supports a memorial to **Les Cadets de Saumur**, the young trainees from the *Ecole de Cavalerie* who died in June 1940 attempting to defend the Gennes river crossing from the German advance. And the views of the river, particularly from the garden of the house to the left, are majestic.

It is worth staying with the **Loire downstream of Gennes**, and the D132 follows its course north-west, passing beneath the handsome *tuffeau* village of (2km) **Bessé**. The 12C parish church lies some way from the village in a subsidiary agricultural hamlet on lower ground, and, aside from the distinction of its eastern belfry, houses a very curious and rustic 17C reredos screen.

Some 3km west you reach **Le Thoureil**, one of the grander river ports of the *ancien régime* and, in this writer's opinion, one of the most beautiful passages of the Loire, where the river is at its broadest and most placid, curving gently west beneath fishing quays, poplars and sand bars. The village took its name from the ruined 11C donjon just to the east at Richebourg, and by 1066 was referred to as 'Turriculum'. Its period of greatest prosperity was the 16C and 17C, the date of the splendid *hôtels particuliers* you find along the eastern section of the river front. The finest of these back onto the low cliffs and support glorious terraced gardens, or have irregular riverside courts. Although not the best, the **Mairie** occupies the earliest, a gable-fronted house begun c 1500. Its ground floor houses a small museum, the **Musée Camille Fraysse**. Fraysse was the local pharmacist and an amateur archaeologist who, in the 1950s, amassed the evidence which has demonstrated that the area just inland of Le Thoureil supported a neolithic tool-making industry. The half-finished or broken flints, arrowheads, burins, knives and scrapers which Fraysse collected are all laid out in small display cabinets to state the case.

The village centrepiece is still the **parish church**, with an unusually narrow 13C belfry the only medieval element incorporated into a building otherwise reconstructed in the mid-19C. A section of 12C blind arcading from an earlier apse has been revealed to the east, but its greatest attractions are two 16C reliquary chests from the neighbouring abbey of St-Maur. These are mounted on plinths to the west of the crossing arch, the beautifully pilastered arcades honouring the 12 apostles, along with reliefs of St-Benoît, St-Maur, and other, inevitably desirable, minor Benedictine saints (key at No. 3, Place de l'Eglise if locked).

What little survives of the **abbey of St-Maur** stands 2km west of here, beyond the wooded cliffs at **St-Maur-de-Glanfeuil**. A Gallo-Roman villa certainly existed here, and the foundation of a monastery is traditionally supposed to have taken place in 543 under St-Maur, a disciple of Benedict of Nursia (the founder of Montecassino, and of 'Benedictine' monasticism). Expanded by a certain Rorigo at the beginning of the 9C, the abbey was deserted in the wake of the Norse raid of 862 and the remains of St-Maur were taken to St-Pierre-des-Fossés, south-east of Paris, which subsequently became known as St-Maur-des-Fossés. Glanfeuil was not reoccupied until the early 10C, when it was downgraded to the status of priory, but a new church is known to have been consecrated in 1036, and the community was once more given autonomy by Pope Urban II in 1096. Its later history was less auspicious, and it was badly damaged by the English in 1368, by the Huguenots in 1560, and by the Allied advance across the Loire in 1944.

The bizarre collection of buildings which remain now acts as a residential ecumenical centre, the majority of these structures being post-war. However, most of the reformed conventual precincts of 1685–1700 stand, with two walks of the cloister forming an angle around the excavated remains of what is described as a 4C shrine to a nymph but which is undoubtedly the foundation of a 12C monastic *lavabo*. This exists at the same ground level as was occupied by the church to the south, the façade of which is partially preserved within the end-wall of a hall of 1955. The arch heads of the portal and window of this façade are 12C, while the gable houses the centre's proudest treasure, the 'Carolingian' **Cross of St-Maur** (visible from a small first floor room off the main staircase). The cross is made up of five panels of superbly carved interlace, and is set within an upper front which itself mesmerises with a marvellous display of decorative stonework, the latter belonging to the church of 1036. Although it is traditionally thought to have been preserved from Rorigo's Carolingian monastery, the context of this cross is probably much more straightforward, and one suspects it was carved shortly before 1036 to embellish the gable in which it is so beautifully housed.

Beyond St-Maur the D132 begins to drift south of the river, climbing above the rough pasture of the old flood meadows and through a number of small villages. At (2km) **St-Rémy-la-Varenne** the 15C and 16C **Logis du Prieuré** has a splendid run of encircled busts across its exterior elevations, and houses temporary summer exhibitions in the rooms around its abundantly carved 16C firebreast. While at (5km) **Blaison** the early 13C collegiate church of **St-Aubin** shelters a good set of 15C choir stalls, among whose heads and sentinel beasts sits a fantastically reformed relative of a tortoise. The rest of the village is no less arresting, the vast stone slabs of a ruined dolmen scattered among the late medieval canonries, and a three-towered 16C manor house standing in the bailey of the former castle.

West of Blaison, the road rejoins the D751 at the pleasant town of (6km) **St-Jean-des-Mauvrets**, whose schist-built houses give notice that one has crossed the great geological divide that separates the limestone formations of north-central France from the granites and slates of the Armorican massif. This geology has a marked effect on the river, pushing a subsidiary channel so far to the south of the main course that it has become known as the river Louet, and narrowing the northern flood plains to bring the river Authion flowing into the Loire at (7km) **Ponts-de-Cé**. The latter town is a succession of bridges over the Louet, Loire and Authion, but its days as a great river crossing and constant battlefield are over and it has become an otherwise unremarkable suburb of Angers. A mid-15C tower survives from the once famous château which, with its 17C southern wing, houses the **Musée des Coiffes d'Anjou**, an assortment of lace and embroidered bonnets collected from most of the towns of Anjou. Now you just need to cross the last of the bridges at (1km) St-Aubin to find yourself within sight of (5km) Angers (see Route 12), one of the truly great cities of western France.

9

The Valley of Le Loir: Vendôme to Angers

ROAD (163km): Vendôme D5, 10km Le Gué-du-Loir; D5/C14, 3km Mazangé; C14, 3km Lunay; D53/D917, 8km Montoire (D108, 2km Lavardin); D917, 6km Trôo; D917/C1, 6km Vieux-Bourg-d'Artins; D10, 5km Couture-sur-Loir; D57/D305, 3km Poncé-sur-le-Loir; D305, 7km La Chartre-sur-le-Loir; D305/N138, 16km Château-du-Loir; D10/D11, 9km La Bruère-sur-Loir; D11/D30, 4km Vaas; D305, 13km Le Lude; D306/D54, 10km Luché-Pringé; D13/N23, 13km La Flèche; N23, 12km Durtal; N23, 35km Angers.

The river Loir rises to the south of Chartres, draining the great plains of the southern Beauce and growing in strength as it flows south from Châteaudun and into the Touraine near Morée. On reaching Vendôme, the river turns west, slowly closing the gap separating it from the broader valley of the river Loire before flowing into the Sarthe to the north of Angers. The above itinerary is concerned with this passage between Vendôme and Angers, seeking to relate an incomparably beautiful valley to the settlements which drew sustenance from the river banks.

Certain themes stand out—the medieval painted churches clustered around Montoire, the great Renaissance towns of Le Lude and La Flèche, the extraordinary depth of early 16C patronage encountered all the way from Couture to Pringé. But what is striking about most of the monuments you encounter, is a stylistic breadth, an ease with which the forms of consecutive eras are juxtaposed. This open, liberal sensibility marks out the entire valley, as apparent in the social inclusiveness of the markets of the larger towns as in their historical structure, and it can be no coincidence that the Loir gave birth to the greatest lyric poet France has produced, Pierre de Ronsard.

If you wish to follow the river downstream, towns such as La Chartre, Le Lude and La Flèche make excellent overnight bases. But whatever your eventual destination, Vendôme is a beguiling place in which to start, and is arguably one of the finest market towns in France.

Vendôme

Anchored between a steep crag to the south and a gentler range of northern hills, the town grew above an island in the Loir, turning the flat valley bottom to advantage by cutting subsidiary channels and canals to facilitate navigation throughout the various quarters. These natural features made the town—giving the centre its present shape—and it was as a substantial walled river crossing astride the road from Chartres to Blois that Vendôme grew in significance. You can see this most clearly from the **Château**, accessible by car along the road to Blois (where a left turn onto the Rue du Château brings you into a shady car-park), or on foot via a steep path which ascends from a flight of steps above the Rue St-Bié.

It was from this spot in 1032 that Geoffroy Martel saw three flaming spears plunge into a fountain below, and determined to found an abbey dedicated to La Trinité where they landed. This decision, and the feudal reforms Geoffroy initiated from the early castle here, established Vendôme as an important medieval centre, for, although the Gallo-Roman town of *Vindocenum* had existed on the site, it was a relatively small settlement which had lapsed during the Early Christian period. Geoffroy was Foulques Nerra's successor as Count of Anjou, and with Anjou passing into the hands of the Plantagenets the Counts of Vendôme became Plantagenet vassals, uneasily bordering the Beauce and the French royal domain. The acquisition of Vendôme by the Bourbons in 1371 brought direct allegiance to the crown, and royal interest served the town well, particularly during the late Middle Ages when the booming tanneries turned their hands to glove-making, and the population quickly doubled. With Marie de Luxembourg married to François, Comte de Vendôme, the town was liable to receive the French court, and one of François I's initial acts on acceding to the French throne in 1515 was to raise Vendôme to the status of duchy. However, a stroll around the town reveals little evidence of widespread 16C patronage, for with the third Duke, the Huguenot Henri de Bourbon, crowned Henri IV in 1589, Catholic Vendôme demurred, sided with the League and was sacked, the majority of its 15C and 16C timber buildings going up in smoke.

This was not the reason for the château's ruination, however. Largely abandoned in the 17C, it was finally pulled apart in 1793, the splendid walks and gardens planted among the ruins an attempt to make the best of a fairly pointless demolition. The foundation lines of the **Chapelle St-Georges** are all that remains of Geoffroy Martel's castle, founded by his wife, Agnès de Bourgogne, and used as a mausoleum by the Counts of Vendôme. Even Henri IV's parents, Antoine de Bourbon and Jeanne d'Albret, were buried here. The rest of the castle is substantially 13C, the northern enceinte walls standing to parapet level and provided with semi-circular bastions reminiscent of those at Angers. The largest of the angle-towers to the east, the **Tour de Poitiers**, was rebuilt as a main keep during the 15C and is the most architecturally detailed of the towers to have survived. But it is the gardens and the view which are the compelling reason for a visit, and on a quiet sunny day the château ranks among the most beautiful sites in western France, a tiny orangery at the edge of the north-eastern terrace providing a space for summer concerts, with the town and valley laid out below.

Returning by the path down to the **town** brings you along the Rue St-Bié and into the Place de la République. West of here lie the engaging market spaces of the **Place St-Martin**, decorated with café tables and awnings and busy in the morning with the shoppers of the Vendômois. While to the east, a gap in the street front allows the Rue de l'Abbaye to curve past the Romanesque bell-tower and Flamboyant west front of **Abbaye de la Trinité**. This gap replaced an earlier archway—destroyed in 1792 after the abbey was dissolved—which originally acted as a gate connecting the monastic precincts with the town. The shape of these precincts becomes apparent as you move towards the church, with three 12C arches surviving from the monastic grain store on the inner face of the earlier west range (the area above and to the south of the old archway having been used as a visitors' wing), and the 16C Sacristan's and Prior's Lodgings at Nos 4–6 Rue de l'Abbaye.

Having been created a parish in 1791 the **monastic church** survived in better order, and what remains is one of the most important late medieval buildings in France. Geoffroy Martel's foundation was confirmed in 1033 and colonised by Benedictine monks from the abbey of Marmoutier, work proceeding swiftly and the church being ready for consecration in 1040, the year of Foulques Nerra's death. Geoffroy endowed La Trinité with more than merely land, for in 1038 he returned with two significant relics, given to him by the Byzantine Emperor Michael IV Paleologus in gratitude for his help in repelling the Saracen invasion of Sicily. The first was an arm of St George, reserved for the chapel Geoffroy's wife, Agnès, founded in the castle. The second, a crystal, in which was sealed a 'Holy Tear' shed by Christ upon the tomb of Lazarus, may stretch modern credulity, but after Geoffroy confided the relic to the care of La Trinité its attested miracle working powers attracted a considerable pilgrimage. This pilgrimage reached its zenith in the wake of the Hundred Years War, when the offerings at the shrine of the *Sainte Larme* (Holy Tear) were sufficient to finance the completion of a new nave.

All that survives of Geoffroy's church are the transept walls, their low crossing capitals now supporting four 13C statues representing the Archangel Gabriel and the Virgin locked into an Annunciation, along with St Peter and St-Eutrope, the latter two saints represented by relics in the abbey. There is certainly evidence of a considerable amount of rebuilding in the late 11C and 12C (see below), but the transepts do not appear to have received their domed-up octopartite vaults until the mid-13C, a campaign which may have precipitated a more general refurbishment. The greater part of the present building is late medieval, however, and its sporadic and extended building programme makes it a monument of particular significance to historians of late Gothic design.

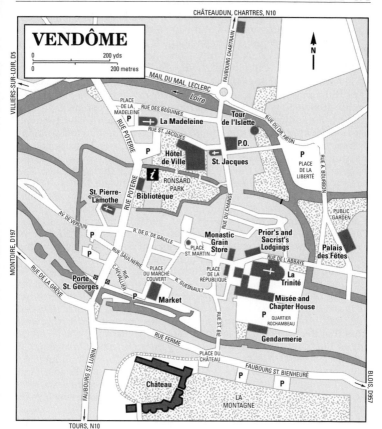

There is some dispute about precisely when work began on the new **choir**. The church was reported to be dilapidated in the late 13C, but the clerestory glass dates from between c 1280 and c 1300, and as this presents a coherent programme it would appear that the conventional date given for the start of work on the choir, 1306, is too late. All that is certain is that the monks of La Trinité gained permission to take stone from the quarry of the Cistercian abbey of Aumône as early as 1271, and that the eastern arm was complete by 1318. The two eastern bays of the nave then followed during the abbacy of Jean de la Buffa (1317–42), after which work ground to a halt, as the effects of the Hundred Years War and a depopulated, plague-ridden countryside conspired to create a climate of violence and uncertainty. The architectural language of this greater eastern area is usually described as late Rayonnant, with a glazed triforium adding an intermediate zone of glass, and the mullions of the clerestory windows run down through this triforium to connect with a row of balustraded quatrefoils above the stringcourse, effectively unifying the upper storeys of the elevation.

The clerestory tracery of the two eastern nave bays has been varied, and instead of a large roundel at the head of the window the patterns are respectively lozenge- or spoon-shaped. But the overall handling is little changed, and it is an approach one might find in the more ambitious mid-13C churches of the Ile-de-France.

This situation changes as you move west along the **nave**, but the shifts are subtle and give an insight into just how conservative French late Gothic architecture can be. The third and fourth bays of the nave date from c 1450, adding fillets to the mouldings of the main arcade to create a leaner-looking profile, and a band of foliage decoration to the string-course. Above, the balustrade of quatrefoils has been transformed by inserting flickering petals of tracery between square panels, while the design of the clerestory tracery is much looser than that to the east. The three western bays are later still, dating from between 1485 and 1507, and here at least the language has begun to take on more liquid character. The bases are taller and the arcade has lost its capitals, creating a seamless transition between vertical and curved surfaces. The triforium has been given a run of ogee arches, and the tracery becomes progressively more elaborate as you move west, culminating in the **west window**, a magnificent *tour-de-force* of shimmering, sinuous form. This final campaign is attributed to Jehan de Beauce, the architect responsible for the north-west spire of Chartres cathedral, on the basis of both a detailed comparison with Chartres and the fact that he maintained a house in Vendôme until 1506. If so, Jehan is revealed as a master of window, as well as tower, design, and it is on this **west front** that the architectural reputation of La Trinité rests. The façade is one of the great statements of Flamboyant architecture, realising not only the potential of tracery to dramatise the interior of a building, but to encompass a form at once symbolic and naturalistic—the tear. And having recognised the tumbling, fluid cadences of repeated tears, they were employed to unleash a miracle of light and shade which rains unquenched across the exterior surfaces.

La Trinité is also justifiably celebrated for the quality and range of its surviving glass and furniture. This is concentrated in the choir, where the high **clerestory stained glass** dates from the last quarter of the 13C, with a superb central panel representing the Trinity spilling across all three lights, and abbots, saints and donors filling gabled panels to both north and south. To the right of the axial window, Pierre d'Alençon, Count of Vendôme (1258–84), is seen offering a new reliquary *chasse* to the abbot of La Trinité, while the arms of his wife, Jeanne de Châtillon (died 1292), are featured next to the figure of St Benedict at the north entrance to the choir. The latest of the clerestory glazing is probably the south-western window, where SS. Barnabas, Philip, Eutropius and Louis (the latter only canonised in 1297) have a heaviness at odds with the crisp and possibly Tours-inspired forms of the hemicycle windows.

The ambulatory chapels were mostly reglazed during the 16C, though they also contain some earlier and more enigmatic glass, including a very fine panel of the head of the Virgin in the east wall of the north transept, the work of a Chartrain glazier and dating from c 1215. Further east, the **Chapel of St-Martin** boasts a late 15C cycle of glass centred around the life of the saint, and stands opposite the sole remnant of the shrine of the Holy Tear, a colossal and rather crude base dating from 1519. The chapel of La Madeleine also houses a proficient, though clumsily restored, cycle of early 16C glass, but it is the **Axial Chapel** which accommodates the most unexpected work, a magnificent Romanesque Virgin and Child, enthroned within a jewelled mandorla and supported by four angels. It is thought to date from c 1140 and was almost certainly made for the axial chapel of Geoffroy Martel's La Trinité, where a considerable amount of work is known to have been undertaken during the second quarter of the 12C. In addition, the chapel houses some good early 16C glass—a series of eight panels illustrating Old Testament scenes, most of which bear later inscriptions, ranging from an Adam and Eve before God to a Daniel in the Lions' Den. The very best of the 16C glazing is to be found in the nave, where a number of saints have been sensitively remounted in the south aisle, one per bay, and where the cellarer, Jean Gallois, was responsible for the north aisle **Chapelle des Fonts**, furnishing it with the wonderful purples of the Raising of Lazarus.

The most remarkable 16C work stands in the choir, where a good number of the **choir stalls**, sold off as scrap wood at the Revolution, have been returned to their original position, although 16 still remain in the parish church of St-Hilaire at Villiers-sur-Loir, which had the foresight to acquire them at sale. They were made between 1522 and 1529, and even in this abbreviated form glory in one of the finest sets of **misericords** still to grace a French great church. These depict the seasons, signs of the zodiac, trades and miscellaneous allegorical figures, with two exceptionally fine end panels, showing Mary Magdalene before a Cross which bears the Instruments of the Passion, and the Resurrected Christ beneath a Pietà. But to learn more of their subject matter and style it is worth making the journey to Villiers.

Leaving the church by the west door takes you beneath the shadow of its most distinctive element—the most visible landmark in Vendôme—the mighty Romanesque **bell-tower** of La Trinité. This was built as a freestanding tower to the south-west of the church, and, though the lowest stage has been altered, it is generally agreed that both tower and spire date from between c 1120 and c 1150, the upper octagon inventively supplied with conically roofed pavilions at the angles. The spire is built of coursed stone, and with its capstone rises to a height of 83 metres, making it the tallest early 12C structure in France. It is also, arguably, one of the most influential. Not only are monumental spires of this date unprecedented, but the manner with which the octagonal base was treated clearly inspired the architect of the south-west spire at Chartres Cathedral to lift pavilions into the angles of the spire itself, and thus was born 13C north French spire design.

The main monastic quarters are to the right of this belfry, where an 18C arch gives entry to all that remains of the **cloister**. The cycles of reform, decline, renewal, and change of use revealed here may interact with those of the church, but the results are of a wholly different order. In 1663 the Congregation of St-Maur was introduced in an attempt to restore monastic discipline to Vendôme, and, as was generally the case elsewhere, the Maurists built themselves a new conventual range while leaving the church itself intact. At La Trinité they went a stage further, and retained the early 14C cloister and chapter house, adding, between 1732 and 1742, the three austere and light-filled wings which now enclose the cloister. The loss of the claustral walks came later, and after the French Revolution the conventual buildings were annexed to act first as a town hall and then as a barracks, the cloister becoming too much of a hindrance to the French battalion billeted here, who demolished three of its arcades in 1907. The only complete walk is to the north, each bay given a pyramidal roof and the tracery mullions having been replaced by solid walling.

This north walk is currently inaccessible but you can visit the superb **chapter house** (key in museum if locked), whose 1972 restoration caused a stir after the 14C stonework of the south wall was removed to reveal a fragmentary band of Romanesque **wall painting** attached to the wall behind. This is just under 6 metres in length and 1.5 metres high, with two episodes you can readily distinguish and three subjects which have been deciphered from partial iconographical clues. The more visible scenes represent the Supper at Emmaus, jammed behind one of the 14C responds to the left, and the Miraculous Draught of Fishes. To the right a few patches of paint survive from an Investiture of St Peter, Christ's Commission to the Apostles, and the Ascension. Where the frescoes escaped damage in the 14C, as in the Miraculous Draught of Fishes, they have survived intact, and, having been protected against surface damage and aerial pollution, are quite astonishingly vibrant and richly coloured.

It is known that the Gothic chapter house stood on the site of its 11C predecessor, and the shape of the latter is known from excavation, giving rise to the possibility that the remaining paintings formed part of a large cycle of the Life of Christ, running from the north-west angle across the east wall and ending with the surviving post-Resurrection scenes. However, it has also been argued that the particular selection of Resurrection scenes may be linked with a movement to enhance the prestige of a reforming Papacy, stressing matters of Investiture and the role of the Church as an instrument of Salvation, and that there is nothing random in the survival of this particular group in the chapter house. Like most other wall paintings to which they compare—they are stylistically very close to those in the western porch at St-Savin-sur-Gartempe and in the apse of St-Hilaire at Poitiers—they are undated. However, they probably belong to the 1090s and are the work of a travelling shop who clearly found employment elsewhere in western France.

The rest of the east range is now occupied by the **Musée**, whose imposing entrance hall makes clear that a considerable body of 11C and 14C material was incorporated into the Maurist wing when it was rebuilt. The main displays are arranged over four floors, with the medieval exhibits on the ground floor, temporary exhibitions above, and the second and third floors given over to local painting, sculpture and furniture, and natural history, respectively. Both of these latter floors are well worth visiting, with the work of **Louis Leygue** perhaps the highlight. Leygue won the Grand Prix de Rome in 1931 and established himself at a forge in Vendôme in 1950, producing a prodigious quantity of work in stone, iron, bronze and copper, some of which he gave to the musée. These donations encompass the full range of his later work, including many studies and preliminary drawings, and a magnificent skeletal horse and rider from the 1970s, all hats, heads and awakening self-consciousness.

The area to the **west of the abbey** belonged to the town, with the grandest of Vendôme's market squares, the **Place St-Martin**, carved out of the space left by the demolition of a parish church in 1856. Its late 15C bell-tower, the **Tour St-Martin**, was retained to form the centrepiece of a splendid rectangle, with a statue celebrating the Marquis de Rochambeau, the last ancien régime *Maréchal de France*, closing the Place to the east. The Marquis was chosen by Louis XVI to command the French contingent despatched to America to assist Washington's campaign for Independence, contributing to the victory at Yorktown in 1781. Although closely linked with Louis XVI's policies, he was acquitted of all charges after the death of Robespierre, and died peaceably down the road at Rochambeau in 1807.

From here, Vendôme's main street, the **Rue du Change**, slides north to cross the 18C Pont Perrin, its handsome terraces of 17C–19C shops and houses broken to the west by a reminder of the street's position on the medieval pilgrimage route from Chartres to Santiago de Compostela. The **Chapelle St-Jacques** was a wayside hospice and chapel, which first opened its doors in 1203 (offering accommodation as well as Mass), before the renewed popularity of the pilgrimage after the Hundred Years War resulted in the chapel's reconstruction. The handsome façade on the Rue du Change dates from this rebuilding of 1452, as do the windows and roof of the interior; the imposing western gallery, which forms such an excellent foil for the temporary exhibitions and concerts now held here, was added somewhat later. But the majority of the stonework along the long walls was retained from the earlier building, hence the half-columns and peculiar late Romanesque capitals visible along the exterior of the north wall.

A small door in the north wall brings you out on to the **Rue St-Jacques**, past the 18C rear elevations of the Lycée Ronsard, to provide a first glimpse of the octagonal spire and belfry of **La Madeleine**. You can get a less inhibited view of this tower from the Rue des Béguines, from where the Flamboyant tracery of the east window is also revealed. Either route will bring you into the Place de la Madeleine and face to face with the west front of the parish church. Prior to 1475 there was no parish of La Madeleine, and the church was originally founded to serve the tanners and glove-makers who had hugely expanded this quarter of the town. The interior makes it clear that large congregations were anticipated, the spacious nave enhanced by a full aisle to the north and a set of subsidiary chapels to the south, the chapels arranged between the buttresses in the manner of a toned-down Spanish hall church. The great wooden roof—and most of the architectural sculpture—was replaced during the 19C, and the best of the late medieval work is to be found in the east window, donated by François de Vendôme and Marie de Luxembourg in the early 16C.

To the south of La Madeleine, the **Rue Poterie** provides a sequence of bridges over the Loir's various channels, creating a north–south axis which parallels that of the Rue du Change. To the east is the delightful **Parc Ronsard**. The focal point of the park is the **Collège des Oratoriens**, a superb 17C school building arranged as four wings enclosing a square *cour d'honneur*, the elevations drawing warmth from the rose-red brick and symmetry from the stonework. The college was founded in 1623 by César de Vendôme, the son of Henri IV and Gabrielle d'Estrées, though the date of 1639 inscribed on the south wing suggests that construction was at a leisurely pace. The rangy north-western spur was added in the early 18C, well before the school's most illustrious pupil, Honoré de Balzac, arrived as an eight-year-old in 1807. Having been transformed into a lycée in 1848, it now houses the hôtel-de-ville. The Parc occupies a considerable bank of land between the Rues Poterie and du Change, and also includes a very fine late 15C manor house, **L'Hôtel du Bellay le Saillant**, which now accommodates the Office du Tourisme, and a 15C wooden laundry platform, known as the **Lavoir des Cordeliers**.

Continuing south along the Rue Poterie takes you past the 19C town library, entertainingly embellished with a floral display which invariably gives the correct date. A left turn onto the **Rue St-Pierre-Lamotte** brings you to a more mysterious structure, the chapel of **St-Pierre-Lamothe** (an 'h' is used here). This tiny building is probably 11C, with some crudely carved foliage capitals and evidence of small circular windows to east and west, the latter probably later inserts.

The quarter around St-Pierre-Lamothe was badly damaged by the air-raids of June 1940, and though the area has been sensitively reconstructed, particularly around the **Place du Marché** where the iron and glass market hall of 1899 has been refashioned, there is comparatively little of interest. What there is belongs to the **Porte St-Georges**, the old southern town gate which the Counts made over to the town to act as an hôtel-de-ville in 1467. Civic ambition resulted in the addition of the window embrasures and machicolations of the southern elevation in the 16C, and Napoleon heightened the gate in 1809, to get his artillery through en route to Spain.

Below Vendôme the Loir throws a series of meanders which snake westwards as far as Montoire, creating a broad valley floor. The swiftest route west is along the D917 but, as with the river, it is more worthwhile to take a winding course, setting out along the D5 to (7km) **Villiers-sur-Loir**. Like many of the villages above these northern shores, Villiers is sited not on the crest of the ridge but on the south facing slopes, with a small central square enclosed by the church and the Mairie, the latter provided with an elaborate clock-tower.

The parish church of **St-Hilaire** was rebuilt in the 15C to serve an increased congregation, and decorated with an intriguing, but ghostly, set of wall paintings c 1500 which juxtapose a huge **St Christopher** with the **Meeting of the Quick and the Dead**. This latter composition, where three huntsmen encounter three corpses in a wood, was a commonplace of late medieval churches, highlighting the certainty of death; but the treatment is so badly decayed here that it is impossible to make out many of the incidental details. Fortunately, this is not the case with the early 16C **choir stalls**, 16 of which retain their carved misericords. This carved group originally formed part of the second tier of stalls from La Trinité, Vendôme, enlarged here by a set of plain stalls from the chapel of St-Jacques, Vendôme, and they extend the known range of the lower set to include some entertainingly proverbial subject matter—racy and vernacular stuff.

West of Villiers, the D5 throws off an occasional glimpse of the 18C **Château de Rochambeau** on the left bank of the river, before skirting the water meadows to (3km) **Le Gué-du-Loir**. The **Manoir de Bonaventure** stands at the edge of the village encompassed by a 15C turreted wall, its lawns generously open to passers-by who wish to gaze at the 16C house within its court. It is a lovely spot, set above the narrow river Boulon, where Ronsard was fêted by Antoine de Bourbon and Alfred de Musset was brought for childhood holidays by his father.

You can also continue along the road here, signposted to Savigny-sur-Braye, and take a right turn to the C14 to bring you into (3km) **Mazangé**. This route takes you tumbling down to a village half hidden within the willows and alders of a sunken tributary stream. The most striking vertical in this descent is provided by the late medieval spire of **St-Lubin**, and the rich russets and browns belong to its superbly tiled roof. This tilework also encloses a magnificent timber roof, raised in 1563 and, for once, not only original but largely unrestored.

Returning west, the C14 breaks through vast fields of wheat and sunflowers, dipping to meet another of the Loir's tributary streams, the Cise, at (3km) **Lunay**. The church here received a new roof at roughly the same time as that at Mazangé, but, unlike its smaller neighbour, **St-Martin** at Lunay was abominably treated during the 19C, and in the 1830s an apse-ambulatory was shoehorned into the 14C square-ended choir and embellished with suitably gloomy paintings. This had the effect of preserving a 14C fresco cycle in what became the sacristy, though to see it you must contact the *presbytère*. The nave came off better, and the fine early 16C portal has been recently restored, the Virgin and Child which came to stand on its trumeau now removed to the safety of the north nave wall.

From Lunay the most direct route back to the Loir is along the D53, cresting a rise to command a glorious panorama of the valley, before descending past the old cliff-dwellings of (4km) **Les Roches-l'Evêque** and picking up the D917 to (4km) **MONTOIRE-SUR-LE-LOIR**. Montoire is the main market centre between Vendôme and Château-du-Loir, a spacious but dreary town aligned around a large square, the **Place Georges Clemenceau**, which lies just to the north-west of the river.

The town rose to prominence in the 12C as a staging-post between Vendôme and Tours, at which date a leper-hospital was established and the ruined keep of the castle—visible beyond the river—was built. The most interesting areas are to be found on the left bank of the Loir, across a bridge from which the overhanging willows and alder of the river banks are most prolific, and where the best of the 16C–18C townhouses survive. It is here, along a narrow alley to the right of the Rue St-Oustrille, that you can find the tiny priory of **St-Gilles**, whose eastern semidome supports one of the finest Romanesque **apse paintings** to have survived in France (if locked the key can be obtained from No. 33 Rue St-Oustrille).

Stepping into this chapel, craning to see into the apses as your eyes adjust to the low light, is a revelatory experience. The date of St-Gilles' foundation is unknown. Legend ascribes it to Charlemagne, who passed through Montoire on his way from St-Calais to visit Alcuin at Tours in 800. But although St-Gilles was a dependency of the Benedictine abbey of St-Calais, there is no documentary evidence for the priory which pre-dates 1411, when we are told Pierre de Gis was prior. Pierre de Gis was variously succeeded by three generations of Ronsards, the poet Pierre de Ronsard being the last of the commendatory priors from 1566 to 1585. And yet there seems no doubt that the present truncated chapel is 11C, a seductive theory being that it was founded in memory of Geoffroy Martel, Count of Anjou and Vendôme, who died in 1060 as he was setting out on a pilgrimage to St-Gilles in Provence.

Whatever the precise date and motive for building the chapel, an intriguing twist has been given to the transepts which are treated in the manner of enclosed apses, i.e. they are rectangular on the exterior and apsidal on the interior. This gives the interior a trefoil east end, the apses shaped like a clover leaf, each of which carries a fairly full body of Romanesque paint.

Each apse centres on a vision of Christ, and the temptation is to see three Christs in Majesty whose gazes meet in the crossing. However, this would be to misunderstand the nature of the imagery. The **Christ to the east** is a beneficent figure, a returning saviour ablaze in glory and surrounded by the four beasts of the Apocalypse. The benign nature of such an image is reinforced by the handling of the angels, swiftly and rhythmically sketched in, and the manner in which they hold the mandorla is one of the most memorable gestures in Romanesque painting. The promise they illustrate is probably that of the Acts of the Apostles: 'This same Jesus, which is taken up from you into heaven, shall so come in like manner as you have seen him go into heaven'. This main apse Christ is the only composition not to have been extensively repainted in the mid-13C and early 14C, its light blues and ochres applied to a fairly light ground. The style of this painting has something of the lyricism of the crypt painting at Tavant, the supporting angels having an almost balletic ease of movement. Like Tavant, it probably dates from the second quarter of the 12C.

The **apse paintings to the north and south** are the work of a very different artist, that to the south being more fully coloured and monumental in feeling, the precious blues and greens having been ground from lapis lazuli and malachite. The figure of Christ in the south apse is a terrifying and minatory image, a **Christ in Judgement**, his hands disposed to separate the blessed from the damned. The depth and radiance of the painting here is clearly intended to evoke Byzantine apse mosaics, an effect which would have been more strongly felt when the subsidiary elements of the composition survived intact. You can still make out a fragmentary **Martyrdom of St Lawrence** (or possibly St

Vincent) on his grid-iron to the left, overlaid by a probably 14C **Wedding at Cana**, and with a good bit of 14C paintwork to the left.

The last of these Christs, in the north transept, depicts **Pentecost**, the Holy Spirit streaming from the hands of Christ and conveying the gifts of teaching, healing and prophecy upon the Apostles. It is perhaps the most stylised of the images, and despite its advanced decay and the heavy layers of overpaint, would seem to be the work of the same painter as was responsible for the Judgemental Christ of the south transept. But then the various styles pursued within these three apse paintings are inseparable from their meaning, and, considered as a whole, the programme has an impressive iconographic clarity, in which the images are intended to work together rather than be seen in isolation. It is the resolution of this desire for integration which is St-Gilles' enduring achievement.

Montoire is also within easy reach of another celebrated cycle of medieval **wall paintings** in the church of St-Genest at **LAVARDIN**, 2km upstream along the D108.

The sign at the edge of the village announces that Lavardin is *un des plus beaux villages en France*, and it is hard to disagree as you approach the banks of steeply tiled roofs from beyond the river, cradled against the cliffs and in the shade of a ruined **castle**. The castle is in the process of being consolidated and is currently closed to visitors, though the road to St-Arnoult offers an impressive view of the 14C gatehouse and concentric systems of defence. As a possession of the Counts of Vendôme, the site was first fortified in the late 11C, from which period the rectangular keep survives. Though the castle was repaired after the Hundred Years War, when Comte Jean VII was buried in the late 15C *logis*, the buildings were dismantled on the orders of the Protestant Prince Conti in 1590 and the site was never again occupied.

The priory church of **St-Genest** was built on lower ground to the east, initially as a dependency of the small collegiate chapel of St-Georges in the castle at Vendôme, subsequently under the Augustinian canons of St-Georges-du-Bois. St-Georges-du-Bois had been reformed in the late 11C by the village's most famous son, the great schoolman, poet and bishop of Le Mans, Hildebert de Lavardin, and despite the archaicism of the choir capitals it seems likely that the present church was built at roughly the same date, and in a single campaign of c 1090–c 1120. These capitals have excited much comment, their block-like shape crudely and powerfully turned into spiralling volutes at the angles, with shallow reliefs hatched out of several of the main faces. Some of the reliefs are arrestingly primitive—the Virgin and Child to the north, for instance—but the most enigmatic sculpture is in the north aisle, where two windows have been treated to four spiral columns and an assortment of capitals and bases, all of them 12C and probably relics of some piece of liturgical furniture.

The paintings are more heterogeneous, ranging from c 1200 to the early 16C, and surviving in considerable quantity. The finest may well be the earliest, a lightly pigmented **Baptism** of c 1200 in the north choir aisle, whose solid modelling and elongated figures are related to some of the paintings at nearby St-Jacques-des-Guérets. To the east of this is a roughly contemporary **Tree of Jesse** in a very much more curvilinear style. The **Christ in Majesty** of the apse, towering above SS Peter and Paul, would seem to be early 14C, while the most extensive survival, the **choir of saints and angels** embellishing the sanctuary vault, is probably slightly later. Beneath the vault is an early 14C **Washing of Feet** and a 15C **Passion cycle**, while the marvellous **Last Judgement** in the south choir aisle is undatable, late medieval being the best one can manage.

Completing this astonishing catalogue is a diffuse group of saints, martyrdoms and commendatory images arranged on the western and inner faces of the nave piers, many of them carrying inscriptions and all of them admirably identified in the explanatory sheet set up to the left of the south nave door.

The rest of the village spills away to the north and east of the church, too small to sustain many cafés and shops, though offering some lovely walks along the river and at least one good restaurant at the bottom of the hill.

West of Montoire the D917 stays to the north of the Loir, sidling beneath the slopes that support the great 18C and 19C arboretum of (2km) **La Fosse** (visits might be arranged for a group; for details phone 54 85 38 63), before alighting on another of those villages that has made this area a haven for students of the Romanesque. This is (4km) **TRÔO**, the ruined 12C façade of the **Maladrerie Ste-Catherine** (the old leper-house) standing opposite the Mairie, as you first enter the riverside precincts. The village itself has been stepped into the hillside, and to reach the centre you can either climb the steep path from the car-park, by the Mairie, or overshoot the bluff on the D917 and cut back along the D8, bringing you through a gap in the medieval ramparts at what was the 15C Porte de Sougé.

The church and famous *butte* are just beyond, with the 148 foot (45 metres) deep town well, known as the **Puits qui Parle**—because of its resounding echo—to your left as you come through the ramparts. The parish church of **St-Martin** was substantially rebuilt in the late 12C, when the aisleless two-bay **nave** was covered by domed-up rib vaults and the lower walls strengthened by enormous relieving arches, in a suitably scaled-down version of the sort of nave pioneered at Angers Cathedral. The apse was replaced in the early 14C, to the east of a crossing which bears a set of Romanesque capitals, though as the church has been recently and harshly restored for a second time much of the finer detail has been lost. The two exceptions to this are to be found in the choir, where a proficient set of early 16C stalls and a fine wooden statue of St-Martin giving half his cloak to a beggar survive, the latter now displayed in a glass cabinet beneath a 13C tomb canopy.

South of the church a 14 metre high mound of earth, known as **La Butte**, was raised as the motte of an 11C feudal castle, from whose flattish top the whole of the Loir from Lavardin to Artins is revealed. You can see little of the town, however. The reason for this becomes apparent as you descend the Rue Haute and strike off down the narrow path to the right. The majority of the earlier houses of Trôo were not simply revetted against the hillside, but were actually built into it, making the town what locals call a *ville troglodyte*. Some of these cave houses can be visited, the rooms cut out of the soft *tuffeau*, with a forward wall and window embrasures thrown across the entrance. A very few also give on to a complex network of secondary caves and tunnels, the so-called *caforts* (or *caves forts*, literally strongholds), which provided an inner refuge in times of war.

The attraction for students of the Romanesque is on the left bank of the river, opposite the village proper, where the late 12C **wall paintings** of the church of **St-Jacques-des-Guérets** act as a magnet for art historians throughout France. The paintings, along with the splendid 16C wooden statues of St James the Pilgrim and St Peter in Papal Vestments, were discovered in 1890–91, when an 18C retable was removed and the whitewash stripped from the walls. The documents which might have helped to interpret St-Jacques-des-Guérets were probably burned in the Revolutionary bonfire made of all church documents found at Trôo and neighbouring St-Georges-du-Bois.

St-Jacques was a parochial dependency of the Augustinian priory at St-Georges-du-Bois, though the church itself is modest, a 12C aisleless box with a clumsy horseshoe apse and a 16C timber roof. Why it should have attracted pilgrims who had travelled south via St-Calais and Trôo, bound for Tours and Compostela, remains elusive. It was almost certainly as a result of this popularity that the wall paintings were commissioned c 1200, from a group of painters whose origins are equally enigmatic and whose work can only be loosely paralleled. There is a little 15C painting, either laid over the earlier work or developed independently of it, but the vast bulk of what survives is late Romanesque, recognisable by the inventive borders with which the scenes are framed.

Two badly faded scenes on the north nave wall depict the **Massacre of the Innocents** and **Nativity**, while, lacking a vault, the dominant imagery of the apse has been applied to the lower walls. The central window embrasure carries figures of St George and St Augustine, with a magnificent **Crucifixion** (above an Angel at the Tomb and a sketchy Resurrection of the Dead) to the left, and a **Christ in Majesty** (above the Last Supper) to the right. The south wall of the apse closes with a curious **St Peter holding the Keys to the Heavenly Jerusalem**, and a **Martyrdom of St James**.

The south nave wall continues the pilgrimage imagery with **St Nicholas throwing three bags of gold** though a poor man's window, to provide his daughters with a dowry (the origin, incidentally, of the three golden balls which act as a pawnbroker's sign), above a **Raising of Lazarus**. Immediately west of this, a vast composition opens out in three tiers. At its centre **Christ descends into Limbo**, witnessed by the Elders of the Apocalypse above, with the Torments of the Damned below. Finally, there is a **crusading joust**, badly decayed but just visible beneath the south nave windows. Not only does this add up to an extensive cycle, it also includes some of the most accomplished late Romanesque painting in western France. The range of colour in the Crucifixion and Christ in Majesty, for instance, is quite unparalleled by wall painting elsewhere, and seems deliberately to emulate the colours of late 12C Limoges enamels. And the figure of Christ descending into

Limbo—much more angular and sharply silhouetted than the work in the apse—remains, in the opinion of this writer, one of the great works of late Romanesque art to survive in Europe.

The most interesting route **west from Trôo** follows the D917 through the cornfields to (4km) Sougé, where a left turn onto the C1 offers a way over the river, passing the picturesque silhouette of the parish church of St-Pierre at (2km) **Vieux-Bourg-d'Artins**. Locally celebrated for the peculiar cavity in its 13C west portal, said to be for lepers to take holy water, it is a bewildering and beautifully situated building, the hangar-like east end overlooking the river bank. The church was built above the site of a pagan temple, which may account for one or two of the odder bits of reused masonry, but though it was substantially refurbished after a fire in 1542, the greater part of its roughly coursed masonry is 11C. (The interior is open to visitors on Sunday afternoons, Easter to end October, but it is worth visiting for its exterior and situation alone.)

Once over the river and into present-day Artins, a right turn onto the D10 quickly brings you to (5km) **Couture-sur-Loir**. Gently angling away from the south bank of the Loir, the town is best reached by cutting up to meet the river (signposted Isle-Verte) and passing the 19C Château du Pin. Diagonally opposite the château, a wooden bridge and a few landing stages mark the site of the **Isle-Verte**, a tiny island lyricised in the poetry of **Pierre de Ronsard** and the place where the poet desired to have his tomb. It is among the loveliest spots of the Loir valley, fringed by overhanging willows and reed beds where the river widens and its pace slows, within sight of the village where Pierre de Ronsard spent his childhood, and where his parents, Louis de Ronsard and Jeanne Chaudrier, were buried. Louis was responsible for refurbishing the nave of the parish church of **St-Gervais-et-St-Protais**, while he was engaged in building the Manoir de la Possonière, but it was Claude, Pierre's brother, who commissioned a tomb after the death of his parents, in 1544 and 1545 respectively. A chapel was built to accommodate them to the north of the 13C choir, in what is now the sacristy, but Revolutionary anger with the seigneurial classes led to the smashing of the tombs, and the eventual removal of the damaged effigies to their present situation beneath the north-western clock tower. The **Manoir de la Possonière** survived in better shape, the 1km journey along the road to Les Essarts worthwhile for a view of its superb early 16C façade, the lintels brazen with moralising Latin inscriptions.

Occupying the **north bank of the river**, and reached along a combination of the D57 and D305 (no more than 3km from Couture), the **Château de Poncé-sur-le-Loir** is certainly a grander building than the manoir, but in its way is no less susceptible to Ronsard's ideals of charmed rural life. The existing structure was begun in the second quarter of the 16C for Jean de Chambray on the site of a medieval moated castle, with a principal entrance to the north and a terraced formal garden extending to the banks of the Loir. One of the consoles of the stair-tower carries the date 1542, by which time the work was probably substantially complete—the flattened forms of the stringcourses and pilasters compare with those of the François I wing at Amboise. The west pavilion was replaced in 1804 by the present low block, denuding Poncé of its elegant symmetry. But although the house was never on the scale of the great early 16C châteaux to the south-east of here, like them the richest architectural treatment was reserved for the **central stair-tower**.

This is regarded by the present owners at least as one of the finest Renaissance stairwells in France, straight ramped and covered by coffered vaults, whose panels carry a wealth of angels, cupids, masks and shields which emerge from the more densely carved floral motifs. It is certainly an impressive stairwell, a little like a scaled-down version of that at Azay-le-Rideau, from which any any tendency towards late Gothic vaulting devices has been expunged. It originally gave on to the gardens of the south front via an open loggia. The removal of this loggia, and the restriction of the formal *parterres* to no more than two splendid terraces by the road, is a great loss, and has deprived the château of its carefully contrived relationship with the river. In fact, you are now more conscious of its relationship with the cliff face to the north, a precipice partially disguised in 1830 by a grandiose retaining wall, with Neo-Gothic brickwork at the base and a battlemented stone arcade above. It was built for Amadée de Nonant, ostensibly to prevent the lesser mortals of the village from peering down on château life, and, in spite of the collapse of its central section in 1985, remains one of the more imposing early 19C initiatives to grace the valley.

The **village of Poncé-sur-le-Loir** is also worth exploring, though more for its heights than for its dull riverside strands. Like many other villages in these parts, Poncé originally occupied the hill, until the 19C brought the railway and the development of the river front. The smaller farms and older houses still cluster around the church of **St-Julien** at the edge of the promontory. The church itself just about warrants the visit (when the signs *à l'église* give out, turn right by the roadside cross), and the late 12C nave carries a faded set of early 13C wall paintings depicting the Infancy of Christ to the south, and the miraculous appearance of Saints George, Demetrius and Mercurius at the Battle of Antioch in 1098, above a Feast of Dives and Lazarus. The 'Romanesque' cycle in the apse is 19C, employing the same banded backgrounds as are on show in the nave to throw the narratives forcefully forward, though the severity of colour and ornament tend to jar.

To the **west of Poncé** the D305 becomes the main valley road, swinging beneath the vineyards to cross the river at the attractive winemaking centre of (7km) **La Chartre-sur-le-Loir**. The town has become understandably popular with visitors intent on exploring this particular stretch of the river. Its handsome central square, the **Place de la République**, hosts a number of cafés and hotels, and there is a large complex of tennis courts and swimming pools just to the south. The slow-maturing white wine produced here, *appellation d'origine contrôlée Jasnières*, is surprisingly little known, and was described by one local as 'all fruit on the palette and flint on the nose'. The vineyards cling to the northern slopes, while the D305 weaves an enthralling path between the southern hills and the river, passing the late medieval bell-tower at (6km) **Marçon** before joining the N138 to reach (10km) **Château-du-Loir**.

All that remains of the once mighty castle which gave the town its name is the ruined hulk of a 15C keep, preserved as an adornment to the attractive **Jardin Public** which surrounds the Maison du Tourisme. This lies to the south-west of a large market square, the **Place de l'Hôtel-de-Ville**, with the town's one other ancient survivor off to the south-east, beyond the Place Le Monnéar. Here, the long low outline of the church of **St-Guingalois** is banked above a shallow rise, with a substantially 13C choir supported by a mid-11C crypt, and a largely 16C nave. Unfortunately, the church was harshly re-cut during a late 19C restoration, and the early Romanesque crypt has been virtually rebuilt. The church possesses some good late 17C sculpture, however, with a terracotta Pietà of 1687 by Barthélemy de Mello in the choir and a slightly later composition by him in the nave, depicting St-Martin dividing his cloak to give to a beggar.

Château-du-Loir grew with the arrival of the Le Mans–Tours railway and its ambience is very much that of a sizeable late 19C industrial town, with few pre-19C houses surviving in the area around the church. When the Place de l'Hôtel-de-Ville is filled with the hurly-burly of a Saturday market, the town becomes an appealing place in which to linger. But on a dull day it is a dull town, and if pressed for time you would do better to make your way to Le Lude or La Flèche, both of which make more congenial bases in which to stay overnight.

West of Château-du-Loir, the best routes again involve meandering along with the river, which here means switching from bank to bank. The most promising route begins by crossing the Loir along the D10, where a right turn onto the D11 by the timberyards at (5km) Le Gué-de-Mézières brings you to (4km) the delightful parish church of **St-Martin** at **La Bruère-sur-Loir**. Enclosed within a cemetery behind the main street, and approached along a north nave wall which encases remnants of a 10C door and 11C window, the church was substantially altered in the mid-16C, when a new choir and nave roof were added. Advantage was also taken of the lavish local patronage to commission a programme of **stained glass windows**, most of which happily survive. A few panels were replaced by Hucher and Fialeix in the 19C, notably the prayerful knight and the St-Martin, but most of the glass is 16C, with the principal compositions often drawn above exquisite small animal studies, confined to the window bases in the manner of *bas-de-page* manuscript illuminations. Clockwise from the north-western window the subjects are: the Annunciation, Visitation, Nativity, Christ among the Doctors, Triumphal Entry to Jerusalem, Agony in the Garden, and Betrayal.

Downstream of La Bruère, a combination of the D11 and D30 brings you back to the north bank of the Loir at (4km) **Vaas**, crossing the river to reveal a wonderful vision of weirs, mills, gardens and water, to the north of which lies the village proper.

Vaas was built above a Gallo-Roman town, and the shape of the fortified medieval *burh* which replaced this is apparent in the narrow streets of the present village, sealed to the west by the apse and late medieval belfry spire of **St-Georges**. St-Georges was founded by Premonstratensian canons in the late 12C, which accounts for its scale, though the decline in importance of the church during the late Middle Ages is evident in the modesty of its 15C nave. Architecturally, it is the choir which seizes the eye, dating in the main from the 13C and covered by a high 'Angevin' vault. Locally, the church is better known for its **17C paintings**. These are indeed excellent, with a Virgin of the Rosary of 1618 at the west end of the nave, and a superb mid-17C Apotheosis of Christ mounted on the south wall, the latter occasionally attributed Philippe de Champaigne.

Beyond Vaas, the D305 sweeps through fields of maize and dairy pasture, bisecting the vast **archaeological site** at (7km) **Cherré**, before a rise to the west brings you into the dense woodland which once covered the whole of this area.

The Gallo-Roman settlement at Cherré is still being investigated, and those areas where excavations are complete are arranged as a *parc archéologique* and can easily be visited. The town clearly served a large community, with a late 1C semi-circular theatre capable of accommodating 3000 and a large early 2C covered market hall to the north of the present road, and a complex of temples and baths to the south. The beautifully coursed masonry of the theatre stands up to a height of 4 or 5 feet, like the rest of the buildings on the site unencumbered by subsequent alterations. It would seem that the abandonment of Cherré in the 4C was relatively sudden and complete.

As the D305 breaks the ridge to the west it reveals a shallow tree-lined slope, levelling out towards a narrow bridge which, in once more crossing the Loir, brings you into the great frontier town of (6km) **LE LUDE**.

Known as *Ludus* or *Luz* during the Middle Ages, the site was extensively fortified by Foulques Nerra at the end of the 10C to act as a border castle, separating Anjou from Maine. It remained an Angevin fastness throughout the Middle Ages, becoming a key English target during the Hundred Years War, and eventually falling in 1425 only to be recovered two years later by Ambroise de Loré and Gilles de Rois. Its present status as one of the grander market towns in the belly of the *département* of Sarthe, and thus technically a part of Maine, was brought about in 1790, when a sliver of what was previously northern Anjou was made administratively accountable to Le Mans. But it was renowned as a major market town as early as the 13C, and then, as now, its fame derived as much from its fairs as from its castle. The great autumn *Foire du Raillon* is still held on the second Thursday in September, and the whole structure of the town, stretching south from the castle through a succession of distinctive squares, seems to have developed with markets in mind.

It is these squares, the **Places François de Nicolay**, **de l'Hôtel-de-Ville**, and **Neuve**, and the narrow streets connecting them, which are the great joy of Le Lude, and strolling among the Thursday market stalls where they spill out of the Places to fill the streets is one of the great experiences of Angevin life. Even empty of traders it is an invigorating townscape, with a number of 17C houses along the **Rue**

d'Orée, and a particularly fine **Town Hall** of 1822 in the Place de l'Hôtel-de-Ville. Little actual medieval building survived the expansion of the town during the 17C and 18C, though the parish church of **St-Nicolas** retains elements of its heterogeneous medieval fabric, behind a cloak of 19C plasterwork, along with an excellent 18C pulpit.

The entrance to the **CHÂTEAU DU LUDE** is just to the north of the church, hidden from the town by an unprepossessing wall which hardly prepares you for the cylindrical bulk of the vast drum towers. Le Lude's present configurations are superficially reminiscent of Chaumont, an essentially square complex pinned at the angles by cylindrical towers, and surrounded by a wide dry moat on all but the river front. The process by which this came about is far from straightforward, and the sudden shifts of style as you walk around the château mask an even greater number of minor alterations, which reflect the attempts of a succession of owners to impose their own identies on the château.

Foulques Nerra's late 10C and early 11C castle was entirely rebuilt in the early 13C, after Anjou had passed into the French royal domain, and when Jehan de Daillon, chamberlain to Louis XI and Governor of the Dauphiné, decided to build anew in 1457 he made extensive use of the 13C foundations. The first area to be built was the **north wing**, with a terrace carried on flattened arches, and steepling dormer windows. The architect was Jacques Gendrot, more used to acting as clerk of works to René d'Anjou, and by Jehan's death in 1480 not only was this wing complete but a large secondary court had been raised to the east supported by the substructures of the 13C keep. The court was demolished by Timoléon de Daillon in 1642 to make way for the superb formal gardens which run down to the river, but the substructure was retained, and by descending into the moat it is possible to gain access to a 13C sexpartite-vaulted cellar, now called the **Salle des Gardes**.

The next enterprise was the **south wing**, probably undertaken during the reign of Louis XII as it sports his porcupines on the lower balustrade, and certainly complete by the death of Jehan's son, Jacques, in 1532. This was extensively restored for the Marquis de Talhouët-Roy in the mid-19C, whose initials TR are carried on the chimney stacks, but both the shape and the nature of the decorative detailing are early 16C. The machicolations and covered sentry walks favoured in late medieval fortifications have been retained, but, as at Chaumont or Blois, large windows have been opened into the outer elevation and form the principal vehicle for architectural embellishment. Each window is framed by Italianate pilasters, while the fuller carving of the lintels serves to continue the decorative interest from window head to sill, creating a series of sharply linked vertical panels.

It is now impossible to judge how the inner elevations of the north and south wings were treated as the **cour d'honneur** was refurbished by Timoléon de Daillon in the 1630s, but there was certainly originally a passageway opening from the *cour d'honneur* to the *basse-cour*. That there is no more is due to the Marquis de Vieuville, who inherited Le Lude in 1785 and commissioned the architect Jean Barré to remodel the early 17C east wing, hence the rather dignified Louis XVI elevation overlooking the river.

The **interiors** were largely refurbished in the 19C, and, despite the survival of the elliptically-shaped **Grand Salon** as Barré had it decorated in the late 18C, it is this 19C work which predominates as you are conducted around the château. However, there is one unexpected 16C survival. In 1853 the architect Delarue stripped out the plaster of an ante-room in the south-west tower to discover a significant cycle of **16C frescoes**, dating from between c 1560 and 1585 and attributed to the itinerant Italian painter Giovanni da Udine. The compositions derived from two manuscripts known to have been in the library here—a copy of Petrarch's *Trionfi*, illuminated c 1515, and a Bible picture-book first printed in 1553. The subjects are Old Testament, of the life of Joseph mostly, but with a stunning Noah's Ark visible through the door.

West of Le Lude, the D306 offers a fast route to La Flèche, though if time allows it is worth slipping to the north, along the D54, to cross the Loir beneath the astonishing silhouettes of (10km) the church at **Luché-Pringé**. A church, dedicated to **St-Martin**, already existed here when the site was confided in the monks of St-Aubin at Angers in 1057. Their establishment of a small priory may account for the architectural accomplishment of the building, but it sheds little light on the bizarre sequence of episodes which conspired to create one of the most distinctive small churches in western France.

At some point between 1166 and 1225, and most likely towards the later date, the monks of St-Aubin were responsible for the superb two-bay **choir**, built along the lines of an Angevin hall church with beautifully sprung octopartite vaults rising above slender columns. This was the only part of the building to survive the Hundred Years War in reasonable condition, and when building work restarted in the late 15C the opportunity was taken to refurbish the narrow transept and raise a square bell-tower over the crossing. The **nave** is more hybrid, dating from the 16C, and the lack of interest in aligning the north and south arcades may relate to the reconstruction necessitated by the Protestant sack of 1557. It had to be reconstructed a second time after a fire in 1921, when the western two bays were lost for good, but the eastern area was replicated in all essentials and the employment of a half-bay to abut the crossing was the original means of creating a wider central vessel. The west wall was also simply moved forward, along with the worn portal relief of St-Martin and the Beggar, but miraculously the great 16C walnut **Pietà** was undamaged, and as one of the most moving 16C sculptures to survive in France is now displayed in the south aisle.

The area to the **west of Luché-Pringé** is one of the most sublime in a valley renowned for its beauty, and as the D13 winds around the hill to (2km) **Pringé** it can seem as if the abounding fertility of the entire Loir has been bequeathed on this one small passage. Characteristically, the village of Pringé itself sustains an attractive **parish church**, sandwiched between the cemetery and a 15C manor house (if locked the key can be obtained from No. 4, Rue de Verron). Although a cursory inspection of the interior uncovers a wealth of half-revealed and abandoned schemes, Pringé remains one of the most satisfying small churches in Anjou or Maine, having been started by a team of masons who enjoyed a close working knowledge of the nave of Le Mans Cathedral. They were responsible for the apse and sanctuary bay, employing exactly the same decoration around the apse windows as is found in the triforium at Le Mans, and equipping the domed-up rib vault with very similar moulding profiles. The transepts were knocked through in the 15C but, as can be seen from the remnants of a blind dado arcade and two window heads to the south, the sanctuary bay was originally aisleless. The greater sanctuary area certainly dates from c 1150–60, whereas the nave employs a very different imagery, and does not seem to have been begun before c 1200.

This nave was evidently intended to be fully aisled and vaulted, in the manner of an Angevin hall church, but only the easternmost bay was ever actually vaulted and, although the provision for aisles was there, these too were swiftly abandoned. Prosperity seems to have returned to the parish after the Hundred Years War, and the late 15C saw the church acquire its transepts and a varied set of **wall paintings**, extending to a vast St Christopher across the south-west wall and a very fine Vision of St Hubert. The latter is probably contemporary with the stained glass, i.e. early 16C, and although the state of the glass is patchy it is where the best pictorial material is to be found.

Just beyond the village, the D13 loops between a splendid medieval fortified farmhouse, firmly of the flood plain, and the **Château de Gallerande**, banked above a moat and sited at exactly the point where the northern ridge begins to rise. The château may not be visited, and, although the actual fabric was mostly rebuilt in the 19C, its classic late 15C dispositions are easily seen, the four cylindrical angle-towers connected by wings to form a considerable rectangular massif. The descent into the watermeadows downstream of Gallerande takes you through the geranium-clad village of (3km) **Mareil-sur-Loir**, before a left turn onto the N23 brings you back to the river itself and (8km), sweeping along the Promenade Foch, into La Flèche.

La Flèche

The glorious views across the weir to the old Château des Carmes are a familiar landmark to travellers along the N23, enlivening the journey from Paris to Angers. The town itself seems less well known, which is surprising given its agreeably spacious 19C atmosphere.

A castle was first built by the river in the mid-11C, when Jean de Beaugency raised a stone donjon to the west of the present weir, and by the end of the century the town had begun to expand to the north, centred on the church founded by Jean's son, Hélie de la Flèche. But although Hélie de la Flèche became Count of Maine, and the town had been a significant frontier post on the border with Anjou (the marriage of Hélie's daughter, Eremburge, to Foulques V of Anjou in 1109 united Maine with Anjou), it was not until the 16C and 17C that La Flèche began to grow, a new château being constructed to the north of Hélie's church of St-Thomas in 1539, in turn becoming the site of an important royal college founded by Henri IV in 1604. Henri placed the college in the hands of Jesuit teachers and the number of students grew rapidly, reaching a peak of over 1200 by the mid-17C, and with René Descartes among its better known alumni.

The presence of a sizeable Jesuit community in the town also encouraged the foundation of a number of convents, that of the Carmelites being given the use of the medieval castle by the river. This they largely demolished, replacing it with a substantial 18C complex, though all that survives is a part of the main accommodation block and one wing of the 15C castle, now known as the **Château des Carmes**, and which acts as the hôtel-de-ville.

The **town centre** lies to the north, along the Rue Gallieni, where the **Place Henri IV** acts as a hub and general meeting place. The church of **St-Thomas** stands at the southern edge of the square, unsympathetically restored in the 19C and left with little more than a handsome early 13C bell-tower and an unusual late 13C cult statue, known as Notre-Dame-du-Chef-du-Pont, to show for its medieval past. The college lies just to the north, along the Rue Henri IV, known as the **PRYTANÉE NATIONAL MILITAIRE** since Napoleon had it refounded as a military school in 1808. The college was further expanded in 1921 when a new building was constructed on the edge of La Flèche, in the *quartier Gallieni*, and it is there that most of the *Baccalauréat* candidates are now taught. The main courts of the Prytanée still accommodate those students destined for the *grandes écoles militaires*, however, and can be visited out of term time, when those pupils remaining in college over the holidays will conduct visitors around the precincts (open 10.30–12.30 and 14.30–17.30).

You assemble by the 17C Porte d'Honneur, being brought into the **Cour d'Austerlitz**, the easternmost of the three great courts which form the heart of the college. When Henri IV founded La Flèche as a royal college in 1604 this was the *cour d'honneur*, closed to the north by the mid-16C Château Neuf. But the château was demolished in the late 18C and replaced by the existing northern elevations as a means of expanding the teaching rooms. With the exception of this area, and the 18C octagonal tower above the chapel, all the surviving buildings are early 17C, and were mostly complete by 1640. It is the very essence of early 17C French architectural design—restrained, modular, rational, even provided with an austerely beautiful formal garden to the rear of the main courts—one of a very few 17C Jesuit colleges to survive in Europe. And at its centre is a carefully weighed extravagance, the sumptuously Baroque **Chapelle St-Louis**, concealing an interior of extreme richness behind a fastidiously plain outside.

The chapel was laid out in 1606 under the architect Pierre Métezeau, but was substantially modified after 1612 when Ange-Etienne Martellange took over, and it is to Martellange that the success of the design is due. The building had a dual function. In addition to acting as the college chapel, it was intended as a mausoleum for Henri IV and Marie de Medici, whose wills specified that their hearts were to be interred in the choir. And so they were, to either side of Pierre Corbineau's magnificent **altar retable** of 1633–37. This retable now houses an equally fine **Annunciation** by Jouvenot, which replaced the original altar painting in 1816 but admirably compliments Corbineau's exhilarating use of coloured marbles. The nave was also given a tribune gallery, placed to the west of one of the grandest 17C organs to survive in France, and positioned above a run of lateral chapels which never received their intended set of screens. This was a rare oversight, but one which scarcely jars in a building which has escaped the ravages of over-zealous restorers and stands as one of the most complete Baroque interiors in France.

The chapelle St-Louis is not the only chapel of note in La Flèche. Just to the west of the town, in a cemetery by the side of the D306 to Sablé, the tiny **Notre-Dame-des-Vertus** amply rewards the ten minute walk it takes to get there. The chapel seems to date from the early 12C, with a sturdy western portal and a freely restored transept and choir, the building having been altered in the 17C when the painted wooden ceiling and columnar sanctuary entrance were added. The spaces are very simple, and embellished with 18C statuary and early 16C wooden panelling, most of the latter obtained from the Château le Verger, including a tremendous Muslim warrior terrorising the inner face of the west door.

La Flèche is considered the capital of the **Maine Angevin**, that area of northern Anjou which administratively became a part of Maine in 1790, and when travelling south-west along the N23 you are certainly conscious of the landscape acquiring a more open and Angevin character. The towns and villages are also more widely dispersed, taking refuge from the flood plains by colonising the wooded heights to the south. The few settlements actually situated on the banks of the Loir tend to have grown out of fortified seigneurial towns.

The first you encounter is (6km) **Bazouges-sur-le-Loir**, with a medieval château and a single surviving 16C rampart tower, visible to the left of the N23 as it swings through the village. The parish church of **St-Aubin** is to the east of this tower, a largely late 12C structure given a splendid early 16C painted roof in which 26 apostles, saints and martyrs alternate with tall single trees in stylised panels.

The **château** is a little further south-east, originally supplying its landward moats from the Loir and directly overlooking the river. As it currently stands, the château is substantially 15C, the machicolated towers having been built on 13C foundations and the central *corps de logis* refurbished during the 17C and 18C, creating an intentionally picturesque silhouette when seen from the opposite, southern, bank of the Loir (open 1 July–15 September only; 10–12 Tues and Fri, 15–17 Thurs, Sat and Sun).

Durtal lies 6km further west, though as you approach from the east, along the N23, the crumbling outline of its two great cylindrical towers becomes visible the moment you cross the present border with Anjou and begin the descent into the town. The *département* of Maine-et-Loire has recently purchased the **Château de Durtal** for use as an old people's home, so there is at last some hope that the catastrophic decay of an important monument may be arrested, and some of the more glaringly insensitive 20C alterations reversed. This promises to be a major undertaking and, short of a glimpse of a few fairly routine 18C frescoes and the marvellous views of the Loir valley from the covered sentry walk in the south-east tower, there is relatively little of interest in the interior. However, there are guided tours.

Elements of Geoffroy Martel's mid-11C castle have been uncovered underlying the present structure, but the **east wing** which so impressively dominates the upstream approaches to the town is substantially 15C, the flanking cylindrical towers faced with banded stonework in what amounts to a revival of the technique used at Angers. The **South Pavilion** was added in the second half of the 16C for François de Scépeaux, and was intended to be the start of a much grander extension, but the scheme was eventually abandoned in the 17C with no more than a few bays of the west wing complete. This abandonment presaged a more general decline, despite the Rochefoucauld family taking up residence in the 18C, and finally gave way to a series of alterations in the 19C and mid-20C, whose dismal partitions and plumbing so disfigure the present château. And there, for the moment, the matter rests.

South-west of Durtal, the Loir grows wider and more sluggish, draining the sparser moorland of north-eastern Anjou, before turning more decisively westwards and embarking on one last great meander to join the Sarthe below Briollay. The N23 disregards this course and touches the river just once, at (15km) Seiches-sur-le-Loir, though the serious château viewer might wish to take a final detour along to the D601 to the **Château le Verger** (3km north of Seiches). The interiors are closed to visitors, your view being restricted to a roadside glimpse of the rump of Pierre de Rohan's superb late 15C residence, commissioned from the architect Colin Byard and, sadly, largely demolished in 1776 on the orders of Cardinal de Rohan.

Returning south to Matheflon and Seiches-sur-Loir will bring you back to the N23, and the road south-west to (20km) Angers (see Route 12).

10

The Sarthe Valley: Le Mans to Angers

ROAD (125km): Le Mans D147/D51, 23km La Suze-sur-Sarthe; D79, 11km Pirmil; D69/D41, 11km Malicorne-sur-Sarthe; D8, 10km Parcé-sur-Sarthe; D57, 6km Asnières-sur-Vègre; D22, 8km Solesmes; D138, 3km Sablé-sur-Sarthe; D309/D27, 10km St-Denis-d'Anjou; D27/D768, 5km Miré; D768/D74/D508, 24km Château le Plessis-Bourré; D107, 14km Angers.

The above itinerary is concerned with the lower reaches of the valley of the Sarthe, picking up the river where it flows south from Le Mans, and continuing downstream as far as the confluence with the river

Mayenne just to the north of Angers. The landscape has much in common with the valley of Le Loir, the river cutting a sinuous path through the underlying limestone to form a succession of gently shelving promontories. Only rarely do these meanders turn against a headland, and where this is so—at Parcé or Sablé-sur-Sarthe for instance—a castle was established to take advantage of the site, and patrol the frontier between Maine and Anjou. Sablé is the only sizeable town, and makes a good overnight base, but the Sarthe is essentially a valley of villages and farmsteads, a valley graced by some of the most bucolic settlements in western France, and, for those looking for the tranquil and the picturesque, virtually all the places mentioned make excellent overnight halts.

The easiest way to break free of suburban Le Mans and pick up the valley of the Sarthe is to take the D147 south-west to Allonnes, and, where it changes designation to the D23, continue across the high ground to (20km) La Suze-sur-Sarthe.

The more appealing route turns left onto the D51 and into the centre of **Allonnes** (5km from Le Mans), though as you track through the high-rise housing its appeal may seem elusive. Despite its being difficult to recognise, Allonnes was an important secondary Gallo-Roman town, its ruined baths and temples buried deep in the woodland between the modern town and the river. To the south, the industrial sprawl has penetrated as far as (5km) **Spay**, an otherwise pleasant village whose largely 12C parish church contains a good 18C retable, a rather touching, and paintless, 15C Virgin and Child, and a 16C seigneurial wooden throne.

Once beyond Spay, the D51 begins to wind through pockets of old grassland, the fields now mostly planted with maize, never losing more than a few hundred metres on a river whose banks support great stands of poplar, ash and alder. At (3km) **Fillé** you can stand above the old river quays, where a weir allows a canalised section of the Sarthe to swing north, while, further west, the lifeless choir of the 19C church at (5km) **Roëzé-sur-Sarthe** has been startlingly built into the base of a 12C castle tower.

The most attractive of the small towns which rise above this stretch of the river is (4km) **La Suze-sur-Sarthe**. The old centre lies along the left bank, host to a Thursday market which spills away to the west of the vast cracked shell of a 15C château. This latter has been part demolished, but the gable of the riverside wing now carries a 19C painted statue, bizarrely mounted above the purer lines of a Renaissance fireplace. It is best seen from the bridge, or the opposite bank, or indeed when taking advantage of the Sunday river cruises which leave from the wharves by the campsite.

From La Suze the D23 offers a fast route south-west, cutting across the wooded plateau as far as Malicorne and avoiding the northerly meanders of the river. But, again, it is the back roads which are the more rewarding, and the D79 (you pick it up just outside La Suze, after following the signs to St-Jean-du-Bois along the D229) takes you through pines and silver birch to cross the river beneath a picturesque huddle of terraced gardens at (5km) **Fercé-sur-Sarthe**. The central square is no less appealing, with another of those narrow 12C belfries which were the mainstay of local parish church design rising opposite an excellent local *auberge*.

It is also worth persisting with the D79, at least as far as (6km) **Pirmil**, the attraction being the Romanesque **carving** in an astonishingly accomplished parish church. Pirmil was the seat of an 11C seigneurial castle, whose chapel was served by Benedictine monks from the abbey of St-Vincent-du-Mans. It was these monks who were responsible for building the parish church of **St-Jouin** and they evidently chose their forms with care, producing a fully vaulted aisleless building which subsequently lost its westernmost bay. The crossing and nave are covered by domed-up rib vaults, supported by small figures, or grotesques, at the springing point of the ribs, as in the choir vault of the abbey of La Couture at Le Mans. Several of these are fine carvings in their own right, particularly the fantastically compacted crossing figures and the elegant Archangel Michael to the south-west, but it is the extraordinary respond capital midway down the north wall of the nave which calls for most comment. This is the only figurative note to break the foliate variations found elsewhere at capital level, and seems to represent, from east to west: a man playing a fiddle while an acrobat turns a one-handed somersault; a cow, playing a recorder and seated on a winged beast while another cow jumps upside down; and a damaged pairing which might represent a man and a demon wrestling over possession of a banderole. It is tremendous stuff, and, like the rest of the main campaign here, late 12C.

To the south of Pirmil, and some 4km along the D69, **Noyen-sur-Sarthe** is another of those small market towns which have tried to improve the attractiveness of their river fronts with a sandy beach and a small landing stage for pleasure boats. Its southern rival, the old pottery-making town of **Malicorne-sur-Sarthe** (7km along the D41), has been more successful, and the island created by the canalisation of the river now supports tennis-courts, jetties and a campsite. These overlook a glorious sweep of the Sarthe, as the river turns north-west, a long weir running diagonally towards a disused 18C watermill and the warm stonework of an earlier parish church climbing to support an octagonal slate spire.

The church is substantially late 11C, dedicated to **St-Sylvestre**, and badly in need of a decision either to strip it of its mouldering 18C plaster or re-whitewash the whole interior. Restoration of the chapel of St-Anne is underway, in the angle between the nave and the south transept, revealing the sumptuous vermilions and ultramarines of a once very fine late medieval wall painting. The early 16C effigy of a seigneur de Chaources, for which the church was best known, has been temporarily removed.

The **château** is only rarely open (Sun, Mon, Thurs and Fri afternoons; July and August only), but the exterior elevations are visible, pinned to the far side of a moat by a pair of round towers, and arranged as two distinct pavilions. What survives was constructed in the early 18C for the Marquis de la Châtre, intended as no more than a set of reception rooms for the 15C château beyond, though, as an economy measure, the earlier main block was demolished in the late 18C, leaving the present buildings to act as the principal residence.

West of Malicorne, the D8 runs through rough pasture, heath and woodland, before breaking a low ridge to reveal the towers and belfries of (10km) **Parcé-sur-Sarthe**, slanting unexpectedly across a narrow bluff. It was this situation which led to the building of a castle, known as the château de Ravadun, whose classic 11C motte still rises between the Rue Basse and Rue de la Motte. The castle, along with the rest of the town, was destroyed in 1370 by an English raiding party under Robert Knolles, and reconstruction was slow. None the less, one cannot fail to be impressed by the wealth generated in France in the wake of the Hundred Years War, and—short of a couple of new suburbs and a few 18C and 19C window embrasures—the town you see today is that which was built in the late 15C and 16C. The grander houses, grouped along the **Rue Basse** and the river front, are splendid, and any stroll through the town will reveal a wealth of 16C vernacular form and detail. The set-pieces are less compelling, though the 12C tower now islanded in the Place de la République, and originally the belfry of a parish church destroyed by Knolle's troops, makes a fine town emblem. A new church was begun at the end of the 15C and dedicated to **St-Martin**, but was to all intents and purposes entirely reconstructed in the late 19C, retaining little more than its wooden Crucified Christ, and a very touching late 16C painting of the Nativity now hung from the south aisle wall.

The Sarthe has been bridged at Parcé, allowing you to cross to the **right bank** and, picking up the D57, accompany the river along one of its most abundant and tranquil passages.

The river loops south-westwards at (3km) Avoise, but it is worth staying with the D57 as it continues north to catch up with a tributary river, the Vègre, at (3km) **ASNIÈRES-SUR-VÈGRE**. Sitting on the parapet of the medieval bridge, watching the dragonflies skim the millpond, or turn through banks of sedge to flit above crumbling riverside walls, one can sympathise with the view which sees the village as the most beautiful in Maine, if not in all western France. Its beauty derives not from any single vista, or even sequence of vistas, but from Asnières as a whole, with its terraced streets weaving between late medieval farmhouses.

The manor of Asnières belonged to the chapter of Le Mans Cathedral, and the so-called **Manoir de la Cour**, or court house, seems to have been built to house the canons' representative in the village, surviving as an extremely rare example of a 13C secular hall. To its north, and overlooking the river, the **parish church** is a more modest structure. The narrow western belfry was added to a probably late 11C nave during the mid-12C, at the same time as the present entrance portal was punched through the south wall, and the church was finally enlarged c 1300, when the present square-ended choir was built. The structure became better known in 1950 however, when, puzzled by the off-centredness of the western belfry and eccentric alignment of the choir, a group of archaeologists and restorers stripped the church of its 18C whitewash to uncover tier upon tier of medieval **wall paintings**.

None of the paintings is dated, and—with the exception of a damaged but very fine late medieval Passion cycle in the choir—it is all fairly schematic work, but the painting in the nave looks to be the earliest, probably belonging to the very late 12C. This encompasses a Harrowing of Hell on the west wall, with an Adoration of the Magi, Presentation in the Temple, Soldiers threatening the Harvest (?), and Flight into Egypt to the north. On the south wall the fragmentary Three Maries at the Sepulchre is 14C or 15C, while the earliest painting in the choir is that featuring the Baptism, probably dating from shortly after the completion of the choir. The fragments of the Passion cycle which survive above this—a Last Supper, Washing of Feet, Arrest and Flagellation—are probably later 14C. This is no more than an outline of the more obvious works; there are also many fragments and over-paintings. But though they fall a long way beneath the quality of the wall paintings which survive in, for example, the Loir valley, the commitment to large-scale pictorial story-telling on show here retains a quietly compelling power.

South-west of Asnières, the D22 passes just to the north of the handsome square at (6km) **Juigné-sur-Sarthe**, before descending to cross the river beneath the fortress-like conventual block of the (2km) **Abbaye de Solesmes**. A priory was founded here in 1010 by Geoffroy le Vieux, seigneur de Sablé, as a daughter-house of the abbey of La Couture at Le Mans, though it is its present status as the revived Benedictine abbey of St-Pierre-de-Solesmes which draws pious Catholics from throughout Europe. The revival began in 1833, when a priest from Sablé, Prosper Guéranger, acquired the semi-ruined priory and drew a small congregation of Benedictine monks to the site. By 1837, Guéranger was elected abbot of what had become an autonomous Benedictine abbey, and work began on enlarging the church and precincts. The choir was built as a three-aisled Angevin hall in 1863, the nave restored and given a set of lateral chapels in the 1870s, and in 1895 the Benedictine architect, Dom Mellet, was invited to draw up plans for the enlargement of the conventual buildings. Work was interrupted by the 1901 law expelling all religious orders from France, when the monks went into exile, establishing the monastery at Quarr on the Isle of Wight. On their return in 1921, Mellet's plans were simply dusted off and construction resumed, resulting in that vast conventual block, modelled on the Merveille at Mont-St-Michel, so visible as you approach Solesmes from across the river.

Only the **monastic church** is open to visitors, a 14C western portal giving entry to a gloomy nave, the art-historical interest lying to the east, in the transepts. These were remodelled during the late 15C, that to the south provided with a large **Entombment Group** by Prior Guillaume Cheminart in 1496. Cheminart's donation seems to have inspired his successor, Jean Bougler, to fill the whole of the **north transept** with a series of colossal carved tableaux, their forms equally indebted to the sculptural illusionism explored in the late 15C work. The tableaux were commissioned between 1530 and 1556, with Bougler himself represented at the feet of the entombed Virgin, and depict the Dormition and Assumption to the north, Christ among the Doctors to the west, and both Mary offered the Eucharist by Christ and Virtues triumphing over the seven-headed Beast of the Apocalypse to the east. As with the rest of the building, their 19C restoration was so harsh as to have virtually denatured a once subtle grouping, and the more inspiring reason for a visit is to listen to the monks chanting the hours (Vespers in summer is at 17.00).

Below Solesmes, the D138 skirts the watermeadows to the south of the river, bringing you under a railway viaduct and into (3km) **SABLÉ-SUR-SARTHE**, an ancient market town and the largest centre of population to stand between Le Mans and Angers. The town's growth was due to the establishment of an early 11C frontier castle on the rocky spur separating the rivers Erve and Vaige, just above the point where they flow into the Sarthe. Two distinct residential quarters developed beneath this castle, the earlier sandwiched between the two tributary streams along the right bank of the Sarthe, and a second enceinte on an island within the Sarthe itself.

The present town centre unites these two areas, with the axis of the old medieval road from Laval to La Flèche, the Grande-Rue and Rue de l'Ile, diverted in the mid-19C by the construction of the Rue Carnot and Place Raphaël Elizé. The diversion was undertaken in 1840 and, coupled with the arrival of the railway in 1860, is responsible for the largely 19C character of the modern town. The succession of monumental three-storey buildings in the **Place Raphaël Elizé**, allying shallow wrought-iron balconies with more thickly worked carving, is probably the most successful of the larger architectural perspectives, and quite unashamedly Parisian in inspiration.

To the rear of the Place, the **Grande-Rue** has retained a more ramshackle collection of 16C–18C houses, and climbs, via a left turn into the Impasse du Château, to the 14C barbican of the **château**. This is virtually the only medieval construction to survive on the heights, and the château as it now stands was built in the first half of the 18C to designs by the architect and garden designer, Claude Desgotz. The principal façade dates from a remodelling undertaken by Georges Lafenestre in 1870, which saw the complete transformation of the interiors and the earlier formal gardens give way to the present open parkland. The château now houses the conservation department of the *Bibliothèque Nationale* and may not be visited, but there is nothing to prevent you from strolling among its splendid grounds.

You get a better view of the 18C elevations of the château from the small marina on the left bank of the river, where the restrained handling and elegant rhythms of Desgotz's façade are crushingly overpowered by Lafenestre's operatic late 19C roof. The marina stands in the old island quarter of Sablé, a quarter which has been extensively redeveloped over the last decade, with a new, and largely empty, shopping precinct, and an attractive jetty where the river cruisers tie up, and from where you take can trips along the river (summer only, the boats usually leaving at 10.00 daily, with occasional evening sailings including dinner—check at the 'port' for details).

The other prominent landmark is the parish church of **Notre-Dame**, built to a Neo-Gothic design in 1895 on the site of the demolished medieval church. The building itself is one of the better Gothic Revival churches to have sprung up in Maine, loosely based on the more conservative mid-13C churches of eastern France, and for once built of extremely fine *tuffeau*. The interior is airy and spacious, and retains one, very considerable, surprise. For the transept windows house that glass which the *Commission des Monuments Historiques* insisted must be saved from medieval Notre-Dame when it was demolished in 1894. The **north transept glass** draws together saints, bishops and donors, and inserts them at the base of a number of scenes from Christ's Infancy and Ministry. The **south transept window**, by contrast, repeats both the form and content of the early 16C axial window of the old church, arranging 11 scenes of Christ's Passion and Resurrection around the finest late medieval Crucifixion to survive in western France.

The D309 offers the best route **south-west from Sablé**, sweeping above the softer contours to the west of the Sarthe, before gently descending to bisect the medieval village of (10km) **St-Denis-d'Anjou**. The larger structures are to either side of the main road, with the 18C **Auberge du Roi René** next door to a richly decorated late 15C townhouse now accommodating the Mairie. These stand opposite a building of quite exceptional interest, and although it is difficult to unravel the processes whereby the parish church of **St-Denis** came to acquire so striking a silhouette, it does at least seem that the originally aisleless nave, transept, crossing tower and sanctuary date from the late 12C. The north aisle, window tracery and subsidiary extension to the choir were added piecemeal during the 15C and 16C.

The church is chiefly renowned for its marvellous array of early 16C **wall paintings**, with a superb group of images on the south wall of the nave, depicting the Feast of Herod and Herodias (Salomé laying the head of John the Baptist on the table), the Vision of St Hubert, and a damaged St Christopher guided across the river by an anchorite with a lantern. To the east are representations of St-Blaise (like Hubert another protector of wild animals, and a reflection perhaps of the medieval hunting traditions of the area), and, on the choir north wall, St-Martin about to divide his cloak to give to a crippled beggar. There are other, more fragmentary, paintings elsewhere in the nave, all of similarly high quality, and, with two good restaurants just outside the church and a 16C wooden market hall to the west, more than enough to sustain an extremely pleasant lunchtime.

5km south-west of St-Denis, **Miré** is another of those larger villages whose church received a set of paintings during the early 16C, in this case applied to the surface of a wooden barrel vault over the nave. Heavily repainted in the 19C, they depict saints and evangelists beneath triangular canopies, the standing figures interspersed with occasional narrative scenes of Adam and Eve, the Annunciation and so on. In their general form, if not their detail, they are a poorer version of the vault paintings at Bazouges-sur-le-Loir.

Once over the departmental boundary the road changes designation to the D768, swooping through a succession of dull roadside towns, and with (10km) Châteauneuf-sur-Sarthe not much better, the temptation must be to head straight for Angers. There is one **detour** worth making, however, and a left turn on to the D74 at La Croix-de-Beauvais, followed by a right on to the D508, just beyond Ecuillé, will bring you to the moated fairyland of the **CHÂTEAU LE PLESSIS-BOURRÉ**. (24km from Miré: open 10–12, 14–18; 15 Feb–15 Nov. Closed Wed and Thurs Mornings except during July and August.)

The château was begun in 1468, on estates acquired some six years earlier by Jean Bourré, Louis XI's minister of finance, and was complete by 1473. At first sight the château appears to be a palatial seigneurial castle, with four cylindrical angle-towers rising from the security of a broad moat, but the *corps de logis* is vulnerable to even the smallest detachment of troops equipped with a bombarde and torches, and any defensive considerations have been relegated to a secondary role. Nonetheless, one of the angle-towers still rises proud of the rest to act as a donjon; and it has been treated to a shrunken upper storey, as at Langeais, where Bourré acted as supervisor of works.

Entry is via an outer court, remodelled from the earlier *communs* during the 17C but largely reconstructed after the French Revolution. This court now channels you across the low-arched bridge spanning the moat, over a working drawbridge and into the *cour d'honneur*. The **Corps de Logis** lies opposite, drawn upwards into a fourth storey by steepling dormer windows, beneath which the main embrasures have been aligned so as to impose a distinctive bay rhythm on the eleva-tion—or so it at first appears. Closer examination reveals elements which seem almost casually off-centred and, as in the entry wing, disturb any sense of a more orderly geometry at work here.

Most of the **interiors** have been decorated and refurnished since the Revolution, and the obligatory guided tours make good sense of the contexts of this later work, but attention should be drawn to at least one possible area of original decoration which survives in the first-floor **Salle des Gardes**. This consists of a large coffered ceiling, whose cells carry an unparalleled sequence of allegorical fables, proverbs, virtues and popular mythologies. These could well be late 15C, i.e. they may belong to the château as Jean Bourré knew it, but their moralising nature must have proved irksome to an 18C owner with a very different sense of humour, as one of the panels carries a superbly salacious interjection in a quasi-late Gothic style.

The remotenes of Plessis-Bourré, mired in the low moors between the Sarthe and Mayenne, becomes more obvious as you head south from the village of (2km) Bourg. Following the D107 south from here you cross the drained marshland and tiny hamlets of Haut-Anjou, before the road (7km) bridges the river Mayenne within sight of its union with the Sarthe, and speeds a last 5km into Angers itself (see Route 12).

11

Baugé and eastern Anjou

ROAD (128km): Baugé D766, 10km Jarzé; C6/C5, 6km Fontaine-Milon; D61/C11, 5km Montgeoffroy; N147, 6km Beaufort-en-Vallée; D7, 4km Brion; D211/D206, 14km Blou; D206/D58, 11km Vernoil-le-Fourier; D206, 10km Gizeux; D749, 21km Château-la-Vallière; D766/D66, 7km Marcilly-sur-Maulne; D66/D138, 10km Broc (D138/D767, 5km La Boissière); D138, 8km Genneteil; D141, 11km Pontigné; D141, 5km Baugé.

Eastern Anjou is not an area which is easy to define. The cantons around Château-la-Vallière and Gizeux were absorbed into Touraine in 1791, depriving Anjou of its old north-eastern frontier, while the economic life of the area around Jarzé and Montgeoffroy is now tilted towards Angers, rather than the established market towns of Baugé and Beaufort-en-Vallée. Topographically, it divides itself into two broad belts: the low-lying flood plains of the Vallée d'Anjou, and the wooded heathland to the south of the valley of the Loir. It is this topography which has had the greatest impact, forcing the southern centres to cling to the low hills above the river Authion and allowing the more northerly settlements to become widely dispersed across a wooded plateau. The suggested itinerary is organised as an irregular anti-clockwise circuit with its centre at Baugé, the principal town of a sparsely populated region and the most agreeable place to stay.

Baugé

Baugé's current situation dates from the first quarter of the 11C, when Foulques Nerra, Comte d'Anjou, began work on a donjon above the north bank of the river Couasnon, some 2km north-east of the earlier centre. Favoured by Yolande of Aragon and her son, René d'Anjou, Baugé enjoyed an illustrious 15C, witnessing the reconstruction of the château, the expansion of the town northwards to occupy the high ground towards the plateau, and the expulsion of the English from Anjou, the decisive battle being fought at le Vieux-Baugé in 1421. The following century brought decline and impoverishment. Even the foundation of an important hospice in 1643 did little to change its reputation—the French saying *'je vous baille ma rente de Baugé'* (I'll send you my rent from Baugé) referring to an empty promise. The population of Baugé is now no more than it was in the 15C, despite the renewed prosperity generated by its position astride the 19C coaching route from La Flèche to Saumur, but what has endured is an unquestionably lively and unselfconscious market town, enriched by the survival of a number of attractive architectural set-pieces.

The most imposing of these is the **Château de Baugé**, whose great southern façade overlooks the largest of the town squares, the Place Ferrières. It was begun c 1430 for Yolande of Aragon and extended northwards after 1440, when it became a favourite residence of René d'Anjou and his first wife, Isabelle de Lorraine. The **north**

pavilion is architecturally the most impressive, with a delicately carved ogee-arched doorway giving entry to the main octagonal stair-tower. Virtually the only late medieval interior decoration to survive is to be found here, where the upper vault carries an array of heraldic bosses, René's claims to Aragon, Jerusalem and Anjou ostentatiously advertised alongside the intertwined initials R and I. Most of the rest of the château was altered between the 18C and 20C, the principal apartments now housing a miscellaneous collection of coins, ceramics, textiles and armour under the title **Musée du Baugeois**.

West of the château, the Rues Victor Hugo and Clemenceau form the main street of Baugé, with Adolphe David's 1863 fountain in the **Place du Roi René** at the centre. The **Rue Basse** will take you straight to the central Place, its varied rooflines sheltering the shabby yards of what, as the Auberge de l'Ecu de France (No. 23), was Baugé's grandest 19C coaching house. The more unusual survivals are to either side of David's granite fountain, but it is also worth climbing north-west to the **Place du Marché**, whose splendid precincts are fringed by a number of fine townhouses. The majority are embellished with the unmoulded brick chimney-stacks which are something of a local speciality, the 18C roofs of No. 41 for instance; but occasionally, as with the pharmacy, they are punctuated by lavish dormer windows, in this case of 1644. There are similarly distinguished houses throughout Baugé and, though undramatic, the varying styles and dates of these domestic buildings make for a consistently interesting townscape.

There are also a couple of survivals of wider significance. The earliest is to be found in the **Chapelle de la Girouardière**, just to the south of the dull late 17C parish church of St-Pierre-et-St-Laurent. Since the French Revolution, the chapel has housed the **Croix d'Anjou**, a relic of the True Cross given in 1241 to Jean d'Alluye, an Angevin Crusader, by the bishop of Crete. The fragment had been fashioned into a rood with two cross-beams, the upper originally bearing an inscription, which Jean gave to the Cistercian abbey of La Boissière, but fears for its safety during the Hundred Years War led to its removal to the château at Angers. Here, shortly after 1359, Louis d'Anjou had it mounted on a gilded base, encrusted with precious stones and set with two superb gilded images of a crucified Christ. After René—Duke of Lorraine in addition to Anjou—adopted the emblem of the twin-armed cross to distinguish his troops at the battle of Nancy in 1477, the relic became known as the Cross of Lorraine, and found its way into modern consciousness as the symbol of the French *Résistance*. But it is not only for its political significance that the cross is worth seeking out (visiting hours are restricted to 15.00–16.30, closed Thursdays). It is also one of the finest examples of mid-14C French metalwork to have survived in Europe, the subtle pinks and blues of its jewels of an extraordinary beauty.

The second surprise lies to the far side of the Place du Roi René, along the Rue Pasteur, where the **Hôpital St-Joseph** retains a mid-17C **Pharmacie**, perfectly intact. The hospital itself was founded by Anne de Melun in 1643 as a hospice for the poor, and is now the modern general hospital, both the main ward block and pharmacy dating from the mid-17C. It is a unique survival, for not only are the various boxes, jars and bottles contemporary, but the shelving, stools, marquetry and painted ceiling are also mid-17C, and of a piece, presenting a Renaissance dispensary within a fully Renaissance context.

The old *chef-lieu de Baugé* is 2km south-west of the present centre, at **Le Vieux-Baugé**, on whose hill Charlemagne established a *vigeurie*, a minor administrative centre from which a *viguier* or provost dispensed justice. Nothing survives of the Carolingian town, but it is worth drifting south-west along the D61 to the earlier settlement for the unusual and heterogeneous parish church of **St-Symphorien**. Having been built alongside a Benedictine priory, St-Symphorien extends to a substantially 11C nave and crossing, a late 12C chapel to the north of the transept, an inventive choir of c 1200—in which radiating chapels are sprung from a single unified space rather than the usual ambulatory—and an early 16C south transept, attributed to the local architect, Jean de l'Espine. The spaciousness of these eastern parts is striking, so much so that one suspects direct intervention on the part of the priory, but the church is locally most celebrated for its curious 18C **spire**. This is known as a heliocoidal spire, a composition in which the octagonal faces corkscrew upwards to create a spiral, its theatricality enhanced by the spire's having an unintentional lean.

The vast **forests** which once ringed Baugé come closest to the town along its western rim, where the forêt de Baugé still sustains 6000 hectares of beech and evergreen oak. The D766 cuts across this forest, and the plain which supports it, passing the classically Romanesque proportions of the east end of (5km) St-Martin at **Echemiré**, before looping north to bypass (5km) **Jarzé**. It is worth slipping south here, initially into Jarzé itself, where the Romanesque belfry of the parish church of **St-Cyr**, visible for miles as you approach from the west, has been incorporated into a complex and very substantial collegiate church. The 11C **belfry** originally stood between the nave and choir of a modest building, but the decision in 1481 of Jean Bourré, Louis XI's finance minister, to construct a seigneurial chapel to the south of the choir initiated a process of radical transformation. This two-bay chapel of St-Martin was designed by Macé Colureau—the mason from Cléry then working on Bourré's now destroyed château here at Jarzé—and given a fairly routine tierceron vault which has been beautifully sprung from the body of the pier. By 1500, Jean Bourré had founded a college of five canons to serve the church and, his stock still very much in the ascendant, charged François Bergier, *maçon de Bazouges*, with 'improving and lengthening the choir'. It would also seem that the nave was rebuilt at roughly the same time.

The result cannot be counted a resounding success, the lack of height in the vaults dictated by the retention of the Romanesque belfry, and the loss of the 16C glass making it impossible to gain a sense of Bourré's aesthetic programme. The choir does at least retain a few figures from a 16C fresco of the **Entombment** on the east wall, along with a splendid set of **choir stalls**. The rear set of these stalls is mostly original (c 1500), with a marvellous chimera to the north, the flesh falling away from its ribs, and an excellent quartet of bench-ends.

There are a number of routes you can take from Jarzé to the great 18C **CHATEAU DE MONTGEOFFROY**. A combination of the C6/C5, D61 and 11C, via Fontaine-Milon is the most direct (11km in total). The château lies just to the west of the village.

Architecturally, Montgeoffroy is one of the most important late 18C buildings to survive in western France, evidence, like the Petit Trianon at Versailles, that the rich Neo-Classicism of the mid-18C was already being pared down and formalised before the death of Louis XV in 1774.

The château was built for Maréchal Louis-Georges-Erasme de Con-tades, Governor of Alsace, by the Parisian architect Jean Barré, work beginning in 1773, with the *corps de logis* finished within three years. The site was previously occupied by a 16C château, and the chapel and cylindrical moat towers from this earlier complex were retained, the latter used as an advance guard to frame a supremely symmetrical design. Barré's formal concerns are rooted in a desire to cleanse architecture of the decorative excess of the mid-century, and, remark-ably, the only relief sculpture to encrust the main elevation is confined to the Contade coat of arms in the pediment. The surfaces are otherwise relatively flat, a few spare mouldings detailing the storey lines, and the formal repertoire kept within a narrow range. In short, the emphasis has shifted from ebullient mass to harmonious profile, towards the balance and decorum of first-rate Neo-Classical architecture.

Inside, carved ornament is also kept to a minimum, and held firmly in check by the reticulated frames of the wood panelling. The furnish-ings of the rooms open to the public, all on the ground floor, are mostly those listed in the 1775 inventory, conceived by their Parisian designers as a foil for the sterner accents of the panelling. They are at their finest in the central **salon**, like all the larger rooms painted in the cool pearl-greys favoured in the late 18C, and for once extending a keen sense of the indivisibility of architecture and décor in the design of a large-scale château. The rooms overlooking the gardens to the rear tend to be freer in their handling, the maréchal and Madame Herrault, his companion, occupying two bedrooms to the west. The Venetian hangings of the **Appartement de Madame Herrault** are one of the few deliberately sumptuous touches applied against the architectural frame, again acting as an excellent counter to the greys of the wood panelling. The largest of the rooms to the east, the **salle à manger**, is a decided innovation in late 18C France, for the usual habit was to eat off trestle tables set up in any room thought convenient. The panelling in the corners has been chamfered, making the room seem oval, with an inner niche occupied by an extraordinary stove, given to the maréchal by the grateful burghers and faïenciers of Strasbourg.

Finally, you will be taken outside and shown the kitchen, warm with the coppery glow of a magnificent collection of pots, moulds, pans and braziers, and given a glimpse of the 16C chapel, illuminated by a stained glass window donated by a previous owner, Guillaume de la Grandière, in 1543. It is a building of unusual integrity and, for those with a serious interest in the late 18C, quite unmissable.

South-east of Montgeoffroy you soon meet the N147, the road marking the northern edge of the flood plains of the river Authion and bringing you into one of the great feudal towns of 'La Vallée' at (6km) **Beaufort-en-Vallée**. Although the Authion is a tributary river, before the first *levées* were built along the north bank of the Loire in the 12C the two rivers would meet when in flood. In other words the valleys of the Loire and Authion are one great valley—the Vallée d'Anjou—more usually known simply as La Vallée. You get a marvellous view of these fertile flood plains from the ruined **Château de Beaufort**, the old motte thrown up by Foulques Nerra in the early 11C and now occupied by the scrappy remains of a late medieval castle. These few fragments, bits of the southern walls of 1346, and a single tower built under René d'Anjou in 1455, are virtually all that remain of medieval Beaufort, though the later town survives in splendid style to the north-east of the château.

This pivots around a handsome market square, at whose centre a 19C statue of Jeanne Laval celebrates the foundation of Beaufort's Renaissance prosperity—Jeanne's granting of rights to free pasturage to all inhabitants of La Vallée. The level of wealth enjoyed in the 16C is reflected in the scale of the parish church of **Notre-Dame**, where the late 15C nave was vaulted between 1527 and 1536. A colossal northern bell-tower was added to the new choir in 1542, the latter under the local architect, Jean de l'Espine. Sadly, the restorers of the 1870s replaced most of the 16C work with a series of very free, machine-cut 'improvements', and the interior has a harsh and muddled quality. The glass is an exception to this, unmistakably late 19C but with a tremendous variety and depth of colour, and a determination on the part of the glass painter, Edouard Didron, to limit the 16C references to incidentals of background and costume.

In the Place Jeanne Laval is the **Musée Joseph-Denais**, a collection of local curios, Egyptian antiquities, weapons and sundry bric-a-brac assembled by the compulsive collector, journalist and native writer, Joseph Denais (1851–1916). But the most exciting aspect of Beaufort lies in the townscape itself, in the mid-17C houses along the **Rue de l'Hôtel-de-Ville**, or the early 19C mansions spilling eastwards from the Place Jeanne Laval. Any stroll will reveal a wealth of minor triumphs and vernacular detail.

To the east of Beaufort a range of low hills signals the edge of La Vallée, and supports the few early settlements that developed where they could be free of the high water marks. 4km along the D7, **Brion** has an extremely fine parish church, dedicated to **St-Gervais-et-Protais** and in the gift of the abbey of St-Aubin at Angers. The choir and transepts were probably built c 1150, with the nave following on in the late 12C, its two bays of Angevin vaulting steeply pitched to frame paired lancet windows. The west front is entirely the work of the restorers of 1849–70, and it is the **east end** which is most interesting. The bays here are articulated by pairs of half-columns, a self-conscious homage to Fontevraud, while the capitals are either the work of the sculptor responsible for the hemicycle capitals at Cunault, or of one of his assistants. The former seems more likely, for however radical the restoration elsewhere, the eastern capitals have not been heavily recut, and the alternation of animals with that very lush Cunault foliage is quite superb.

South-east of Brion, the D211 drifts through fields planted with maize and asparagus, cutting into the spacious 19C market square at (8km) **Longué**, where a left turn on to the D206 will bring you to another of the older settlements which rise above the levels at (6km) **Blou**.

The village curls around three sides of its principal monument, the parish church of **St-Christophe**, whose dumpy late 12C crossing tower acts as a navigation mark for the surrounding region. The main body of the church probably dates from c 1130, and boasts an unusual **north transept front**, with a diaper pattern cut into the area above the blind arches and a gabled and buttressed window sunk into the proud stonework at the centre. As with the bundling of the shaftwork at the angles of the crossing tower, this has a decidedly Poitevin feel to it, but may have grown out of a local tradition, as the blind arcading of the choir interior readily compares with that of Vernoil. The rest of the village is equally attractive, the low and widely-spaced houses opening on to small courts or, in the case of the mairie, the old village square.

Vernantes lies another 9km along the D206, the market centre for the rich horticultural produce you pass when moving north-east towards the town. The **Mairie** now occupies the rump of the 12C town church, whose nave was demolished shortly before 1867, when the present parish church was built, in what was the old cemetery to the south. The late 12C belfry and 15C stone spire are nevertheless the most interesting structures in an otherwise dull town, and you are better off travelling 2km east to **Vernoil-le-Fourier**, where the church and late medieval priory buildings of **St-Vincent** form an unexpectedly handsome group.

The church was given to the abbey of the Ronceray in Angers in 1101, by Geoffroy Foulcrade, *sénéchal d'Anjou*, and the west front, south wall of the nave and richly decorated south transept probably date from shortly after this. The northern elevations, crossing tower and vaults are all later, hence the strange disjunctions in the axiality of the building obvious at vault level. The interior of the **south transept** must once have been splendid, however, with larger arches framing the windows, while the inventive geometric ornament of the narrower runs of blind arcading would originally have been highlighted in paint.

Beyond Vernoil, the D206 winds above the sparse heaths of **north-eastern Anjou**, crossing the present border with Touraine just to the west of the pleasant village of (10km) **Gizeux**. Since 1791, when the cantons of Bourgueil and Château-la-Vallière, both previously in Anjou, were incorporated into the new *département* of Indre-et-Loire, this area has been known as the Touraine-Angevine. A glance at the tiny church of **Notre-Dame** reveals Gizeux's historical credentials to be impeccably Angevin, for there, in the transepts, lie two magnificent tombs of the du Bellay family, seigneurs of Gizeux, barons of Les Landes, high chamberlains of Plessis-Macé. The overall design of each tomb is identical, and both were commissioned by Martin du Bellay from the Tours-based sculptor Nicolas Guillain. That to the south shows René du Bellay (died 1611) kneeling before a lectern, prayerful and

accompanied by his wife, Marie du Bellay. The north transept repli-
cates this arrangement, but depicts Martin du Bellay (died 1627) and
his wife, Louise de Savennières, updating the dress so that both sport
fashionable ruffs.

The du Bellay **Château de Gizeux** (open June to mid-Sept; Sunday
afternoons only) was probably built for René, rather than Martin,
c 1600, and is an excellent example of the grander manor houses
favoured in the 17C, designed so that the *cour d'honneur* opens
towards the village. The principal architectural feature is the two
polygonal towers at the angles of the main courtyard, its grandest
accomplishment a long L-shaped stable-block, *les communs*, the latter
only added in 1741 with a set of hay-lofts illuminated by a superb run
of dormer windows.

North-east of Gizeux, the D749 tracks across the heaths and forests
of the Landes, the woodland now much diminished and the cleared
land given over to rough pasture and the inevitable maize. The principal town of the northern Touraine-Angevine, (21km) **Château-la-
Vallière**, is an important crossroads, but—apart from the traffic—idles
peacefully above the **Etang du Val Joyeux**. This latter is a small lake
formed by the river Fare, whose shores accommodate a campsite and
beach, and are now equipped for boating and fishing. The town itself
was raised to a duchy in 1666 by Louis XIV, in favour of his mistress,
Louise de la Beaume le Blanc, a lady-in-waiting to Charles I of England's widow, Henrietta Maria. Her days as a royal mistress ended the
following year, when she gave way to the imperious Mme de Mon-
tespan, and she retired to the Carmelite convent on the Rue St-Jacques
in Paris. The ducal estates remained in the family, however, to be sold
eventually to the English industrialist Thomas Stanhope-Hollond in
1816. It is a tranquil place, cradled within a great crescent of oak forests,
and lying to the north of the ruinous feudal castle which once controlled
the frontier here.

The **Château de Vaujours**, stands just to the right of the D34 as you
head south, its improbably romantic bailey overrun with ivy and
evergreen oak. Although closed to visitors, the picturesque qualities of
its fractured walls are easily viewed from the track which runs alongside the remains of the 13C barbican. The shape of the once
magnificent 15C *logis* is visible to the right. The *logis* was an overnight
halt much favoured in the itineraries of Louis XI.

West of Château-la-Vallière, the D766 runs fast and straight, across
the plateau to Baugé. A sinuous alternative would be to turn right off
the main road onto the D66, slipping past (7km) the 13C church and
cylindrically towered 16C châtelet at **Marcilly-sur-Maulne** to pick up
the valley of the Maulne. One of the most isolated and beautiful
tributary valleys of the Loir, the river drains the gentle slopes of the
north-easternmost corner of Anjou, running beneath (5km) an imposing farm-cum-hamlet, itself known as **La Maulne**, but otherwise flowing through virtually uninhabited country.

Short of accompanying the river most of the way to the Loir and
cutting up to Le Lude, you should follow the signs to (4km) **Broc**, the
latter an enticement to visit its intriguing parish church of **Notre-Dame**.

Founded by Benedictine monks from La Trinité, Vendôme, in 1060, the church has undergone a series of changes of identity, with much of the fabric of the north wall of the nave belonging to the late 11C, the choir and bell-tower to the late 12C, and the nave crowned by a very fine set of vaults in the early 16C. Apart from an excellent early 17C wooden figure of Christ Crucified, the church is best known for its late 12C **apse paintings**; a monumental Christ in Majesty above an extremely vivid Annunciation and fragmentary Virgin and Child, the whole loosely related to the wall paintings at St-Jacques-des-Guérets.

Broc is also only 5km north-east of the site of the Cistercian abbey of **La Boissière**, and at Easter and in August when the now private precincts are open to the public (check for details with the Tourist Offices in Le Lude or Baugé), it is worth dropping south along the D767. The abbey was founded on the banks of a narrow stream, the Marconne, in 1131, and became a considerable pilgrimage centre after 1244, when the Crusader, Jean d'Alluye, gave the Cistercian monks charge of a relic of the True Cross—a fragment which subsequently became known as the Croix d'Anjou. Clearly disturbed by the prospect of pilgrims flocking to the abbey church, the monks built a pilgrimage chapel to the west of the monastic precincts as early as 1246, the **Chapelle des Etrangers**, whose beautifully vaulted rectangular spaces housed the Cross. The relic is now in Baugé (see above), but the chapel, along with the mostly 18C conventual buildings and a part of the 12C choir, survived the Revolution, the conventual buildings converted into a private house in 1833. Even when closed the site has a beguiling power, the weathered *tuffeau* and deep slate-blue of its roofs together with the woods of the Marconne creating a consummate balance of nature and architecture.

Otherwise you might push on along the D138, past the handsome outlines of the church at **Chigné** (6km from Broc), whose early 13C apse vault is part-sprung from a pair of attenuated column figures representing the dedicatory saints, Peter and Paul.

Genneteil is another 3km further west, and the attraction is again ecclesiastical, but unusual. **St-Martin-de-Genneteil** is entered via a weathered and excellent mid-12C portal, enlivened with interlace, masks, hunting scenes and signs of the zodiac, and studded with those curious ornaments, like pyramidal jelly-moulds, that initially found favour at St-Aubin, Angers. The north choir chapel also houses a late 12C cycle of **wall paintings**, with a Baptism of Christ to the west and Virgin and Child to the east, the two linked by a procession of adoring virgins in the vault. The intrados of the arch giving entry to the chapel also carry a Sacrifice of Cain and Abel, a theme found at St-Savin-sur-Gartempe and in Berry, which, together with the restricted colour palette, reinforces the suspicion that the cycle is the work of an itinerant painter from the Poitou.

To return from Genneteil to the **Couasnon valley** and Baugé you should take the road signposted Lassé, and turn right on to the D141 before crossing the river. This route takes you through (11km) **Pontigné**, the village stacked around the spiralling faces of a superb heliocoidal spire. The latter belongs to the distinguished parish church of **St-Denis**, a mostly mid-12C structure which received a new nave vault in the early 13C. It is best known for its lavish Romanesque transept capitals, and should be better known for the **wall paintings** of its two subsidiary transept chapels. These are first-rate productions of c 1220, that to the north focusing on a Virgin and Child, beneath which a Nativity cycle has been marvellously interfused with the two larger censing angels. In the southern chapel, a Christ in Majesty surmounts the Raising of Lazarus, to the right of which a late medieval seigneurial couple have ingratiated their way into the scene. The handling of the paint is astonishingly fluid, the rich loopy folds of drapery outlined in red ochre, and the painter's obvious predilection for well-grounded figures has given rise to his identification as the 'Master of the Big Feet'.

Finally, following the river westwards, the D141 will bring you back into (5km) Baugé by the southern façade of the château.

12

Angers

With a population of around 140,000, **ANGERS** is one of the major cities of western France, and, along with its great regional neighbours—Le Mans, Tours, Nantes and Poitiers—exercises considerable economic and political clout. Its historical strength lay in its situation, a towering outcrop of Armorican shale overlooking the Maine valley, just below the junction of the rivers Loir, Sarthe and Mayenne, and sufficiently north of the Loire for the surrounding plateau to be largely flood-free. Natural strongpoints controlling major transportation routes tend to prosper, and, though the Gallic *Andecavi* were more inclined to exploit the Bronze Age tin trade from the confluence of the Maine and Loire, Augustus' Roman administrators established Gallo-Roman *Juliomagus* on the site of the present city.

History. Until the recent (and continuing) excavations, comparatively little was known about the physical shape of *Juliomagus*, but it appears that it was an open city with a population estimated to have been about 9000 by the 2C, extending from the present Rue du Mail southwards as far as the railway station. Its main west–east axis is mimicked by the Rue St-Aubin, with the major north–south route, the *vicus senior* of the Middle Ages, followed by the Rue St-Laud. Within this greater area an amphitheatre was built beneath the current Rue des Arènes and a forum provided where the Place de l'Académie now sits, while no less than four thermal baths have been discovered, the grandest beneath l'Esvière and the Place du Ralliement.

In common with its larger contemporaries, Tours and Le Mans, *Juliomagus* adopted the title of its indigenous Gallic peoples, becoming known as *Civitas Andecavorum*, and, following the first invasions by the Franks and Suevi during the late 3C, the city retreated behind a wall at the top of the promontory. Substantial elements of this wall survive, particularly along the Rue Toussaint, but by shrinking the city to a rectangular enclosure above the high ground it had a profound impact on the subsequent development of Angers. In the first place, there was little domestic settlement *extra-muros* until the late 9C; in the second, the dispositions of the wall were often aped by the later medieval fortifications. Christianity seems to have arrived during the 3C, and by c 380 Angers had a bishop graced with the title 'defensor' and the role of civic administrator, but the origin of his powers and the site of his see remain unresolved. The cathedral was only moved within the city walls in 470, giving rise to a wave of new foundations, the abbeys of St-Aubin in the 6C and of St-Serge in the 7C, the church of St-Martin in the 7c, and a secondary rash of funerary chapels around the present Place du Ralliement, where the early bishops of Angers were buried. This modest early Christian infrastructure came under threat during the Norse invasions of the mid-9C, and Angers was sacked in 853–54, and briefly occupied in 872, before Charles the Bald successfully retook the city after what was reported to be a lengthy siege.

By this date, Angers had acquired a 'count' as administrative governor—precisely when is uncertain, but with the death of Charles the Bald in 877 and the effective breakdown of Carolingian government, a struggle for secular power broke out. This struggle was not confined to Angers but it founded a peculiarly powerful dynasty in Angers when, in 898, Foulques le Roux seized power. His son, Foulques le Bon, promptly marched into southern Maine, and his grandson, Geoffroy Grisegonelle, exacted fealty from the counts of Nantes. But it was **Foulques Nerra** (987–1040) who embarked on the definitive expansion of the county of Anjou, and from his base in Angers first annexed the Mauges and then encircled Tours with a great ring of castles, at Langeais, Montbazon, Loches and Ste-Maure-de-Touraine. Saumur fell in 1026, and, with the eventual acquisition of Tours by his son, Geoffroy Martel, in 1044, the whole of Touraine was subsumed into the greater county of Anjou. The city also began to grow once more. A number of new dwellings were built to the east of the wall, referred to as the *suburbium civitatis*, and a *faubourg* constructed along the river, described as *Val de Maine* and probably protected by a second wall. Furthermore, the right bank of the Maine was colonised by religious foundations, first St-Nicolas c 1010, and then Notre-Dame-de-la-Charité in 1028, the latter becoming universally known as the abbey of the Ronceray. The Ronceray provoked the construction of a large new quarter, *La Doutre* (the other side), connected to the left bank by a bridge while, within the old town, there was new building work at the château and the cathedral, and the foundation of a school by bishop Hubert of Vendôme.

The 12C saw Angers briefly flicker at the centre of a vast empire. In 1109 Foulques V managed to acquire Maine by marriage, and in 1128 negotiated the marriage of his son, Geoffrey (called Plantagenet because he wore a sprig of broom—or *planta genesta*—in his helmet while hunting), to Mathilda, daughter of Henry I of England and Normandy. Geoffrey seized Normandy in 1144, dying a year before the marriage of his son, Henry Plantagenet, to Eleanor of Aquitaine added Poitou, Périgord, Limousin, Saintonge, Angoumois, Gascony and Toulouse to the Plantagenets' already vast north-western French territories. And in 1153 Henry forced Stephen of Blois to recognise him as the legitimate heir to the English throne, and succeeded, in 1154, as Henry II, King of England. So powerful an Angevin dynasty was not an unmixed blessing for the city, however. Geoffrey preferred Le Mans, and Henry—in so far as he stopped moving—favoured Woodstock or Chinon. The population boomed nonetheless, prompting Henry to found the hospital of St-Jean on the right bank in 1175, and construct a second bridge, 'de Treilles', whose system of tolls and subsidiary watermills became a valuable revenue raiser. Raoul de Diceto, writing c 1150, described the city as prosperous, its western slopes planted with vines. He was also taken with the 'Great Bridge' and its parade of shops, 'seeming like a street on solid ground, always open to all who want to cross it. The wanderer will find in abundance whatever need requires and whatever luxury requests'.

Plantagenet interest in Angers crumbled with John, and the absorption of the city into the royal domain of Philip Augustus transformed it into a frontier post, angled to meet the threat posed by Brittany and Poitou. In 1230 Blanche of Castille, Louis IX's mother, had a new castle built and encircled Angers with a colossal outer wall, its 4km circuit readily identifiable in the 19C boulevards which ring both the modern centre and the Doutre. The city's liberties were also scaled back, despite Louis IX's granting of a measure of independence with the re-creation of the county of Anjou for his brother, Charles, in 1246. Charles went on to take Sicily and southern Italy during the late 1260s, ostensibly in the name of the Papacy, and Angers languished, a neglected outpost of a new Mediterranean empire, only its cathedral finally nearing completion.

It was the second wave of royal sibling preferment that made for the city, for between 1360 and 1364 King Jean le Bon distributed a number of royal appanages among his four sons, with Anjou being raised to the status of duchy and given to Louis. Although Louis was more inclined to live at Saumur and was a far from pleasant character, the cruellest and most avaricious of Charles V's brothers, he was not immune to the metropolitan attractions of Angers. Not only did he encourage the growth of a university and reinvigorate the administrative *corps* in the city, he seems to have restored Angers' sense of itself, and implicitly acknowledged its urban pleasures when commissioning the cycle of Apocalypse tapestries not for his wonderland at Saumur but for the château here. And his grandson, René (1409–80; titular king of Sicily as well as duke of Anjou, and popularly known as 'good king René'), must have seemed like a draft of the true vintage. Fluent in Latin, Greek, Italian, Catalan and French, an accomplished poet and musician, a good mathematician, the gardener responsible for introducing the carnation and Provins rose to northern France, founder of the chivalric Order of the Croissant, brilliant organiser of tournaments and fêtes, René was one of the most talented and mercurial aristocrats of the 15C. He launched a new programme of works at the château c 1435, before the death of his first wife, Isabelle de Lorraine, and, after his

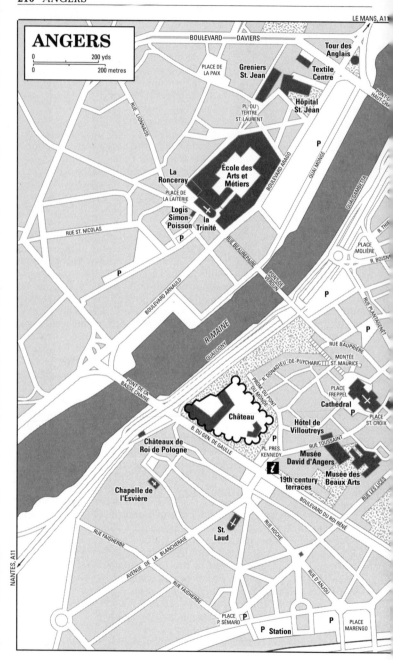

LE MANS, A11

ANGERS

| 0 | 200 yds |
| 0 | 200 metres |

BOULEVARD DAVIERS

PLACE DE LA PAIX

Greniers St. Jean

Tour des Anglais

Textile Centre

Hôpital St. Jean

PL. DU TERTRE ST. LAURENT

RUE LIONNAISE

École des Arts et Métiers

BOULEVARD ARAGO

QUAI MONGE

QUAI GAMBETTA

La Ronceray

PLACE DE LA LAITERIE

Logis Simon-Poisson

la Trinité

RUE ST. NICOLAS

RUE BEAUREPAIRE

PLACE MOLIÈRE

R. THIE

R. BOISN

PONT VERDUN

P

RUE PLANTAGENET

BOULEVARD ARNAULD

R. MAINE

QUAI LIGNY

RUE BAUPRIÈRE

MONTÉE ST. MAURICE

R. DONADIEU DE PUYCHARIC

PROM. DU PONT

PONT DE LA BASSE CHAINE

DU MONDE

Château

PLACE FREPPEL

Cathédral

PLACE ST. CROIX

Hôtel de Villoutreys

B. DU GEN. DE GAULLE

Châteaux de Roi de Pologne

PL. PRES. KENNEDY

RUE TOUSSAINT

Musée David d'Angers

19th century terraces

Musée des Beaux Arts

RUE LES LICES

Chapelle de l'Esvière

BOULEVARD DU ROI RÉNÉ

RUE FAIDHERBE

St. Laud

RUE HOCHE

AVENUE DE LA BLANCHERAIE

RUE FAIDHERBE

RUE D'ANJOU

NANTES, A11

PLACE P. SÉMARD

P Station

P

PLACE MARENGO

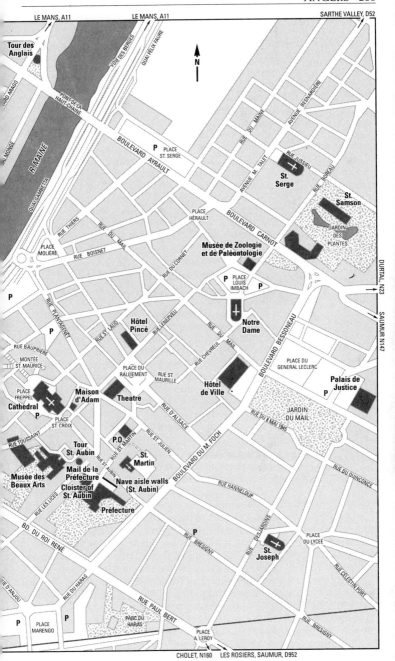

LE MANS, A11   LE MANS, A11   SARTHE VALLEY, D52

Tour des
Anglais

R. MAINE

N

VOIE DES BERGES

QUAI FÉLIX FAURE

PONT DE LA
HAUT-CHAINE

RD ARAGO

ALLONGE

QUAI GAMBETTA

BOULEVARD AYRAULT

P PLACE
ST. SERGE

RUE DU MAINE

AVENUE BESNARDIÈRE

RUE JUSSIEU

St.
Serge

AVENUE M. TALET

RUE BOREAU

St.
Samson

PLACE
HÉRAULT

BOULEVARD CARNOT

JARDIN
DES
PLANTES

RUE THIERS

RUE DU MAIL

RUE BOISNET

PLACE
MOLIÈRE

RUE DU CORNET

Musée de Zoologie
et de Paléontologie

P PLACE
LOUIS
IMBACH

DURTAL, N23

SAUMUR N147

P

RUE PLANTAGENET

RUE ST. LAUD

Hôtel
Pincé

RUE LENEPVEU

RUE DU MAIL

Notre
Dame

BOULEVARD BESSONNEAU

RUE BAUPRIÈRE

MONTÉE
ST. MAURICE

PLACE DU
RALLIEMENT

RUE ST.
MAURILLE

RUE CHEVREUL

PLACE DU
GENERAL LECLERC

Palais de
Justice

PLACE
FREPPEL

Cathedral

P

PLACE
ST. CROIX

Maison
d'Adam

Theatre

Hôtel
de Ville

RUE D'ALSACE

JARDIN
DU MAIL

RUE DU 8 MAI 1945

P

RUE TOUSSAINT

Tour
St. Aubin

P.O.

RUE ST. MARTIN

RUE ST. JULIEN

St.
Martin

BOULEVARD DU M. FOCH

RUE DU QUINCONCE

Musée des
Beaux Arts

Mail de la
Préfecture

RUE ST. AUBIN

Nave aisle walls
(St. Aubin)

Cloister of
St. Aubin

Préfecture

RUE HANNELOUP

RUE LES LICES

BD. DU ROI RENÉ

P

RUE BRESIGNY

RUE DES JARDINS

St.
Joseph

PLACE
DU LYCÉE

RUE CÉLESTIN PORT

TE D'ANJOU

P PLACE
MARENGO

P

RUE DU HARAS

PARC DU
HARAS

RUE PAUL BERT

PLACE
A. LEROY

RUE BRESIGNY

CHOLET, N160   LES ROSIERS, SAUMUR, D952

marriage to his mistress, Jeanne de Laval, in 1454, promoted the expansion of the university law school, then by the Place du Ralliement, so as to admit over 1000 students.

Louis XI brought Anjou back into the royal domain in 1474, forcing René to retire to Provence, but, although it was not until Louis' death in 1483 that Angers gained a mayor with a modicum of freedom from crown control, the mercantile and intellectual energies that René had unleashed proved resilient. The first printing press in the Loire valley was set up in the booksellers' quarter around the Rue Chaussée-St-Pierre in 1476, and the Arts faculty of the university began to draw students of the calibre of François Rabelais, Joachim du Bellay, Ambroise Paré and Jean Bodin. The following century saw large-scale expansion, as Angers' traders exchanged linen for silk and spices from Lyon, wine, slate and *tuffeau* for luxury goods from Paris, Orléans and Spain. A new hôtel-de-ville was built abutting the ramparts in 1530, the magistracy effectively freed itself of royal nominees, and the population climbed to 28,000. A number of the city's finest surviving townhouses date from this period, buildings such as the Logis Barrault, Hôtel Pincé, Hôtel de la Godeline, and Hôtel de Guesclin, the majority either built by, or for, senior civic officials.

But, as Charles Ménard's 1638 topographical view of the city makes clear, Angers had still not broken through Blanche's 13C walls, a situation which continued throughout the 17C and 18C. In 1619 Richelieu described the city as full of 'uncouth and hard to manage people, due as much to their numbers as to their natural temperament'. By the late 17C, after repeated outbreaks of plague and the brief and bloody Angevin Fronde of 1649–52, the population had shrunk by 25 per cent. The 18C was little better, and, in the 1769 census 10 per cent of Angers' citizens were classed as 'poor' or 'very poor', and a quarter were in domestic service. A powerful ecclesiastical and aristocratic class remained, however, concentrated around the cathedral and in the central parishes, while the poor were mostly in the Doutre and the former *faubourgs*, an economic distribution that has changed very little to this day.

The walls were finally demolished in 1807 on the authorisation of Napoleon—though those encircling the Doutre remained in place until the 1830s—and a series of broad boulevards were laid in their place. This was more of a piecemeal process than it now appears, the last of the realignments only taking place in 1839, just as the property developers began to move in. The best of these was undoubtedly Alexandre Richard-Delalande who, like Haussmann in Paris, designed the great terraces of townhouse along the Boulevard Roi René behind integrated Neo-Classical elevations. The arrival of the railway in 1849 provoked a second wave of big civic projects, when the area around the Place Ralliement was remodelled, and the Rues d'Alsace and Voltaire created. Early industrial expansion was concentrated around the station, in the *quartier St-Laud*, and, as the big railways yards grew, the river port declined, a condition accelerated by the virtual abandonment of freight shipping along the Loire after World War Two. Postwar industrialisation was more promiscuous, and Angers is now ringed with factories, research institutes, and food-processing plants, the vast 1950s and 1960s dormitory suburbs at Montplaisir, Belle Beille, and La Roseraie reducing what had become chronic overcrowding in the city centre.

City Tour. The obvious place in which to begin an exploration of the city is the **CHÂTEAU**. If you approach the castle from the Place Kennedy you will probably notice the base of a tower from the Gallo-Roman wall, just above the point at which the wall moved from a north-west to south-east axis on to a west to east axis. A second base has been uncovered beneath the gallery currently housing the Apocalypse Tapestry, and it is clear that the promontory which supports the château lay just within the westernmost corner of the Gallo-Roman enceinte. This is a strategically significant point, at the very top of the bluff overlooking the river Maine and downstream of the city centre. This site was first adopted as a residence by the counts of Anjou in 851, a place described by a cathedral chronicler as 'where it is opportune to live', and which allowed advance warning of Viking longships on the Maine. A chapel dedicated to St-Geneviève is mentioned in a charter of 886, and the *aula*, or ceremony hall, features in a number of 10C texts, but it is likely that these early structures were of wood.

The excavations at the south-western corner of the present château are principally aimed at establishing the shape of the castle Foulques Nerra rebuilt in stone in the early 11C, and are proving successful, reinforcing the view that Foulque's château consisted of a great hall on the cliff-edge side of a small rectangular enclosure. Additions were made to this between the mid-11C and the late 12C, namely an aisleless chapel, dedicated to St-Laud and served by a college of canons, an octagonal kitchen, subsidiary chambers attached to the west of the hall, and a fortified gate. Moreover, one wall of Foulques' **Grande Salle** (great hall) still stands, though the handsome entrance arch and blind arcading were added c 1150.

What is clear is that the castle Blanche of Castille commissioned on behalf of her son, Louis IX, in 1230, represented a massive expansion, on a scale to rival even the biggest of Henry II's French castles at Chinon. Blanche created the outlines of the castle you see today, an irregular five-sided enceinte which backs onto the cliffs to create a vast inner bailey, the whole colossal enterprise being structurally complete by 1240. The most imposing features of this complex are the walls themselves, reinforced by a total of 17 towers and, unusually for a 13C castle, pierced by two great gates. The rationale for this was simple. The Porte-de-la-Ville was rarely used by the standing royal garrison; instead they turned to the **Porte-des-Champs**, which, as it name suggests, gave on to cultivated land, allowing the soldiery access without risk of attack from Angevin 'loyalists' within the city. The defensive arrangements here are formidable, with two linked portcullisses between the main drum towers, and a series of vaulted chambers giving onto to the castle bailey proper. Entrances were always vulnerable however, and it is the **curtain wall** which offers the greatest insight into Angers' strength in depth. The 17 towers which lie along this wall appear from the exterior to be semi-circular projections. A stroll along the sentry walk reveals that they are fully cylindrical, continuing through the wall to emerge on the bailey side as shallow apsidal projections. Before they lost their two upper storeys and conical roofs in the 17C, they rose a full 10m above the wall—creating the type of silhouette Viollet-le-Duc attempted to recapture at Carcasonne in the mid- 19C—and intimidated the surrounding area with what amounts to a serial exhibition of donjons.

Nothing survives of the internal arrangements of the 13C château, and the structures which you see today were mostly built under ducal patronage in the 14C and 15C. Louis I d'Anjou launched the earliest of these works c 1370, when Foulques Nerra's old hall was refurbished and provided with the tall, simply moulded windows which now overlook an inner court. North-east of this, and at a right angle to the old hall, Louis II d'Anjou constructed what became known as the **Logis Royal**, the principal ducal residence, which was further refined between 1435 and 1453 when René d'Anjou added a magnificent northern gallery, the **Galerie du Roi René**. This north wing was destroyed in 1944 and the present structure is a replica, but its detailing is reasonably faithful, a superb vault closing off the staircase with a canopy of eight triradials, and the fretted tracery lights closed to the interior by small wooden shutters.

The interiors now house a collection of 16C tapestries, one pair relating legends from the lives of St-Maurice and St-Martin, with the far better Flemish **millefiori tapestries** of c 1500 next door (so-called because they situate the principal players in a glade of flowers, here inhabited by a menagerie of smaller animals). They depict angels holding the Instruments of the Passion, and are displayed so that you can compare the techniques used in Flanders, the gauges of wool aimed at producing a very consistent overall effect, with those made use of in mid-16C Arras, whose **Passion of Christ Tapestry** continually exploits differences of texture and dye to suggest diaphonous and veiled dress, and extremely subtle transitions of light and shade.

To the east of the *logis royal*, Louis II also added a new **Grande Chapelle** between 1405 and 1413, its dedication to St-Geneviève recalling that of the earliest chapel within the castle (the old canons of St-Laud had been expelled *extra-muros* by Blanche in the early 13C). The new chapel was built to house the *Vrai Croix de la Boissière*, the twin-armed cross that Jean d'Alluye had ceded to the Cistercians of La Boissière after his return from the Crusades in 1244, and which was adopted by Louis as the 'Croix d'Anjou'. The cross is now preserved in Baugé, but the keystone of the eastern bay mimics its form, the domical geometry of the vaults also reflecting the durability of this originally local vaulting type well into the late Middle Ages.

The chapel is otherwise architecturally modest, a simple three-bay rectangle with a good east window, whose tracery patterns owe much to the curvilinear forms originally developed in the Lady Chapel of Wells cathedral. A splendid seigneurial oratory was provided to the south-east for Louis and his wife, Yolande of Aragon, from where they could witness the high mass, but its external blind tracery patterns have been stripped, leaving a ghostly design where the medieval paint could not penetrate. This is not the only polychromy to survive, for along the east wall a number of geometric designs were incorporated to either side of arcaded saints, and the remnants of a once excellent painted alabaster reredos—an Arrest, Crucifixion, and Resurrection—have been mounted above the altar. All these appear to date from the early 16C. The most striking object is an interloper, however, the **Tomb of Donadieu de Puycharic**, which was brought here from its original resting place in the church of the Jacobins. Puycharic was governor of the château between 1585 and 1607—volatile times— and was responsible for skimming the mural towers so as to mount artillery platforms in their stead. His memorial was carved by Jacques Sarrazin in 1607, a piece of studied piety in marble, and now allows the solemn Puycharic to gaze on the altar, while just avoiding any glimpse of the seigneurial pomp to the south.

To the south of the chapel the seigneurial court was closed off by a grand **Châtelet**, an inner gate René had built in 1450–51 to dignify the transition between the outer courts and his own ducal apartments, whose entrance towers were given similar pilasters to divide the cylinders into vertical panels as his grandfather had used at Saumur. These outer courts are now planted with a garden, and they lead you east towards the last of the medieval structures in the enceinte, the **Logis du Gouverneur**. The core of this dates from c 1480, after Louis XI had taken Anjou back under direct royal control, with the upper storey reached via a striking octagonal stair-tower. It was substantially rebuilt during the 18C, hence the present window arrangement. There is an excellent small café in its lower chamber.

Despite its considerable architectural merits, the château is best known for the **APOCALYPSE TAPESTRY**. Since 1954 this has been housed in a specially built gallery to the south of the châtelet, the construction of which revealed the apse of the chapel of St-Laud, visible at the west end of the gallery in the form in which Henry II (Plantagenet) had it refaced c 1155. The documentation of the tapestry, though incomplete, is unusually good. From this we know that it was commissioned by Louis I d'Anjou some time before April 1377, when the first payment for two *draps*, or hanging sections, was made to Nicolas Bataille, a Parisian weaver or merchant. Nicolas Bataille seems to have received 1000 francs for each of the six sections, the last recorded payment being made for the fifth at Christmas 1379, with instructions to distribute 20 francs to provide wine for the assistants of Robert Poinçon 'who had worked on the tapestry', suggesting that some of the weaving was sub-contracted.

The cartoons were supplied by Jean Bondol, Charles V's court painter, and Charles' royal library was pressed into service to provide the pictorial models, taken from a surviving 13C illustrated Apocalypse manuscript (Bibliothèque Nationale MS Lat. 403) which, in the inventory of 1380, is described as having been 'lent to Monsieur d'Anjou to make his fine tapestry'. Jean Bondol was trained in Bruges, and variously appears in a number of documents as 'Jehan de Bondolf, dit de Bruges', or (as when receiving payment for the Angers tapestry in 1378), 'Hennequin de Bruges'—Hennequin being a Flemish late medieval form of John. Certain heraldic details suggest the sixth, and final, section was not delivered until 1382/83, and, as Louis I died in 1384, he can only briefly have seen the tapestry in full.

Precisely where the tapestry was first displayed is a mystery, the obvious candidate being Foulques Nerra's great hall, which Louis I had recently refurbished and better illuminated with tall, square-headed windows. But late medieval tapestries were known to travel for feasts and tournaments, and the earliest mention of the tapestry's display dates from 1400, when it was set up in the entrance court to the archbishop's palace at Arles to celebrate the marriage of Louis II to Yolande of Aragon. Bertrand Boysset, merchant of Arles, commented 'no man is able to describe the expense, the beauty, the *noblesse* of these hangings'. René d'Anjou certainly kept the tapestry in the château here at Angers, only moving it to Baugé in 1476 so as 'not to leave it to the mercy of Louis XI and his royal officers'. He pointedly left it to Angers Cathedral in his will, where it became a more specifically religious object, being displayed at the feasts of St-Maurice, Christmas, Easter and Whitsuntide. In the 17C, however, the third section was cut in two, the better to display it across both the nave and the choir. In the 18C, the tapestry's entire usefulness was called into question, and the chapter resolved to sell it in 1767 'excepting those parts necessary for the Maundy Thursday service', and when no buyer came forward most of it was put into store. Seized at the Revolution, it was repossessed by the bishop in 1806, but then languished in the *évêché* until Canon Joubert rescued it in 1848, and between 1849 and 1863 laboured to restore what remained.

Joubert's restoration has been followed by others, but what does remain is sublimely impressive—76 out of the original 84 scenes, the backgrounds alternating between red and blue and intended to be seen in six horizontal sections. Each *tableau* represents a scene from the Apocalypse, the whole cycle introduced by a majestic vision of Christ, beneath whom St John prostrates himself. The gallery has provided an excellent set of texts elucidating the iconography, so it only remains to comment on the style and focus. Although Bondol was true to his 13C models, he changed the figure modelling and colour in exactly the way you would anticipate from a late 14C artist. The heads are tilted, the shading is graduated, the perspectival architecture is suitably fantastical and the expressions of torment have been sharpened. The figures also move powerfully across space, his draughtsmanship possessing a very real sense of depth, though it is evident from his handling of the compositions that Bondol himself was a manuscript illuminator. In this respect it is interesting to observe that what has been described as 'the most monumental decorative enterprise of Northern European 14C art' was entrusted to an illuminator and not a panel painter. A final reflection is prompted by the subject, and the unanswerable question of why Louis commissioned an Apocalypse and not the more usual Arthurian cycle or Story of the Golden Fleece. Sudden pangs of conscience are an unlikely explanation, particularly since Louis instigated a fashion among his brothers for Apocalypse tapestries (Jean de Berri commissioning a cycle in addition to Philip the Bold), and perhaps it was simply the potential for the strange, gruesome, savage and splendid that inclined Louis to invest in the greatest of all accounts of the visions of St John.

The **streets to the north of the château** have been recently pedestrian-ised, and having largely escaped the bombardments of 1944, retain the densest concentration of 15C–18C houses to survive in Angers. The grandest is to be found on the Rue St-Aignan, where the **Logis de l'Estaignier** of 1448 accommodates a small collection of 16C–19C silver and pewter behind a street façade half of timber and half of stone. But the most beguiling street is the **Rue Donadieu-de-Puycharic**, whose gap-toothed run of gable-fronts curves gently east, obscuring the canonries behind tall schist walls before depositing you on the **Montée St-Maurice**. The latter is a monumental stairway, driven through the late medieval quarter in the mid-19C to provide a processional route linking the river with the **CATHÉDRALE ST-MAURICE**.

Although there is documentary evidence for the existence of a bish-opric by the beginning of the 4C, nothing is known about the earliest cathedral of Angers, and the church was only moved within the Gallo-Roman walls c 470. Again, we are ignorant of the forms the late 5C building took, and know comparatively little about its 6C successor, but its earliest recorded dedication to a 4C bishop, St-Maurille, is an important clue to the outlook of the early Christian community in Angers. The most popular cults in Early Christian Gaul were Mediter-ranean in origin, and even the 4C cathedral of a major centre such as Tours was originally dedicated to St-Maurice, the Egyptian soldier-martyr (the same St-Maurice as was so enthusiastically adopted at Angers in the late 12C, see Galerie St-Maurice below). But, as with neighbouring Le Mans, Angers took a founding bishop as titular saint, a move which fitted neatly with the late 4C bishop's role as 'defensor' of the city.

The 6C cathedral made way for one built under Bishop Hubert de Vendôme between 1020 and 1025, and, though it is not at first apparent that much of this structure survives above ground, it had a considerable impact on the subsequent development of the church. Hubert's cathe-dral possessed a wide, single-aisled nave with a wooden roof, a not uncommon form in early Romanesque western France. When the present **nave** came to be rebuilt under Bishop Ulger, some time before 1148, the single-aisled formula was retained, and the eastern sections of the walls incorporated those of the early 11C church, evident in the shallow strip buttresses of the exterior. The easy amplitude which derives from this arrangement is one of the most striking characteristics of Angers Cathedral, inviting you not only to become involved in a stately progress from west to east, but also to move laterally across the spaces—or at least this would have been the effect before chairs and pews were set into the nave. But though its breadth is due to Hubert, its height—24.68 metres from pavement to crown—is not, and the slowing of the architectural rhythms owes much to the distinctive vaulting strategies adopted by Ulger's successor, Bishop Normand de Doué, some time between 1148 and 1153. Despite the controversies over the precise dating of their design, the vaults were definitely up by 1162, and are the earliest known examples of domed-up rib vaulting to survive in France.

Conventionally, 12C French rib vaults are ribbed groin vaults, i.e. the two diagonal ribs are used both to centre and to strengthen the vault and, though simplified, the geometry is still ideally formed by the intersection of two barrel vaults, meaning that the crown of the vault is at the same height as both the transverse arches and the wall arches. At Angers, the crown of the vault is considerably higher than this, and the geometry is slightly domical. French historians call these vaults 'Plantagenet', Anglo-American historians prefer the term 'Angevin'. Either way, they had a profound impact on the development of late 12C and 13C building in western France, and are one of the guiding forces behind its architectural style.

Attention seems to have switched to the west front after the completion of the nave, and the **transepts and crossing** were only begun c 1190, that to the south having been designed by the architect Etienne d'Azé. Though the formal and proportional language of this area is similar to that established further west, with tall paired lancets above a high dado and a passage run around the structure at clerestory sill level, Etienne introduced a series of innovations. In the first place, he inscribed a rather more delicate blind arcade across the dado wall, and, in the second, he heightened the vaults by 40cm, just enough for their tendency to create distinct spatial compartments to be felt more forcefully. Moreover, the thick diagonal ribs were concealed within the webbing of the vault and eight slender ribs laid across its surface, lending an altogether more calligraphic and 'Gothic' quality to the centre of the church. The first bay of the choir seems to have been laid out at much the same time, but the campaign was hindered by the subjection of Anjou to French royal control, and it was not until 1236 that the north transept was finally completed.

The continuation of an aisleless format into the **choir** was implicit in Ulger's mid-12C nave, and gave rise to the sort of east end one associates with a good number of Romanesque and early Gothic buildings, but which is unparalleled in the mid-13C great church architecture of northern France. This colossal and simple apse has a stillness and grandeur which sets it apart from its northern contemporaries, drawn from the same fount of architectural form as inspired many a Mediterranean church, and, whatever the nature of that tantalising relationship between Angevin architecture and San Franceso at Assisi, the east end of Angers comes closer in spirit to a mendicant church than that of any other cathedral in northern Europe. In the event, the apse was developed just as the new Franciscan and Dominican preaching churches were beginning to make their presence felt, and the conventional date of 1274 has been persuasively discounted in favour of a date closer to c 1250.

The **stained glass** for which the cathedral is so well known has been much moved around, and the major restoration project launched in the 1980s has now reached the choir, bringing in its wake a systematic re-evaluation of both the dating and likely original situation of most of the glazing. There are helpful descriptions beneath a number of the more important windows, which relate the subjects but have yet to catch up with the work of the restorers. The earliest glass is in the north wall of the nave, where three windows dating from c 1180 depict the lives of St-Vincent, Ste-Catherine, and the Dormition and Glorification of the Virgin. They are closely related to contemporary windows in

Poitiers and Le Mans cathedrals, using deep cobalt blue backgrounds to throw the narrative scenes into high relief, and are at their best in images such as the beheading of Ste-Catherine, where the figures have an intense, dancing vitality. The famous Virgin and Child, now in the westernmost north nave bay, seems to date from c 1210, having been originally made for the south transept, an intentionally majestic and conservative image beneath which bishops Raoul and Guillaume de Beaumont offer up their croziers and prayers.

The majority of the 13C glass has found its way to the choir, with a life of St-Martin from the west front (now divided between two windows) being the best preserved. The glass here probably dates from c 1220, the figures enclosed in thick outlines and treated to heavy and rather schematic drapery patterns. The glaziers responsible for this window probably belonged to a local shop and were behind the style adopted by the main series of choir windows, whose large compartments are best seen from a distance. They include a Tree of Jesse, a Childhood and Passion of Christ, and a number of saints' lives, namely those of Peter, John the Baptist, Lawrence, Eligius and Maurille. Two other windows, dedicated to the lives of St-Julien and Thomas Becket, stand out. These seem later, perhaps of c 1235–40, and are the work of two quite different glazing shops, both of which were indebted to recent work at Chartres cathedral. The St-Julien cycle is the more refined, its elegant figure style indebted to the work of the 'St-Chéron Master' of Chartres, while the Becket window looks to the Chartres choir glass and the iconographical schemes outlining Thomas Becket in the southern radiating chapel.

The very finest glass was reserved for the transepts, where the late medieval glazier André Robin was largely responsible for the superb **rose windows**, between 1434 and 1465. That to the south depicts a Christ in Majesty surrounded by signs of the zodiac and musical angels, the white glass occasionally drilled so that 'jewelled' inserts (roundels of deep colour), might be mounted in glittering profusion within the individual panels. To the north, an image of Christ bearing his wounds is encircled with labours of the month, angels carrying the Instruments of the Passion, and Apocalyptic signs of the end of the world. Finally, in 1499 the north transept east window was endowed with a memorial to bishop Jean de Rély, a magnificent Pietà, whose exquisite blues and silver yellows shine above the main northern altar.

The **internal fittings** were less liable to re-arrangement, simply being replaced as and when changes in ceremonial fahion or the liturgy demanded. Few medieval furnishings came through, and those that did are now in the sacristy (an excellent 14C wash-basin) or the treasury to the north of the nave (open only by special arrangement; miscellaneous collection including Bishop Ulger's damaged wooden shrine, the 1296 heart casket of Marguerite d'Anjou, Bishop Hardouin de Bueil's early 15C crozier, and a good late 16C gilded silver chalice).

The nave is dominated by an enormous gothic revival **pulpit**, carved by the founder of the St-Joseph atelier in Angers, René Choyer, and displayed at the 1855 Paris exhibition as a 'mountain of wood'. The cathedral authorities refused it a place in the nave until 1871, ostensibly on the grounds of size, only relenting after its peculiar vein of militant neo-medieval imagery found favour with the late 19C religious revival.

The best work is to be found in the choir, where Antoine-Denis Gervais' superb colonnaded **High Altar** of 1757–59 combines baroque extravagance with architectural translucency to stunning effect. David-d'Angers added a marble **statue** of **Ste-Cecile** to the east of this altar, a profoundly personal work he completed in 1822, modelled on a girl he had known in Rome, Cecilia Odescalchi, who refused his proposal of marriage to enter a convent, dying the following year.

The rarest work is hidden behind the 18C choir stalls, however, where the suspicions of Angers' senior *conservateur*, Antoine Ruais, were marvellously realised when he stripped back an 18C whitewash to reveal an exquisite cycle of **wall paintings of the Life of St-Maurille**. Work on this project started in 1984 and has only recently been completed, but the bringing to light of such an important medieval cycle has presented the cathedral authorities with a dilemma. The wall supporting these paintings is just over one metre behind the 18C wooden choir backs, themselves a listed *monument historique*, and, with little room for permanent scaffolding, inspection for the moment is confined to small parties by prior arrangement.

The cycle consists of 20 scenes from the life of St-Maurille, opening with his ordination and continuing—via an elaborate account of his flight to England—to the miraculous resurrection of an infant, René, who had died before Maurille had performed the sacrament of baptism. The paintings are a good 4 metres above pavement level, composed as a horizontal band between the colonettes of the choir dado arcade, and have been laid directly on to the stone. The colours are extraordinarily vivid, a rich palette of coppery greens, cobalt blues, vermilion, tyrian purple and a rich rose-orange. Even more unusually, oil has been added to the medium, lending a translucency to the images, and at the sort of date which would place these paintings among the earliest oils in western Europe. That date is uncertain, but certain details do find parallels in a number of late 13C northern French manuscripts, and the stress on baptism, and the positioning of the cycle just above the shrines of St-Maurille and St-René in the apse, suggest it may have been commissioned by the reforming bishop Nicolas Gellent (1260–91), probably towards the end of his episcopacy.

Of the exterior, the **west front** is the most rewarding. At first sight this is not an especially compelling, or cohesive, composition, but first impressions give way to a qualified admiration, particularly when you begin to examine the sculpture. A drawing of 1699 shows the façade to have been preceded by a very grand 13C porch, but this was demolished in 1808, and, as they now stand, the exposed lower storeys date from the mid-12C nave campaign. A splendid single **west portal** was inserted c 1160, clearly modelled on the middle doorway of the Portail Royal at Chartres Cathedral, arranging the Angels and Elders of the Apocalypse in the archivolts around a central Christ in Majesty. The lintel was knocked out in 1745, leaving just four seated apostles beneath the inner orders of the arch, with eight standing jamb figures below. Not all the latter can be identified, but the Queen of Sheba (?) and Moses stand to the right of the south jamb, and David can be seen playing his harp to the north. Whereas the tympanum area is modelled directly on Chartres, the jamb figures have been varied, but the style of all is extremely close to that of the 'Chartres Archivolt Master', and further evidence, if evidence be needed, of the activities of Chartrain sculptors in mid-12C western France.

The handling of the upper superstructure is less of a piece. The present arrangement dates from after a fire of 1831 and, though the aim was to approximate the west front's 16C appearance, substantial modifications were made. The two spires are reasonably close to those of 1530–40, but the architect Jean l'Espine's unusual central lantern of c 1545 has been narrowed and the delicacy of its relationship to the flanking towers lost. L'Espine's lantern rises above the most striking feature of the upper area of the façade, the **Galerie St-Maurice**, a superb run of eight figures carved by the Angevin sculptors Jean Giffard and Antoine Desmarais in 1537 to replace the earlier gable. It shows St-Maurice and seven martyred companions in 16C battle-dress, beneath a Latin inscription which reads: 'Grant us peace in our time, Lord, and disperse those nations seeking war.' Maurice was *Primicerius* (leader) of a Christian military corps recruited in Egypt, referred to in a 5C text as the 'Theban legion', which accompanied Maximian into Gaul after he had been made co-Augustus by the emperor Diocletian. The 5C hagiography maintains they were martyred after refusing to join in pagan sacrifices at Agaunum (now St-Maurice-en-Valais, near Lausanne) during the Great Persecution of 303–5. While, in this form, the story is historically untenable, certain of its details seem to derive from a mutiny by some Christian soldiers during Maximian's 286 campaign. His adoption by Angers dates from the late 12C, and though it may have been eased by the similarity of his name to that of Maurille, it was probably motivated by rivalry with neighbouring Tours, whose cathedral was originally dedicated to St-Maurice. By the late Middle Ages he was routinely invoked whenever Angers was under threat, and the vigorous posture the 16C sculptors gave him might have alarmed a malcontent from as far away as the river.

The east end of the cathedral overlooks the **Place Ste-Croix**, one of the main commercial centres of the medieval city and, despite the loss of space to Chauvel's late 19C statue of Bishop Freppel, a pleasant spot in which to linger. The Place is most celebrated for the **Maison d'Adam**, a superb half-timbered house of c 1500, so-called from the statues of Adam and Eve which, until the 19C, stood to either side of the Tree of Life on the main angle post. Unusually, the house occupies a corner site, giving it two street façades and multiplying the number of gables. This advantage was also exploited in the curious forebuilding along the Rue Montault and in the polygonal stair-tower above the street corner, both motifs which ape the architectural projections of aristo-cratic *hôtels particuliers*, and which are unprecedented in a timber built mercantile house. The carvings are equally ostentatious, inter-weaving a vivid cast of wine-bibbers, monkeys and bare-arsed va-grants with more conventional biblical or typological representations, such as Samson and the Lion, the Annunciation, or a Pelican Feeding her Young.

To the south-west, the **Rue Toussaint** follows the line of the Gallo-Roman wall, evident in the exposed banks of schist which provided a solid platform for the later houses which populate its flanks. The most dramatic, indeed the earliest, is the **Hôtel de Villoutreys**, a cacophony of gables and chimney-stacks directly opposite the important Augustinian church of Toussaint, but there are others further down the street which also command respect. The church of **Toussaint** remains the most significant structure in the area, however, originally founded as an oratory in 1040 by Girard, a canon of the cathedral, but taken over by a chapter of Augustinian canons from Airvault (Poitou) in the wake of the Gregorian reform, and by 1103 reconstituted as an Austin priory. The present building dates from c 1230, with a four-bay nave and elegant *en-delit* shafts rising above small canopied statues of apostles and saints. The shafts supported what must have been a splendid run of early Angevin net vaults, sprung from two attenuated shafts where they cross the transepts, but the vaulting would have gone no further, as the present choir is a pseudo-Gothic addition of 1730 and 13C Toussaint was built to a T-transept design. Deserted at the Revolution, its vaults and roofs had collapsed by 1810, leaving what was until recently a simple shell.

The decision to restore the building to accommodate the **Galerie David-d'Angers** was taken in 1981, and the architect Pierre Prunet engaged to spruce up the walls and launch a steeply pitched roof of steel and glass from a new concrete wall-plate. The result is a great success, for subjecting David's often intricate relief carving to abundant natural light has revealed a breadth of detail easily missed in the originals. Pierre-Jean David was born the son of a cabinetmaker in Angers in 1788, and, after enrolling in the studio of the Paris-based sculptor, Roland, was awarded an annual grant by the city of Angers. Thereafter he won the 1811 Prix de Rome for his Death of Epaminondas, which he subsequently asked the city council to accept on behalf of the Musée des Beaux-Arts. Overcome with gratitude he also added the title 'd'Angers' to his surname—'the name of the son next to the name of his mother'—an undeniably deeply felt move which had the useful effect of distinguishing him from his older contemporary, the painter Jacques-Louis David. By 1817 he had obtained his first major commission, for the statues along the Pont Louis-XVI (now Pont de la Concorde) in Paris, and, after his appointment to a teaching post at the Academy of Art, began soaking up commissions. His Republican sympathies, and eventual involvement in the 1848 Revolution, made for an uneasy relationship with many of his patrons, however, and he was exiled in 1851, only returning to Paris shortly before his death in 1856. Throughout this period he despatched plaster-casts of his works to Angers, some for display at the museum and some to maintain a studio collection and inventory, and by 1839 a gallery devoted to David-d'Angers' works was inaugurated in the Musée des Beaux-Arts.

All this work was transferred to Toussaint in 1984, the portrait medallions for which he was renowned displayed in an open gallery above the choir, while the larger statuary dominates the nave. It is these grand public monuments which seize the eye, the casts extending to the magnificent Strasbourg memorial to the Gutenberg Press of 1840, as well as the great political figures such as Larrey and Bonchamps. The transepts house the exhibits most likely to be of use to specialists, with casts of the various stages of the evolution of the great pediment frieze of the Panthéon in Paris.

It is also worth visiting the old conventual precincts to the south, where two and a half walks of an excellent 17C cloister survive, and the municipal library, gardens and a playground jostle for space. The **gardens** are the most tranquil spot in Angers, planted with a variety of trees and enclosed by a singular mixture of architectural styles.

To the rear of the gardens, the **Logis Barrault** has accommodated the Musée des Beaux-Arts in one of the finest late medieval townhouses in Anjou since 1807, although its interior has been stripped and its elevations were vastly extended during the 17C, when it was briefly called on to act as a seminary. What stands of the *logis* is best viewed from the courtyard, where the lower storeys of the east wing, stair-tower and north gallery survive to give one a general sense of its architectural values, though the insertion of early 19C Neo-Gothic windows into the main south wing can cloud the issue. The house was built between 1493 and 1495 for Olivier Barrault, mayor of Angers, as a 'handsome, honest and luxurious building that would embellish and honour the city'. It entertained some illustrious guests—Cesare Borgia in 1498, Mary Stuart in 1548, and Marie de Medici in 1619—but was unsuited to its subsequent uses as seminary, prison and museum, and consequently lost all its internal fittings, with the exception of a fire-place in the east wing and the marvellous staircase vault. The force-fulness with which the external elevations are treated is striking, the great angle tower rising through coats of arms to a secondary upper stair-turret, and the north gallery vaulted with a snaking run of triradial vaults.

The **MUSÉE DES BEAUX-ARTS** itself is in a state of transition, while the stair-tower of the Logis Barrault is restored and the collections of the old Musée Archaeologique assimilated to form the Musée d'Anjou. The following description is therefore provisional, although the ground floor will continue to house temporary exhibitions while the first foor concentrates on the substantial holdings of 12C–16C furniture and metalwork. These open with a number of 15C and 16C carved wooden chests, a few lengths of panelling, and a superb late 16C terracotta Virgin and Child, **La Vierge de Tremblay**, the child caught and gently tugged back towards the Virgin's lap in what is one of the most delicate devotional images to have survived from the period. The larger room contains a miscellaneous array of Limoges enamels, metalwork and ivory carving, enhanced by two magnificent early 16C oak chests. The first arranges arcaded female saints above two fish-like serpents, while the second, intact even to the signed locks of their Swiss maker, Michaud Girart, glories in an inverted *danse macabre*, where monks, clerics, nobles and merchants join forces to aim bows and arrows at an impassive grim reaper. The metalwork is more conventional, but in-cludes a rare late 13C gilded mask from a tomb effigy and an excellent fragmentary collection of architectural canopies from a mid-12C bronze candelabra, one of the great 'crowns of light' of which Honorius of Autun spoke so eloquently and which is thought to have come from the same shop as was responsible for the Geoffrey Plantagenet enamel in Le Mans.

The paintings which make up the Beaux-Arts collection are on the second floor, and at the time of writing were arranged chronologically across five rooms. The earliest work, in the so-called **Salle des Primitifs**, is not the most exciting, juxtaposing a Tuscan *Virgin and Child* of c 1360 by Francesco Pisano with a bewitching mid-15C *Maestà* attributed to the Sienese Sassetta and an important small triptych of c 1370, the latter indebted to Simone Martini and probably painted in Avignon. Flemish painting is oddly represented by a number of early 16C works, of which one might single out the Hoogstraeten Master's *Crucifixion* of c 1505 and a tiny portable triptych centred on the *Virgin and Child* of c 1520.

The majority of the 16C holdings are in the adjoining room, grouped around a small panel painting of the Holy Family entered in the museum catalogue as by **Raphael**. It is a very beautiful image, a warm landscape before which Mary and Joseph are clothed in the light pinks and blues associated with Raphael and Perugino's work, but its similarity to a painting by Raphael in the Prado, Madrid, has led several scholars recently to see in this a studio copy, made as the major (Prado) commission was finished c 1515. Otherwise, it is the 17C Flemish painting which stands out, an excellent personification of *Autumn* by Jan Brueghel of 1595 next to a *Baccanalia* by his frequent collaborator, Hendrik van Balen. And among the inevitable mid-17C genre scenes of David Teniers the Younger, two darker, more enigmatic, works stand out: an unattributed 17C nocturnal *Crucifixion*, and Louis de Caulery's strange allegory of penance and lust—the *Concert Espagnole* of 1600.

The museum's collection of **French 18C and 19C painting** is its greatest accomplishment, most of the 18C work having been initially brought together by the Marquis de Livois. As these have been in the museum since 1799, a mere three years after it was first formed, and were originally either purchased 'first-hand' or from Parisian dealers, they mostly sit in the frames in which Livois bought them. This can prompt a number of reactions, from approval of the sensitivity with which **Antoine Watteau**'s delightful c 1716 *Fête de Campagne* (or rustic marriage proposal), is enclosed, to astonishment at the waves of gilded stucco which threaten to engulf two beautifully muted small-scale still lifes of the 1760s by **Jean-Baptiste Chardin**. Livois was very much in favour of still lifes, and the sort of mythological scenes which might include a fair amount of naked female flesh. The total of 11 paintings he acquired by Chardin testifies to the former, and **Jean-Baptiste van Loo**'s *Renaud dans les bras d'Armide* of c 1735 is the most licentious example of the latter. On seeing **Jean Honoré Fragonard**'s 1755 pairings of *Jupiter and Callisto*, and *Cephalus and Procris*, one is surprised to learn that Livois did not in fact own them, but, as he already had **Jean-François de Troy**'s 1727 *Bathing of Bathsheba* in his collection, perhaps even he felt that the similarity in the poses of the passive Bathsheba and Procris would have been too much.

The largest of the French 18C canvases is currently reserved for the space which first greets you as you open the doors at the head of the stairs, **François Boucher**'s colossal *Réunion des Arts* of 1761. The situation becomes it, allowing you to draw back from the bravura brushwork to examine the way Boucher piles up the allegorical motifs, strewn across the foreground by winged putti beneath the incomplete coffered semi-dome of 'Architecture'.

The highlight of the 19C holdings is **Ingres'** *Paolo Malatesta et Francesca da Rimini*, painted while he was staying at the Villa Medici in Rome in 1819, and by far the most successful of the variations Ingres painted of a commission he first received from Caroline Murat in 1814 (the original commission is now in the Musée Condé, Chantilly). The story is taken from Dante's *Inferno* and shows the couple's shy embrace just moments before their murder, the colours orchestrated to force your eyes to look deep into the surrounding gloom. To this one might add **Jean-Baptiste Corot'**s excellent 1826 sketch of the Temple of Minerva Medica, and **Jean de Fleury'**s panorama of Angers and the Pont de Treilles of c 1840. The latter is an extremely good example of the type of picturesque river scene popular with early 19C buyers, with a broken bridge and fantastical huddle of islanded timber houses beneath a great sweep of foreground genre detail, and the north-west spire of the cathedral in the process of being rebuilt up above the hill.

A right turn from the Musée des Beaux-Arts on to the Rue du Musée brings you into the Place St-Eloi where the **Tour St-Aubin** is the most substantial, if not the most significant, remnant of Angers' premier Benedictine abbey. This was founded c 535 by Germain, bishop of Paris, and initially dedicated to St-Germain d'Auxerre, only taking the title St-Aubin in the 7C, in memory of an early 6C bishop of Angers. Little is known of the early history of the abbey. Canons replaced the monks in the wake of the Norse attack of 853, a situation which endured until 966, when Count Geoffroy Grisegonelle reintroduced a congregation of Benedictines and gave the counts of Anjou titular control as abbots. The abbey was damaged by fire in 1032, reconstruction being supported by Geoffroy Martel during the 1050s, and by 1100 Foulques Réchin had bowed to the pressures of the Gregorian reform and ceded to the monks the right to elect their own abbot. The 12C witnessed a high point in the abbey's fortunes. The conventual buildings were hugely expanded, the bell-tower completed, and with more than 100 monks the monastic congregation counted among the largest in western France.

The Tour St-Aubin was begun under Abbot Robert de la Tour-Landry c 1130 with the massive strip buttresses and raised doorway of contemporary donjons. It was always freestanding, acting as a defensive enceinte tower to the west of the monastic church, and, like the tower of La Trinité at Vendôme, grew to house the abbey belfry. These upper bell stages date from the late 12C, rising above an excellent ribbed dome and quartered at the angles with elongated octagonal turrets. To the west of here, the **Mail de la Préfecture** has been driven along what was the axis of the abbey church, a few blocked window arches on the north side having once belonged to the 11C aisle wall.

The more significant remains are to the south, where the **Préfecture** is accommodated in what was the conventual precinct, rebuilt between 1688 and 1740 in the crisp and austere vernacular of the Maurist reform movement. As with St-Serge (see below)—also reformed by monks from the Congregation of St-Maur at the end of the 17C—the monastic quarters were subject to a lengthy and ambitious rebuilding programme, brought to a superb conclusion under the architect Pierre Baudriller in the second quarter of the 18C. The finest of these later buildings is the **lavatorium** in the south wing, whose interior surfaces carry a restained programme of relief carving culminating in a glorious Baptism of Christ keyed into the vault. This is rarely open to the public, but the **cloister walks** can always be entered during office hours. The early 18C campaigns here followed the plan of the 12C cloister and, in places, simply interred the inner walls and arcades behind rubble and plaster. When these were stripped during the 1850s alterations which saw the old Maurist buildings transformed into the Préfecture, a considerable body of medieval work was uncovered, including some of the greatest Romanesque sculpture to have survived in the Loire Valley.

The **chapter house wall** of the east walk is virtually intact, the arches originally opening into a rectangular *capitulum* no less than 20m x 15m in size. The arches to the north of the entrance to this chapter house are narrower than the paired arches to the south and are earlier, dating from c 1130, and supported on files of columns originally six deep. Although scarred by ramping arches from a vanished 15C cloister vault, most of the carving is in good condition, and seems to be the work of local sculptors. The paired arches to the south are very different, for here the lunettes formed by the relieving arches invite relief carving, and have been given a subtle iconographical programme: to the right David and Goliath are attended by a number of Labours of the Month in the archivolts; in the centre a half-destroyed tympanum features a man leading a dragon by a leash (St-Romain? St-Philibert? St-George?), a combat mimicked by two dozen posturing warriors in the archivolts; and on the left a Virgin and Child are attended by angels arranged across the archivolts in virtually every kneeling pose imaginable.

This latter arch had its iconographical range expanded towards the end of the 12C, when the lower arches were painted so as to allow an Adoration of the Magi to take place. This painted programme, tiny as it is, must rank among the finest medieval **wall paintings** of France; compressing a Massacre of the Innocents as well as an Adoration into the left-hand arch, and a Journey of the Magi and the Magi before Herod on to the right, an irregular space of less than a square metre painted with the finesse of an illuminated manuscript. The whole of this southern end is later than its counterpart to the north, probably dating from c 1150, and seems to be the work of sculptors from south-western France. Finally, the chapter house entrance was carved in yet a different style, with beautifully framed relief sculpture across the unmoulded archivolts of the portal, and two powerful historiated capitals in the jambs: Samson and the Lion, and Samson killing the Philistine and rescued by Delilah.

A second quite magnificent portal survives off the old south walk of the cloister, in what is now the **Salle Jeanne de Laval**. This originally formed the entrance to the monastic refectory, its distinctive iconography, like its sculptors, imported from the Saintonge c 1160, and the whole portal carved with a brilliance and verve which defies description. It depicts the Pascal Lamb, crowned by the uppermost pair of six female virtues shown plunging swords into demons, and accompanied by angels bearing incense and palm branches. The inner arch further qualifies the theme of the victory of good over evil with a representation of two lions (guardians of the Resurrection) mauling a pig (Satan) and two figures who, like Samson, are seen in the act of breaking a lion's jaw, so prefiguring Christ's ultimate triumph.

To the south and east of the Préfecture the great boulevards constructed after Napoleon ordered the demolition of the city walls still frame the centre of Angers. The best of the 19C domestic architecture lines the **Boulevard du Roi René**, where, between 1837 and 1850, the architect-developer Alexandre Richard-Delalande was responsible for the majority of the town houses which line the northern street front. Like Haussmann in Paris, Delalande expanded the façades to embrace three or four internally distinct houses, and embellished the fronts with exquisite wrought-iron balconies often, as in Nos 3–7, incorporating neo-Renaissance portrait busts.

The **Boulevard du Maréchal Foch** was developed in more piecemeal fashion, its broad, tree-lined pavements, populated with spacious cafés, leading north to the banks of administrative offices around the **Jardin du Mail**. The symmetrical gardens here constitute Angers most imposing public park, inaugurated in their present form in 1859 but built above a popular promenade first established outside the city walls as early as 1619. The effect of 19C development on Angers is most apparent around the edges of the Jardin, where vast secondary squares were opened up, the old Hôtel-de-Ville of 1691 remodelled, and Charles-Edmond Isabelle's Neo-Classical Palais de Justice finally completed in 1875. As early as 1834 V. Vincent reported: 'Gone are the sad, dark walls which made Angers seem like a dungeon, gone are the multitude of convents, churches, chapels and cemeteries. In place of these monuments of another age have arisen new streets embellished with elegant shops, filled with all the products of modern industry'.

A few more 'sad, dark walls' are in the process of being demolished just to the north of the Préfecture, on the Rue St-Martin, though in this case to reveal rather than to dissolve an old church, which, since it was first founded as an oratory in the 7C by St-Loup, has been known as **St-Martin**. Until recently the church functioned as the chapel of the Lycée St-Martin, the school which grew out of an earlier college on the site, but has been acquired by the département who intend undertaking the sensitive restoration it so urgently requires. Its importance lies in its **crossing**, a majestic square outlined by four piers of *opus mixtum*, alternate bands of stone and brick, which dates from a reconstruction financed by Foulques Nerra between 1012 and 1020. The quarter-columns in the angles and upper stages belong to a series of modifications made in the 1060s, but as a rare example of a building dating from Foulques Nerra's Anjou, and one with the sort of spacious transepts and square crossings favoured in contemporary Ottonian Germany, its return to the public domain is much to be commended. The plan is to provide access directly from the Rue St-Martin.

Just beyond the post office at the bottom of the Rue St-Martin, the **Place du Ralliement** was refurbished and given a big new central café in 1994, regaining much of the dynamism that made it the social hub of late 19C Angers. Like the boulevards to the south and east, the Place was largely developed in the 1840s and surrounded by handsome blocks of rented housing, the variety of whose wrought-iron balconies testify to a similarly wealthy clientele. The one major public building to grace the square, Botrel and Magne's **Théâtre Municipal** of 1868–71, has extended a curious twist to the theatrically favoured Louis-XIII-style sweep of columns, niches, arches and relief sculptures by raising a huge semi-circular window at the top of the façade, in a self-conscious reference to the Constantinian basilica in Rome. The theatre is still closed for repair but, when reopened, it would be worth strolling through its magnificent public foyer, modelled on the reception halls of 17C châteaux, and into the auditorium, whose ceiling was painted by the artist responsible for that of the Paris Opéra, Jules Lenepveu.

North of the Place, a warren of pedestrianised streets compete with the Rue St-Aubin as the main shopping centre of Angers. The **Rue Lenepveu** is the most prominent, running north-east to the older mercantile quarters around the Place du Pilori, and accommodating the lavish early 16C **Hôtel de Pincé** on its western flank. Built for the Lieutenant Criminel (King's Prosecutor) and ex-mayor of Angers, Jean de Pincé, the hôtel was clearly intended to rival the Logis Barrault, and, in certain particulars, is actually modelled on it. The left wing and stair-tower were built first, between 1530 and 1535, the latter provided with the same sort of branching vault employed by René d'Anjou at the château, and subsequently brought into the bourgeois repertoire at the Logis Barrault. Then, between 1535 and 1538, the local architect Jean Lespine was called on to design the right wing, eschewing the richer decoration which had seen the main wing planted with busts of Jean de Pincé and his wife, Renée Fournier, in favour of simple friezes of ox-skulls and foliate scrolls. Both façades and interiors were rather hammed up in Magne's restoration of 1880–89, but Lespine's ornamental runs of balustrade shafts remain original, a decorative pastiche of what in an earlier château would have been the sentry walk.

The last private owner was the Angevin painter Guillaume Bodinier, who in 1861 presented the house to the city in order to display the collections of the local antiquarian Count Turpin de Crissé, since when it has been called the **Musée Turpin de Crissé**. De Crissé's collection of classical sculpture and ceramics are housed on the ground floor, boasting an excellent Etruscan engraved mirror of c 250 BC, and an exceptional group of Greek black-figure vases, all augmented by exemplary brief art-historical notes. The first floor concentrates on Egyptian antiquities, while the upper two floors are given over to Japanese and Chinese art respectively. The Japanese work includes a fine series of 18C 'Yukiyo' prints, images of the floating world of actors and courtesans, while the Chinese work includes one of the highlights of all Angers' museums, the exquisite silk brocade of an 18C mandarin's robe.

The Rue Lenepveu eventually runs down to the **Place Louis-Imbach**, once the medieval market square and now supporting, at its north-western angle, a small natural history museum, the merged collections of the **Musées de Zoologie et de Paléontologie** (open Tues–Sun, 2–5 only). To the left of the museum the Rue Botanique and its continuation, the Rue Boreau, bring you past the sole surviving enceinte tower of the 13C city walls, and then cut to the west of a superb botanical garden, the **Jardin des Plantes**, first laid out in 1789. The garden was redesigned early this century by Edouard André around a sequence of waterfalls, and now includes a good children's playground, in addition to the banks of azaleas, succulents and exotic trees. One of its most appealing features is what appears to be a vast and run-down potting shed, festooned with ivy and wisteria, and which turns out to be the shell of a parish church, St-Samson, founded in the 12C to serve the laity drawn to the estates of the august Benedictine monastery just down the Rue Jussieu, the abbey of St-Serge.

St-Serge was the second of Angers' monastic communities to take root, having been founded in 654 by Clovis II, King of the Franks, and dedicated to two 3C soldiers martyred in Syria, SS-Sergius-and-Bacchus. The shrine of St-Sergius at R'safah-Sergiopolis on the Euphrates was one of the more important early Christian pilgrimage centres of the Levant, but the cult seems to have been overshadowed here by the arrival in 851 of the relics of St-Brieuc, the great evangelist of Brittany, and though Sergius was not dropped from the dedication Bacchus was. What has survived the French Revolution is a rambling and heterogeneous structure, but one whose great hall-choir stands among the definitive statements of Angevin architecture of any era.

The earliest part of the existing fabric is in the **transepts**, where the bands of masonry and brick originally belonged to the crossing of a church consecrated under Abbot Ulgrin, an ex-prior of Marmoutier, in 1059. Much of the masonry further out into the transepts is also mid-11C and, like the crossing, was remodelled when it was decided to construct a new choir shortly after a portion of the Breton saint's relics was returned to the bishop of St-Brieuc in 1210.

The elegance of this new **choir** is quite extraordinary, its basic rectangle divided into twelve bays by six slender columns, and amplified to north, south and east by an échelon of chapels. As in Angers Cathedral, the vaults are sharply domed-up, with each bay carrying eight ribs except where they meet the eastern wall, where the two easterly diagonals only run as far as an arch angled across the corner, which in turn is ribbed with a triradial. This is not achieved without cost, and from the outset there was a potential for discord in the disparity between the thickness of the walls and the elegance of the internal shafts, columns and vaults. St-Serge overcame this by concentrating light at the eastern end of the choir (and it was evidently intended to be very light, as the one surviving 13C window in the centre of the north wall is grisaille), and inviting the eye to look to the vault and not to the walls as the major determinant of space. This has a number of effects, most obviously making a small area seem spacious, and the equality of treatment extended to the ribs dividing the individual compartments brings the choir together into a single, tightly-knit composition. But, however one argues the case, it is the combination of a hall church format with extremely light vault cells which is the triumph of St-Serge, and though only locally influential it had implications one can see explored throughout late medieval Europe. Precisely what hindered a wider reception for St-Serge's particular range of effects remains an open question, for the eastern vaulting bays have a beauty and complexity which makes one wonder why they were not endorsed beyond western France, a bafflement which is only increased by the carved **bosses**.

Given our existing knowledge, these would look odd outside a regional context, but however wayward the handling of the supports they allow subtle iconographical programmes to be woven into the fabric of the vault, which is useful if your glass is grisaille. Except for the four bosses of the central aisle, which depict Abraham holding two souls, the Resurrected Christ, a Coronation of the Virgin and the Lamb of God, all the bosses carry apostles. The smaller sculptural plaques, sitting at the junction between ribs, carry a rich New Testament programme, with scenes from the Incarnation, the Parable of Dives and Lazarus, and the Apocalypse, augmented by a veritable choir of angels.

The archaeology and dating of this choir is problematic, and a number of authorities maintain that the walls of the southern chapel belong to an earlier, mid-12C structure, concerned for its apsidal form, distinctive bases and the pointed arches of its windows. But the briefest of glances at the lopsided arch connecting the western bay of the choir with the north chapel is enough to confirm that the handling is quite eccentric. This writer is inclined to see the south chapel as the earliest part of a choir whose design was altered during the course of construction, and which was probably only finally completed around 1225.

The late Gothic **nave** can scarce compete with so bold a choir, and was anyway hurriedly put together, having been built under the abbacy of Jean de Berné (1445–66) to replace a structure damaged during the Hundred Years War. It was originally aisleless, a series of side chapels having been punched through the lower walls in the 16C, which in turn had arches knocked through their transverse walls in 1832 to facilitate the present aisle. Most of the original late 15C clerestory glass survives, however, with apostles to the south exchanging banderoles with a splendid run of Old Testament prophets to the north.

The area west of St-Serge is dominated by an old railway marshalling yard, beyond which the Boulevard Ayrault sweeps you down to the river, over the Pont de la Haute-Chaine and into **Doutre**. The atmosphere here is very different to that in the '*cité*', the old artisans' houses located along crabbed streets, staggering between a wealth of medieval religious foundations established when it was a simple *faubourg*. The first of these you encounter is the **Hôpital St-Jean**, a magnificent hospital founded in 1175 by Etienne de Marsay in the name of the count of Anjou, Henry II (Plantagenet). The foundation charter provided for lay control, but this did not prevent an Augustinian takeover, and government became swiftly vested in a college of canons regular under the rule of a prior. Its prerogatives were further clarified in the statutes of 1267, which guaranteed a welcome to patients 'of every country and every religion' except for foundlings, who were to be cared for at the abbey of the Ronceray, and the incurably ill, who were the responsibility of the leper house of St-Lazare. Resentment at the levels of taxation levied by the prior was finally assuaged by two acts of parliament in the mid-16C, which brought the hospital back under lay control and began to improve its medical reputation. Female nursing staff were brought in and, with a system of visiting doctors, the hospital was treating up to 500 patients at any one time by the mid-17C. St-Jean was finally superceded by the big Ste-Marie hospital at Reculée in 1854, but its adoption as an archaeological museum saved it from demolition, and it stands as one of the most important medieval hospital buildings to survive in northern Europe.

Its architectural organisation is of a type once relatively common in 12C and 13C Europe, with a vast sick ward, the Salle des Malades, divided into three aisles by slender columns, a conventual precinct for the canons, storehouses on the rise of the hill, and a chapel to the east. The cloister only ever seems to have had three walks, those to the north and east surviving from the late 12C arrangements, with a Cistercian austerity in the arrangement of the paired columns and tightly carved waterleaf capitals. The south walk was replaced during the 16C. The **chapel** lies off the north walk, small and irregular, the peculiar treatment of its eastern wall evidence that it was once intended to be single aisled and oriented. It post-dates the sick ward by about 20 years, and adopts both the major forms of Angevin vaulting to be developed in the early 13C—the octopartite, and the octopartite with subsidiary triangular cells. Its internal decoration is now a disappointment, the three northern windows serving as a graveyard for a fragmentary collection of 13C–16C stained glass, and the east wall littered with a number of tomb effigies left over from its days as an archaeological museum, the two 15C figures of the châtelain of Passavant-sur-Layon and his wife being the best.

The **Salle des Malades** remains majestic, an airy basilican hall covered by an elegant canopy of rib vaults. It is closely related to another recipient of late 12C Plantagenet generosity, the Maison-Dieu de Coëffort outside Le Mans, and, like its contemporary, originally laid curtains across the bays to screen the patients in small groups. Since 1967, the ward has acted as a setting for Jean Lurçat's celebrated cycle of **tapestries**, the **Chant du Monde**, and is open to the public. Inspired by Jean Bondol's late 14C Apocalypse Tapestry, Lurçat began work on the Chant du Monde on his own account in 1957, the ten completed hangings variously woven by the Tabard, Goubely and Picaud shops at Aubusson. It was intended as a secular homily on the destructive and spiritual potential of mankind, weaving fierce colours on a black ground in one of the most moving modern pictorial cycles to grace a European gallery. The cycle progresses from images of war and holocaust to celebrations of rural life, poetry, peace and exploration; complex allegorical epiphanies which Lurçat's death in 1966 has left sadly incomplete. The individual scenes unfold as follows: the Great Threat; the Man from Hiroshima; the Charnel House; the End of Everything; Man in Glory in Peace; Fire and Water; Champagne; the Conquest of Space; Poetry; 'Ornamentos Sagrados' (literally 'sacred ornaments', but better in Spanish where it evokes a domestic meaning in addition to the quasi-religious one).

The initial decision to install Lurçat's Chant du Monde in 1967 inspired the **Musée de la Tapisserie Contemporaine** just to the north of the sick ward. This is mostly given over to temporary exhibitions, but Jean Lurçat's widow donated a number of the artist's works which are separately displayed on the first floor. The themes are similar to those of the cycle, though their origins in poetic texts are here quite explicit, and perhaps most revealing in the marvellous 'Liberté', which Lurçat had secretly woven at Aubusson in 1943 to illustrate Paul Eluard's great 1942 resistance poem of the same name.

To the **west of the hospital**, the Rue Gay Lussac climbs past the splendid shell of the **Greniers St-Jean**, a vast 13C complex of hospital cellars and storerooms, whose upper storey came to be rented out to local shop-keepers by the late middle ages. Opposite, in a corner of the Place du Puits-Rond, rise the ruins of 12C St-Laurent, while the Rue de la Censerie hugs the 18C western enceinte walls of the Ronceray, bringing you into the commercial centre of the Doutre at the **Place de la Laiterie**. Like much of this whole quarter, the Place has been restored over the last decade, its superb concentration of 15C and 16C timber houses now stripped of clogging 19C plasterwork to reveal one of the most handsome squares in Angers.

The most luxurious residence is the **Logis Simon-Poisson** of 1582 (No. 67 Rue Beaurepaire), a four-storey townhouse on a narrow site, embellished with personifications of Science, Friendship, Generosity and Munificence. And the south-eastern corner of the Place is occupied by much the most important complex of Romanesque buildings to survive in the city. The most prestigious is **Le Ronceray**, founded as the monastery of Notre-Dame-de-la-Charité by Hildegarde, the wife of Foulques Nerra, in 1028. An early account of the foundation states that a ruined Merovingian abbey stood on the site, and that Hildegarde and Foulques wished to restore it by refounding it. Whatever the merits of the account, Notre-Dame-de-la-Charité became established as the sole Benedictine abbey for women in Angers, and, until its dissolution in 1790, was known more simply as the Ronceray (literally 'the bramble patch').

Entry is via a minor south door, bringing you into a low aisle which serves as a prologue to the temporary exhibitions of 20C textiles held in the nave. What is initially most striking about this **south aisle**, its flattened barrel vault and low galleries, turns out to be the result of a later intervention. The abbey was originally built as a hall church, its aisles rising to be covered by high transverse barrel vaults, and the galleries were inserted in the early 17C in an attempt both to provide additional accommodation, and to arrest the tendency of the **nave vault** to distort the upper walls. This did not prove a successful strategy, and the nave vault was only finally stabilised between 1956 and 1964, when the surfaces were also stripped to reveal fragments of once magnificent late 12C geometric paintwork. The transepts and choir were screened off in 1815 and fell into ruin, but what survives is one of the most significant late 11C naves in the lower Loire Valley.

Work seems to have started c 1060 and proceeded from west to east, with the easternmost transverse arch reached c 1080. The choir east of here may have been damaged by a fire in the Doutre in 1088 and rapidly rebuilt, but the whole complex was solemnly consecrated by Pope Calixtus II on 7 September 1119. As such the nave stands as evidence of the early adoption of hall churches north of the Loire, the high barrel vault reinforced by transverse arches and abutted in the aisles with subsidiary barrel vaults at right angles to that of the main vault. This particular treatment is unusual, but the hall church format was widely taken up in 12C and 13C Anjou, maturing into the most inventively handled alternative to the more usual aisleless churches.

One such aisleless church actually shares a wall with the Ronceray, for, unlike the *cité*, the Doutre was a single parish during the early Middle Ages, controlled by the feared Ronceray abbesses. They began building a new church of **La Trinité** c 1160 to replace an 11C building damaged in the 1088 fire, and which was anyway inadequate for the needs of a fast-growing population. With the exception of Jean Lespine's **belfry** of 1540, which deftly crowns the earlier crossing, the fabric is wholly mid-12C. The plan is stunningly simple, with an apse and shallow transept separated from the nave by a thick chancel wall, which has in turn been pierced by two subsidiary *Berrichon* doors.

The **nave**, however, has been amplified, not merely westwards, as would suit parochial needs, but outwards, the lower walls hollowed out into a succession of undulating niches. These niches are framed by superbly varied registers of ornament, and are set beyond the lines of a vault which shares certain quirks of handling with mid-12C vaults in Normandy, suggesting that the masons, and quite possibly the designer, came from Normandy or the Seine valley. Sadly, Joly-Leterme's breathtakingly harsh restoration of 1870 has wrecked the building's subtleties, but at least one earlier fitting came through unscathed, the splendid early 16C carved wooden staircase which offers access to the organ loft. To the right of this stair, by the damaged tomb slab of Abbess Renée Sarazin (died 1499), a set of stone steps descends to the **Crypt of the Ronceray**, a rather severe Romanesque hall crypt divided into three minor vessels by a total of 16 intermediate supports, rarely opened to the public but of interest to specialists.

At the bottom of the Rue Beaurepaire, the **Pont de Verdun** returns you to the *cité*, with the finest of all views of Angers' cliffs, towers and banks of mural schist.

Beyond Angers

Angers is a good centre from which to explore both the Loire Valley downstream of Saumur, and the lower valley of the Sarthe, as well as the northern Mauges, all of which are covered elsewhere in this guide. There is one major monument which should be covered here, however— the **Château de Plessis-Macé**, easily accessible along the N162 (14km) and worth a detour for its crooked fanfare of towers and gables alone.

The complex was begun in the late 12C with a large square keep to the left of the present entrance, which was linked to the main enceinte wall and protected by a moat. This outer moat in turn fed a second moat, which separated the keep from the inner bailey, wherein were built two large halls. That closest to the keep was the manorial residence (i.e. the residence of the seigneur and his family except in times of war, when they would decamp to the keep), while opposite was a building occupied by servants and workshops.

The greater part of this impressive castle was destroyed during the Hundred Years War and was only rebuilt after c 1450 for Louis de Beaumont, but it was rebuilt above the existing foundations and followed the late 12C shape of things. The earlier keep had survived reasonably well, as had large sections of the enceinte wall, but the actual fabric of the rest of the complex, with exception of a number of 19C windows punched through the moat side of the *corps de logis*, is almost entirely that raised between c 1450 and c 1500. It is an ambitiously detailed structure, the main walls constructed of the local schist, while the quoins, lintels and embrasures are cut from the same soft *tuffeau* as the more sumptuously carved decoration. This is at its most demonstrative in the magnificently corbelled balcony which sits above the north-west angle of the *logis* and was even extended to a second gallery connecting the guardroom to the main servants' block.

With one notable exception, the **interior** has been completely refurbished, mostly under the 19C ownership of Countess Walsh de Serrant, though the new décor includes a splendid 18C Aubusson tapestry woven to a cartoon by Jean-Baptiste Huet and depicting a game of blind man's buff. The exception is the **chapel**, given a very fine Flamboyant east window and a quite outstanding internal tribune platform, fretted about with wooden tracery lights and accessible by a delightfully miniaturised octagonal stair-turret.

13

Cholet, the Mauges and the Layon Valley

ROAD (197km): Cholet D20, 13km Maulévrier; D25, 23km Vihiers (D960, 3km Château de Coudray-Montbault); D54/D170, 15km Passavant-sur-Layon; D170/D77, 12km Le Puy-Notre-Dame; D77, 8km Montreuil-Bellay; D761, 12km Doué-la-Fontaine; 23km Brissac-Quincé; D55, 16km Beaulieu-sur-Layon; D54, 7km Rochefort-sur-Loire; D751, 9km Chalonnes-sur-Loire; 22km St-Florent-le-Vieil; D752, 19km Beaupréau; 18km Cholet.

Although the *département* of Maine-et-Loire approximates to the county of Anjou, those parts of the *département* south of the Loire were only absorbed into Anjou during the early 11C. First, in 1026, Foulques Nerra annexed the Saumurois, a strategically desirable area previously within Touraine, and only then did he begin chipping away in earnest at the northern frontiers of Poitou, eventually bringing the whole of the

Mauges into greater Anjou. The historical boundary between the Mauges and the Saumurois is reinforced by geology, for the valley of the river Layon marks out an important frontier, separating the limestones of central France from the granite country at the southern end of the Armorican massif. The difference is pronounced, the self-sufficient villages and lush vineyards of the Saumurois giving way to the thin, acid soils of the Mauges, with its few spare towns set amidst the dense coppices of the *bocage*.

This underlying geology also finds an uneasy parallel in the later history of the region, for, whereas Foulques Nerra's conquest of the Saumurois during the 1020s is reflected in the largely medieval infrastructure of the fiefdoms he established, at Montreuil-Bellay and Brissac for instance, the earlier identity of the Mauges towns is less apparent. Overwhelmingly Catholic and agricultural, and lacking the mercantilist ambitions of the Loire valley towns, the Mauges was unsympathetic to the aims of the French Revolution. The role it played in the Vendéen War of 1793–95 led to the destruction of most of its towns and, though reconstruction often followed the earlier property lines, the rebuilding was wholesale. Indeed, it is difficult to think of a Mauges town which is not predominantly 19C or 20C.

The above itinerary is arranged as a clockwise circuit centred on Cholet, the modern capital of the Mauges, but the area covered is large and anyone intent on spending a few days in the region may find Montreuil-Bellay or St-Florent-le-Vieil more congenial bases.

Cholet

What little survives of pre-1793 Cholet is to be found around **Le Mail**, the name given to the granite platform overlooking the river Moine on which the first 11C castle was built. A couple of sections of the 13C curtain wall still stand at the base of the rock and a 17C portal has been re-erected to the north, which now acts as an entrance to the gardens of the late 19C Palais de Justice. Except for a few late 18C houses around the Place Travot, that is more or less it. The modern town centres around the huge and eclectic Neo-Gothic church of **Notre-Dame**, built between 1854 and 1885 to a design which combines elements of Le Mans and Beauvais cathedrals with a twin-spired Norman west front. The areas around the church have been pedestrianised and the big squares to the north and east—the **Place Travot** and **Place Rougé**—bustle with well-used cafés and pavement terraces. It is an extremely sympathetic and spacious town, brimming with evidence of the industrial prosperity which has seen the population of Cholet expand from an admittedly artificial low of 2162 in 1797 to around 60,000 today.

The most startling evidence for this prosperity lies in the impressive ranks of new municipal buildings; the superb library and town hall of 1976–84 along the Rue Travot, and the recently opened **Musée d'Art et d'Histoire**, which has successfully united the various town collections in a single building at the bottom of the Mail. The historical work occupies the right wing of the gallery, opening with a crude 14C granite cemetery cross from the parish church of St-Pierre in Cholet, and assembling a miscellany of pots, tiles, mantelpieces and firebacks from prominent houses in the locality. But the museum's main theme is a beautifully orchestrated account of the **Vendéen War**, presented from a number of viewpoints and stretching, chronologically, from the storming of the Château d'Angers on 17 July 1789, to the last of the *Chouan* uprisings in 1815.

The Vendéen War proper lasted no more than three years, the opening shots being fired at St-Florent-le-Vieil in March 1793, when a regiment of locally conscripted soldiers mutinied and gave the signal for a pro-Royalist uprising which engulfed the whole of the Vendée and southern Anjou. The summer of 1793 saw the Royalist 'whites' score a number of notable victories, but the defeat of Henri de la Rochejaquelein's Royalist army by the Republican Général Marceau at Le Mans in December 1793 effectively ended any hopes the Vendéen rebels entertained of unseating the Revolutionary government. The following year saw the Revolutionary Convention appoint Général Turreau to 'cleanse' western France of dissent, a brief he interpreted with ferocious zeal, unleashing waves of troops, the *colonnes infernales* of hated memory, to scorch the countryside and destroy the Vendéen towns. By 1795 any large-scale resistance was at an end, but a guerilla movement persisted and sporadic outbreaks of sabotage, rioting and general mayhem on the part of the Royalists, who referred to themselves as *Chouans*, continued into 1799, with a last rebellion of 1815 still drawing on the old *Chouan* rhetoric.

With a few obvious exceptions, the artefacts on display are of little artistic value, but the cumulative effect of all these banknotes, weapons, prints and pamphlets, knick-knacks, maps and sealing-wax adds up to a sociology of late 18C revolution and warfare, all given a generous context by the explanatory historical notes which accompany each display area. It is the story that is told here which justifies the visit—the brutal, incendiary pitilessness of it all. There were gestures of clemency—Bonchamps' at St-Hilaire-le-Vieil, for instance—and moves towards reconciliation under Charette and Stofflet in 1795, but it is the passionate cruelty of both the uprising and its extinction which underscores most of what is on show: Henri de la Rochejaquelein's desperate and bloody marches north of the Loire where thousands died, and the Republican Turreau's 'infernal columns' which all but emptied the villages of the Mauges.

The **Vendéen leaders** were eventually depicted in poses of heroic vanity in a series of **portraits**, commissioned by Louis XVIII to decorate the Château de Versailles in 1816, when not one of them was still alive. The cycle of ten paintings was not finally completed until 1827, and then for Charles X, but the entire group has been gathered together and now forms one of the centrepieces of the Musée d'Histoire. The artists concerned, Anne-Louis Girodet-Trioson, Paulin and Pierre-Narcisse Guérin, Robert Lefèvre, Amable-Paul Coutan and Jean-Baptiste Mauzaisse, worked to a standard format; the main figures are lifesize and shown in 'vigorous', though not necessarily war-like, poses. In the light of the great Revolutionary portrayals of Napoleon by David and Gros, this later work seems weak and derivative, and even Girodet's 1824 portrait of Jacques Cathelineau, the most skilfully painted of the group, has nothing of the panache of his Roman paintings of the 1790s.

The collections of the **Musée d'Art** are to be found in the opposite wing. Given that **François Morellet**, co-founder of the *Groupe de Recherche d'Art Visuel* in 1960, was born in Cholet, and was active in post-war abstract and op-art circles, the greater part of the available space is given over to a display of recent painting and sculpture. Here given the umbrella term 'geometrical abstraction' it brings together a quite varied collection of work by such as Jean Arp, Victor Vassarely and André Hearteaux, and juxtaposes them with a body of far narrower abstract work from the 1970s and 1980s.

The pre-World War Two paintings are not the result of a definite acquisitions policy, and their quality is patchy. The earliest work on display is a fairly routine early 16C Flemish Virgin and Child, but the majority of paintings are French and date from the 18C and 19C. The best is probably **Carl van Loo**'s unfinished *Family of Darius before Alexander of 1755*. Of the rest one might single out **Philippe de Loutherbourg**'s 1767 *Battle Scene*, a rather beautiful small painting of a nun offering a prayer above a dying soldier by **Horace Vernet** of c 1830, and a good late 19C view of the Bosphorus by **Jules-Achille Noël**.

The area to the **east of Cholet** was sparsely populated even before the rural depredations of the Vendéen war, and the damage caused to the larger villages has lent the region a rather battered 19C air. Nevertheless, on a fine day it is worth taking the D20 to the border with Poitou at (13km) **Maulévrier**, for a stroll among the Japanese gardens of Alexandre Marcel's **Parc Oriental**. Marcel began landscaping the grounds of the early 19C Château Colbert at Maulévrier in 1899, and, between then and 1913, planted over 180 Japanese and east Asian trees and shrubs along the banks of the river Moine. It is an unusually beautiful and disciplined design, the various elements—lanterns, bridges, a pavilion and pagoda, gardens within gardens—subject to a specific set of meanings, and teasing an almost architectural rhythm from the natural contours of the landscape.

Beyond here the D25 will take you east, pushing through the long horizons and open woodland of the eastern Mauges. The major market town of the area, (23km) **Vihiers**, was destroyed in 1793, and having been rebuilt in workaday 19C fashion cannot be counted among the more attractive towns of southern Anjou. It does, however, lie within easy reach of the **Château de Coudray-Montbault** (3km west along the D960; open 1 July–8 Sept only, closed Tues).

The present château is substantially late 15C, though the bases of two cylindrical towers beneath the principal façade originally formed part of a 13C circuit of eight drum towers. The form and silhouette are familiar—conical roofs above earlier cylindrical towers, a central *corps de logis* and a squared moat—but, like the materials, something of an import in southern Anjou. (The château, along with Vihiers, was only brought within the département of Maine-et-Loire after the French Revolution. Historically it formed a part of the Poitou.) The upper elevation arranges lozenges of enamelled brick (originally green and since oxidised to black) against a pink brick ground, very much in the manner of the smaller châteaux of Touraine and Blésois. The oxidation of the brickwork was doubtless exacerbated by the burning of the château in 1793, a sack which destroyed the roofs, entrance gate, most of the right wing and the southern gallery. The château was sensitively restored by the Baugeois family in the late 19C, but the loss of the first storey southern gallery is telling, and, though you can glimpse the magnificent carved stag which originally graced a rear fireplace, it is difficult to visualise the original arrangement which would once have been like a miniaturised arcade from the Louis XII wing of the château at Blois.

Coudray-Montbault has an oratory rather than a chapel, as an Augustinian priory had been founded just beyond the skirts of the early medieval castle in the second half of the 12C, and the seigneurs had use of its nave. This **prieuré** was a daughter-house of La Réau (Vienne), and though it is now a shell you can visit the roofless late 12C nave and adjacent chapel of St Barbara. The latter was once the prior's lodging, and recent work has revealed fragments of the sumptuous **13C wall paintings** which decorated the room while it was a *logis*. Consecration as a chapel came in 1527, and it was presumably then that the stunning **Entombment Group**, occupying a niche in the north wall, was installed. This may have been damaged in 1793–94 but the detailing and, most importantly, the subtle early 16C paintwork is largely intact, with Nicodemus and Joseph of Arimathea wearing the curious snub-nosed sandals favoured by François I's court and Mary Magdalene given a similarly fashionable embroidered floral gown. It is absolutely marvellous and probably out of Michel Colombe's sculptural shop in Tours.

From Vihiers the more rewarding route takes you towards the headwaters of the **Layon valley**, best reached by taking the D54 to Cléré-sur-Layon and, just before you enter the village, turning left on to the D170 to (17km) **Passavant-sur-Layon**. Not only does this bring you through the vineyards but the road provides a splendid view of the ruined cylindrical towers of the 13C **Château de Passavant**, a crumbling quadrangular fortress whose 16C bridge now connects its present owners with the simpler outlines of an 18C residential wing. The village lies above the castle, drawn against the flanks of a 12C parish church which, unusually for this area, sports a square-ended choir within a wholly Romanesque idiom.

The D170 continues to follow the river valley as far as (2km) Nueil-sur-Layon, but beyond here it is better to strike east along the D77, the road climbing to meet the 15C spire of (10km) **Le Puy-Notre-Dame**. The impressive **collegiate church** from which the town takes half its name was probably built to house a relic of the girdle of the Virgin Mary, brought back from the Holy Land by the late 12C Crusader, Guillaume, Comte de Poitiers. The importance of this relic during the Middle Ages lay in its reputation for ensuring a safe confinement and birth, and the copy of Queen Anne's 1638 letter to Louis XIII displayed in the south transept, requesting that he persuade the canons to lend her the girdle, is testimony to its enduring power.

These royal loans were not unusual. Both Prato Cathedral (Italy) and Westminster Abbey (London) also laid claim to possession of the relic, and the various girdles would seem to have sporadically circulated among the noble houses of Europe, presumably one at a time. The most startling aspect of Le Puy's situation is that there is no mention of the girdle before 1392, and the foundation of a college of canons to serve the church did not take place until 1482, when Louis XI effectively relaunched the cult. Yet there can be no doubt that the church dates from the first half of the 13C, and that its size and splendour suggest it was conceived as a pilgrimage centre.

This is most evident in its architectural affiliations, for Notre-Dame is a scaled-down version of Poitiers Cathedral, with a six-bay hall church nave closed to the west by a screen façade, narrow transepts and a square east end. The domical webbing of the **vaults** is supported by simply moulded ribs, octopartite in the nave and transepts, quadri-partite in the aisles, whose transverse members are sprung above very beautiful, small, standing figures. These vaults are among the most elegant of any so-called 'Angevin' vaults to have survived in France, and their potential for creating effects of extraordinary spatial delicacy has been magnificently realised in the **choir**. Here, above a frieze of owls and dragons, the main field of the vault has been teased upwards, so as to allow two triangular cells to grace the outer angles which are then filled with their own arrangement of three ribs, giving rise to a type of fan within the corner known as a triradial. It is difficult to describe, though easy to see, and in both its general handling and its specific motifs contains the seeds of late Gothic vaulting.

The choir vault also acts as a canopy above a fine set of 16C **choir stalls**, whose western bench-ends are embellished with reliefs of St-Georges killing the Dragon and St-Martin dividing his Cloak. These stalls were the last of a series of late medieval additions, which saw the octagonal spire raised above an otherwise 13C belfry in the early 15C, and a set of subsidiary rooms opened off the south aisle. Perhaps most surprising of all, the **Virgin's Girdle** is still exhibited in the church, behind a glass screen in the south transept, though what in fact you are able to see is a recently embroidered pouch which sheaths the linen and silk of the 'original'.

East of Le Puy, the D77 descends through vineyards renowned for producing the best red *Saumur*, levels out, and then, through a gap in the trees, reveals a first glimpse of the château at (8km) **MONTREUIL-BELLAY**. The town which grew up to the south-west of this fastness is the last of the 32 known walled medieval towns in the medieval county of Anjou to retain the greater part of its defensive circuit, and is gloriously situated, on a steep bluff overlooking the river Thouet. But it is understandably the **Château de Montreuil-Bellay**, rather than the town, which draws the visitors.

The site seems to have been first occupied in 1026, when Foulques Nerra, having conquered the Saumurois, raised a donjon to defend the frontier with Poitou and confided the castle as a vassalage in one Berlay, subsequently corrupted to Bellay. This early castle was partially razed by Geoffroy Plantagenet in 1150, and its successor more comprehen-sively sacked in 1214, as a result of which it passed into the hands of the Melun-Tancarville family. It was they who were responsible for the surviving early 13C **barbican**, to the north of which you can make out elements of 13C stonework built above the *petit appareil* of what must have been the base of Berlay's early 11C hall. The rest of an unusual complex dates from the 15C.

The first of the late medieval areas to be resolved was the **Château-Vieux**, to your right as you pass through the main castle gate. When it was acquired by the powerful Harcourt family from Normandy during the Hundred Years War, the château must have been in a fairly poor state, and their first move c 1420 was to build a new residential wing to the east of the earlier donjon, flanked by octagonal towers and embellished with elaborate dormer windows. West of this, a splendid freestanding **cuisine** was built, and given a central chimney which superficially resembles that of Fontevraud, but, like the rest of the kitchen, dates from c 1450. Beyond the kitchen lies the château's rarest accomplishment, an L-shaped wing designed to accommodate the four canons who served the castle chapel in four separate apartments, each with its own towered stairwell and set of chambers. The assumption is that this is contemporary with the collegiate chapel of **Notre-Dame**, built to an aisleless design between 1472 and 1484 and, since the collapse of the old parish church of St-Pierre in 1810, serving as the town church, hence the wall which now divides the chapel from the castle bailey.

Finally, a second residential wing, known as the **Château-Neuf**, was arranged in the north-west angle of the bailey between 1485 and 1505, and it is this block which forms the focus of the obligatory guided tours. It is without doubt a handsome *logis*, peppered with the conical roofs and turrets which play such an exhilarating role in the overall design when seen from afar, but seen close to it bears the heavy marks of Joly-Leterme's late 19C restoration. The **interiors**, except for the superlative run of cellars, were mostly refurbished at the same time, and now act as a repository for the present owners' collections of 16C–18C furniture and tapestries, along with a few late medieval curios (small coffers mostly). The **oratoire** was restored with greater sensitivity, revealing its deposit of fine late 15C wall paintings, where the main Crucifixion is accompanied in the vault by angelic musicians reading the score of a motet by the itinerant Scottish monk, Walter Fry.

The **town** developed to the south-west of the castle, encircled by rampart walls which in their present guise are 15C. The finest of the town gates, the massive **Porte St-Jean**, lies to the south, while the best of the 16C town houses are to be found in the centre, particularly around the Clos Gaudrez. The most picturesque elements in a beautifully modulated townscape are grouped along the river. The château was originally protected by no less than three curtain walls on this northern flank, the outermost of which, breached by the Porte du Moulin, formed part of the main town enceinte. Once inside these walls, and on the banks of the Thouet, the whole structure of the lower town begins to unfold, with ruined sections of enceinte wall crumbling to reveal glimpses of the river, and the remains of the old parish church of St-Pierre consolidated beneath the cliffs, the sad relics of its Romanesque apse and 15C aisles a peaceful setting for a riverside picnic.

The region to the **north-west of Montreuil**, between the Layon and the Loire, is marked by a barely undulating plateau, once thickly forested but now largely planted with vines, maize and sunflowers. Pockets of ancient woodland do survive, particularly towards the southern bank of the Loire, but even here you are more conscious of managed stands of oak and poplar plantations run wild than of ancestral forest. The easiest way to cross this plateau is to take the fast D761 as far as Brissac-Quincé, though in summer a brief detour to take in the old Tironensian abbey of **Asnières** is worthwhile. (7km from Montreuil, open 10–12, 14–17.30, July and August only. Closed Tuesdays.)

The church was founded as a priory in 1114 on land donated by Giraud Berlay, seigneur de Montreuil, and evidently prospered, being raised to the status of abbey in 1129. Sadly, its post-medieval experience was one of loss, amputation even, and after the roofs were burned by Huguenots in 1566 it was mostly downhill. With no more than two monks in 1789, the abbey was sold off, the conventual precincts being taken over by a local farmer for use as outbuildings. The complex was otherwise gradually plundered for its building stone, with the nave finally demolished in 1853. Nevertheless, what does survive is impressive, and probably reflects two building campaigns. The south transept and crossing bay seem to have been built between c 1160 and c 1180, while the north transept and choir, along with the crossing tower, date from the first quarter of the 13C.

It is the **choir** which excites the specialists, as, for once, it has not been extensively restored, and supports the delicate rib profiles of its vaults on two astonishingly slender colonettes, 8 metres high. It is explicitly modelled on the choir of St-Serge at Angers, and carries a vivid set of fully painted vault bosses, grouping portraits of the evangelists around a central figure of Christ and confining narrative scenes to the aisles, which unusually include a Cleansing of the Temple. Elements of the 13C choir pavement also survive, a fairly typical collection of addorsed birds, foliage and geometric patterns, but good to see in its original setting. The south-eastern **Chapelle de l'Abbé** was extensively refurbished during the 15C, acquiring a marvellous late medieval canopy which supports a Man of Sorrows on the east wall, and two tomb effigies. That to the left is 14C, but that to the right is indebted to the broad, bed-like tombs found at Fontevraud, and may well represent the abbot responsible for completing so splendid a choir.

Otherwise, the only sizeable settlement you pass is **Doué-la-Fontaine** (12km from Montreuil), a pleasant town, with a couple of spacious market squares, a number of good 16C houses and a large zoo on its outskirts. It is best known for its huge sunken amphitheatre, known as the **Arènes** and long thought to be Gallo-Roman, though in fact created during the 15C out of a disused medieval quarry. The idea was to create a centre for theatrical spectacles, a theatre which became sufficiently celebrated to be mentioned by Rabelais, though its present claim to fame is as a setting for the Journées de la Rose. This is an exhibition of commercially grown roses held in mid-July, drawn from the local rose-growers who, since the late 19C, have provided Doué with its primary source of wealth.

Beyond Doué, the D761 paces out a swift 23km to the steepish natural mound occupied by **Brissac-Quincé**. The town was built on the crest of this rise, revolving around a drab market square which eventually peters out before the east end of the parish church of **St-Vincent**. The main body of this church was begun in 1532 and financed by René de Cossé, whose reward was to appear as a donor, along with his wife, at the base of a heavily restored Crucifixion in the east window.

The **Château de Brissac** lies at the base of the mound, overlooking the banks of the river Aubance, and is much more interesting than the town. It was begun in 1455 by Pierre de Brézé, a close confidant of both Charles VII and Louis XI, as a straightforward quadrangular castle with four cylindrical angle-towers, but was sold to René de Cossé in 1502 and subsequently found itself attacked by both Huguenots and the Catholic League during the Wars of Religion. As René's grandson, Charles de Cossé, had opened the gates of Paris to Henri IV in March 1594, a grateful monarch raised Brissac to the status of a duchy, and Charles eventually retired here to begin building above the dilapidated core of de Brézé's 15C château.

Work began in 1606, and by Charles de Cossé's death in 1621 the garden (south) and main entrance (east) wings had been completed, both under the supervision of the architect Jacques Corbineau. Corbineau's **entrance façade** must be the most extraordinary architectural elevation of 17C France, its compellingly faceted stonework shoehorned between the great drums of de Brézé's 15C castle. And this is just the starting point, for the extravagant mannerism of the main volumes suggests that even the decision to slant the axis, so as to reveal more of the south-east tower, was not forced on Corbineau, but was a knowing ploy. Whether you are sympathetic to its peculiar range of effects or not, it is impossible to deny it is an exciting design, continually scoring the surface to create patterns of light and shade which can seem almost crystalline against a turning sun. The five storeys of the **staircase tower** are so arranged as to steadily reveal the five orders of classical architecture, the trick being to encase these in banded stonework towards the base. The lowest, barely visible behind the coursed channels, is Tuscan, and the façade progressively rises through Doric, Ionic and Corinthian to a Composite order from which all banded stone has been banished. But perhaps the most wilful reshaping of classical decorum is reserved for the left-hand section of the elevation, where the pediments of the dormer windows have been embraced beneath a single supra-pediment.

Charles de Cossé's death in 1621 brought work to a halt, though a second campaign was eventually initiated under his son, Louis, which saw the more routine north wing built. The **interiors** reflect the sensibilities explored in the exterior elevations, and both the Grand Salon and the *salle à manger* remain substantially as Corbineau designed them in the early 17C, with a superb chimneypiece framing a portrait bust of Charles de Cossé in the Grand Salon, and a musicians' gallery in the *salle à manger*. The portable work was acquired in the 18C and 19C, and includes a good set of 18C Gobelins tapestries and a number of portraits scavenged from the break-up of the Duc de Maine's collections in 1861. The most surprising embellishment is entirely 19C, for the sumptuous second floor **théâtre** was only added in 1883 for the Marquise de Brissac, a noted amateur opera singer and friend of Debussy, though its studied 17C decor was adopted with more of an eye to the overall shape of the château than to the needs of the Marquisse's full soprano voice.

Brissac-Quincé is within easy reach of Angers by the D748. If you are heading west, towards the lower Layon valley and the Mauges, take the D55 through the vineyards to (16km) **Beaulieu-sur-Layon**. Other than buying wine from one of the village *caves*, the chief interest in Beaulieu lies in the **ancienne église**, easily missed along the Rue de la Mairie and not to be confused with the 19C neo-Romanesque church in the main square. All that survives of the 12C parish church is the east end, across whose apse semi-dome an itinerant painter essayed a beneficent **Christ in Majesty** c 1200.

Beyond Beaulieu, the D54 descends the escarpment to (7km) Rochefort-sur-Loire, but it is worth slipping into **St-Aubin-de-Luigné** (7km from Beaulieu and reached along one of several possible left turns off the D54, a combination of the D125 and D106 being the best), self-proclaimed *Perle du Layon* and much the most attractive village in the valley. The hills away to the west of the river form a natural bowl here, ideal for vines, and the white *Côteaux du Layon* produced in St-Aubin has recently become quite fashionable. The village rejoices with all the *domaine* and *dégustation-vente* signs you might expect, but more unusually a good number of these *caves* are located in handsome 16C houses, such as **La Noue** and **La Bouellerie**. The finest of these town-based manor houses now accommodates the **Mairie**, having been built in the early 16C as a presbytery and given the arms of the Borgia pope Alexander VI above the main lucarne, in recognition of the commissioning priest's father, Jean de Pontoise, who made his fortune as the pope's doctor.

Below St-Aubin, the old medieval *bourg* of **Rochefort-sur-Loire** was destroyed in the course of the Wars of Religion, and was unremarkably rebuilt around the surviving 16C belfry of Ste-Croix. But the town has the advantage of bringing you on to the **Corniche Angevine**. This is the old road from Rochefort to Chalonnes, the D751, bedded into the northern slopes of the steep stretch of land which separates the Layon from the Loire (or, more precisely, the Louet, a subsidiary channel the Loire has spun off to the south). The views are majestic, reaching out across the vineyards to the silent, marshy islands of the Loire, tussocked with grass and fringed with scrubby poplars.

The corniche eventually brings you down to cross the river Layon at (9km) **Chalonnes-sur-Loire**, an important centre for the manufacture of wine-presses, with a large market square to the south of the Hôtel-de-Ville. The old centre was closer to the river, and a few 18C houses survive along the banks, but in no great concentration. Even the medieval parish church of **St-Maurille** is mostly late 19C, though the mid-12C domed choir bay and early 13C north chapel came through— the latter, as at Asnières, incorporating a Virgin and Child in the east wall and evangelist portraits on the vault bosses.

West of Chalonnes, the D751 maintains a discreet distance from the south bank of the Loire, rarely affording a glimpse of the river and favouring the vine-covered slopes, or steering a course clear of the flood meadows unless forced back to the banks to serve a succession of once thriving ports. (9km) **Montjean-sur-Loire** is the first you encounter, its neo-Gothic church of 1858 visible for miles but its river quays long silent. An **Ecomusée** has been established in an old forge down towards the river, housing a series of exhibits concerned with boat-bulding and navigation on the Loire, and now starting to develop a secondary theme touching on the hemp-growers, sail-makers and coal-merchants who were an integral part of the industrial ecology of the river.

The most spectacularly sited is (13km) **ST-FLORENT-LE-VIEIL**, rising above a great schist promontory to survey the whole of the Loire valley from Chalonnes to Ancenis, some 15km across the border in Brittany. The site was known to the early Celtic settlers as *Glonna*, meaning 'eminence', and was chosen by the 4C hermit, Florent, as a base from which to convert the peoples of the Mauges. A monastery housing his tomb is known to have existed here by the 7C, but the incursions of first Nominoë, Chief of the Bretons, in 849, and then the Norse raiding parties of 853, persuaded the monks to join the general monastic exodus up the Loire. Like the Benedictines of Noirmoutier, they eventually reached Tournus (Burgundy), but any peace enjoyed by the relics of St-Florent was short-lived, and their odyssey took in Angers and Roye (Picardy) before a portion of the saint found rest outside Saumur. The new monastery founded there c 950 was known as St-Florent-le-Jeune to distinguish it from the mother-house of St-Florent-le-Vieil, but seniority counted for little in uncertain times, and the tremendous growth enjoyed by the Saumur house during the 12C led to '*le vieil*' being downgraded to the status of a priory.

None of this is reflected in the current fabric of the church, despite its being untouched by a fire which destroyed most of the rest of the town in 1794. The pretext for this fire, a deliberate act on the part of the Revolutionary Directoire, was the crucial role St-Florent played in the Vendéen uprising of 1793–95. On 12 March 1793, the mostly Catholic farmers and tradesmen of the town mounted a protest against the mass execution of priests, inciting a mutiny by a group of local conscripts and igniting the revolt of the whole of the Mauges and Vendée. The local peasants readily offered themselves to fight against the Revolutionary directives of Paris and, whipped into an army by a local nobility who were calling for the restoration of the monarchy, the opening skirmishes of an extremely bloody war were fought along the Loire valley. By late summer the whole of Anjou had embraced the Vendéen cause, but the terrible defeat at Cholet on 17 October seriously checked the Royalists' ambitions. The following day, an astonishing 80,000 Vendéen combatants, women, children, ageing sympathisers and the infirm, equivalent to almost a third of the population of the Mauges, crossed the Loire at St-Florent. Even Napoleon was caused to marvel that only one woman drowned. The Royalist general, the Marquis de Bonchamps, was, however, fatally wounded at Cholet and died in St-Florent, shortly after giving his famous order to swallow vengeance and halt any planned massacre of the 5000 Republican prisoners held by the Vendéen army.

These events are well recounted in the small **Musée d'Histoire et des Guerres de Vendée**, housed in the late 17C Chapelle du Sacré-Coeur to the east of the church. But on the whole it is the church, known for purely sentimental reasons as the **Abbaye**, which holds the greater interest. The crossing tower, nave and west front survived the Revolution, having been begun in 1710 to a relatively austere neo-Classical design enlivened only by the relief carving above the main arcades. The earlier choir was replaced in the late 19C by a sizeable neo-Gothic complex, whose handsome crypt now houses a miscellaneous collection of sculpture and stonework, which includes four excellent vault bosses from the 13C choir.

The greatest **sculpture** is to be found upstairs, however, in a chapel to the north of the easternmost bay of the nave. There, rising like an antique warrior from a *sigma*, Charles Melchior Artus, Marquis de Bonchamps, gestures *Grâce aux Prisonniers*. This superb neo-Classical tomb was designed and carved in 1825 by David-d'Angers, himself the son of one of those pardoned by Bonchamps, and though the base was heavily reworked at the end of the 19C the effigy has lost none of its thrilling sense of movement and drama. Bonchamp's hand is invested with an eloquence to rival that of Michelangelo's Adam, a cloak raked across his right arm to suggest the *peplos* of a Greek philosopher-rhetorician, his torso drawn sharply upwards. Any single element might be considered part of the common stock of Revolutionary art, yet it is testimony to David-d'Angers' vision of Bonchamps that not only does the work avoid seeming clichéd, but it retains its power to shock.

St-Florent is the northernmost town of the Mauges, and, like most Mauges towns, suffered grievously for its Vendéen sympathies. Elements of the old ramparts survive along the **Rue du Clos-de-Ville**, and a number of pre-19C houses still stand along the steep and tortuous streets that spill eastwards from the abbey down towards the river. A vestige of the old, and hated, **Tour de la Gabelle**, even lours above the river bank, within the same block as the hotel, and acts as a backdrop to a particularly lovely terrace along the river.

South of St-Florent, the landscape begins to roll, the river valleys deepen and the tightly folded contours take on a higher relief in anything other than the harshest light. Away from the main D752, along the **Cirque du Courossé** for instance (3km west of la Croix-Baron and best reached along the D201), or in the splendid grounds of the **Château du Bas-Plessis**, you can catch a glimpse of this at its most pronounced, where the underlying granites and mica-schists have conspired to create a landscape more akin to that of northern Maine than to anywhere else in Anjou.

The one sizeable town the D752 passes, (19km) **Beaupréau**, was the major town of the Mauges until eclipsed by the industrial rise of Cholet during the 19C. By 1565 the old county had been raised to a duchy and a great château overlooking the river Evre was constructed, incorporating elements of the earlier medieval complex. But, once again, the old centre was destroyed in the Vendéen War, and, though it was rebuilt above the existing street lines, it now lacks atmosphere. The château is resolutely closed to the public, but you can catch a marvellous view of the south elevation from the far bank of the river, after you cross the bridge along the old main road south, back to the new heart of the Mauges at (18km) Cholet.

INDEX

The index lists all of the places described in the book. Châteaux can be found under their individual names. Entries for historical figures, and for artists and architects are limited to those references which are of particular interest or importance.

BLUE GUIDES

The Blue Guide series was founded in 1915 by Muirhead Guide-Books Limited. In 1918 the first Blue Guide, London and its Environs, was published. Findlay and James Muirhead already had extensive experience of guide-book publishing: before the First World War they had been the editors of the English editions of the German Baedekers, and by 1915 they had acquired the copyright of most of the famous 'Red' Handbooks from John Murray.

An agreement made with the French publishing house Hachette et Cie in 1917 led to the translation of Muirhead's London guide, which became the first 'Guide Bleu', Hachette had previously published the blue-covered 'Guides Joanne'. Subsequently, Hachette's Guide Blue 'Paris et ses Environs' was adapted and published in London by Muirhead.

In 1931 Ernest Benn Limited took over the Blue Guides, appointing Russell Muirhead, Findlay Muirhead's son, editor in 1934. The Muirheads' connection with the Blue Guides ended in 1963, when Stuart Rossiter, who had been working on the Guides since 1954, became house editor, revising and compiling several of the books himself.

The Blue Guides are now published by A & C Black, who acquired Ernest Benn in 1984, so continuing the tradition of guide-book publishing which began in 1826 with 'Black's Economical Tourist of Scotland'. The series continues to grow: there are now more than 60 titles in print, with revised editions appearing regularly, and many new titles in preparation.

BLUE GUIDES ORDER FORM

Blue Guides are available through all bookshops or can be obtained directly from A & C Black by writing to: **A & C Black, PO Box 19, Huntingdon, Cambs PE19 3SF** or telephone (01480) 212666, fax: (01480) 212666. Access and Visa are accepted. Availability and published prices are correct at the time of going to press, but are subject to change without notice. For information on our other travel guide series, please contact our sales department.

BLUE GUIDES   ISBN prefix: 0-7136

Albania 3785-4	£12.99
Amsterdam 3228-3	£8.99
Athens 3rd ed 3506-1	£12.99
Austria 3rd ed 3383-2	£12.99
Barcelona 3229-1	£8.99
Belgium & Luxembourg 8th ed 3732-3	£13.99
Berlin and Eastern Germany 3871-0	£13.99
Boston and Cambridge 2nd ed 3170-8	£14.99
Burgundy 3384-0	£8.99
Channel Islands 2nd ed 2835-9	£6.95
China 3027-2	£16.99
Churches & Chapels of:	
Northern England 3171-6	£14.95
Southern England 3029-9	£14.95
Corsica 2nd ed 3589-4	£9.99
Country houses of England 3780-3	£15.99
Crete 6th ed 3588-6	£11.99
Cyprus 3rd ed 3274-7	£9.99
Czechoslovakia 3230-5	£13.99
Denmark 3474-X	£10.99
Egypt 3rd ed 3590-8	£17.99
England 11th ed 3874-5	£14.99
Florence 6th ed 4073-1	£10.99
France 3rd ed 3386-7	£16.99
Gardens of England 3389-1	£14.99
Greece 6th ed 3250-X	£16.99
Holland 5th ed 3654-8	£11.99
Hungary 3030-2	£12.95
Ireland 7th ed 3870-2	£13.99
Istanbul 3rd ed 3275-5	£12.99

Jerusalem 2944-4	£11.95
Literary Britain & Ireland 2nd ed 3152-X	£12.95
The Loire Valley 3872-9	£9.99
London 15th ed 3972-5	£12.99
Madrid 4106-1	£9.99
Malta & Gozo 4th ed 3954-7	£9.99
Midi-Pyrénées 3853-2	£10.99
Morocco 2nd ed 3592-4	£9.99
Moscow & Leningrad 2nd ed 3387-5	£12.99
Museums & galleries of London 3rd ed 3168-6	£12.95
New York 2nd ed 3169-4	£17.99
Normandy 3730-7	£9.99
Northern Italy 9th ed 3276-3	£14.99
Oxford & Cambridge 4th ed 3904-0	£9.99
Paris & Versailles 8th ed 3581-9	£10.99
Portugal 3rd ed 2966-5	£8.95
Rome & environs 5th ed 3939-3	£13.99
Scotland 10th ed 3426-X	£16.99
Sicily 4th ed 3784-6	£11.99
Southern Italy 7th ed 3141-4	£12.95
South-west France 3910-5	£9.99
Spain 6th ed 3731-5	£14.99
Sweden 3935-0	£12.99
Switzerland 5th ed 3559-2	£11.99
Turkey 2nd ed 3829-X	£16.99
Tuscany 3388-3	£12.99
Umbria 3705-6	£9.99
Venice 5th ed 3873-7	£9.99
Victorian architecture in Britain 2842-1	£14.95
Wales 8th ed 4074-X	£12.99
Western Germany 2nd ed 3278-X	£14.99

Please send me the following *Blue Guides:*_____

_____

_____

____ I enclose a cheque for: £_____ made payable to A & C Black *(please add £1.50 for p&p)*

____ Please debit my credit card Access/Visa ☐☐☐☐☐☐☐☐☐☐☐☐☐☐☐☐

Expiry Date: ☐☐☐☐☐☐

Name: _____

Address: _____

_____

☐ *I do not wish to receive information about **Blue Guides** in the future.*